Programming Concepts in Java

Second Edition

J. N. Patterson Hume

Christine Stephenson

D1263292

Holt Software Associates, Inc.
Toronto, Canada

in association with
IBM's Centre for Advanced Studies

Publisher:

HOLT SOFTWARE ASSOCIATES INC.

203 College St., Suite 305

Toronto, Ontario, Canada M5T 1P9

(416) 978-6476   1-800-361-8324

http://www.holtsoft.com/java

ISBN 0-921598-32-7

Second Edition

Printed in Canada by the University of Toronto Press

Table of Contents

Preface

This textbook, *Programming Concepts in Java*, is intended to be used in a first course in computer science. It emphasizes the basic concepts of programming and the object-oriented programming paradigm. No previous knowledge of programming is needed, although some contact with computers and operating environments, such as *Microsoft Windows 95, 98* or *NT* would be an asset.

The programming language used in this book is Java. The environment presented is the IBM *VisualAge for Java, Professional Edition for Windows, Version 2.0* system. The primary focus of this book is computing concepts with the ultimate goal of facilitating the broadest possible coverage of the core computer science curriculum. (Additional references should be consulted if a complete syntax of Java or the Java class libraries is required.) Also, some of the more advanced notions of concurrency, exception handling, and graphical user interfaces have had to be omitted or discussed in an abbreviated way. To begin, Java standalone application programs are used exclusively. Applets are covered in considerable detail in later chapters. The final chapter provides a detailed example of building a graphical user interface to an application using the Java class libraries.

This textbook package includes a CD containing the full professional version of IBM's *VisualAge for Java, Professional Edition for Windows, Version 2.0* software. In addition, the publisher has provided a collection of Java classes to facilitate the teaching of Java. These include the *Console* class which enables students to do text and graphics I/O without having to master the intricacies of the *Java Abstract Windowing Toolkit*. As well, the collection includes the *Stdin* class, which allows students to read all of Java's primitive data types from the standard input stream without having to master Java data type conversion. There are also classes for pretty printing (paragraphing) Java programs, reading Java primitive data types from text files, and submitting programs for marking. A complete set of the classes presented as examples in this book is also available on the CD.

Overview

This book covers the material in standard curricula for first courses in computer science. As well, it emphasizes the object-oriented paradigm.

The list of chapter titles outlines the arrangement of materials.
1. Programming Paradigms
2. The VisualAge for Java Environment
3. Basic Programming Language Concepts
4. Input of Data
5. Control Constructs
6. Strings
7. Methods
8. Classes and Inheritance
9. Applets and Graphical User Interfaces
10. Arrays
11. Records in Java
12. Algorithms for Sorting Lists
13. Self-Referential Classes and Linked Lists
14. Trees
15. VisualAge for Java Visual Builder
16. Advanced GUIs: the Console Class

Chapter 1 introduces the difference between the two major programming paradigms: the procedure-oriented paradigm and the object-oriented paradigm which is the paradigm of the Java programming language. Abstraction is introduced as a way of making programs easier to create and to understand. A number of the basic elements of the Java syntax are introduced, particularly the idea of a class and a method. These are illustrated by graphic examples using the *Console* class. The details of all these concepts are explored in later chapters.

Chapter 2 presents the IBM *VisualAge for Java, Professional Edition for Windows, Version 2.0* environment. The way to begin a project in the *Workbench* using the *SmartGuide* of *VisualAge for Java* is outlined, as is the way to enter standalone Java program classes with methods. The chapter also covers how syntax errors are reported when programs are saved and can be corrected by editing. The use of a shared computer system is explained.

Chapter 3 presents the EBNF metalanguage for formally describing the syntax of a programming language. The primitive data types of the Java language are defined along with the way to declare variables of these types. Expressions for each type are also defined and the assignment statement The chapter explains how values of the different types are output and formatted using a *Console* class. The role of comments in providing internal documentation to a program is also discussed.

Chapter 4 discusses how data can be input to a program. Ways in which a list of data items can be input by counted or conditional loops are shown. Input from the standard input, the keyboard, and input from a file are discussed. Ways to generate data using random numbers for purposes of testing programs are presented. The statistical analysis of numerical data is also described.

Chapter 5 deals with program structure. Algorithms can be programmed using three basic forms of control structure: linear sequence, repetition, and selection. The Java syntax for each of these is defined. The use of diagrams such as flow charts to supplement the program itself is discussed and shown to be unnecessary for a structured program which is properly paragraphed, and internally documented. Tracing execution of a program before trying to run it on a computer is encouraged. The *VisualAge for Java Debugger* facility is described.

Chapter 6 introduces the *String* data structure which is implemented using the *String* class. Strings in Java are objects instantiated from the *String* class. Methods of the class are shown. The *StringBuffer* class is introduced as useful when the contents of a string are to be changed. The *StringTokenizer* class which permits the breaking of a string into tokens is introduced.

Chapter 7 provides details about methods – components of a object that can be used by other objects to operate on the data of the original object. As with subprograms of earlier programming languages, methods fall into two principal classes: procedure-type methods that perform some action and function-type methods that yield a value. The differences in the way these two types of methods are defined and invoked is detailed. The relation between formal and actual parameters is explained. The scope of identifiers in a program is outlined. The signature, header, and specifications of a method are defined. Methods that call themselves – and iterative methods that accomplish the same result – are dealt with.

Chapter 8 shows how an object can encapsulate data and the methods that operate on the data, and illustrates how other objects that use that object are prevented from interfering with the encapsulated data. The class is the template from which an object is instantiated. A constructor method of the class is used to create a new instance of the class – the object. Examples are given of using and creating a class. Inheritance is introduced as a means by which new classes are created through modifications of a base class. By using the Java library of classes, multiple objects of the class can be created or new classes produced.

Chapter 9 introduces Java applets. Applets are invoked by using a browser, such as *Netscape Navigator*, and can be accessed through the *World Wide Web*. It is this feature of Java that is at the root of much of its popularity, as well as its being an object-oriented programming language. The *VisualAge for Java* method of creating Graphical User Interfaces (GUIs) is introduced. This chapter covers many of the classes in Java's **Abstract Windowing Toolkit** (awt).

Chapter 10 introduces the structured data type called an array. Individual elements of an array share the same name and data type but are distinguished from each other by having an index. An individual element of an array can be passed by value to a method whereas an entire array is passed, as any object is, by reference. When the method alters its array parameter the actual array is altered. The efficiencies of searching an array by a linear search and a sorted array by a binary search are compared.

Chapter 11 describes implementing records as objects and the reading from and writing to binary files. In Java, there is no standard way to store an object's fields in a fixed length record. As a result, it must be programmed The ways records can be input from or output to a file are shown, as is the storage of records in a binary form so that random access to individual records is possible. A simple linear search of an array of records is introduced as an example of using records.

Chapter 12 presents algorithms for sorting lists of data stored in arrays. The time complexity of sorting algorithms is explored and big O notation introduced. The chapter also explains how methods depending on recursion prove to be more efficient than simple exchange algorithms.

Chapter 13 gives details of self-referential classes and how they can be used to instantiate nodes to link objects together in simple linked lists. A *List* class is created and then modified to produce an *OrderedList* class by inheritance.

Chapter 14 introduces the binary tree as a data structure that has a recursive definition and is easily implemented by having two links in a node. The chapter demonstrates how the efficiency of searching achieved with a sorted array using a binary search, and the ease of insertion and deletion of elements in a linear linked list is possible with a binary search tree. The heap sort is introduced as a recursive method of sorting which uses trees defined somewhat differently than binary search trees.

Chapter 15 introduces *VisualAge for Java, Professional Edition for Windows, Version 2.0* Visual Builder tool by guiding students through the construction of a movie ticket seller applet. The chapter demonstrates how student-created methods can be integrated with visual design tools.

Chapter 16 provides a detailed example of building a graphical user interface. It examines a simplified version of the *Console* class to introduce Java's *Abstract Windowing Toolkit*.

Conventions

This book uses a number of naming conventions for identifiers. These are not part of the Java language but are used to make programs understandable.

- All identifiers that are multiple words use an upper case letter to begin all words after the first
- Class names have the first letter capitalized.
- Variable and method names have identifiers beginning with a lower case letter.
- Constants have identifiers all in upper case.

Flexibility

Programming Concepts in Java has been organized to provide an introduction to the fundamental concepts of computer science. The object-oriented paradigm of the Java programming language is used to illustrate basic principles.

Differing course demands and student populations may require instructors to omit certain chapters or parts of chapters, or to insert additional material to cover some concepts in greater detail. For example, the discussion of algorithm complexity and big O notation can easily be omitted from the course of study. The instructor may wish to provide other resources if more than an introduction to program correctness or the use of Java on the Internet is desired.

The Java Programming Language

Java is a programming language that was developed at Sun Microsystems. Java standalone application programs provide all the features of other general purpose languages such as Pascal or C. Java applets add the flexibility of sharing programs via the World Wide Web and Internet. Java is an object-oriented programming language and has been provided with an extensive library of classes that can be used in creating programs. This library is being rapidly extended by its many users.

The language is portable; it can be used on any computer platform that has a Java interpreter. Attempts are made to make the use of shared programs safe. For security, for example, no applet may read from or write to a file on the system on which it is being executed.

Java syntax is based on the C syntax but many of the difficult and error prone parts of C and C++, such as pointers, operator overloading, and multiple inheritance have been eliminated. In this book we have eliminated still more of the "tricks" that some C programmers delight in. Our approach is based on the fundamental principle of structured programming, namely keeping programs easy to understand.

Java and its class libraries have many additional features which are not part of C or C++. It provides for strings, graphics, concurrency, and exception handling, as well as a large number of data structures in its class libraries. Java also provides graphical user interface classes.

All of these features contribute to Java's attractiveness as both a commercial software tool and a means of addressing the core computer science concepts.

IBM VisualAge for Java

While this book may be used with any Java product, the Java environment discussed and included with the book is IBM's *VisualAge for Java, Professional Edition for Windows, Version 2.0*. This environment provides a convenient way to enter and save Java programs, both standalone applications and applets. The creation of the files for classes is handled automatically by the environment. It also has a debugging facility.

Perhaps, more significantly, *VisualAge for Java, Professional Edition for Windows, Version 2.0* provides an excellent graphic interface which allows students to create applets which support graphical user interfaces (GUIs).

For more information and educational resources see:

www.ibm.com/java/academic

Comments

Your comments, corrections, and suggestions are very welcome. Please feel free to contact us at:

Distribution Manager
Holt Software Associates Inc.
203 College Street, Suite 305
Toronto, Ontario, Canada M5T 1P9
E-mail: books@hsa.on.ca
USA or Canada phone: 1-800-361-8324
World Wide Web: http://www.holtsoft.com

Acknowledgments

This book would not have been produced without the enthusiasm and help of Tom West who was invaluable in ironing out the technical details of Java, testing the programs, assembling the appendices, and formatting the final text. Dr. Ric Holt also provided valuable feedback on early versions of the text.

Inge Weber entered much of the copy from handwritten drafts, Harriet Hume created the index, and Catharine Trenchard did our final page check. The book cover was designed by Brenda Kosky.

It was our good fortune again to work with such a cooperative and competent team.

We would also like to offer our sincere thanks to a number of members of IBM's VisualAge for Java team for their support of this textbook, most specifically Gabriel Silberman, Program Director of IBM's Centre for Advanced Studies; Arthur Ryman, Solution Architect for VisualAge for Java; Karin Roos, Program Manager, Java Developer Community, Java Marketing; and Sheila Richardson, Coordinator, IBM Retail Publishing Programs.

J. N. Patterson Hume
Christine Stephenson

Chapter 1

Programming
Paradigms

This book introduces the concepts of computer programming. Many new technical terms must be introduced. These are general terms and as such are independent of the particular programming language used. In order to really understand concepts, however, there is no substitute for writing actual programs that can be entered into a computer and executed. In this chapter we begin by introducing technical language as well as the programming language Java. These will become better understood as the book unfolds so do not worry if everything is not immediately clear.

1.1 What is Java?

Although in the popular press Java is most closely linked with the growing phenomena of Internet use, at its basis Java is simply an object-oriented programming language. What is special about Java, however, is that it is an object-oriented programming language that is particularly well-suited to the growing need for tools which fit the way software programmers actually work today.

The increasing size and complexity of computer programs has driven the demand for reusable, off-the-shelf programs and parts of programs that allow programmers to create large applications without constant writing from scratch. The Java class library contains an extensive collection of classes or packages which can be imported directly into an existing program to perform a number of (often complex) tasks. This reduces programming time and the likelihood of introducing new errors (**bugs**).

Lack of standardization across hardware platforms, operating systems, and software applications has been a major stumbling block for software developers, requiring them to develop and maintain multiple versions to meet differing machine requirements. Because the Java compiler generates bytecode rather than native machine code, Java programs are platform-independent, that is, they can run on any platform that supports Java. This portability is also what makes Java so well-suited to use on the Internet.

Another of Java's strengths is that it has been designed to reduce the opportunity for programmers to make common programming errors. Specifically, Java eliminates pointers, which are a major cause of problems in C and C++ programs. It also checks array and string bounds (unlike C or C++). Together these (and other) features make Java more suitable for learning how to program than other languages.

1.2   What is Programming?

Programming is the activity of:

- **Analyzing** a problem to be solved.
- Preparing a **design** for the steps in a set of instructions (an **algorithm**) that together with the data, will solve the problem.
- Expressing the algorithm in a language that the computer can ultimately execute.
- Ensuring that there is adequate **documentation** so that other people, and not just the original programmer, can understand the computer program.
- **Testing** and **validating** the program to ensure that it will give correct results for the full range of **data** that it is to process.
- **Maintaining** the program over time so that any changes that are needed are incorporated.

A program is called **software**; the computer itself is **hardware**.

Large software development projects can go through a sequence of these steps one after the other in a **software life cycle** as shown in Figure 1.1. This series of steps is sometimes called a **waterfall model** because it looks like water cascading down from one level to the next.

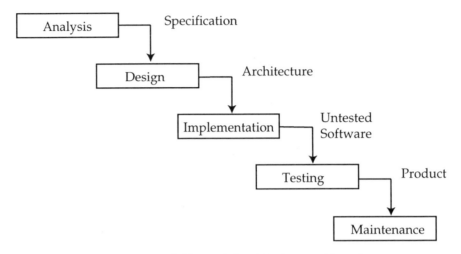

Figure 1.1 Waterfall Model of Software Development

In the early days of computing the first three parts of the programming activity were sometimes called analyzing, programming, and coding. Each of these activities might have been done by a separate person with special qualifications. Over time, however, the increasing complexity of the software being developed has required that greater emphasis be placed on the analysis of problems to be solved and the resulting design of programs and applications.

The implementation stage (once called coding because most early programs were written in machine code) has also evolved to meet the need for programs which can be understood by anyone with some knowledge of the nature of programming languages. Programmers today are much more likely to use a high-level programming language. The advantage of a high-level language is that it is easier to understand.

The waterfall model is an idealization of the programming process. In reality the process is closer to that shown in Figure 1.2.

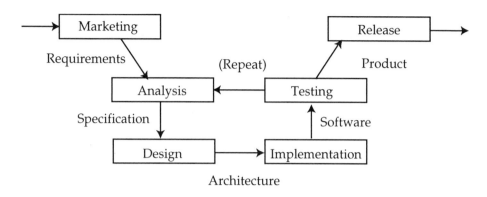

Figure 1.2 Iterative Model of Software Evolution

There is a certain amount of backtracking in the actual evolution of a piece of software of any complexity, particularly if the software is constantly being updated.

In many ways we try to prepare programs that are self-documenting by using variable names such as *netPay* to indicate that the variable contains information concerning the net pay of an employee.

The programming language Java has a number of words called **keywords** that are used for various operations, such as **if** for selection or **while** for repetition. These have been chosen to be brief but expressive. When a programmer invents names to identify entities (**identifiers**) it is best if they are as brief as possible without sacrificing understandability. Abbreviations should be used only when they are well-understood, such as *GST* for Goods and Services Tax and *FBI* for Federal Bureau of Investigation.

1.3   Abstraction in Programs

Programs can become very complex and hard to understand and so we are constantly seeking ways to simplify them. Procedural abstraction and data abstraction are two commonly-used systems for reducing program complexity.

Procedural Abstraction

One way of making a program simpler is to divide it into a number of smaller programs or **subprograms**.

A subprogram that:

- performs some action or actions which may cause the input or output of data, or
- changes the values of data stored in the computer's memory is called a **procedure**.

A subprogram that:

- is given the value, or values, of some data stored in memory and yields a value is called a **function**.

In mathematics we say y is a function of x and write

$$y = f(x)$$

where x is the data value given to the function and y is the value returned. As an example, if the square root function

$$y = \sqrt{x}$$

is given a value $x = 4$, it yields the value $y = 2$.

In this chapter we use the word procedure as a general term to include the function subprogram as well. In the C language the word **function** is used for both procedures and functions. In Java the word **method** is used for both.

For procedure-oriented programming languages certain subprograms are **predefined** so that they may be used in any program. These subprograms have been created by another programmer and placed in a **library** of subprograms available to all users. Reusing existing software components allows programmers to build on the work of others and thus speed up the programming process.

A programmer using a predefined procedure never has to read the actual procedure or even know the details of its operation, as long as she or he knows what data must be provided and what will be accomplished by it.

This is referred to as a **procedural abstraction** since we know what to expect, but do not need to know the procedure's inner workings. The details of such a procedure are **hidden**; only the

interface to use or **call** the procedure must be known. Abstraction helps to simplify programs by providing the essential information about how to use the procedure without irrelevant details.

Data Abstraction

As programs become larger and more complex, it becomes necessary to share the task of creating a large program among a team of people. This sharing helps to ensure that the task can be completed in a reasonable amount of time. When procedural abstraction is used, often one programmer's procedure modifies the same data as another's, and the programmers must be careful about such overlapping. It seems reasonable, therefore, to isolate the procedures of each programmer or team along with the data they operate on in an airtight compartment and to **encapsulate** them in a **module** (a software **object**) that explicitly controls any use of its components by another module.

This is referred to as **data abstraction**. Modules that encapsulate data with the procedures that operate on the data are called **abstract data types** or ADTs.

For example, an abstract data type might be created to manage a **list** of entries that are to be kept in alphabetic order. The data in this module would be the representation of the list. There would be procedures which would allow the user of the module to add a new entry to the list, to delete an entry, to output the list in alphabetic order, and so on. These procedures, with their interfaces, are made known to a user of the module by explicitly labelling them as **public**. The way in which the data is stored in memory and the way the operations are implemented are not made available to the user. The implementation and the way the data is stored can be changed as long as the external behavior of the abstract data type remains the same.

1.4   Programming Paradigms

Two well known systems or **paradigms** (pronounced *paradimes*) used for creating large-scale programs are **procedure-oriented programming** and **object-oriented programming**.

Procedure-Oriented Programming

This paradigm is based on the system of designing programs in a **top-down** manner. The programmer starts by writing the specification of the problem to be solved and gradually refines the solution by breaking it into parts, each of which can in turn be broken into parts. These parts are often solved (implemented) as procedures.

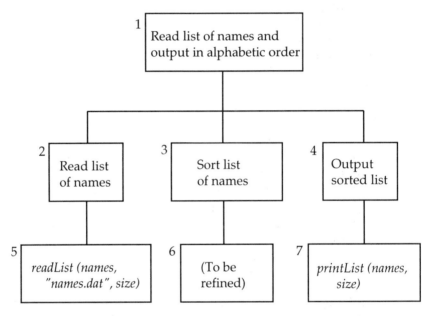

Figure 1.3 Top-Down Programming

Figure 1.3 is called a **structure chart**. It illustrates how the procedures activate (call) each other.

This structure chart shows how a program is **refined step by step** starting at the top (1), with a statement of what is required, here sorting a list of names alphabetically. This top node in the diagram is expanded or refined into three nodes 2, 3, and 4. The computations represented by these three nodes, carried out sequentially, satisfy the top node's specification. The nodes 5, 6, and 7 are further refinements in the procedure-oriented programming language.

In procedure-oriented programming, the data upon which the various procedures operate is commonly kept centrally in a **main program** as illustrated in Figure 1.4. When one procedure is changed it may cause an effect that alters the way another procedure works if the two procedures share the same data.

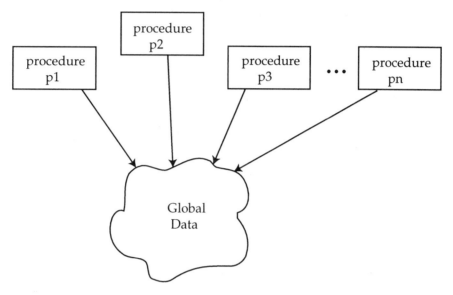

Figure 1.4 Shared Global Data in Procedure-Oriented Programming

Object-Oriented Programming

In abstract data types, data that are operated on by a set of procedures are grouped with the procedures in a module. The module encapsulates the data and procedures (methods in Java) so that no other procedures can have direct access to the data. Modules which encapsulate the data and procedures are called **objects**. These objects very often correspond to actual objects, such as a list of names with all the operations that can be performed on the list.

Creating a program as a number of objects is referred to as **object-based programming**. True object-oriented programming in a language such as Java involves a further idea – the idea of **classes**. The class acts as a **template** from which any number of

instances can be created. Object-oriented programming involves objects that can be **instantiated** from classes.

As well, object-oriented programming allows programmers to create a new class from an existing class. The new class **extends** an existing **base class**. In the process of **inheritance**, additional methods may be added to those of the base class or existing methods can be changed or **overridden**. This makes the new class different from its **parent** base class, and yet saves a great deal of the original, thus reducing the effort to create the new class.

Object-oriented programming makes it convenient to reuse existing program components (classes). A language such as Java has a **library of classes** that can be used. In this way programmers do not constantly have to "reinvent the wheel". Large programs can be made from off-the-shelf components just as computers are created from basic electronic components and chips.

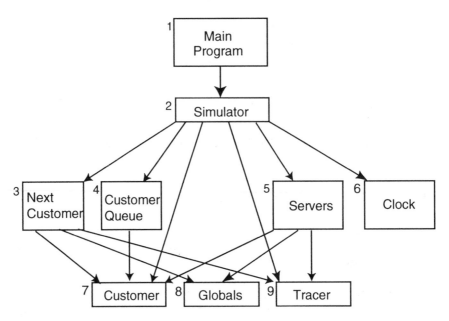

Figure 1.5 Landscape of Queue Simulator

Just as the structure of procedure-oriented programs can be represented by diagrams such as structure charts, the structure of object-oriented programs can be represented by diagrams such as **landscapes**. Figure 1.5 shows the landscape of an object-oriented program that simulates the queueing of customers in a bank. The arrows indicate the fact that some objects **import** other objects' capabilities, that is, use their methods. For example, the *CustomerQueue* object (4) uses the *Customer* object (7) but no other.

Now it is time to look more closely at the object-oriented paradigm that we will be using with Java.

1.5 Key Concepts in Object-Oriented Programming

There are three fundamental concepts in object-oriented programming which every Java user needs to understand. They are objects, classes, and inheritance.

Objects

An **object** is a set of data and the methods which operate on that data. In Java, an object's data are called the **fields** of the object. One example of an object might be an *Employee* object, where the object's data would be the employee's name, employee number, home address, position, hours worked, rate of pay, and income tax paid this year. The object's methods would include retrieving the employee's number, home address, position, hours worked, rate of pay, and income tax paid this year. As well, there would be methods for changing the object's data, for example, adding to the income tax total paid this year. There could also be a method to create the forms necessary to send to the government for tax purposes.

When using objects, a programmer only needs to know what the objects do, and not how they do it. In other words she or he does not need to see the data and how the methods are implemented. In this way, programmers are able to make use of pre-existing classes without ever having to study the internals of these classes.

Classes

A **class** is a **template** for creating objects. From a class, you can create objects, each of which will have its own data and an identical set of methods that apply to that data.

For example, an *Employee* class would be used as a template for creating a new *Employee* object every time an employee was added to the employee database. This employee database would consist of hundreds of *Employee* objects. Each object, when it was created (**instantiated**), would use a special method of the *Employee* class called the **constructor** method to set the data in the object appropriately for the particular employee. Once the objects were created, they would be completely separate entities.

Inheritance

Inheritance incorporates all of the methods and data fields from one class into another class. Data fields may then be added and existing methods changed.

For example, we might want to have a new class for employees called *PartTimeEmployee*, which could have some additional fields (such as the percentage of full time equivalent) and some additional methods (such as a method to set the percentage of full benefits the worker receives). Instead of rewriting the *Employee* class from scratch to make it into the *PartTimeEmployee* class, the *PartTimeEmployee* class will **inherit** from the *Employee* class. When one class inherits from another it keeps all the same data fields and methods of the original class. From there, we can add data fields and methods or can redefine already-existing methods of *Employee* class (for example, the calculations of taxes might be different for part time employees). In Java, if the *PartTimeEmployee* class inherits from *Employee* class, we say that the *PartTimeEmployee* class **extends** the *Employee* class.

1.6   Programming in Java

For many years the procedure-oriented paradigm was the usual way programs were created. Programmers trained in this tradition often find it difficult to adjust their thinking to a different paradigm such as object-oriented programming. This means that potential advantages are not achieved. It is hoped that students who learn the object-oriented approach at the same time as they learn programming may be able to learn these ideas in less time than someone who is entrenched in a different approach.

The language we will be using is the **Java programming language**. We will begin by looking at the concept of a **method** (function or procedure) in Java. After that we will examine the creation and use of classes.

To illustrate the idea of methods we will use the methods of a class developed by Holt Software Associates called **Console**. This class allows the user to write programs that create an **execution window** in which a program may display **graphics**. Later we will see that the *Console* class can also be used to display **numbers** or **text** and permit a user to enter data of various types.

Locating a Figure in the Console Window

The *Console* class can be used to write programs to draw lines, rectangles, ovals, and so on in the console window.

Any figure on the screen actually consists of a number of tiny dots. These dots are called **pixels**. Because the dots are very small, when placed one after the other they appear to form a solid line.

The position and size of figures drawn in the console window must be specified as integral numbers of pixels. For example, if the center of a circle is specified as the point (150, 100), it would be 150 pixel positions to the right of the left-hand side of the window and 100 pixel positions below the top of the window. The origin of coordinates (0, 0) is at the upper-left corner of the window (see Figure 1.6).

It is not possible to specify fractions of pixels. For example, the center of the circle cannot be set at

(150.5, 100.2)

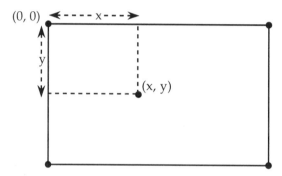

Figure 1.6 The Console Window

Drawing a Colored Rectangle in the Console Window

Drawing graphics requires the use of the methods that are part of the *Console* class. In the *Console* class there is a method called *fillRect* which is characterized by the **signature**

fillRect (**int** *x*, **int** *y*, **int** *width*, **int** *height*);

After the method's name, in parentheses, is a list of **parameters** of the method and their data type, which here is **int** for integer. (We make a practice of showing keywords in Java such as **int** in boldface type.) The explanation given with this signature is that the upper-left corner of the rectangle is at (*x*, *y*), the rectangle has a given *width* and *height*, and it is filled with the current color. The color is set by the *Console* method *setColor* whose signature is

setColor (*Color clr*);

The signature and the explanation of the meaning of the parameters together constitute the **specification** of the method.

In order to use these methods it is first necessary to create or instantiate a *Console* object named *c* from the *Console* class. The program statements that will do this are

```
Console c;
c = new Console ();
```

It is our convention to have class names such as *Console* begin with an upper case letter. Object and method names begin with lower case letters. Notice that each statement in the program fragment is terminated by a semicolon.

The first statement declares that *c* will identify an object of type *Console*. The second statement actually creates the object *c*. This second statement is an **assignment statement**. In it a new object of class *Console* is assigned to the identifier *c*. The **new** is a keyword in Java. Each class has a special method called a **constructor** which is used to create an object that is an **instance** of the class. We say that the constructor method **instantiates** an object of the class. The name of the constructor method is the same as the name of the class. The constructor method for this class has no parameters. When this is the case, the parentheses that follow the constructor method's name are still required but have nothing between them.

Now that we have created and instance *c* of *Console*, we are in a position to use the methods of object *c*. To use a method of object *c* we must precede the method's name by *c* followed by a dot. The two statements to draw a blue rectangle of width 50 pixels and height 100 pixels with its upper-left corner in the upper-left corner of the window are

```
c.setColor (Color.blue);
c.fillRect (0, 0, 50, 100);
```

In the first statement the **actual parameter** (**argument**) of the *Console* method *setColor* is a constant provided by the *Color* class. Certain classes in the Java class library are usually not instantiated. The class *Color* is such a class. In this case the class' name (rather than the object's name) followed by a dot, precedes the field's or method's name.

In order to have the computer produce such a blue rectangle these statements must be incorporated into a complete program.

1.7   Standalone Programs in Java

In Java there are two quite different types of programs: **standalone application programs** and **applets**.

- Standalone application programs can be executed independently of an Internet browser.

- Applet programs are executed through a network browser and are capable of being shared. In applets, for security reasons, no use can be made of files of data.

Initially we will restrict our programs to standalone application programs since applets require an understanding of the Java **graphical user interface** (GUI) class library.

Here is a complete application program that draws the blue rectangle.

```
// The "BlueRect" class.
import java.awt.*;
import hsa.Console;

public class BlueRect
{
    static public void main (String args [ ])
    {
        Console c;
        c = new Console ();
        c.setColor (Color.blue);
        c.fillRect (0, 0, 50, 100);
    } // main method
} /* BlueRect class */
```

While it is probably easier to simply accept all the parts of the program that surround the four statements that instantiate the *Console* object *c* and draw the blue rectangle using the *Console* methods, a few words of explanation might be helpful. To begin, there are two **import** statements that indicate that both the **Java Abstract Windowing Toolkit** (awt) and the *Console* class of Holt Software Associates (hsa) are going to be used.

After the **import** statements there is a statement that what follows defines a *class* called *BlueRect* that is to be publicly available. The **body** of the class is enclosed in curly braces { }. The opening brace is placed directly below the *p* of **public** and the closing brace is placed in the same column in the last line of the program. We think this alignment of corresponding opening and closing braces makes the program easier to understand. Often programs are written with the opening curly brace at the end of the previous line. The next line of the program

static public void *main* (*String args* [ ])

should, at this stage, be accepted as indicating that what follows is the **main method**. All *main* methods have exactly this same line. (Notice that there is no semicolon at the end.)

The body of the *main* method is enclosed in curly braces, the opening brace being written under the *s* of **static** and its matching closing brace lined up at the end of the method. The four statements that constitute the body of the *main* method are indented one level to the right of the *main* method's enclosing braces. This system of **paragraphing** a program makes it easier to read and understand. It is not necessary to its successful execution.

After the closing brace of the *BlueRect* class definition is a **comment**. This consists of any text enclosed in /* followed by */. Comments are included to **document** the program and to help the reader understand it. An alternative form is to begin the comment with two slashes // and end with a Return (end of line).

In choosing appropriate sizes for drawings it is helpful to know how large the console window is. This information is available through two *Console* class methods. The method *maxx* has a value which is the width of the window in pixels. The method *maxy* has a value which is the height of the window in pixels. Although there are no parameters for *maxx* and *maxy* their names must be followed by empty parentheses ( ). The methods *maxx* and *maxy* are function-type methods and each produces a value. The coordinates of the center of the window would be

(*c.maxx*() /2, *c.maxy*() /2)

In Java a single slash / is used for division and dividing one integer by another produces an integer value. For example,

5/2

produces the value 2, the result of division with any fractional part chopped off (**truncated**).

Changing the program *BlueRect* so that it draws a green rectangle that fills the bottom-right corner of the window would require the last two statements of the *main* method's body to be changed to

> c.setColor (Color.green);
> c.fillRect (c.maxx() / 2, c.maxy() / 2, c.maxx() / 2, c.maxy() / 2);

A list of available colors in the *Color* class can be found in the Appendix.

1.8   User-Defined Methods

There are a number of drawing methods that can be used in the *Console* class. So far only the *fillRect* method has been presented.

Here are some other commonly-used methods:

> *drawLine* (**int** *x1*, **int** *y1*, **int** *x2*, **int** *y2*)

draws a line from the point (*x1, y1*) to the point (*x2, y2*).

> *fillOval* (**int** *x*, **int** *y*, **int** *width*, **int** *height*)

draws an oval which could be enclosed in a rectangle whose upper-left corner is at (*x, y*) and whose width and height are given. (The rectangle is not drawn.) The oval is filled with the current color. There is a corresponding method *drawOval* that draws an oval outline. The method *drawRect* is similar to *fillRect* except that it draws the rectangle in outline.

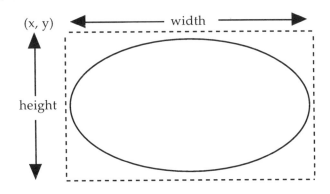

Figure 1.7 Drawing of Oval

Figure 1.7 shows an oval drawn using *fillOval* or *drawOval*.

Simple Examples of User-Defined Methods

The programmer can also create graphics methods that do not already exist in the *Console* class. For example, there are no methods for drawing a circle or a filled circle. The *drawOval* and *fillOval* methods of the *Console* class must be used with equal values for the parameters *width* and *height*.

We will define a method for drawing a circle of a given *radius* with its center at (*xc, yc*) in color *clr*.

```
// Method for drawing a circle.
static public void circle (int xc, int yc, int radius, Color clr)
{
    int width = radius * 2;
    int height = radius * 2;
    int x = xc - radius;
    int y = yc - radius;
    c.setColor (clr);
    c.drawOval (x, y, width, height);
} // circle method
```

Any methods used by a method labelled **static**, for example the *main* method, must also be labelled **static**. Since the *circle* method is to be available for use by other classes, it is also labelled as **public**.

It does not produce a value so the keyword **void** precedes *circle* which is the method's name. The parameters follow in parentheses. These are all of type **int** except the color *clr* which is of type *Color*.

In order to use the *drawOval* method of the object *c*, the *width*, *height*, and top-left corner at (*x, y*) have to be computed from the parameters *xc, yc*, and *radius* of the *circle* method. This is done in the first four statements of the method's body. In the first statement an integer variable *width* is **declared** and **assigned** a value of twice the radius. The * stands for multiplication.

Because the object identifier *c* is used in this method, the declaration of *c* as of type *Console* must be outside the body of the *main* method. Since it is now to be used by **static** methods such as the *circle* method and the *main* method, it too must be labelled **static**.

Here is the entire application program for drawing a red circle with its center at the window's center, touching the top of the window.

```
//The "RedCircle" class.
import java.awt.*;
import hsa.Console;

public class RedCircle
{
    static Console c;

    static public void main (String args [ ])
    {
        c = new Console ();
        int xc = c.maxx() / 2;
        int yc = c.maxy() / 2;
        int radius = c.maxy() / 2;
        circle (xc, yc, radius, Color.red);
    } // main method

    static public void circle (int xc, int yc, int radius, Color clr)
    {
        int width = radius * 2;
        int height = radius * 2;
        int x = xc - radius;
```

```
        int y = yc − radius;
        c.setColor (clr);
        c.drawOval (x, y, width, height);
    } // circle method
} /* RedCircle class */
```

In the *main* method the *circle* method is **called** or **invoked** by the statement

circle (xc, yc, radius, Color.red);

The **arguments** of the calling statement in this case have the same names as the **parameters** in the definition of the *circle* method but this is not necessary as long as they are in one-to-one correspondence and of compatible data types.

The diagram of Figure 1.8 illustrates the structure of the program. The *main* method uses the user-defined *circle* method. The *circle* method, in turn, calls the *drawOval* predefined method of the *Console* class.

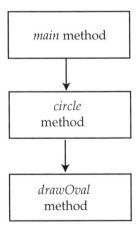

Figure 1.8 Structure Chart of Program

A user can create methods such as *circle* to perform a variety of tasks. For example, he or she could define a method called *ball* to create a filled circle. The *drawRect* and *fillRect* methods of the

Console class could be used to produce methods *square* and *block* in the same way.

A More Complicated Example

We will show how to program a method for drawing a square that is tilted relative to the console window. For this we cannot use the *drawRect* method because the *drawRect* method always produces a rectangle whose sides are parallel to the sides of the console window. Instead, we use the *drawLine* method to create a square by drawing four lines to outline the tilted square. If the four corners of square are at the points (x1, y1), (x2, y2), (x3, y3), and (x4, y4), we can write the instructions to draw the four lines as follows.

```
c.drawLine (x1, y1, x2, y2);
c.drawLine (x2, y2, x3, y3);
c.drawLine (x3, y3, x4, y4);
c.drawLine (x4, y4, x1, y1);
```

Determining the values of the coordinates of the four corners requires some knowledge of trigonometry. The first step is to define the last three points in terms of the point (x1, y1), the size of the square *size*, and the angle of tilt *angle* in degrees (see Figure 1.9).

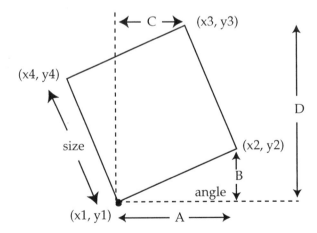

Figure 1.9 Tilted Square

Here is the definition of the *tiltSquare* method.

```
static public void tiltSquare (int x1, int y1, int size, int angle, Color clr)
{
    // Change angle to radians.
    double rAngle = angle * Math.PI / 180;
    // Compute four constants to help compute corners.
    final int A = (int) Math.round (size * Math.cos (rAngle));
    final int B = (int) Math.round (size * Math.sin (rAngle));
    final int C = (int) Math.round (size * Math.sqrt (2) *
                    Math.cos ((Math.PI/4) + rAngle));
    final int D =(int) Math.round (size * Math.sqrt (2) *
                    Math.sin ((Math.PI/4) + rAngle));
    // Compute corners.
    int x2 = x1 + A;
    int y2 = y1 – B;
    int x3 = x1 + C;
    int y3 = y1 – D;
    int x4 = x1 – B;
    int y4 = y1 – A;
    // Draw square.
    c.setColor (clr);
    c.drawLine (x1, y1, x2, y2);
    c.drawLine (x2, y2, x3, y3);
    c.drawLine (x3, y3, x4, y4);
    c.drawLine (x4, y4, x1, y1);
} // tiltSquare method
```

It is not necessary to follow all the details of the calculation but certain programming details should be noted. The constants *A, B, C,* and *D* are defined using the keyword **final** followed by the constant's data type, then its name, then an equal sign, then an arithmetic expression that produces its value. In this arithmetic expression the asterisk * is the multiplication sign. By convention the names of constants are expressed in upper case letters. Notice that the constant *PI* is defined in the *Math* class. The angle in radians *rAngle* is defined as a double length real number by the keyword **double** and assigned the value produced by multiplying the angle in degrees (*angle*) by *PI* and dividing by 180.

Programming Concepts in Java

The expression

Math.cos (rAngle)

is the cosine of the angle expressed in radians,

Math.sin (rAngle)

is the sine of the angle expressed in radians, and

Math.sqrt (2)

is the square root of 2. The three identifiers *cos*, *sin*, and *sqrt* are methods of the *Math* class that produce values.

The lines beginning with the // are **comments** to help explain what is happening in the program. These explanations are an essential part of the internal documentation of the program.

The final thing that should be noted is that each of the expressions for *A*, *B*, *C*, and *D* is enclosed in parentheses and preceded by *Math.round*. This means that the *Math* class *round* method is used to **round off** the values of each expression to the nearest integer since all values of coordinates (*x*, *y*) must be integers. The *round* method of the *Math* class produces a double length integer of type **long** and, in order to assign the value to an **int** variable, the result must be **cast** as (changed to) an **int** value by preceding it by (**int**).

The *tiltSquare* method could be used in a *main* method in this way.

tiltSquare (c.maxx () / 2, c.maxy () / 2, c.maxy () / 4, 30, Color.green);

This would produce a green square with one corner at the center of the window, of size *maxy*/4, tilted at an angle of 30 degrees to the horizontal.

A more interesting method called *moon* might be defined to use the *tiltSquare* method. It draws a series of tilted squares all having a common (*x1*, *y1*) with angles of tilt at 10 degree intervals from tilt 0 to tilt 350. The result is a lacy circular pattern (see Figure 1.10).

Here it is.

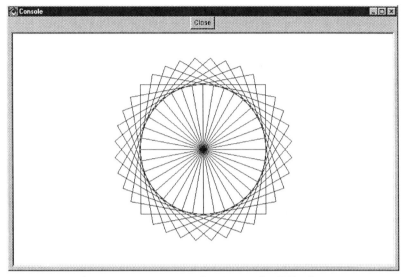

Figure 1.10 Moon in Console Window

```
// Method to draw a moon.
static public void moon (int xc, int yc, int size, Color clr)
{
    // Draw a series of tilted squares at intervals of 10 degrees
    // going from a tilt of 0 to a tilt of 350 degrees.
    for (int angle = 0; angle <= 350; angle = angle + 10)
    {
        tiltSquare (xc, yc, size, angle, clr);
    }
} // moon method
```

The body of this method contains a **repetition construct** which begins with the keyword **for** followed in parentheses by a series of three components separated by semicolons. The first component, namely **int** *angle* = 0, defines an integer variable *angle* that acts as the **counting index** and is initialized to zero. This part is called the **counting index initialization**. After the index initialization is the **continuation condition**: that the value of *angle* is less than or equal to 350 expressed by *angle* <= 350. The third component is the **incrementation** of the index:

  angle = angle + 10

The angle is increased by 10 each time the repetition is executed. So, on the first repetition the angle is 0, then on the second it is 10, on the third it is 20, on the fourth it is 30, and so on. When the angle becomes 360 the continuation condition is false and repetition ceases. This kind of repetition is called a **counted repetition**.

The *tiltSquare* instruction in the **body** of the **for** repetition construct will be executed for values of *angle* going from 0 degrees to 350 degrees at intervals of 10 degrees. This will draw 36 squares at various tilts.

The *main* method that draws a green moon centered in the center of the window would contain the statement:

  moon (c.maxx () / 2, c.maxy () / 2, c.maxy () / 4, Color.green);

Figure 1.11 shows a structure chart to illustrate the connection between the methods.

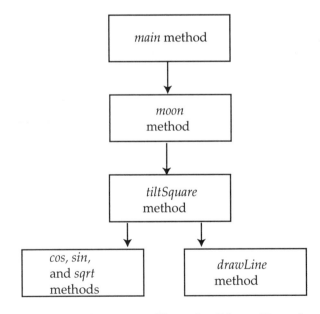

Figure 1.11 Structure Chart for Moon Drawing

1.9   The Form of Application Programs

In this chapter we have shown several complete application programs. All application programs contain a *main* method. The form of these has been:

```
//The "name-of-application" class.
import java.awt.*;
import hsa.Console;

public class name-of-application
{
    static Console c;

    static public void main (String args [ ])
    {
        c = new Console ( );
        details of application
    } // main method

        details of any user-defined methods
} /* name-of-application class */
```

The *main* method is labelled as **static** as are any methods called by the *main* or any other **static** method. If methods other than the *main* method use the *Console* variable *c*, the variable is labelled **static** and is declared outside the *main* method.

Rather than repeat all these parts we will show for many applications only those parts that provide the **name of the application class** as a comment, the **details of the particular application**, and **the details of any user-defined methods**. The remaining parts of the program are identical for every standalone program and we will include them only for larger programs in this book. It is, however, necessary to add them each time they are not already there or the program will not run.

This sort of pattern is similar to the use in legal firms of what is called **boiler plate**, namely standard material that can be copied into a particular legal document. With a computer editor this can be a simple operation.

In the programs presented in this book different typefaces are used for different components. This is to try to make the programs easily readable and understood. Keywords of the Java language are in **boldface**; identifiers of classes, objects, methods, and variables are in *italics*; comments, digits, and quoted strings are in plainface type. In the computer (when using *VisualAge for Java, Professional Edition for Windows, Version 2.0*) all these components are in the same typeface and in a typefont in which each character takes the same amount of space. The characters are in black on white with the exception of keywords which are in blue, comments which are in red, and quoted strings which are in green. (Many books show programs in this computer font.)

The typeface used to show the results of executing a program is the same with boldface being used to show what the user types during execution. Where output formatting is important a constant space font is used.

1.10 Chapter Summary

This chapter has introduced numerous programming concepts and has shown two important patterns or **paradigms** for creating programs. These paradigms are especially important when programs are large.

Steps in Programming

The process of programming can be divided into a series of steps.

- Working out the **specifications** of the problem to be solved.
- Designing an **algorithm** or set of instructions by which the problem will be solved.
- Expressing the algorithm in a high-level programming language.
- Ensuring that the algorithm (or program) is as understandably expressed as possible with additional documentation as required to make it so.

- Testing the program on a full range of data so as to eliminate errors.
- Maintaining the program by making changes as required over time.

Procedural Abstraction

Dividing large programs into smaller subprograms simplifies them. Subprograms are of two basic types:

- **procedures** which cause actions or change values of data stored in memory, or
- **functions** which map one value or set of values into another. For example, the *sqrt* function maps a number into its square root.

To use a subprogram, the programmer needs to know what its **parameters** are to be and what action or change in values is to be expected. This information is given in its **specification** and provides an interface so that it can be used without knowing the details inside the subprogram. These details are **hidden** from the user. This abstraction simplifies the program.

In Java all subprograms are called **methods**.

Data Abstraction

Often several methods of a program share the same data and the programmer must ensure that the actions of one method do not interfere unexpectedly with the actions of another method.

The data and all the methods that can modify them may be hidden in a **module**. This **encapsulation** creates an **object** that other parts of the program can use. This encapsulation is called **data abstraction**. To use this object, other parts of the program must first **import** it. The module itself must also declare as **public** the methods that can be used.

Object-Oriented Programming

Programming based on data abstraction is called **object-based programming** since the module corresponds to an object such as a list. True object-oriented programming requires encapsulation, the concept of a **class,** and **inheritance**. A **class** is a **template** from which multiple **instances** of objects are created. For example, several objects which are lists can be created from a class called *List*.

In Java there is a large library of predefined classes. From these, objects can be instantiated. The value of having these software components available is that programs can be built from off-the-shelf components. This saves much effort, particularly in creating large programs.

Objects, Classes, and Inheritance

There are three fundamental concepts in object-oriented programming which every Java user needs to understand. They are objects, classes, and inheritance.

An **object** is a set of data and the methods which operate on that data.

A **class** is a **template** for creating objects. From a class, you can create objects, each of which has its own data and an identical set of methods that apply to that data.

Inheritance incorporates all of the methods and data fields from one class into another class. Data fields may then be added and existing methods changed.

Graphics Procedures

Methods that can be used to create graphics are encapsulated in a class called *Console* which can be imported into (available to) any Java program. In the program an object of the class *Console* can be created (instantiated). Calling any of its methods requires the programmer to preface the method's name by the object's name, followed by a dot.

The colors used in drawing are encapsulated in the *Color* class and can be referred to by the names *red*, *green*, *blue*, and so on preceded by the class name *Color* followed by a dot.

User-Defined Methods

The programmer can also define methods. The form of the method definition used in this chapter is

static public void name (parameter declaration list)
{
    body of method
}

Each parameter declaration consists of its data type followed by its name. The list is separated by commas.

Structure Charts

The body of our user-defined methods contained calls to the methods of the *Console* object. A **structure chart** illustrates how the *main* method uses our *circle* method which in turn uses the *Console* *drawOval* method, illustrating the relationship between the *main* method, our method, and the *Console* object. Charts such as this are helpful in understanding program structure.

Other Java Syntax

The method is only one of many Java features we have introduced in this chapter. Here are others:

- Comments can be added to a program by having a // followed on the same line by the comment and then a Return. These do not affect the execution of the program and are there to help make the program more understandable – to document it. An alternative form of a comment is to preface the comment text by /* and follow it by */.
- Constants can be defined using the keyword **final,** followed by a data type and the name or identifier of the constant,

then an equal sign, then, in the example we showed, an **arithmetic expression** that gives a value to the constant.

- Arithmetic expressions have the usual mathematical symbols + for plus and – for minus. For multiplication we use *, and for division the slash /.

- In order for arithmetic expressions involving real values to have an integer value, they must be enclosed in parentheses and preceded by *Math.round*. The function *round* is predefined in the *Math* class and yields a value which is the rounded off value of its parameter. This value is of type **long**, the double length integer type. In order to change such a value to the type **int** it must be preceded by (**int**) which then **casts** it as type **int**.

- The division of two integers yields an integer. This has the effect of truncating any fractional part of the quotient.

- Other methods of the *Math* class: *sin, cos,* and *sqrt* were used in the calculation of the coordinates of the tilted square.

- The repetition construct or **for** loop was used to draw the moon. Later chapters will discuss this construct in more detail.

1.11 Exercises

Note: The following exercises require the writing of Java programs. Read Chapter 2 to see how to run them on the computer.

1. Write the method *square* with the signature

    void *square* (**int** *x*, **int** *y*, **int** *size, Color clr*)

    which when called, draws a square of *size* pixels in color *clr*. The upper-left corner of the square will be at (*x, y*). Use the method in an application program to place a yellow square of size about one quarter of the window width with its center in the center of the window.

2. Write the method *block* with the signature

    void *block* (**int** *x*, **int** *y*, **int** *size*, *Color clr*)

    which produces a filled square. Use this in an application program to draw a series of blocks of four different colors across the bottom of the window.

3. Use a repetition construct in a program to draw a pattern of three black blocks separated by three red squares of the same size across the top of the window. Make the squares or blocks as large as will fit into the width of the window. This size will be *maxx*()/6. **Hint:** Use this construct to draw the three black blocks:

    ```
    int size = c.maxx () / 6;
    for (int xcorn = 0; xcorn <= 4 * size; xcorn = xcorn + 2 * size)
    {
        block (xcorner, 0, size, clr);
    }
    ```

4. Write a program that uses the *moon* method of this chapter to draw three blue moons spaced apart and centered on the window. Choose an appropriate size for the radius of the moon.

5. Create a circle of red balls arranged like beads on a string. To solve this problem, begin by creating a method that draws a ball of *radius*, positioned so that its center (*xc, yc*) is at the end of a stick of length *size* whose other end is at the point (*xp, yp*), and which makes an angle *angle* with the x-axis (the horizontal). Figure 1.12 shows this.

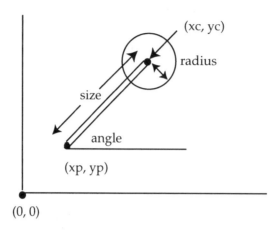

Figure 1.12 Ball on a Stick

The method would have the following signature.

   void *ballOnStick* (**int** *xp*, **int** *yp*, **int** *size*, **int** *radius*, *Color clr*)

Note that the point in the *tiltSquare* method of this chapter
(*x2, y2*) corresponds to the center of the ball.

   Use the *ballOnStick* method to create a method that draws a
circle of balls using the **for** repetition construct. Decide what
the step size in the angle must be in order for the balls to just
touch. What happens if it is smaller than this size?

Chapter 2

The VisualAge for Java Environment

In the first chapter a number of technical terms were introduced and some of the elements of the Java programming language were presented. There were enough details to show the basic structure of a Java standalone application program. Java programs can run in many computer **platforms**. Although Java programs themselves are independent of the environment used, this book shows how they can be run on a PC using **Microsoft Windows 95, 98** or **Windows NT** under the **VisualAge for Java, Professional Edition for Windows, Version 2.0   Environment**. The user may require an alternative reference if another environment is used.

2.1   Beginning to Use VisualAge for Java

Most students these days have had experience running computer applications such as word processing programs or spread sheets. The basic notions of menu bars, pop-up menus, selecting items, clicking or dragging a mouse, entering information in a dialog box, selecting a radio button, and so on are reasonably understood.

Many will already be familiar with the *Windows 95, 98*, or *NT* operating system. So we will be using these terms freely.

To begin, after any local **login**, click the *Start* button in the lower-left corner.

Now select *Programs* from the menu by dragging up to it and then select *IBM VisualAge for Java for Windows* from the sub-menu. Again select *IBM VisualAge for Java* from the sub-sub-menu (see Figure 2.1).

Now release the mouse button. At this stage, after a splash screen, the **Workbench** window appears with a dialog box labelled *Welcome to VisualAge* above it (see Figure 2.2). Select the button *Go to the Workbench* radio button and click the *OK* button. The *Workbench* window is now visible (see Figure 2.3).

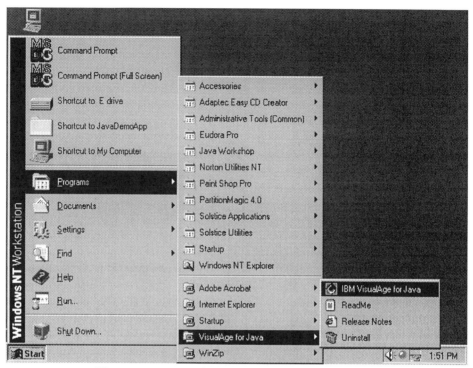

Figure 2.1 Starting up VisualAge for Java

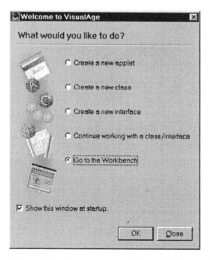

Figure 2.2 The *Welcome to VisualAge* dialog box

The *Workbench* has a sub-window, the **lower pane** at the bottom, in which programs can be typed. Under the word *Workbench* is a **menu bar** with the labels:

File Edit Workspace Selected Window Help

These labels allow you to select the commands necessary to enter, edit, and save your Java program.

Below the menu bar is a row of **icon buttons**, called the **tool bar**. Each of these buttons can be clicked. When you place the mouse over any button, a message describing the function of the button appears. For example, clicking the first button from the left (the runner) will run the program.

Below the icon buttons is a set of tabs that says:

Projects   Packages   Classes   Interfaces   All Problems

These tabs are different ways of organizing the elements in the workspace. We will always use the Project organization. The Project tab should always be selected. At startup time the **upper pane** of the *Workbench* window will have a list of all current projects. This list also includes a large collection of ready-made classes known as the Java class libraries.

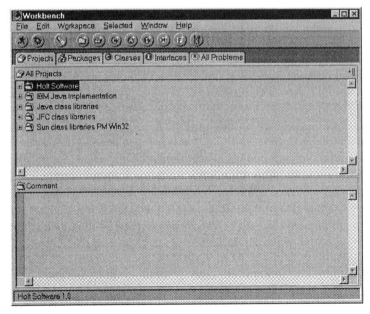

Figure 2.3 The VisualAge Workbench

Organization of VisualAge for Java

Java programs are all **classes**. But not all classes are programs. Classes contain **methods**. If a class contains a *main* method it is a Java standalone application program. A standalone program may use other classes that are not programs. Classes can be grouped together in a **package**. Classes in the same package can use each other. They do not need to be **imported**.

Programs that were shown in Chapter 1 imported classes in the *Java abstract windowing toolkit (awt)* package by including the statement:

import *java.awt.*;*

The asterisk indicates that all the classes in the *awt* package could be used. The *Console* class of Holt Software Associates (hsa) was imported by the statement:

import *hsa.Console;*

In order to avoid having to import any classes that you create, it is best to keep them all in a package called the **default package**.

The top level for organizing Java programs is the project. Any number of packages or classes may be placed in a project. On a multi-user system, it is best if each user has a single project whose name is the user's name. This simplifies what must be done when a user starts (**logs in**) and stops (**logs out**) using the computer.

VisualAge for Java provides a number of projects. These are the **class libraries** that are part of the Java specification.

The projects are called:

IBM Java Implementation
Java class libraries
JFC class libraries
Sun class libraries PM Win32

In the top pane of the *Workbench* window, any project, package, or class with contents has a small plus or minus sign to the left of it. When the contents are hidden, the sign is a plus. When the contents are displayed, the sign is a minus sign. In Figure 2.4, the method *circle* of the *RedCircle* class of the project *JNP Hume's* default pack-

age has been selected and is displayed in the lower pane of the
Workbench window.

To display the packages in a project, click on the plus sign
beside the project icon. The packages are displayed underneath the
project. To hide them, click on the minus sign beside the project.

To display the classes in a package, click on the plus sign
beside the package. To display the methods in a class, click on the
plus sign beside the class.

When a single class or method is highlighted in the upper pane,
the lower pane displays the text of the class header or method.

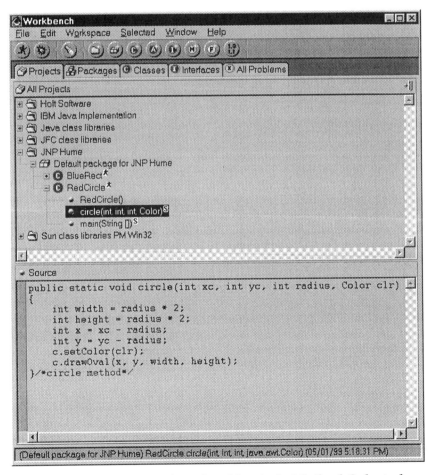

Figure 2.4 The Workbench with *circle* Method Selected

Starting a Project

It is time now to start a project. As mentioned above, all of your programs should be placed in a single project. This not only prevents work from being lost, but ensures that you only have to go through the work of setting up a project once.

To start a project, click on the *Project* icon button (the fourth from the right) on the top of the *Workbench* window, selecting

Add New or Existing Project to Workspace.

A window labelled

SmartGuide - Add Project

appears (see Figure 2.5). In this window, the radio button labelled *Create a new Project named:* is already selected. Type in a name. It is probably best to use your own name. When this is done, click the *Finish* button. Your project is thus added to the list of projects in alphabetical order among the other projects in the list.

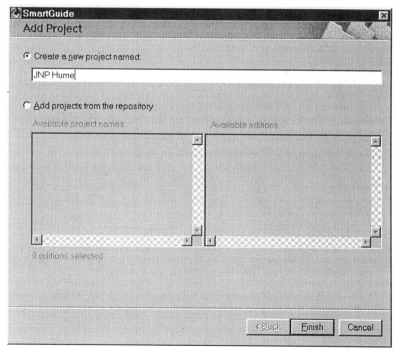

Figure 2.5 The *SmartGuide - Add Project* Window

2.2 Entering an Application Program

To begin to enter an application program which, remember, consists of a class, click on the *Classes* icon button (fifth on the left) thus selecting

Create Class

This causes the

SmartGuide - Create Class

dialog box to appear (see Figure 2.6). Leave the *Package* text field blank and type in the name of the class, which for the first program of Chapter 1 would be *BlueRect*.

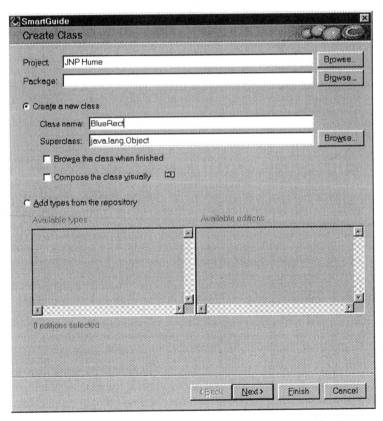

Figure 2.6 The *SmartGuide - Create Class* Window

There are two check boxes beneath the class name, labelled *Browse the class when finished* and *Compose the class visually*. Make certain neither are checked and then click *Finish*. The class is then created and the class name is now shown in the *Project* list as a sub-heading under the default package which is under your project name.

In the program entry window at the bottom of the **Workbench** there appears a skeleton of an application program preceded by this comment

```
/* This class was created in VisualAge */
```

The class is written without any body as

```
class BlueRect {
}
```

The opening curly brace of the class is placed after the class name. This is not the style we will be using, so place the mouse just in front of the opening curly brace and click. Now press **Return** (the Enter key) and the curly brace will be on the line below the letter *c* of **class**. Notice that the keyword **class** is in blue. All keywords are shown in blue. We make a practice of putting the keyword **public** in front of the keyword **class**. To do this, click in front of the *c* of **class** and type in the word "public". Editing in the *VisualAge for Java* environment is similar to most word processors.

Now enter the import lines from the *BlueRect* class. Move the cursor line just after the comment and enter

```
import java.awt.*;
import hsa.Console;
```

The rest of the class *BlueRect* can now be entered. First enter the *main* method. Pressing return after the opening curly brace of the class in its new position will cause automatic indentation so the line

```
static public void main (String args [])
```

can be typed. Type **Return**, then the opening curly brace of the *main* method's body, then **Return**. Again automatic indentation occurs. The body of the *main* method stays at this same level of indentation until the closing curly brace is typed, then it moves over to the left automatically. This automatic indenting greatly assists the paragraphing of programs without affecting their execution, making them easier to understand. Enter the rest of the *main* method.

```
static public void main (String[] args)
{
    Console c;
    c = new Console ();
    c.setColor (Color.blue);
    c.fillRect (0, 0, 50, 100);
} // main method
```

When the *main* method has been entered, select *Save* in the *Edit* menu at the top of the *Workbench*. When the program is saved, *VisualAge for Java* separates the *main* method from the class header. The upper pane now shows the *main* method in the *BlueRect* class. The class header no longer has the *main* method in it. To edit the *main* method, select it in the upper pane. The text of the *main* method will appear in the lower pane where it can be edited.

2.3   Errors in Programs

When a program is saved it is automatically **compiled**, that is, translated into Java **bytecode** that can then be run on any computer platform that has a Java **interpreter**. If there are no syntax errors in the program, it can be run immediately. At this stage in the programming process however, program fragments usually contain syntax errors (commonly omitted semicolons or curly braces).

VisualAge for Java highlights these errors and displays an error message describing the nature of the error in the **status line** at the bottom of the *Workbench* below the program itself. When a method with an error is saved, its name in the *Project* list has a red X beside it and the class containing it has a grey X.

The user can correct these errors using standard editing methods and the *Edit* menu.

2.4   Running Programs

An error in a program is called an **unresolved problem**. When all errors are corrected, by editing, the program can be **run**.

If a class is runnable (it has a *main* method or its an applet), a running person icon appears beside the class name in the upper pane. To run a program, the class or any of its methods must be selected in the upper pane. Next, click the **running person icon** from the icon buttons at the top of the *Workbench*.

The program starts to execute. When the *BlueRect* class is successfully executed the *Console* window appears with the blue rectangle in the top-left corner (see Figure 2.7).

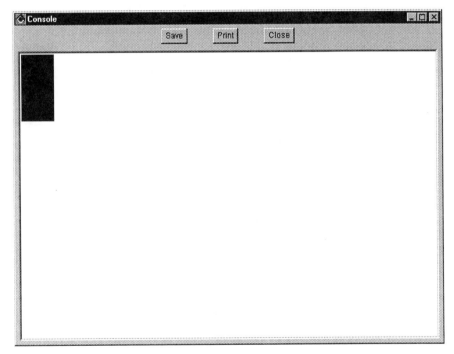

Figure 2.7 The Output from *BlueRect*

To go back to the program, either click *Quit* in the *Console* window or close the window by clicking on the small box, marked x, in its upper-right corner.

As more programs are created their class names will be listed under your project name. To execute any one of the programs:

- Select the program's class name or any of its methods.
- Click on the run icon.

2.5 Modifying an Existing Program

Sometimes a programmer needs to create a new program that is very similar to one that is already saved. This new program can be produced by editing the old one. To do this, select the class name of the existing program in the upper pane, then choose *Reorganize* from the *Selected* menu at the top of the *Workbench*. This brings up a sub-menu from which you select *Copy*. A dialog box appears asking where the copy is to go (Figure 2.8). Just click *OK*.

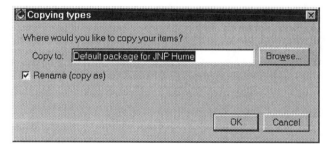

Figure 2.8 The *Copying types* Dialog Box

A second dialog box then appears (see Figure 2.9). In it the present name of the class is highlighted. Change this to a new name then press *OK* to save the copy under this new name.

Figure 2.9 The *Copy* Dialog Box

Now the copy can be changed without the risk of changing the original program. This process can be used if you first create a simple program in your project with a class called *BoilerPlate* then copy it as the basis for all other application programs. Here is the *BoilerPlate* program.

```
// The "BoilerPlate" class.
import java.awt.*;
import hsa.Console;

public class BoilerPlate
{
    static Console c;

    static public void main (String args [])
    {
        c = new Console ();
        // Replace the following line.
        c.println ("BoilerPlate");
    } // main method
} /* BoilerPlate class */
```

Once this program is saved in memory all other programs can be entered without resort to the *SmartGuide* by copying the *BoilerPlate* program and modifying it to suit the particular application at hand. This can save a great deal of time.

2.6 Programs with Several Methods

So far each program that we showed has only a *main* method in its class, namely the *BlueRect* class or the *BoilerPlate* class. Now we will see what happens when a program like the *RedCircle* class of Chapter 1 is entered. *RedCircle* has a *main* method and a *circle* method.

Programs with several methods are often entered one method at a time. The first method to be entered is the *main* method since it is what makes the class a program. The class *RedCircle* would be entered just as the class *BlueRect* was entered but the *circle* method would not be entered at this stage. After the *main* method in its class is entered, click *Save* in the *File* menu. An unresolved problem will be noted, namely that there is no *circle* method and the listing of the *RedCircle* class in the *Project* list will be marked with an X.

Now the *circle* method must be entered since the incomplete class with the unresolved problem cannot be run.

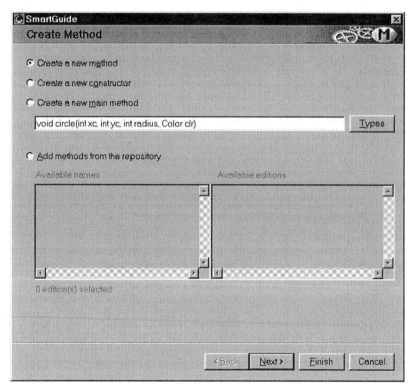

Figure 2.10 The *SmartGuide - Create Method* Dialog Box

First be sure that the class with the *main* method is selected. To enter another method, click the **M** (for method) **icon** at the top of the *Workbench*. A dialog box (Figure 2.10) labelled *SmartGuide - Create Method* appears asking for the signature of the method to be typed in. Part of this is already entered under *Method Name*. It says *void newMethod()*. This should be replaced with the return type, name, and parameters of the actual method you want to enter. Do not enter any of the **visibility modifiers: public, private, protected, static**, or **synchronized**. For the *circle* method, the method name must be changed and the parameters with their data types placed in the parentheses.

```
void circle (int xc, int yc, int radius, Color clr)
```

Because you need to change the method attribute to **static**, click the *Next>* button instead of *Finish*. The brings up a second dialog box labelled *SmartGuide - Attributes* (Figure 2.11). Click the *static* check box and then press the *Finish* button.

Click the **static** button and the **public** button and edit the rest of the header for the *circle* method. Then click *Finish*.

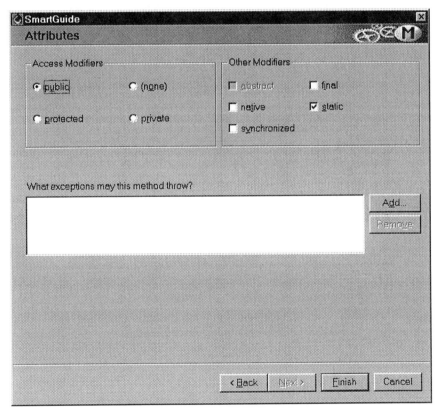

Figure 2.11 The *SmartGuide - Attributes* Dialog Box

The method is created and appears in the upper pane. The text of the *circle* method appears in the lower pane. It has the curly braces enclosing its empty body. Insert the rest of the *circle* method between the curly braces.

The actual body of the *circle* method is then entered and the method saved. Its name then appears in the upper pane. If there are no syntax errors in *circle*, the *RedCircle* class should now have no unresolved problems and can be run in the same way as *BlueRect* was run.

A faster way to enter programs with several methods is to enter other methods at the same time as you enter the *main* method. Be sure the additional methods are placed inside the closing curly brace of the class containing the *main* method.

2.7   Running on a Shared Computer

When a number of people use the same computer, it is not possible for each user to maintain files of programs and data in the same area of memory.

In the *VisualAge for Java* environment all projects are stored in a **Repository**. It would be very confusing if a number of different users' work were kept in the same Repository. It is thus necessary to store each user's work in some form of back-up storage, either off-line on a floppy disk, or on a preallotted part of the computer's hard disk. Work is stored as a number of text files.

This means that at the end of a session on the computer, users must arrange to **export** their work to this back-up store. Then, when users begin a new session on the computer, their work, or the part that is of interest, must be **imported**. If you are not working in a shared environment, you need only import and export files when you want to bring files into or out of *VisualAge for Java*.

Importing Files into *VisualAge for Java*

In general, when you start up a session in *VisualAge for Java*, the Repository does not contain any of your own work. To import files, you must select *Import* from the *File* menu. This causes a dialog box to appear labelled *SmartGuide - Type of Import* (see Figure 2.12).

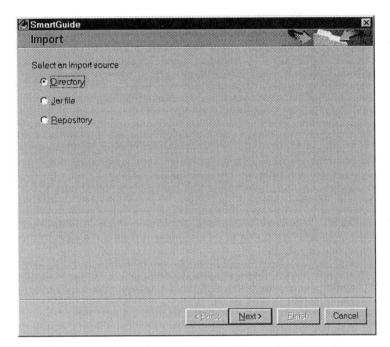

Figure 2.12 The *SmartGuide - Import* Dialog Box

Select the *Directory* radio button and click *Next>*. A dialog box labelled *SmartGuide − Import from a directory* appears (see Figure 2.13).

Enter the directory containing the Java files in the *Directory* text field and the name of your project (likely your own name) in the *Project* text field. Note that your project does not have to exist as the importation procedure will automatically create it, if necessary.

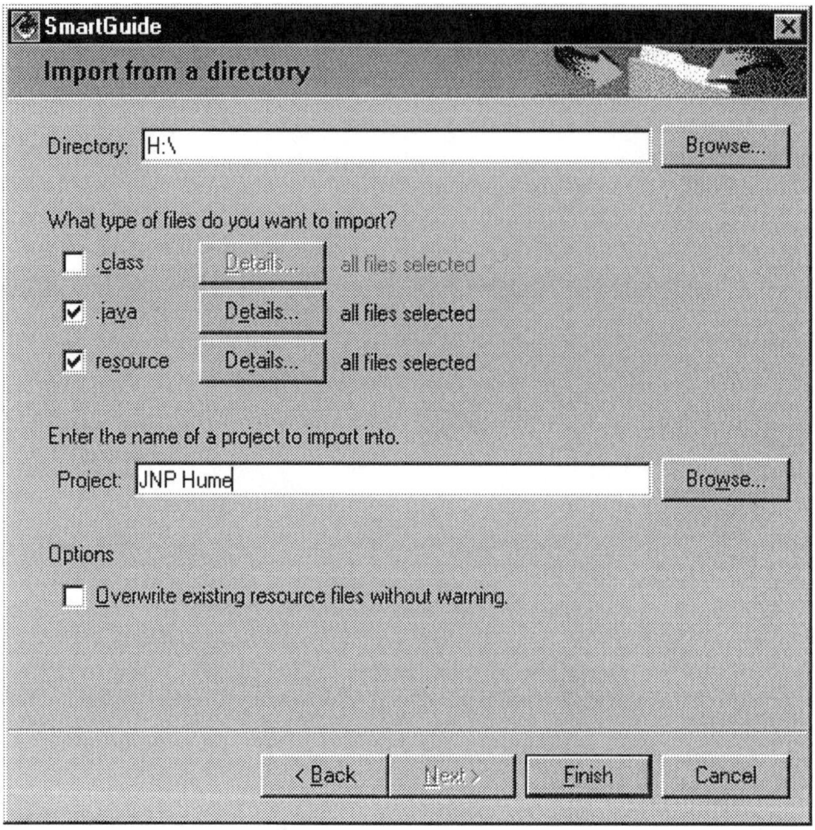

Figure 2.13 The *SmartGuide - Import from a directory* Dialog Box

If you need to import data files as well (for example, to be read in by a program), leave the *resource* check box selected, otherwise uncheck it. Finally, click the *Details* button beside the *.java* check box. A dialog box labelled *Source file import* appears (see Figure 2.14). Select the Java files you want imported into your project and click OK.

Beside the *Details* button, the numbers of files to be imported is listed. If you are importing data files, click the *Details* button beside the *resource* check box and select the data files you want imported.

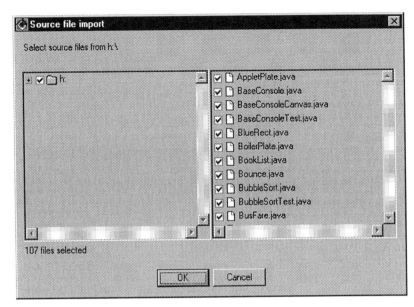

Figure 2.14 The *SmartGuide - Source file import* Dialog Box

Once that is done, click the *Finish* button to start the
importation process. If you are importing to a project that does not
yet exist, a *Question* dialog box appears asking you to confirm the
creation of the project (see Figure 2.15).

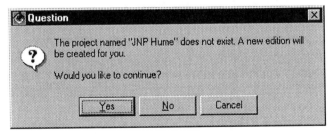

Figure 2.15 The *Question* Dialog Box

Once you confirm the project creation, all the files are
imported into the Repository and compiled. The project and all
the classes appear in the Workbench where they can be edited.

Exporting Files from *VisualAge for Java*

When you are finished working on your files in a shared environment, you must export your work or it will be lost. To export your files from *VisualAge for Java*, select your project in the upper pane and select *Export* from the *File* menu. A window labelled *SmartGuide – Export* appears (see Figure 2.16).

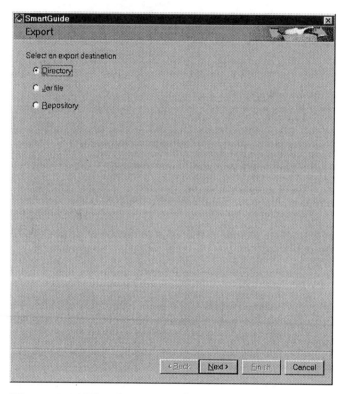

Figure 2.16 The *SmartGuide - Export* Dialog Box

Select the *Directory* radio button and click *Next>*. A second dialog box labelled *SmartGuide – Export to a directory* appears (see Figure 2.17).

Enter the name of the directory into which the *.java* files should be copied. Unless you specifically need the *.class* files or have modified the data files, unselect the *.class* and *resource* check box. Click the *Finish* button. *VisualAge for Java* copies the files from the

Repository to the specified directory. The *.java* files are text files that can be copied onto diskette and used in other Java environments.

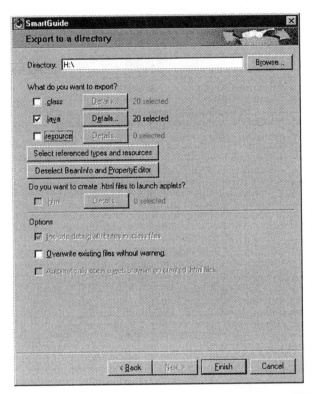

Figure 2.17 The *SmartGuide - Export to a directory* **Dialog Box**

2.8 Manipulating Classes or Methods

Once a class or method has been created, *VisualAge for Java* provides a number of facilities for manipulating it. These facilities allow users to print paper copies, to remove classes that are no longer needed, and to create new ones more quickly by copying and renaming.

Printing

Any classes or methods in the workspace can be printed. Select the class or method in the upper pane then select *Print* from the *Selected* menu. This brings up a dialog box (Figure 2.18) labelled *Print*. The check boxes that are usually wanted are already checked by default, so just click OK.

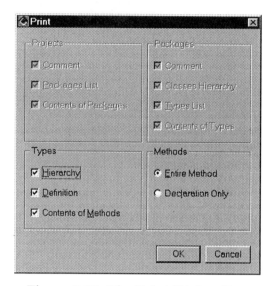

Figure 2.18 The Print Dialog Box

Deleting a Class

To delete a class, select the class in the upper pane and select the *Delete* command from the *Selected* menu. A dialog box asks if you really want to delete the class including its methods. Press "Yes". You should note, however, that this may cause unresolved problems in other classes that use the class you delete.

Copying a Class

To copy a class, select the name of the existing class in the upper pane of the Workbench, then choose *Reorganize* from the *Selected* menu. This brings up a sub-menu from which you select *Copy*. A dialog box appears asking where the copy is to go. Click *OK*. A second dialog box then appears. In it the present name of the class is highlighted. Change this to a new name and press *OK* to save the copy under this new name.

Renaming a Class

To rename a class, select the class to be renamed in the upper pane of the Workbench, then choose *Reorganize* from the *Selected* menu. This brings up a sub-menu from which you select *Rename*. A dialog box then asks for the new name. Fill it in and click *OK*.

All these last three operations can be applied to a method by selecting it in the upper pane as you did the class name.

2.9   List of Commands in Workbench Menu

The following is a list of all the commands in the *Workbench* window. It does not describe all the commands in detail, but indicates which commands are available and where they are found. This list is placed here for future reference and you may wish to skip past it at this stage.

File menu

Quick Start	Bring up a dialog box to perform basic operations such as creating classes, applets, and so on.
Import	Import text versions of Java programs into *VisualAge for Java*.

Export	Export projects, packages, or classes from *VisualAge for Java* into text form.
Print Setup	Set up the printer that *VisualAge for Java* uses.
<Set of items>	The last five projects, packages, or classes that can be brought up instantly from the File menu.
Save Workspace	Save the current workspace.
Exit VisualAge	Leave *VisualAge for Java*.

Edit menu

Revert to Saved	Undo any changes in edited item since last save.
Undo	Undo the last change in the text.
Redo	Redo an undone change in the text.
Cut	Copy the selected text to the paste buffer and delete the selection.
Copy	Copy the selected text to the paste buffer.
Paste	Paste the contents of the paste buffer.
Select All	Select all the text in the lower pane.
Format Code	Indents the code in the lower pane. The placement of the open brace (open brace on the same line or the next) can be controlled as an option (see *Option* in the *Window* menu).
Find/Replace	Find specified text in the lower pane. Replace it with specified replacement text.
Search	Search for the item in the workspace that bears the name of the selected text. Finds classes, methods, and fields with a specified name in any project, package, or class in the workspace.
Print Text	Print the text in the lower pane.
Save	Save the edited text in the lower pane. If the method definition has changed, add this new definition to the class.
Save Replace	Save the edited text in the lower pane. If the method definition has changed, replace the original definition.
Breakpoint	Insert or remove a breakpoint on the line where the cursor is located.

Workspace menu

Open Project Browser   Display a list of projects to open into a *Project* window.

Open Package Browser   Display a list of packages to open into a *Package* window.

Open Type Browser   Display a list of classes to open into a *Class* window.

Search   Search for the item selected in the upper pane in the workspace. Finds classes, methods, and fields with a specified name in any project, package, or class in the workspace.

Search Again   Repeat a previously occurring search.

Search Results   Bring up the search window.

Tools   A hierarchical menu with a sub-menu with one item called *Fix Manager*. This gives the current fix level of *VisualAge for Java*.

Selected menu (for Classes)

Open   Open the selected class into a *Class* window and place it in the *File* menu for easy access.

Open To   Open the selected class into a *Class* window with a specified tab set. This is a hierarchical menu with the sub-menu specifying the tab to be set.

Go To   This is a hierarchical menu with the sub-menu specifying the type of items to go to. A dialog box listing all of the items of the specified type (project, package, or class) appears. Selecting the desired item then causes the upper pane to display the specified item, expanding projects and packages if necessary.

Add   This is a hierarchical menu with a sub-menu allowing you to create a new project, class, interface, applet, method, or field.

Method Template   Create a generic method in the class that can then be edited.

Import   Import text versions of Java programs into *VisualAge for Java*.

Export	Export the selected class from *VisualAge for Java* into text form.
References To	This is a hierarchical menu allowing you to search for references to the selected class or a field in the class.
Replace With	Replace the class with a different edition of the class. This command is *very* useful if you have made catastrophic changes to a class and want to revert to some previous save. It helps to remember *when* the last save was, as that is how the different saves are sorted.
Delete	Delete the selected class.
Reorganize	This is a hierarchical menu with a sub-menu with three items: Copy, Move and Rename. This allows for copying, moving and renaming of the selected class.
Manage	This is a hierarchical menu with a sub-menu with one item: Version. This sets the version number of the selected class.
Compare With	Compare the contents of the class with another edition of the same class. This command is very useful if you have made changes to a class and it has now stopped working and you cannot remember what you did.
Run	This is a hierarchical menu with a sub-menu to run a class that is an applet or has a *main* method.
Document	This is a hierarchical menu with a sub-menu with two items: Print and Generate javadoc. This allows for printing of the selected class or generating the javadoc documentation of the selected class.
Externalize Strings	Used to create String resources. Very advanced.
Tools	Used for Remote Method Invocation and database access. Very advanced.
Properties	Examine and modify the properties of the selected class, such as the command line arguments to be used when it is run, or the properties of the applet.

Selected menu (for Methods)

Open	Open the selected method into a *Method* window and place it in the *File* menu for easy access.
Open To	Open the selected method into a *Method* window with a specified tab set. This is a hierarchical menu with the sub-menu specifying the tab to be set.
Go To	This is a hierarchical menu with the sub-menu specifying the type of items to go to. A dialog box listing all of the items of the specified type (project, package, or class) appears. Selecting the desired item then causes the upper pane to display the specified item, expanding projects and packages if necessary.
Add	This is a hierarchical menu with a sub-menu allowing you to create a new project, class, interface, applet, method, or field.
Method Template	Create a generic method in the class that can then be edited.
References To	Search for references to the selected method in the workspace, project, package, or class. This command is very useful if you want to know where your method is used.
Declarations Of	Search for where the selected method is declared in the workspace, project, or package.
Replace With	Replace the method with a different edition of the method. This is *very* useful if you have made catastrophic changes to a method and want to revert to some previous save. It helps to remember when the last save was, as that is how the different saves are sorted.
Delete	Delete the selected method.
Reorganize	This is a hierarchical menu with a sub-menu with three items: Copy, Move and Rename. This allows for copying, moving and renaming of the selected method.

Compare With	Compare the method with another edition of the same method. This command is very useful if you have made changes to a method and it has now stopped working and you cannot remember what you did.
Run	This is a hierarchical menu with a sub-menu to run a class that is an applet or has a *main* method.
Print	Print the selected method.
Properties	View the properties of the method.

Window menu

Clone	Create an identical copy of the active window which can then be manipulated independently.
Switch To	Switch to any other open *VisualAge for Java* window.
Refresh	Refresh (redraw) all the windows in *VisualAge for Java*.
Lock Window	Make the active window unclosable. This can be turned off when you try to close a locked window, but stops you from closing the window accidentally.
Maximize Pane	Make the selected pane (upper or lower) the whole window. This menu item becomes Restore Pane to split the window into the upper and lower pane again.
Orientation	This is a hierarchical menu with a sub-menu allowing you to split the window horizontally or vertically. The book assumes a vertical split.
Show Edition Names	Toggle the display of the version and edition numbers in the upper pane.
Workbench	Open and display the *Workbench* window.
Scrapbook	Open and display the *Scrapbook* window.
Repository Explorer	Open and display the *Repository Explorer*.
Console	Open and display the *Console* window. (Note that this is not the *Console* window of the *hsa* class *Console*.)
Log	Open and display the *Log* window.

| *Debug* | This is a hierarchical menu with a sub-menu allowing you to open the Debugger window with either the trace panel or breakpoint panel visible. |
| *Options* | Set the options for *VisualAge for Java*. Controls behavior such as how the automatic code formatter works, the font sizes and colors, and the workspace class path. |

Help menu

All *Help* menu items bring up the online help in an Internet Web Navigator (likely *Netscape Navigator* or *Microsoft Internet Explorer*).

Help Home Page	Display a visual depiction of the *Help* menu with the same choices.
Concepts	Explain the basic concepts that underlie the *VisualAge for Java* environment.
Tasks	Display instructions on how to perform tasks such as navigating the workbench, building programs, and running and debugging programs.
Reference	Display instructions on common tasks such as resizing windows, a list of all icons and windows used by *VisualAge for Java*, and the complete documentation to the Java class libraries.
Getting Started	Display a tutorial introduction to *VisualAge for Java* using the visual design tools.
Glossary	Display a list of technical terms and definitions used by *VisualAge for Java*.
Search	Search the online help for a phrase or word. The *VisualAge for Java Search Engine* must be started for this to work.
Samples	Display a list of help samples.
PDF Index	Display a list of PDF Help files available.
Support	Load IBM's *VisualAge for Java* web page into the Internet Browser.
Help on Help	Display the help on the help system.
About VisualAge	Display the version number and trademark information about *VisualAge for Java*.

2.10 Chapter Summary

This chapter explained how to enter a Java standalone application program into a PC computer using the IBM *VisualAge for Java* environment. Knowledge of standard computer editing operations using a **mouse** in the *Windows* environment and related tasks is assumed.

Workbench

Programs are entered and edited using the **Workbench** window. It has a **menu bar** across the top. Below is a bar of **tool icons** that can be clicked for various actions. Below that, is the **upper pane** of the window which contains a list of projects, classes, and methods in the current **Workspace**. The **lower pane** is used to enter and display classes and methods. At the bottom of the window is a **status line** used to show error messages. The relative sizes of the upper and lower panes can be changed by dragging the boundary between them.

Starting

The first time the computer is used, the name of the **project** must be selected. We advise users to start a single project, using as its name their own name. It is also wise (and simpler) to use the **default package** to contain all of your classes. Your project name will appear in the list of projects in the upper pane. This list of projects also contains all the Java class libraries available for use.

Creating Classes and Methods

Classes and methods can be entered by following the *SmartGuide* path of dialog boxes.

The *SmartGuide* lets you enter methods of an application program class other than a *main* method separately from entering the class. This is perhaps slower than entering all methods at one time.

Running Programs

The act of saving a class causes it to be **compiled** into **Java bytecode** that can be executed on any computer platform having a Java **interpreter**. **Syntax errors** are reported in the **status line** and the line (or part of it) in question is highlighted. A program cannot be run until all such errors are corrected. Errors are cataloged in the list of **unresolved problems**.

To run a program, click the running person icon button. If a class uses the *Console* class, the *Console* window appears. This is the Holt Software *Console* developed by Holt Software Associates and is not to be confused with the Console referred to in the *VisualAge for Java Window* menu commands.

Using the *BoilerPlate* Class

Users can save time entering Java application programs that use the *Console* class by modifying a class called *BoilerPlate*. This contains a skeleton program with a *main* method. The one statement in its body can be replaced by the actual body of the new *main* method.

To use this *BoilerPlate* system:

- Select the *BoilerPlate* class in the *Projects* list.
- Choose the *Copy* command from the *Reorganize* sub-menu of the *Selected* menu.
- Insert the class name of the new application in the second dialog box that appears, then press OK.
- Make the changes in the copy of the *BoilerPlate* class that appears in the lower pane, then save it.
- Be sure to change the one line body of the *main* method in *BoilerPlate* to the new *main* method body and the final comment to reference the new application class name.

Including More Methods than a *main*

Once the class with the *main* method has been saved, programmers can add additional methods using the *SmartGuide* and the *M* icon button. It may be faster, however, to enter all the methods of an application class at one time.

Running on a Shared Computer

In *VisualAge for Java* all projects are stored in a **Repository**. Individual users' work will probably be kept on a floppy disk or in prealloted limited disk space on the computer.

When a user begins a computer session, his or her own project must be **imported** and at the end of the session the project is **exported**. This process is easiest if a single project name is involved and the same **home directory** is always used.

Manipulating Classes or Methods

Classes or methods can be copied, renamed, printed, or deleted using commands in the *Selected* menu. Menu commands are listed in this chapter.

Chapter 3

Basic Programming Language Concepts

In the first chapter we looked at two programming paradigms: the procedure-oriented paradigm and the object-oriented paradigm and illustrated these using graphic examples. We showed how to use simple predefined classes. In addition we introduced constants, arithmetic expressions, comments, and repetition. The programming language used was Java.

Now we must begin a more systematic examination of the Java language. We will start by introducing a language for defining the Java programming language. Then the various primitive data types will be presented along with the way variables of the different types are declared, how expressions are formed, how values are assigned to variables, and output. Comments are explained as a method for documenting a program and making it more understandable.

3.1   Metalanguage for Defining Syntax

High-level programming languages have a formal structure that allows the computer to translate programs into instructions to implement algorithms. Just as any **natural language** like English has a **grammar** and a **vocabulary**, so too does a programming language like Java.

The vocabulary of Java includes words that are **reserved** by the language. These are the **keywords** of the language such as **if, while,** and **for.**

Java programmers also create their own words as **identifiers,** or **names,** for user-defined methods, classes, constants, and variables. There are rules for creating these identifiers.

- An identifier should be a sequence of letters, digits, and underscores beginning with a letter.
- Reserved words may not be used as identifiers.

Upper and lower case letters are distinct in keywords and identifiers. So *Tax* is distinct from *tax*. By convention we have class names begin with an upper case letter, method and variable names with a lower case letter. Constants have identifiers that are all upper case.

Extended Backus-Naur Form or **EBNF** grammar is a commonly-used **syntax** notation. It is a language that records the syntax rules, that is, rules for writing or **producing** acceptable statements in the Java language. EBNF is a **metalanguage** for expressing these **production rules**.

Each rule defines a **syntactic variable** such as an *identifier* in terms of other syntactic variables, and strings of characters that will ultimately form part of the Java program. These strings of characters are called **terminal tokens**. Terminal tokens in EBNF are shown in boldface type. Here is the definition of an identifier.

identifier ::= letter {letterOrDigitOrUnderScore}

In this definition the identifier is defined as being a *letter* followed by zero or more instances of *letterOrDigitOrUnderScore*. The symbol ::= means "is defined by". The curly braces {} in EBNF mean that what is enclosed can occur zero or more times. Square brackets [ ] in EBNF mean that an item is optional. This use is quite separate from the use of curly braces or square brackets in a Java program. A vertical line | means "one of". For example, the syntactic variable *letterOrDigitOrUnderScore* is defined by

letterOrDigitOrUnderscore ::= letter | digit | underscore

The syntactic variables *letter*, *digit*, and *underscore* are defined by these production rules containing terminal tokens (in bold):

letter ::= **a** | **b** | **c** ... | **z** | **A** | **B** | **C** ... | **Z**
digit ::= **0** | **1** | **2** ... | **9**
underscore ::= **_**

3.2   Primitive Data Types

The programs we introduced in Chapter 1 concentrated on graphics. To use a graphics method we had to specify the coordinates in pixels of points in a window. These were integers.

We will now consider the primitive types beyond the **int** type that are available in Java.

- There are two basic **numerical types**: the **int** type for integers, both negative and positive, and the **float** type for numbers that can have decimal points. These are often called real numbers.

- For integers there are, as well, the **byte** type (a byte is equal to 8 bits), the **short** type, and the **long** type which use one quarter, one half, and twice the number of bits as the **int** type respectively.

- For float numbers the **double** type uses twice the number of bits as the **float** type.

- Another type is the **boolean** type which has only two possible values, **true** and **false**.

- The **char** type represents a single character in **unicode**. Each unicode character is represented by 2 bytes or 16 bits.

3.3   Declarations of Variables

The different types of data used in a program require different amounts of space in memory to store them. In order to store data of a particular type in the computer's memory, enough space must be reserved to hold the value. This is done by including a **declaration** that establishes the identifier by which the data can be referenced and the data type of the value.

For example, to reserve space for a person's year of birth we might write

   int *yearOfBirth*;

The declaration begins with the keyword **int** which gives the data type; the identifier comes next. Notice that when an identifier is a compound word, the convention in this book is to capitalize the first letter of words other than the first word. Underscores, which are like hyphens (but not the same), could be used instead, for example,

   year_of_birth

Any later reference in the program to a variable must be spelled exactly the same way. If the variable is not spelled consistently, the compiler generates an **error message** indicating that the variable has not been declared. This happens when the identifier used and the declared identifier are not the same.

The declaration of a variable in a program must precede the use of the variable declared.

As well as allocating the proper amount of storage space in memory, the declaration of the data type of a variable establishes what operations will be possible on that variable.

3.4   Expressions: Arithmetic and Boolean

Arithmetic Expressions

Numbers or numerical variables of type **int**, **short**, **byte**, and **long** or **float** and **double** can be combined using the arithmetic operators +, −, *, and /. The * is for **multiplication** and the / for **division**. In an expression such as

1.34 * 7.8 + 2 / 12.2

the multiplication (*) is evaluated first, then division (/), and finally the addition (+). When there are two operators with the same **precedence**, such as * and /, they are evaluated left to right. It is sometimes better to enclose subexpressions in parentheses to indicate the intended order of evaluation since expressions in parentheses are evaluated first. In the preceding example, the expression, written with parentheses

(1.34 * 7.8) + (2 / 12.2)

makes the order of evaluation explicit.

When integers are combined in an expression, the result will be an integer. If there is a division operator / in an integer expression, the result is automatically truncated to be an integer. For example, 5/2 gives the result 2. It is possible to **cast** an expression such as this, that normally would yield an integer to produce a **float** result by writing

(**float**) 5/2

This causes the 5 to be treated as a float number. If there is any float number in the expression, the result will automatically be float. The expression 3 + 6.2 gives the **float** result 9.2. If, instead, the *round* method of the *Math* class is used, the value of

   Math.round (3 + 6.2)

will be 9. The result is rounded to the nearest integer.

   The % operator can be used to obtain the remainder on division of two positive integers. For example, the value of

   14 % 5

is 4, which is the remainder when 14 is divided by 5. This is often referred to as the **modulo** operator.

Boolean Expressions

   Boolean expressions can have only two possible values, **true** or **false**.

   A Boolean expression may be a single boolean variable or consist of a **comparison**. A simple comparison has the form

   expression comparison-operator expression

To be compared, the values of the two expressions must be of the same or compatible data types, that is, both numbers.

   The comparison operators are:

Symbol	Meaning
==	equal to
!=	not equal to
>	greater than
<	less than
>=	greater than or equal to
<=	less than or equal to

Boolean variables, or comparisons can be combined using the boolean or **logical** operators && for **and**, and || for **or**. If two boolean expressions are combined using the operator && then both expressions must be true before the compound expression is true. If they are combined using the || operator then at least one of the two must be true before the compound expression is true.

Here is a boolean expression which will test whether an exam mark submitted is a number between 0 and 100.

> 0 <= *mark* && *mark* <= 100

The value is **true** if *mark* occurs in this range.

3.5   Assignment Statements

The value of an expression can be stored in a variable in memory. The variable must have been declared and its data type must be the same or compatible with the data type of the expression. This is done using an **assignment** statement. The assignment statement has the form:

> variable = expression;

To illustrate, here is an application program that uses the assignment statement. It is presented as a program fragment that must be placed as the body of a *main* method in the *BoilerPlate* class defined in Chapter 2.

Here is the boiler plate for a Java program. The details of an application can be placed into the boiler plate to produce a complete application program.

> **import** *java.awt.*;*
> **import** *hsa.Console;*
>
> **public class** name-of-application
> {
>   **static** *Console c;*

```
static public void main (String args [ ])
{
    c = new Console ( );
    details of application
}
details of any user-defined methods
} /* name-of-application class */
```

Here is the program fragment that provides the "details of application".

```
int hoursWorked;
double payRate;
double totalPay;
hoursWorked = 40;
payRate = 21.50;
totalPay = hoursWorked * payRate;
c.println ("Totalpay = " + totalPay);
```

A real numerical constant like 21.50 is of type **double** and cannot be assigned to a variable of type **float**. A **float** value could, however, be assigned to a variable of type **double**.

In the last statement the **string constant** in double quotes causes the value of *totalPay* to be converted to a string and concatenated to it. The + here is the **concatenation operator** not the addition operator. When the list of output items in a *print* or *println* statement begins with a string constant, this conversion of subsequent items to strings takes place. For example, the statement

```
c.println ("Here are two integers " + 2 + 3);
```

will produce the output

```
Here are two integers 23
```

To produce a space between the 2 and 3 another string constant consisting of a space surrounded by quotes is required as in this statement:

```
c.println ("Here are two integers " + 2 + " " + 3);
```

Integer values can be assigned to **float** or **double** variables but the converse is not true unless the **float** or **double** value is cast as an integer. For example,

```
int hoursWorked;
hoursWorked = (int) 12.3;  //Converts 12.3 to 12.
```

Here is a boolean example of an assignment statement.

```
boolean correct;
correct = 7 < 10 || 5 > 7;
c.println (correct);
```

The boolean variable *correct* will have the value **true** stored in it since the expression assigned to it is true. In evaluating a compound expression, such as that on the right-hand side of the assignment statement here, if the first of the two boolean expressions separated by the || determines the value of the whole expression by being true, the evaluation is **short circuited** and the second boolean expression is not even evaluated. Similarly with the && operation, if the first expression is false, the second is not evaluated.

The && operator has higher precedence than the || operator.

Initializing Variables in their Declarations

An assignment statement can be combined with a declaration to give a variable its initial value. For example,

```
int sum  = 0;
```

declares a variable *sum* and sets its value as 0.

Constants

Some values stored in memory called **constants** remain the same throughout the execution of a program.

A constant must be initialized in its declaration. Declaring it as a constant with the keyword **final** before its data type means that its value cannot be changed. Any subsequent attempt to assign a value to a constant is a violation of its definition.

For example,

```
final double INTEREST_RATE = 7.5;
```

defines the constant *INTEREST_RATE*. By convention, constants are given identifiers of upper case letters.

Syntax of Assignment Statements

The syntax of the assignment statement expressed in EBNF is

assignment-statement ::= variable = expression;

Notice that the symbol = is a terminal token in the assignment statement, but the symbol ::= is a symbol in the EBNF metalanguage. The data type of the expression after the = must be the same or compatible with the data type of the variable or else a syntax error will be reported and execution terminated. An integer-valued expression is compatible with a real variable but not the reverse.

Variable Names on Both Sides of an Assignment Statement

The assignment statement is not an equation as is obvious when an assignment contains the same variable identifier on both sides. For example, these statements might appear in a program.

int *sum* = 1;
sum = sum + 1;

Here *sum* is given an initial value of 1 in its declaration. In the assignment, the expression on the right-hand side is evaluated to give the value 2. This value is then assigned to the variable *sum*. This gives *sum* the value 2 after the execution of the assignment statement.

This sort of assignment occurs frequently in programs and can be written in abbreviated form as

sum += 1;

A still shorter form of this particular assignment statement is

sum ++;

Similarly the assignment

*sum = sum * 10;*

can be written in short form as

sum *= 10;

The assignment

sum = sum − 1;

can be written as either

sum −= 1;

or

sum −−;

3.6   Output Statements

The hsa *Console* class provides the *print* or *println* methods for producing output. When a string is output it may consist of a series of string constants and other data types concatenated using the + operator. In general, each output item is output by a single statement. To output two items requires two output statements. If the *print* method is used these are on the same line. If two calls to the *print* method are given, such as in

c.print (15);
c.print (12);

the result is 1512. The items are both on the same line and there are no blanks output between the items. The *print* statement continues the output on the current output line. The statements

c.println (15);
c.println (12);

produce these two lines of output.

15
12

The method *println* causes a Return after its output.

Boolean values are output as *true* or *false*. For example,

c.println (7 > 2);

produces the output *true*.

By default a call to *print* or *println* sends output to the screen.

Output Formatting

As previously noted, the space around an output item can be controlled by outputting an accompanying **string constant**.

For example, the statements

int *mark* = 86;
c.print ("Here is a mark ");
c.println (mark);

result in this output.

Here is a mark 86

The blank after "Here is a mark" causes a space before the value of *mark*. The same result could be obtained by the single statement

c.println ("Here is a mark " + mark)

The + sign here causes the *mark* to be converted to a string and concatenated to the string constant. In statements of this sort a string should be the first output item in a list separated by the concatenation operator. For example, the statement

c.println (2 + 3 + " is five");

produces the output

5 is five

whereas the statement

c.println ("Twenty-three is "+ 2 + 3);

produces the output

Twenty-three is 23

Another way to control the format of an output item is to follow its name or value by a **format item**. The format item is either an integer or an integer variable. The value of the format item controls the size of the **field** in which the **output** item is displayed. Numerical items are right justified in the field. For example, the statements

> *c.print* (35, 6);
> *c.print* (12, 3);
> *c.println* (2, 3);

would result in this output. The blank spaces are represented by the symbol Δ.

> ΔΔΔΔ3 5Δ12ΔΔ2

The first item output is in a field of size 6 spaces and is at the right-hand side of the field. This leaves four blanks to the left of it. The second item is in a field of size 3 which gives one blank to the left of the 12. The third item has two blanks to the left of the 2. Because the third statement is a *println*, the line is ended.

A **float** or **double** number is output with the decimal place and as many as sixteen digits to the right of the decimal point. Trailing zeros in decimal places are omitted. For example,

> *c.println* ((**double**) 5/16, 12);

would result in the output

> ΔΔΔΔΔΔ0.3125

All digits after the fourth decimal place are zeros. Note that the decimal point takes one of the spaces. Another easy way of getting the effect of casting an integer value as a **double** value is to add a decimal point after it.

The output of real numbers can be messy unless the number of decimal places is controlled. To control the number of decimal places output, as would be required in outputting a bank balance in dollars and cents, a second format item can be provided for a **float** or **double** value. For example,

> *c.println* ((**double**) 5/3, 6, 2);

would produce the output

           ΔΔ1.67

Here two decimal places are output and the value is rounded.

Very large or very small real values are output in **exponent form**. For example, 1.3E7 is the exponent form for 13 million. For string values, the string is output left justified in its field. For example, the statements

> *c.print* ("Balance", 10);
> *c.println* ("Interest", 10);

would produce the output

           BalanceΔΔΔInterestΔΔ

Output formatting is very useful for producing neat tables of results.

3.7   Comments in Programs

Internal documentation is an essential element of good program design. Parts of a program used to document the program are called **comments**. Comments may be placed anywhere in a program between other statements or on the same line after a statement. In one form the comment is preceded by // and terminated by the end of the line. The other form of a comment is to precede it by /* and follow it by */. In this form the comment may continue over any number of lines.

Here is an example showing a comment going over several lines.

> /* Here is an example of a comment
> that goes over several lines of
> a program. */

The other form for a comment would look like this:

> // Here is an example of a comment
> // that goes over several lines of
> // a program.

We tend to use the second form more frequently. Notice that in either case there are no semicolons at the end of the lines although, in fact they would do no harm. The first type of comment is perhaps more prone to error since if the closing */ were omitted the comment would just run on and on. Lines in a program can be temporarily deleted by prefacing them with //. This changes them to a comment.

3.8 Chapter Summary

This chapter has introduced a number of basic concepts of programming. The primitive data types were presented along with the form of expressions of the various types.

Metalanguage for Syntax Definition

To define the syntax in a programming language we could use natural language such as English. Often, however, definitions in natural language are relatively easy to understand but not precise enough. Instead a formal language is introduced to define the programming language. This acts as a **metalanguage. Extended Backus-Naur Form** or **EBNF** is a metalanguage commonly used in computer science for describing a programming language.

Syntax variables such as **identifiers** are defined in terms of other syntactic entities and **terminal tokens**. To **produce** a syntactically correct program in a particular programming language we use these definitions, or **production rules**, replacing each syntactic variable by its definition until only terminal tokens remain.

Primitive Data Types and Declarations

The primitive data types of Java include: **byte, short, int,** or **long** for integers, **float** or **double** for real numbers, and **boolean.** A variable is declared as of one of these types by writing a **declaration** such as

    int *age*;

A declaration starts with the data type followed by the identifier of the variable. The variable must be declared before it can be used.

Arithmetic Expressions

Numbers, both real and integer, or numerical variables can be combined using the **arithmetic operators** to form arithmetic expressions. The order of evaluation in expressions is:

- expressions in parentheses,
- the multiplication and division operators * and /,
- the addition and subtraction operators + and −, and
- operations with the same precedence are evaluated from left to right in the expression.

Integers can be assigned to real variables but real numbers may not be assigned to integer variables.

Integer division always results in an integer. Any fractional part is truncated.

The % operator produces the remainder on integer division. It is called the **modulo operator**.

Boolean Expressions

A Boolean expression can be:

- a boolean variable,
- a comparison,
- comparisons or boolean variables compounded by using the boolean or logical operators: && (for **and**) and || (for **or**), or
- boolean expressions in parentheses.

The comparison operators are >, <, ==, <=, >=, and !=.

In a compound expression, each individual comparison or boolean variable is evaluated left to right. If the left value immediately determines the value of the compound, the remaining evaluation is **short circuited** and not done. For example, in the compound expression

$$7 < 9 \parallel 8 > 5$$

the fact that 7 is less than 9 will cause the whole expression to be true no matter what the next comparison might yield.

Assignment Statements

The value of an expression can be assigned to a variable using the form

variable = expression;

The value of the expression must be the same as, or compatible with, the data type of the variable. An integer expression can be assigned to a real variable but not the converse.

Initial assignments of values to variables can occur in their declarations. For example,

int *sum* = 0;

The expression assigned to a variable can contain the same variable. For example,

sum = *sum* + 2;

means that the value stored in *sum* is increased by 2 and stored back in *sum*. A short form for this assignment is

sum += 2;

The particular short form

sum ++;

is the same as

sum += 1;

and

sum --;

is the same as

sum -= 1;

Output Statements

Output statements use the *print* or *println* method of the *Console* class with an output item as a parameter. By default these methods place the output item in a **field** that is just large enough to hold it. A *println* statement causes a new line after the output item is output.

To control the format of output the values can be interspersed with the output of string constants that have extra blanks preceding or following them. Several output items that begin with a string constant can be concatenated using the + operator. Items that are numerical or boolean values are converted to strings.

Another way to control the format is to follow the single **output item** in a *print* or *println* statement by a **format item** which is separated from it by a comma. This controls the size of the field used for output. Numbers are right justified in their field. Strings are left justified. Real numbers can have the number of decimal points output controlled by following the first format item by a comma and a second format item. Very large or very small numbers appear in **exponent form**.

Comments

Comments can be placed between or at the end of statements to make a program understandable. They may begin with // and end at the end of the current line. They may alternatively be preceded by /* and followed by */. Variables and constants should not require comments since the names chosen for identifiers should explain their contents. Comments are not followed by semicolons.

3.9   Exercises

1. Which of these identifiers is syntactically correct?
    a) *sum*
    b) *3rdPage*
    c) *two+two*
    d) *Fixed_Price*
    e) *high-level*

2. The arithmetic expression

    $$3 * 5 + 7 - 2/6$$

    has a value 21.666.... What value would be computed? Write
    the same expression with all parentheses included.

    What are the values of the following expressions?

    (a) $3 * ((5 + 7) - 2)/6$
    (b) $3 * 5 + (7 - 2)/6$
    (c) $((3 * 5) + 7 - 2)/6$

3. Write a program that computes the interest on a bank balance
    to the nearest cent and stores the result in a variable called
    newBalance. Prove that the new balance is stored to the nearest
    cent by an output instruction that prints *newBalance* with three
    decimal places. Test the program using a variety of values
    assigned to the balance and the interest rate.

4. What is output by the following statements involving boolean
    expressions?

    ```
    c.println ( 5 > 3 && 7 > 9 || 6 < 8);
    c.println ( 2 < 6 && 5 < 10 && 7 > 3);
    ```

5. What is output by this program segment?

    ```
    int sum = 0;
    for (int count = 1; count <= 10; count ++)
    {
        c.println ("sum = " + sum + " count = " + count);
        sum += 1;
    }
    c.println ("sum = " + sum);
    ```

    What would be the output if the incrementation part of the **for**
    were *count* += 2? See what happens if an attempt is made to
    output *count* in the last *println* statement.

Chapter 4

Input of Data

In the programs so far there has been no input of data. The output was produced by graphic statements in the program such as *drawLine* or by the output statements *print* and *println*. In this chapter, we will be looking at the various ways of inputting data. Input statements will be shown for input from the keyboard, the standard input device, or from a file. Ways to input numerical data and string data will be discussed and programs that involve repetition are presented for inputting sequences of similar data items. As well, methods of generating data for purposes of testing programs, and ways to analyze numerical data statistically are given.

4.1   Entering Programs

Programs can be directly entered using the editing environment of the computer as described in Chapter 2. This allows programs to be created in the input window by typing on the keyboard. They can be edited to correct typing errors, then run. If the instructions in a program are not syntactically correct, syntax errors are reported. These syntax errors must be corrected, using the **editor** of the environment, before the program is run again. When the program gets past the stage where there are syntax errors, that is, to the **execution phase**, the output can be examined to see if it is what is expected.

At this stage the errors that remain are usually **semantic errors**. What the programmer wanted and what was actually produced were not the same. For example, the program might have a statement to *drawLine* instead of a *drawRect* statement. Such errors in **meaning** can only be detected by examining the output and so are not reported to the user by *VisualAge for Java*. Semantic errors are corrected by editing the program in the same way as syntax errors are corrected.

Just as the keyboard is used to input the program and any editing changes, it is also the **standard input** device for entering the data on which the program operates. The program itself must contain one or more statements to read or input the data from the keyboard. We will now show how input of various data types can be accomplished using Java standard input and afterwards how it is done using methods of the *Console* class.

4.2   Standard Input and Output

Java provides a way of reading input from the standard input device (the keyboard) and writing to the **standard output** device (the screen) but its built-in facilities for this are quite primitive. They provide the ability to read in either single characters or entire lines of data from the keyboard but there is no built-in facility to read any other data types, for example integers and booleans.

The facilities for output are somewhat better. All of Java's primitive data types can be output directly. There are, however, no methods for printing numbers into fixed-length fields or with a specified number of decimal places.

In later sections, we use Holt Software's *Console* class. This class has methods for reading in all of Java's primitive data types directly and for outputting data into fixed-length fields. The *Console* class also has facilities for doing basic graphics. This means that you only need to read the rest of this section if you want a better understanding of doing input and output without the hsa *Console* class.

Reading from standard input uses a predefined object called *System.in*. This is an object of class *InputStream*. An *InputStream* can only read in single characters. To be useful, *System.in* must be converted to a *BufferedReader*, from which an entire line of input can be read at a time. The statement

> *BufferedReader stdin =*
> **new** *BufferedReader* (**new** *InputStreamReader* (*System.in*));

performs the conversion. Once this is done, the *readLine* method is used to read a line of input from the standard input device.

In *VisualAge for Java*, the first statement actually using standard input or output causes the system console window to be displayed, allowing input to be entered. This is not to be confused with the hsa *Console* class window.

The *VisualAge for Java* console window has three panes. The top pane labelled *All Programs* displays a list of all the programs whose input and output are available in the window. Selecting a program listed in this pane displays the input and output of that program in the bottom two panes. Once a program has finished execution, clicking the *Clear* icon (the left-most icon that looks like a brush) eliminates the program from the list. The center pane displays anything sent to standard output. The bottom pane is for entering standard input. Whenever a program reads from *System.in*, the input must be entered in the bottom pane. Note that whatever is typed in the standard input pane is not echoed in the standard output pane.

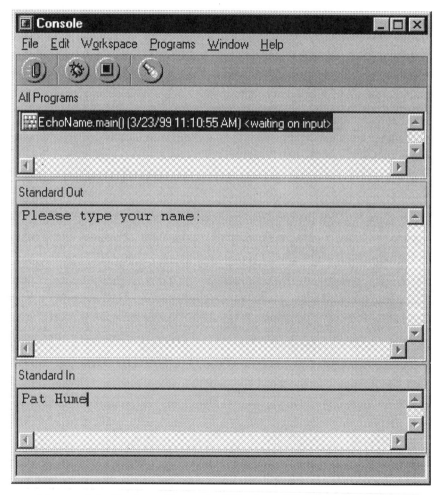

Figure 4.1 System Console Window Waiting for Input

The *System.out* object's *print* and *println* methods send data to the standard output device. The *print* and *println* methods take an item of any Java primitive data type or a *String* object as an argument. The *print* method outputs the item to the standard output without following it with a Return. The *println* method outputs the item following it with a Return. The statement

   System.out.print (s)

outputs a string *s* not followed by a Return while

   System.out.println (i)

outputs an integer *i* followed by Return.

   Here is a small application program using standard input to read a name and standard output to repeat it.

```
// The "EchoName" class.
// Asks for a name and echoes it back.
import java.awt.*;
import java.io.*;

public class EchoName
{
    static public void main (String args []) throws IOException
    {
        String name;
        BufferedReader stdin =
            new BufferedReader (new InputStreamReader (System.in));
        System.out.println ("Please type your name:");
        name = stdin.readLine ();

        // Output the reply.
        System.out.println ("Your name is \"" + name + "\"");
    } // main method
} /* EchoName class */
```

In the *EchoName* class,

   BufferedReader stdin =
       new *BufferedReader (***new** *InputStreamReader (System.in));*

converts *System.in* into the *BufferedReader* object *stdin* from which entire lines from standard input can be read. The next line writes the message "Please type your name" to standard output to prompt for a name. The line after that reads an entire line of input from standard input into *name* (not including the end-of-line character at the end). The last few lines of the *main* method display a single line in the *StandardOut* pane which echoes what is typed in the *StandardIn* pane.

The *main* method header has the words

throws *IOException*

in it. This phrase must be used whenever a BufferedReader is used.

4.3   Input of Numerical Data

The most common and simplest form of input used in programs is by reading lines. A line is a series of characters terminated by **Return** (the **enter** key).

A line that represents an integer consists of an optional sign (+ or −) followed by one or more digits. For example, −375 and 258 are integers. When Java standard input is used, the line of characters representing an integer must be parsed and converted to a numerical value. This is a complicated process and, for this reason, we use the methods of the *Console* class to handle input and output. Applications using the Console class must have the form illustrated in the *BoilerPlate* class shown here.

```
import java.awt.*;
import hsa.Console;

public class name-of-application
{
    static Console c;

    static public void main (String args [ ])
    {
        c = new Console ( );
        details of application
    } /* main program */
```

> details of any user-defined methods
> } /* name-of-application class */

Now, here are the details of the body of a *main* method that inputs an integer. It is to be part of the *NextYear* class.

```
// The "NextYear" class.
// This tells you how old you will be next year.
int age;
c.print ("Please enter your age: ");
age = c.readInt ();
c.print ("Your age next year will be ");
c.println (age + 1);
```

Notice that the way the *Console* method *readInt* is used is different from the way the *println* or *print* methods are used. The method *readInt* here yields a value that is assigned to the variable *age*. The method has no parameters but must be followed by parentheses with nothing between them.

In terms of the classification of methods as either functions or procedures the *print* or *println* methods are procedures: they cause output, whereas the *readInt* method is a function: it has a value.

Whenever input is expected from the user, the program should assist the user by outputting an input **prompt**. The prompt in this program is:

Please enter your age:

Because the *print* instruction rather than *println* is used for the prompt, the cursor remains at the end of the prompt, just after "age", waiting for the user's input. Notice that the prompt message has a space after it. At this stage the user enters his or her age and presses Return. The Return signals the computer that the input is complete. The user can also correct an input error by backspacing and retyping the value before pressing Return.

Here is a sample *Console* execution window from the program.

Please enter your age: **21**
Your age next year will be 22

The user's input **21** is shown in boldface type. On the computer screen there is no difference in appearance between what the computer outputs and what is **echoed** on the screen as the user types input data.

Real numbers are entered in the same way as integers, except that they may contain a decimal point. Here is a program that calculates the area of a floor. The real numbers are of type **double**.

```
// The "FloorArea" class.
// Find the area of a floor given its length and width.
double len, width;
c.print ("Enter length in meters ");
len = c.readDouble ();
c.print ("Enter width in meters ");
width = c.readDouble ();
c.print ("Area is ");
c.print (len * width);
c.println (" square meters");
```

We can also combine the last three statements into a single statement this way.

```
c.println ("Area is " + len * width + " square meters");
```

The + sign indicates that the value of *len * width* is to be converted to a string and concatenated to the other two strings.

When two or more variables such as *len* and *width* are of the same data type they can be declared in a single statement, listed separated by commas, as in "**double** *len, width*".

4.4   Input of String Data

String data can be read as lines using the *Console* class method *readLine*. Here is a program segment that inputs a line of characters, namely a string, and echoes it. Compare this with the *EchoName* class (Section 4.2).

```
// The "NameInOut" class.
// Read a name and output it.
String name;
c.println ("Please enter your full name");
name = c.readLine ();
c.println ("Your name is \"" + name + "\"");
```

Here is a sample console execution window.

> Please enter your full name
> **Bill Gates**
> Your name is "Bill Gates"

Again the user's input is in boldface type.

In the *println* statement that outputs the name there are three components: a string constant which acts as a **label**, a string variable *name*, and another string constant. The label indicates what the output represents. At the end of the labelling string constant that is enclosed in double quotes are the characters \". This indicates that a double quote mark is wanted in the labelling string itself. In the program the name is joined to the label string, then a second double quote is concatenated to result in a quote following the name.

The backslash \ is used with other special characters like a double quote as well. To get a backslash itself in a string two backslashes are required. The statement

> *c.println* ("Here is a backslash character \\");

would produce the output

> Here is a backslash character \

The meaning of the + operator is very different when it is used with strings. While with numerical values the + operator indicates addition, with strings it means to concatenate, or join end to end. We say the operator + is **overloaded**, that is, used with different meanings in two different contexts. The statement

> *c.println* (4 + 5);

would output the integer 9. Here the + is interpreted as the addition operator.

4.5   Input of Sequences of Data

One of the most common operations in computing is to read a sequence of data items of the same type. This requires the repetition of the input operation.

Counted Repetition

Suppose the average of a series of 10 exam marks is to be calculated. Here is a program segment that does this.

```
// The "TenAvg" class.
// Compute the average of 10 marks.
int mark;
int sum = 0;
c.println ("Enter 10 marks one to a line");
for (int count = 1 ; count <= 10 ; count++)
{
    mark = c.readInt ();
    sum += mark;
}
c.println ("Average of 10 marks is " + (double) sum / 10);
```

The repetition construct which begins with the keyword **for** is called a **counted loop** or a **for** statement. In parentheses following the **for** are three components separated by semicolons. These are

- the declaration and initialization of the counting index,
- the continuation condition, and
- the incrementing of the counting index.

The counting is recorded in the **counting index** *count* and has a **range** from 1 to 10. The index *count* will start with a value 1 and then each time the **body** of the loop is executed it is increased by 1. This continues until the 10th time through the body at which point *count* has a value 11 and the loop terminates. The instruction after the loop body is then executed. To see the value of *count* on each repetition insert a

c.println (count);

statement inside the loop.

In order that the average will be output as a real number, with decimal places, the variable *sum* is cast as **double** by having the keyword **double** placed in parentheses ahead of it. The average otherwise would be truncated since both *sum* and 10 are integers.

The usual style for writing a loop is to indent the statements in the loop's body a few spaces from the column where the body's enclosing curly brace is located. This is known as **paragraphing** or **pretty printing** the program. The final output statement concatenates the label "Average of 10 names is" to the output value using the + operator. The output value is automatically converted to a string then concatenated.

The program that was presented is not very general; it works only with a sequence of 10 marks. To make it more general, the number of marks in the sequence could be input along with the actual sequence. Here is a modified version of the program segment which asks the user for the number of marks, reads them in and prints the average.

```
// The "HowManyAvg" class.
// Compute average of a sequence of marks.
int howMany, mark;
int sum = 0;
c.print ("How many marks are there? ");
howMany = c.readInt ();
c.println ("Enter " + howMany + " marks one after the other");
for (int count = 1 ; count <= howMany ; count++)
{
    mark = c.readInt ();
    sum += mark;
}
c.println ("Average of " + howMany + " marks is " +
    (double) sum / howMany);
```

Again the various output items in the final *println* statement are concatenated using the + operator.

This program is an example of processing each data item as it is read. Although the programs in this chapter do not check for bad input, if the user entered a real number in reply to the prompt

How many marks are there?

in this program, a run-time error would be reported and execution terminated.

Conditional Repetition

A sequence of data items can be processed by a different kind of repetition construct called a **while** statement. Here, reading and processing continues until a data item is entered that is a **signal** or **sentinel** to stop the processing, rather than having a predetermined number of data items. This type of repetition is called a **conditional loop**; repetition continues until a certain **condition** becomes false.

For example, here is a program segment that reads a sequence of words until it reads the sentinel word "stop". When it encounters the word it stops the repetition. The fact that the sentinel word is "stop" has nothing to do with what happens. If the sentinel word was "banana" repetition still would stop but the user might not see clearly why this happened.

```
// The "LastLetter" class.
// Read a sequence of words and output the last letter
// of each word until the sentinel is read.
String word;
final String SENTINEL = "stop";
c.println ("Enter a sequence of words, end with " + SENTINEL);
// Words must have at least one letter.
word = c.readLine ();
while (!word.equals (SENTINEL))
{
    c.println ("Last letter of " + word + " is " +
        word.charAt (word.length () - 1));
    word = c.readLine ();
}
c.println ("This is the end of the sequence");
```

As with the sequence of numbers, each line is input and then processed before the next line is input. Note that the input statement for strings is *readLine* rather than *readInt* which is for integers. The repetition construct begins with the keyword **while**. Action of the loop stops when the word input is equal to the sentinel. The continuation condition

(!word.equals (SENTINEL))

is a boolean expression which is either true or false. The exit from the loop occurs when it is false. The condition uses the *equals* method of the *String* class. The exclamation mark means **not**. As well, the methods of *charAt* and *length* of the *String* class are used in the output statement. These three methods of the *String* class will be explained in more detail in Chapter 6.

4.6   Input from a File

So far all the input has been from the keyboard, which is the standard input device. This allows the program to read data directly from a user. In many cases, however, programs are required to receive data input from a file. **Reading** data from a file or **writing** data to a file is possible in application programs but not possible in applets.

To read data from a file, the program must establish a connection to the particular file that is to be read. This is done in this example by statements which **open** a stream called *input* from the file named *fileName*.

```
BufferedReader input;
input = new BufferedReader (new FileReader (fileName));
```

Here is an example program which asks the user to enter the name of the file where the data to be read is stored and then reads and processes the data. The program reads positive integers until *input.readLine* () returns **null** (indicating the end of file has been reached) and then finds their average.

```
// The "FileAvg" class.
// Input a sequence of integers entered originally one to a line
// from a file whose name is to be read in from the keyboard
// and find their average.
String fileName, line;
```

```
int number;
int sum = 0, count = 0;
c.println ("What is the name of the file of integers?");
fileName = c.readLine ();
BufferedReader input;
input = new BufferedReader (new FileReader (fileName));
line = input.readLine ();  //Read a line of characters.
while (line != null)  //File is terminated by a null.
{
    number = Integer.parseInt (line);  //Change to an integer.
    count++;
    sum += number;
    line = input.readLine ();  //Read next line.
}
c.println ("Average of " + count + " numbers is " + (double) sum / count);
```

Notice that *input* is declared to be an object of class *BufferedReader*. If the opening operation is not successful, the program execution will be stopped. We say that this class is capable of **throwing** an I/O exception. When this is the case, the words

throws *IOException*

must be added to the *main* method's header.

The *BufferedReader* class is part of the *java.io* package. To use the class (and the other file reading and writing classes in this chapter) the package must be imported into the class, just as *hsa.Console* and *java.awt* were imported into the previous classes. This is done by adding the line

import *java.io.*;*

to the other import statements in the class.

Each integer is recorded as a line of characters and is parsed and changed to an integer by the statement

number = Integer.parseInt (line);

Reading and writing a file is similar to using the Java standard input and output *System.in* and *System.out*.

4.7   Output to a File

Data produced as the output of a program can be output to a file. Output of data to a file is similar to input from a file except that the class for output is *PrintWriter* (or *PrintStream*) if text output is wanted. The *PrintWriter* class is connected to *FileWriter* by the chaining of objects. To output to a text file, the *print* and *println* methods are used, just as in the *Console* class.

Here is a program that stores the odd integers from 1 to 361 in a file that is named by the user. We will use the text output form.

```
// The "OddInts" program.
// Produce a file of data consisting of the odd integers
// from 1 to 361 inclusive.
PrintWriter output;
String fileName;
c.println ("What is the name of the file for the integers?");
fileName = c.readLine ();
output = new PrintWriter (new FileWriter (fileName));
for (int number = 1 ; number <= 361 ; number += 2)
{
    output.println (number);
}
// Close file.
output.close ();
```

The statement

output.println(number);

outputs *number* as a string of characters followed by a Return. A **null** string is automatically placed at the end of the file.

If a file is to be read again after it has been output, it should be closed. This allows the file to be opened again as input later in the program if required. At the end of execution of a program all files are automatically closed so that the file in this example need not have been closed. Note that once again, *main* must be modified to indicate that it can throw an *IOException*, and the *java.io* package must be imported.

Files may also be kept in binary form. The use of binary output of files will be discussed in Chapter 11.

Here is a program that inputs text stored in a file named *"poem.dat"* and outputs the same text to a file called *"poem2.dat"* with the lines numbered.

```
// The "NumberLines" class.
// Read the file named "poem.dat" line by line
// and output the lines, numbered, to a file named "poem2.dat".
String text;
int lineCount = 0;
BufferedReader input;
PrintWriter output;
input = new BufferedReader (new FileReader ("poem.dat"));
output = new PrintWriter (new FileWriter ("poem2.dat"));
text = input.readLine ();
while (text != null)
{
    lineCount++;
    output.println (lineCount + "  " + text);
    text = input.readLine ();
}
output.close ();
```

When the *readLine* method reaches the end of file, it returns a **null**. To see the result of the program's action, the file "poem2.dat" can be brought into the *Notepad* of *Windows*.

4.8   Generated Data

Often a large amount of data is required to test programs. This is particularly true if the data is being analyzed statistically. Rather than try to input vast quantities of data through the keyboard, it is possible to produce or **generate** the data artificially for testing purposes.

The *random* method of the *Math* class is very useful for generating simulated data. A real randomly-chosen value between

0 and 1 (but not including 1) can be generated and assigned to the variable *randomReal* by these statements.

> **double** *randomReal*;
> *randomReal* = *Math.random* ();

To produce a random integer, say between 1 and 6 suitable for the result of a cast of a die (one of a pair of dice), we could use these statements.

> **int** *die*;
> *die* = (**int**) (*Math.random* () * 6) + 1;

By multiplying a real random number between 0 and 1 by 6 we produce a real number between 0 and 6 (but not including 6). When this is cast as an integer, as it is by preceding it by (**int**), the real value is truncated, leaving a random integer between 0 and 5 inclusive. By adding 1 the result becomes a random integer between 1 and 6 inclusive.

Here is a program that produces a file called "dice", simulating the throw of two dice 300 times.

```
// The "DiceData" class.
// Simulate the throw of two dice 300 times
// and store the generated data in file "dice".
int die1, die2, roll;
PrintWriter output;
output = new PrintWriter (new FileWriter ("dice"));
for (int count = 1 ; count <= 300 ; count++)
{
    die1 = (int) (Math.random () * 6) + 1;
    die2 = (int) (Math.random () * 6) + 1;
    roll = die1 + die2;
    output.println (roll);
}
output.close ();
c.println ("Simulated data of 300 throws now in file 'dice'");
```

4.9   Statistical Analysis of Data

One way of characterizing a sequence of numbers is to compute their **average** value. Another commonly-used statistical characteristic is the **variance**. This is defined as the mean (average) of the square of the differences between each data item and the average value. The variance measures the extent to which individual numbers differ from the average. If there are n data items each of which will be called x_i their average $\bar{x}$ is produced by the formula

$$\text{average} = \bar{x} = \frac{1}{n} \sum_{i=1}^{n} x_i$$

where the Σ means to add up the individual values x_i for i going from 1 to n.

The variance is defined as

$$\text{variance} = \frac{1}{n} \sum_{i=1}^{n} \left(\bar{x} - x_i \right)^2$$

This can be rewritten as

$$= \frac{1}{n} \sum_{i=1}^{n} \left(\bar{x}^2 - 2\bar{x}x_i + x_i^2 \right)$$

$$= \bar{x}^2 - \frac{2\bar{x}}{n} \sum_{i=1}^{n} x_i + \frac{1}{n} \sum_{i=1}^{n} x_i^2$$

$$= \frac{1}{n} \sum_{i=1}^{n} x_i^2 - \bar{x}^2$$

This shows that the variance can be computed as the average of the squares of the x_i minus the average value squared.

Here is a program to compute the mean and variance of the generated data for the dice throws stored in the file "dice".

```
// The "DiceStats" class.
// Compute the mean and variance for the simulated dice throws
// in file "dice" prepared by the data generation program.
int roll;
int count = 0, sum = 0, sumOfSquares = 0;
String line;
BufferedReader input;
input = new BufferedReader (new FileReader ("dice"));
line = input.readLine ();
while (line != null)
{
    roll = Integer.parseInt (line);
    count++;
    sum += roll;
    sumOfSquares += roll * roll;
    line = input.readLine ();
}
double average = (double) sum / count;
double variance = (double) sumOfSquares / count − average * average;
c.println ("Average=" + average + " Variance=" + variance);
```

4.10 Chapter Summary

This chapter discusses the input of data from the **keyboard**, which is the **standard input** device, and from files. As well, the output of data to files is presented.

Entering Programs

Programs are entered using an Environment such as that provided with *VisualAge for Java*. **Syntax errors** are reported at compilation time and corrections can be made. When there are no errors, the program can be run. If results do not match what is expected, the program must contain **semantic errors**. These errors must be found and corrected.

Input of Data

Java provides a way of reading data from the standard input device (the keyboard). There are no built-in facilities for reading primitive data types. Only single characters or entire lines can be input. This is done using a predefined object *System.in* of the *InputStream* class. *InputStream* provides only for the reading of single characters. To achieve the reading of entire lines, *System.in* must be converted to a *BufferedReader* with the statement

> *BufferedReader stdin =*
>   **new** *BufferedReader* (**new** *InputStreamReader* (*System.in*));

which provides the *readLine* method.

Input and output is through a system console window with three panes: the top for output, the bottom for input, and the middle to display threads waiting for input. Input entered is not echoed in the output pane.

The hsa *Console* class was devised to make input and output of data much simpler. A single pane shows both input and output and methods of the hsa *Console* class permit the input and output of all primitive data types. Moreover, output can be formatted.

Input of Sequences of Data

Many computer applications involve the input of a sequence of data of the same data type. This requires the use of a **repetition construct** in the program. There are two basic types of repetition constructs.

- In the **counted loop** an **index** changes incrementally as each data item is input. The form of this construct is:

> **for** (index declaration and initialization; continuation condition;
>   index incrementation)
> {
>   body of **for** loop
> }

The body of a **for** loop consists of the statement or statements in curly braces. The usual style is to indent the body a few spaces from the beginning and ending braces of the construct. This paragraphing makes the program easier to understand. If the body contains only one statement the curly braces are not necessary but can be used nevertheless. For consistency, we tend to use them in many cases where the body has only one statement.

- In the **conditional loop** used in this chapter, data items are processed until a continuation condition becomes false. Then control exits from the loop to the statement after the loop's enclosing curly brace. The loop begins with the keyword **while** followed by a **continuation condition** in parentheses.

Input from a File

To read **text data** from a file, an *input* object of class *BufferedReader* is instantiated by a statement such as

> *input =* **new** *BufferedReader (new FileReader (fileName));*

All output to a text file is as strings of characters. Files of strings are terminated by **null**.

Output to a File

To write text data to a named file, an object of type *PrintWriter* is declared and instantiated by chaining to a class *FileWriter* by statements of this type

> *PrintWriter output;*
> *output =* **new** *PrintWriter (new FileWriter (fileName));*

Generated Data

Instead of preparing files of data from actual problems, large quantities of data can be automatically **generated**. This can be done using the method *random* from the *Math* class. These values are **uniformly distributed**, meaning that if many values were generated, there would result approximately the same number of each of the possible subranges of values. A program that produces simulated data for throws of two dice was shown.

Statistical Analysis of Data

A program was shown for computing the **average** and **variance** for a sequence of numerical data items stored in a file. These statistical measures are useful in understanding how data is distributed among possible values.

4.11 Exercises

1. Write a program that generates a student's exam mark out of 100 by producing 10 random numbers ranging from 0 to 10 and adding them. Output the sequence of 10 marks and their average.

2. A series of marks for an examination is to be averaged. Write a program that first asks the user to enter the number of marks in the series then generates this number of marks by the method shown in Exercise 1. Test it for the extreme cases where the number is 0 or 1.

3. Prepare a file called "exammark" of 100 generated exam marks using the method of Exercise 1, that is, where each mark is a sum of 10 random integers between 0 and 10. Find the average and variance of the marks stored in the file "exammark".

4. Generate a file called "dicegame" that contains data generated to represent the throw of 2 dice 100 times. Write a program that analyzes the data in file "dicegame" by computing its average and variance.

Chapter 5

Control Constructs

So far we have introduced many of the basic concepts of programming: primitive data types, assignment statements, input and output statements, and comments. In this chapter we will look at **structured statements**. These **constructs** can change the flow of execution of a program from a linear sequence of execution of statements to either **repetition** or **selection**. We have already made simple use of some of these **control constructs**, namely repetition, which includes both the counted **for** loop and the **conditional while** loop. In this chapter we will examine the loop constructs in more detail, and present several selection constructs.

5.1   Structure within Methods

Within the methods of a program there are groups of statements that form substructures. These are the **control constructs**. The three basic kinds of control constructs are:

- **Linear Sequence** where statements are executed one after the other in the order in which they are written.

- **Repetition** where a group of statements is to be executed repeatedly.

- **Selection** where one group of statements is selected for execution from a number of alternatives, depending on a test upon data.

The realization that all algorithms could be expressed in terms of using these three basic control constructs appeared in the early 1970s and formed the basis of what is known as **structured programming**. Before that time, the structure of programs could be quite complex and trying to follow the sequence of execution in a program was like untangling a plate of spaghetti. It was therefore the custom to provide charts along with the program to show the sequence of execution or **flow of control**. Figure 5.1 shows the **flow chart** for a program with nested **while** loops.

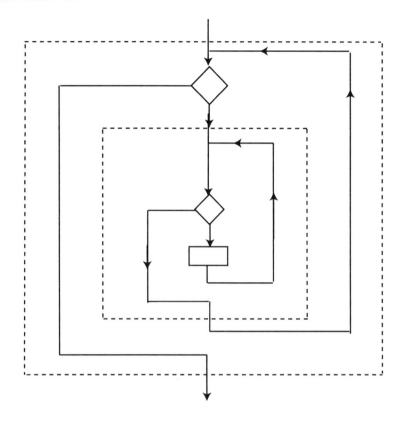

Figure 5.1 Flow Chart of Nested While Loops

Dotted lines forming a box surround each loop, one nested inside the other. There is a single flow line entering each box and a single line leaving. This would be true for any of the three basic control constructs.

Flow charts are not really necessary in structured programs. High-level languages were developed to make it easy to use the three basic control constructs, which when used exclusively, make it impossible to create "spaghetti programs".

Programmers now use **structure charts** or **landscapes**. These charts express the relationships and the **flow of data** among objects and methods, rather than flow of control. (See Chapter 1 for a more complete description of structure charts.)

5.2   Repetition Constructs

We have already introduced the two basic repetition constructs: the counted **for** loop and the conditional **while** loop. In this section we will provide a more detailed description of these kinds of repetition.

The Counted Loop

In Java, the counted loop begins with the keyword **for**. The body of the loop is enclosed in curly braces. It is thus easy to spot the **scope** or extent of the loop. To make it even easier, the style in writing programs is to indent the **body** of the loop. This is called **paragraphing** or **pretty printing** the loop structure.

The syntax of a **for** construct is:

```
for (index declaration and initialization;
        continuation condition; incrementation statement)
{
    body of repetition
}
```

Note that the three components in parentheses after the **for** are separated by semicolons and that the line does not have a semicolon after the right parenthesis. The index is sometimes called the **control variable** or **counter**.

In most of the counted loop examples we have shown so far, no particular use is made of the **index** of the loop except to count the number of times the loop has been repeated. Within the scope of the loop, its value can be used in the statements of the loop body. Its value should not be altered however.

Here is an example program to compute the sum of the squares of integers from 1 to 100 inclusive.

```
// The "SumSquares" class.
// Compute the sum of the squares of integers from 1 to 100.
int sum = 0;
for (int number = 1 ; number <= 100 ; number++)
{
```

sum += number * number;

}

c.println ("Sum of squares of numbers from 1 to 100 is " + *sum*);

Here the index *number* is used to calculate the square to be added to the sum. Notice that the index *number* is declared as an integer variable. It has a **scope** that is the extent of the loop construct and it is not known outside the loop. To ask for the output of *number* outside the loop would result in a syntax error.

The amount by which the index changes on each repetition is controlled by the incrementation statement. If, in the previous example, only the sum of the squares of the odd numbers was wanted, the first line of the construct would be

for (**int** *number* = 1; *number* <= 100; *number* +=2)

Here the index *number* would be in turn 1, 3, 5 ... 99. If the increment 2 were added to 99 it would be 101, which would exceed the upper limit of the **range**, so the last iteration happens with *number* set to 99.

An endless loop can be achieved by using the **for** loop with blank initialization, continuation, and incrementation as in

for (;;)

The semicolons separating the three blank components remain.

The Conditional Loop

There are two forms of the conditional repetition. One is referred to as a **while** construct and it has this form:

while (continuation condition)
{
       statements of **while** construct
}

The other is referred to as a **do** construct and it has this form.

do
{
       statements of **do** construct

```
}
```
while (continuation condition);

The difference between these two is where the continuation condition is tested. In the **while** the continuation condition is tested at the beginning and in the **do** it is tested at the end. Notice that in the **do** loop there is a semicolon after the continuation condition.

If the body of a **for, while,** or **do** construct contains only one statement then it need not be enclosed in curly braces. In this book, however, for consistency we use braces even if there is only one statement.

It is possible to write programs using just conditional loops and no counted loops. Here is an example where a conditional loop does the same thing as a counted loop. The problem is similar to one we solved before using a counted loop: to sum the squares of the first 100 integers.

```
// The "Sum100" class.
// Sum the first 100 integers.
int sum = 0;
int number = 1;
while (number <= 100)
{
    sum += number;
    number++;
}
c.println ("Sum of first 100 integers is " + sum);
```

In this example the index *number* is declared as an integer and initialized to 1 outside the loop. Inside the loop, at the beginning, the *index* number is tested to see if it has reached the upper limit of the range. At the end of the loop's body the index *number* is increased by 1. The counted loop does these operations:

- setting the initial value of the index,
- testing to see if it has reached its upper limit, and
- increasing it by 1 on each iteration.

The counted loop is definitely convenient, but not essential.

The principal difference between the **while** and **do** constructs is that the **while** loop can be executed zero times but the **do** loop must be executed at least once. We will show more examples of the **while** loop in later sections of this chapter.

Testing of Loops

It is important to make sure that a loop produces the desired results. The loop should be tested to see that the program works properly when the loop body is executed zero times, once, a typical number of times, and where an attempt is made to have it execute an inappropriate number of times.

As an example, consider a program that uses a conditional loop to find the sum of the first *n* integers, where the user enters the value *n*.

```
// The "SumInts" class.
// Find the sum of the first n integers.
int n;
c.println ("Enter a positive integer or 0");
n = c.readInt ();
int sum = 0;
int number = 0;
while (number < n)
{
    number++;
    sum += number;
}
c.println ("Sum of first " + n + " integers is " + sum);
```

Values of *n* should be tested for at least 0, 1, 10, and –2. The program should be run for these values and the results checked against known answers. It is helpful that we know the answer is given by the formula

$$n (n + 1) / 2$$

where *n* must be a positive integer. The result could be calculated by hand if a formula were not available.

In testing programs with loops it is often helpful to insert an output statement in the body of the loop to print the value of the index of a counted loop or the variables that are changing on each iteration. This can be removed when the program is working properly.

Proving Loop Correctness

One way of verifying correctness of the loop is to check that a certain condition called an **invariant** is true:

(1) as the loop is entered,

(2) at the beginning of execution of each loop iteration, and

(3) as the exit occurs, (assuming the exit is at the beginning of the loop body). In other words the invariant is an **assertion** that conceptually appears at the beginning of the loop body. It is required to be true whenever it is encountered at run time.

For the loop in the example, at the beginning of the body these must be true:

(a) *sum* gives the sum of integers from 0 to *number*, and

(b) 0 <= *number* and *number* <= *n*.

This is the invariant. We know that this invariant is always true at the top of the loop body for two reasons.

(1) On entry into the loop *sum* is 0, the sum of integers from 0 to *number* is 0 since *number* = 0, so both (a) and (b) are true.

(2) At the beginning of 2nd execution, when the loop has been executed once, the value of *number* will be 1 and *sum* will be 0 + 1 which is the sum of the integers from 0 to *number* which is 1.

The normal way of proving the invariant is true for every iteration is to assume that it is true for one iteration, say the *i*th, and show that it is true for iteration *i* + *1*. This is **proof by induction**. Since as a base case it is known to be true for the first iteration by step (1), we can conclude that it is true for the second iteration; then, since it is true for the second, by deduction it must be true for the third iteration, and so on. With this inductive proof we know that the invariant is true every time execution reaches the beginning of the loop body.

5.3 Basic Selection Constructs

The basic form of the **if** selection construct is:

```
if (condition)
{
      statements of if clause
}
else
{
      statements of else clause
}
```

The condition is evaluated and, if it is true, the sequence of statements in the **if clause** is executed. Alternatively, if the condition is false, the sequence of statements of the **else clause** is executed. Only one of the two alternative sequences is executed, depending on the truth or falsity of the condition. The condition is, of course, a boolean expression. If there is only one statement in a clause it need not be surrounded by curly braces.

Here is an example in which a selection construct is nested in a repetition construct.

```
// The "PassFail" class.
// Read a sequence of exam marks and indicate whether each mark
// is a pass or fail.
// The sequence of marks is terminated by a sentinel –1.
int mark;
final int SENTINEL = –1;
c.println ("Enter marks of exams, end with " + SENTINEL);
mark = c.readInt ();
while (mark != SENTINEL)
{
      if (mark >= 50)
      {
            c.println ("The mark " + mark + " is a pass");
```

```
    }
    else
    {
        c.println ("The mark " + mark + " is a failure");
    }
    mark = c.readInt ();
}
c.println ("The end");
```

Notice that the first mark must be read outside the **while** construct since it must be tested in the continuation condition. The next mark is read on each repetition at the end of the body of the **while** construct.

Here is a sample execution window for this program.

```
Enter marks of exam, end with −1
68
The mark 68 is a pass
35
The mark 35 is a failure
−1
The end
```

When the sentinel is read, the statement following the **while** construct would be executed. In the program the sentinel is labelled **final** in its declaration. This means its value is constant and cannot be changed.

If there is nothing to be done in the **else** clause of a selection then the keyword **else** is omitted and the selection becomes either executing the **if** clause, or doing nothing. Here is an example.

```
// The "PassPercent" class.
// Compute the percentage of pass marks in a sequence of exam marks.
int mark;
final int SENTINEL = −1;
c.println ("Enter marks of exams, end with " + SENTINEL);
int countOfPasses = 0;
int countOfMarks = 0;
mark = c.readInt ();
while (mark != SENTINEL)
{
```

```
    countOfMarks++;
    if (mark >= 50)
    {
        countOfPasses++;
    }
    mark = c.readInt ();
}
c.print ("Percentage passed is ");
c.print ((double) (countOfPasses * 100) / countOfMarks);
c.println ("%");
```

Selection can be made among more than two alternatives. A three-way selection is done using one **if...else...** construct nested inside a second.

Here is an example of a three-way selection where people riding buses are classified by age as: students (12 years old or less), adults, or seniors (65 years old or more).

```
// The "BusFare" class.
// Read sequence of ages counting
// the number of students, seniors, and adults.
final int SENTINEL = –1;
int student = 0, adult = 0, senior = 0;
c.println ("Enter ages, end with " + SENTINEL);
int age;
age = c.readInt ();
while (age != SENTINEL)
{
    if (age >= 65)
        senior++;
    else
        if (age <= 12)
            student++;
        else
            adult++;
    age = c.readInt ();
}
c.println ("senior=" + senior + " adult=" + adult + " student=" + student);
```

In the loop a second **if...else...** construct is nested in the **else** clause of the first **if...else...**. Since an **if...else...** construct is considered to be a single statement, the nested **if...else...** does not require curly braces.

In each of the previous examples **while** loops were used. In the continuation condition of each, a variable's value was compared to a sentinel. In order for this condition to be evaluated at the beginning of the execution, an initial value of the variable had to be read in outside the loop. Then, at the end of the loop, a new value of the variable in the condition was read in. The statements that did this were identical: one outside the loop and one inside. There is an alternate form of a conditional loop that makes use of the **if** and **break** statements. This can provide an **exit** from the loop anywhere between the beginning and end.

Here is a program equivalent to the last example using the **if** and **break** statements.

```
// The "BusFare2" class.
// Read sequence of ages counting the number of students,
// seniors, and adults.
final int SENTINEL = -1;
int student = 0, adult = 0, senior = 0;
int age;
c.println ("Enter ages, end with " + SENTINEL);
while (true)
{
    age = c.readInt ();
    // Test exit condition.
    if (age == SENTINEL)
        break;
    if (age >= 65)
        senior++;
    else if (age <= 12)
        student++;
    else
        adult++;
}
c.println ("senior = " + senior + " adult = " + adult + " student = " + student);
```

Rather than testing a continuation condition involving a variable at the beginning of the **while** loop, this form of the **while** loop uses the continuation condition **true**. This means that the loop would keep running endlessly unless there were an **exit condition** somewhere inside the loop's body. The exit here is

```
if (age == SENTINEL)
    break;
```

Note that the **exit condition** is the opposite of the continuation condition. The **break** statement gives control to the statement following the loop's body if the exit condition is true. In other words, execution then continues from the statement following the loop's body.

This variation means that conditional loops can be written with an exit anywhere that is convenient, rather than being restricted to the beginning, as in the ordinary **while** loop, or the end in the **do** loop. Notice that this simplifies the program.

In writing this version of the program a slightly different kind of paragraphing was used for the nested **if...else** statements. When there are many layers of nesting, this format prevents the program listing from "drifting" to the right. We have not used curly braces since the **if** and **else** clauses consisted of only single statements.

The **continue** statement is similar to the **break** statement except that rather than going to the statement following the loop, as **break** does, it merely goes to the end of the loop body.

5.4   Flow Charts

Producing correct programs requires programmers to understand flow of control. Although paragraphing of programs makes it unnecessary to draw a diagram showing the flow of control through a program, producing a diagram for each of the basic control constructs can be very helpful.

A sequence of instructions can be represented by a box with an arrow entering the box and an arrow leaving it (see Figure 5.2).

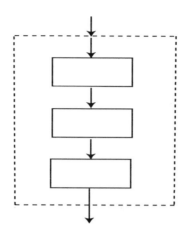

Figure 5.2 Flow Chart of Sequence

A **while** conditional repetition construct can be represented by the diagram in Figure 5.3. When the continuation condition is true, the remaining statements of the loop are executed and control returns to the beginning of the loop. When the continuation condition is false, control leaves the construct.

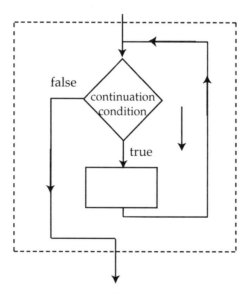

Figure 5.3 Flow Chart of While Conditional Repetition

A two-way selection can be represented by the diagram in Figure 5.4.

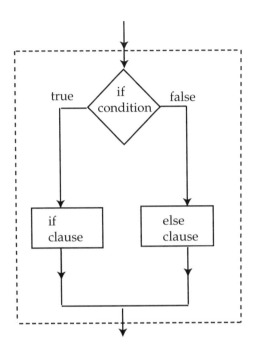

Figure 5.4 Flow Chart of Two-way Selection

Around each of the basic diagrams there is a dotted box. There is only one entry point into each box and one exit point from each box.

Any one of the three constructs can be nested inside the box of another construct. For example, the **if** clause of a selection may have a sequence nested in it. Any one of the boxes of the sequence may, in turn, contain a repetition construct. One of the boxes of the repetition may contain another repetition construct, and so on. The flow chart of Figure 5.1 shows one loop nested inside another.

5.5   Tracing Execution

In trying to write programs that are correct, it is very helpful to simulate the action of the computer and follow the sequence of execution of the statements. As the process proceeds, the user records the values of variables that are changed after any statement that changes their values. As well as variables, the values of any **for** loop indexes are recorded.

This process of tracing is usually done on paper away from the computer and is known as **desk-checking** a program. The hope is to spot any errors and eliminate them before the program is run on the computer.

In programming a loop, a common error is to have one too many, or one too few, repetitions. These are called **off-by-one errors**. Loops should be traced with data that tests extreme conditions.

Frequently a programming environment contains a **debugging** facility that executes the statements one after the other at slow speed or at a one-statement-at-a-time pace. The values of the variables and indexes are displayed as the process goes on. For a debugging facility to be useful, the programmer must already have a good idea of what to expect at each stage so that when an error occurs, it can be spotted and the error corrected. Quick fixes at the keyboard often prove disastrous so that a little forethought is, in the end, the best course of action.

Using the VisualAge for Java Debugger

The *VisualAge for Java* Environment provides a **debugging** facility that allows the user to execute programs line-by-line and, at each step, to examine the values of variables. It is necessary to stop continuous execution at a certain **breakpoint** so that line-by-line execution can begin.

To set a breakpoint, in the upper pane of the *Workbench* select the method where there is to be a breakpoint, then in the lower pane move the cursor to the line at which the breakpoint is to be placed. Next, select the *Breakpoint* command from the *Edit* menu. A blue circle appears at the line to indicate that the breakpoint has been placed. The breakpoint is removed by the same process.

When a breakpoint is reached during execution, the program halts and the *Debugger* window appears (see Figure 5.5).

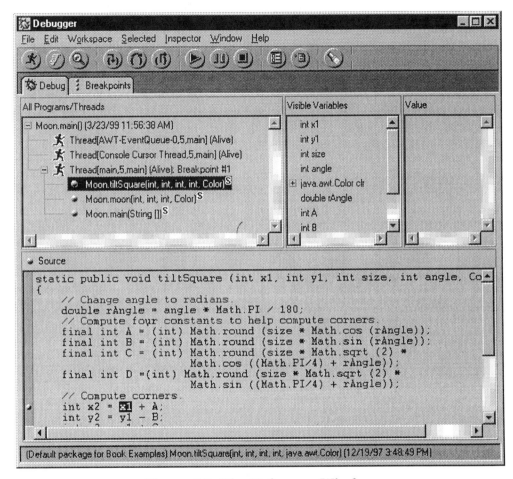

Figure 5.5 The Debugger Window

The tool bar of the *Debugger* window resembles other tool bars in *VisualAge for Java* with a few special functions. There is a *Display* button that looks like a piece of paper beside the *Run* button and an *Inspect* button that looks like a magnifying glass beside that. The next three buttons are used to control stepping of execution (*Step Into, Step Over*, and *Run to Return*). Following these are three more buttons to handle execution (*Resume, Suspend*, and *Terminate*).

When a program halts after hitting a breakpoint, the part being debugged appears in the lower pane of the *Debugger* window labelled *Source*. All the executing threads in the program are listed in the pane labelled *All Programs/Threads*. The *main* thread is the only one of concern. It has a trace of all the methods called to get to the current line. In Figure 5.5, the *main* method of *Moon* called the *moon* method, which in turn, called the *tiltSquare* method.

The *Visible Variables* pane displays all the variables available at that point. The *Value* pane shows the current value of the variable selected in the *Visible Variables* pane. By clicking on the variables listed in this pane, the values of the variables in the program can be determined.

In Chapter 8 and onwards, you will be using reference data types. In the *Visible Variables* pane, reference data types have a plus sign to the left of the name (see the *clr* variable in Figure 5.5). Clicking the plus expands the reference variable allowing the examination of its contents. This allows the inspection of individual elements of an array or the fields of an object.

The *Step Into* button can be used to execute the next line. If the line to be executed is a call to another method, then the new method is entered, the *All Programs/Threads* pane is updated, and the *Source* pane shows the new method. If the *Step Over* button is selected, any call to a new method is fully executed and the line after the call to the new method is highlighted.

Any number of breakpoints can be set and the *Resume* button, the seventh from the left, continues regular execution until the next breakpoint or until the program ends. All breakpoints can be removed at once by clicking the *Clear All* button (the one with the three breakpoint circles).

5.6   Another Selection Construct

Any multi-way selection can be programmed using nested **else** ...**if**s but under certain circumstances there is a possible alternative. This is the **switch** or **case construct**.

Here is an example program fragment that assigns a letter grade to exam marks. If there are several case values that require the same

action, these cases can be listed, separated by colons, before the
action required.

```
// The "LetterGrades" class.
// Produce letter grades from marks for test.
int A = 0, B = 0, C = 0, D = 0, F = 0;  //These are not constants.
int mark;
c.println ("Enter marks end with –1");
mark = c.readInt ();
while (mark != –1)
{
    switch (mark)
    {
        case 8: case 9: case 10:
            A++;
            break;
        case 7:
            B++;
            break;
        case 6:
            C++;
            break;
        case 5:
            D++;
            break;
        case 0: case 1: case 2:  3: case 4:
            F++;
            break;
        default:
            c.println ("Mark is incorrect, enter again");
            break;
    }
    mark = c.readInt ();
}
c.println ("A = " + A);
c.println ("B = " + B);
.. and so on
```

In the **switch** construct the statements in each **case** clause are
not enclosed in curly braces. If the **break** statement is omitted then

the statements of the following alternative are also executed. The **default** clause must be the last alternative and is executed when no earlier match occurs.

When several cases have the same requirements, the different cases are separated by colons preceding the statements that are to be executed. In the example, this is equivalent to having no statements in the **case** 8 clause or the **case** 9 clause. Since there is no **break** statement, the statements of the **case** 9 clause are executed. Thus all three cases: 8, 9, and 10, have the statements of **case** 10 executed.

Here is another example program using the **switch** construct. It is somewhat simpler since each input produces a different response. In the previous example a grade of F could be produced with any one of 5 different marks. This program displays a **menu** to the user of possible inputs: 1 - sing, 2 - cry, and so on.

```java
// The "Respond" class.
// Choose a response.
import hsa.Console;

public class Respond
{
    public static void main (String args [])
    {
        Console c = new Console ();
        int command;

        while (true)
        {
            c.print ("Choose from 1–sing, 2–cry, 3–laugh, 4–stop: ");
            command = c.readInt ();

            if (command == 4)
                break;

            switch (command)
            {
                case 1:
                    c.println ("La la la");
                    break;
```

```
                    case 2:
                        c.println ("Boo hoo");
                        break;
                    case 3:
                        c.println ("Ha ha ha");
                        break;
                    default:
                        c.println ("I don't understand");
                        break;

            }

        }
    } // main method
} /* Respond class */
```

It is also possible to use single characters rather than integers as the **case** labels. For example, this program asks the user to enter a number to indicate the selection and then executes the **switch** statement using that number. The programmer could instead have written the program to accept a single character. This would require changing the **switch** statement and the statement which reads the input. The program might then display this menu.

> *c.print* ("Choose from 's' - sing, 'c' - cry, 'l' - laugh, 'f' - finish: ");

Then the individual cases are labelled as **case** 's', **case** 'c', and so on. Note that the single character labels are in single quotes and each one must be different.

Here is an example program where constants, such as LEFT_VOTE, that have integer values are used to identify the different cases. This perhaps makes the program easier to understand. Java only allows integers or single characters as case labels.

```
// The "Voting" class.
import hsa.Console;

public class Voting
{
    static final int LEFT_VOTE = 1;
    static final int MIDDLE_VOTE = 2;
    static final int RIGHT_VOTE = 3;
```

```java
public static void main (String args [])
{
    Console c = new Console ();
    int vote;
    int left = 0, middle = 0, right = 0;
    final int SIGNAL = -1;

    c.println ("Vote 1 for Left, 2 for Middle, 3 for Right, end with " +
        SIGNAL);

    while (true)
    {
        c.print ("Enter vote: ");
        vote = c.readInt ();

        if (vote == SIGNAL)
            break;

        switch (vote)
        {
            case LEFT_VOTE:
                left++;
                break;
            case MIDDLE_VOTE:
                middle++;
                break;
            case RIGHT_VOTE:
                right++;
                break;
            default:
                c.println ("Invalid vote");
                break;
        }
    }
    c.print ("Left", 8);
    c.print ("Middle", 8);
    c.println ("Right", 8);
    c.print (left, 8);
    c.print (middle, 8);
    c.println (right, 8);
} // main method
} /* Voting class */
```

5.7 Checking Input Data

Runtime errors occur in programs if input data is not appropriate and preparation in the program has not been made for such inappropriate or **bad data**. In the *LetterGrades* class program, if the user enters an integer that is not in the range 0 and 10 or the sentinel −1, the **default** option of the **switch** statement gives the user the error message

Mark is incorrect, enter again

We say that such a program is **forgiving** − that the user has a second chance to enter appropriate data rather than having execution stop.

This would not work however if, by mistake, the user entered the letter *B* instead of the mark 7. An **exception** would be **thrown** when the statement

mark = c.readInt ();

was executed and the system attempted to interpret *B* as an integer and failed. An error message would appear and execution would stop.

Handling such exceptions is possible in Java with a little more programming. This technique of handling bad data is based on the fact that any input data, whether an integer, a real number, or a string, can be read as a string by *readLine*, without causing an exception. After it has been read in as a string, it can be **parsed** to see if it is an integer (**int**) or a real number (**float** or **double**). In the *letterGrades* class program a variable *markStr* would be declared as a *String* and the statement

mark = c.readInt ();

would be replaced by these statements

```
while (true)
{
    try
    {
        String markStr = c.readLine ();
        mark = Integer.parseInt (markStr);
```

```
        break;
    }
    catch (NumberFormatException e)
    {
        c.println ("Bad mark, try again");
    }
}
```

The input statement

$markStr = c.readLine ();$

is in a **while (true)** loop where the exit occurs with the **break** if the string *markStr* can be successfully parsed as an integer. The attempt to read and parse it is preceded by the keyword **try**, and parsing occurs in the statement

$mark = Integer.parseInt (markStr);$

In this statement the *parseInt* method of the *Integer* class tries to produce an integer from the string *markStr*. If it succeeds, it exits from the **while** loop at the **break**. If it **throws** an exception, the instructions in the **catch** clause are executed. The **catch** statement has a parameter that specifies the type of exception that is being caught, which in this case is a *NumberFormatException*.

In Java there are different kinds of exceptions that can be caught and **exception handling** is extremely important in software that is to be **user friendly** and able to cope with errors made by the user without having them stop execution.

In the *LetterGrades* class program the input statement

$mark = c.readInt ();$

occurs twice, once just before the **while** and again at the end of the loop body. If we leave the loop this way the "forgiving input loop" must be included twice. It is perhaps simpler to use the form

```
while (true)
{
    forgiving input loop
    if (mark = -1) break;
    switch statement
}
```

5.8   Common Programming Errors

Many of the simplest programming errors involve semicolons. These are:

- Forgetting the semicolon after a statement.
- Using a semicolon after the header of

    a **do** or **while** loop,

    an **if** condition, or

    a **switch** construct.
- Using a semicolon after a closing curly brace.

Other errors involve the use of curly braces. Common ones are:

- Omitting curly braces when there is a single statement in an **if** or **else** clause or in a **for** loop and later adding another statement without adding the curly braces.
- Forgetting a closing curly brace particularly when constructs are nested and two curly braces are required, one after the other.

Common errors in **switch** constructs are:

- Not using a colon after the case label.
- Not repeating the keyword **case** before each value of the label when a number of values share the same statements.
- Forgetting to include the **break** as the last statement of each alternative except when it is specifically intended that the next alternative also be tested.

Common errors in **for** loops are:

- Forgetting to include the data type of the index variable in its declaration and initialization.
- Having the continuation condition count one too few or one to many executions by confusing the relations $<=$ and $<$ or $>$ and $>=$.
- Not using semicolons between the initialization, continuation, and incrementation components.
- Attempting to change the value of a counting index inside the body of the loop.
- Attempting to output the value of a loop's index outside the body of the loop.

Common errors in conditional loops are:

- Forgetting the parentheses around the continuation condition.
- Forgetting to initialize any variable in the continuation condition of a **while** loop outside the loop itself.
- Forgetting to alter the value of a variable in the continuation condition inside the loop so that it changes from one iteration to the next.
- Forgetting that the body of a **do** loop will be executed at least once.
- Forgetting the semicolon after the continuation condition of a **do** loop.

Common errors in selection constructs are:

- Forgetting the parentheses around the condition.
- Forgetting the relationship of the **if**s and **else**s when selections are nested. An **else** always belongs to the nearest **if** preceding it in the program.

5.9   Chapter Summary

Control Constructs

This chapter discusses the structure within methods. Ultimately all methods can be created out of three basic **control constructs**:

- **linear sequence** where statements are executed one after the other,
- **repetition** where certain statements are repeatedly executed for a fixed number of times (**counted repetition**), or until some condition is false (**conditional repetition**), and
- **selection** where one sequence of statements is selected from alternative sequences depending on a condition.

Flow Charts

The **flow of control** in the execution of a method can be represented by a **flow chart**. Diagrams of this sort were prevalent before structured programming became the accepted style for programs. At that time, many programs had complicated sequences of execution of their instructions. These programs were referred to as "spaghetti" programs.

The control structure of structured programs can be easily followed by reading the program itself, without a supplementary flow chart, particularly if the body of each construct is indented to indicate its **scope**.

The flow charts of the three basic control constructs: sequence, repetition, and selection were shown.

Repetition Constructs

Of the two basic repetition constructs, the **conditional loop** is the primary one in that a **counted loop** can be programmed using a conditional loop, whereas the reverse is not possible. Counted loops begin with the keyword **for**. Following the **for** in parentheses are three components separated by semicolons. These are:

- the declaration and initialization of the index,
- the continuation condition, and
- the increment of the index on each execution of the loop.

The value of the index can be used in statements inside the loop but is not available outside the loop.

Conditional loops may begin with the keyword **while** followed in parentheses by the continuation condition. The body of the loop is in curly braces. The other form of the conditional loop begins with the keyword **do** and ends with **while** followed in parentheses by the continuation condition followed by a semicolon.

A variation of the conditional loop, where an exit is achieved at any place inside the body of the loop, can be done using the header

while (true)

and having within the body the statement

if (exit condition) **break**;

Selection Constructs

The form of the basic selection construct is:

```
if (condition)
{
    statements of if clause
}
else
{
    statements of else clause
}
```

If the condition following the **if** is true, the statements of the **if clause** are selected and executed; if false, the statements of the **else clause** are executed. If there are no statements in the **else** clause, the keyword **else** is omitted.

The basic selection is a two-way choice between two alternatives. To achieve multi-way selection, nested **if...else** constructs are used for additional alternatives.

Tracing Execution

Following the sequence of execution of the statements for a variety of input data helps produce correct programs even before they are run. This process, called **desk checking** or **tracing**, helps the programmer find errors. The process of finding and fixing errors is called **debugging**.

Often programmers are tempted to run a program immediately on the computer and fix errors without much thought. This often prolongs the process of producing a correct program.

When tracing loops, extreme values of the test data should be tested. If a sequence of data items is to be processed, sequences of length 0 and 1 should be checked.

The Switch Construct

Multi-way selection can be achieved using a **switch** or **case construct**. The keyword **switch** is followed by a selection expression whose possible values of the selection expression correspond to the values following the keyword **case** in a sequence of alternatives in the form

>   **case** value of selection expression : statements for this alternative

If two selection expression values require the same consequences, they are listed, separated by colons, each preceded by the keyword **case**. After the statements of an alternative, the statement

>   **break**;

must appear unless it is intended that the statements of the next case also be executed.

The selector variable can be an integer or a character. The final alternative can have no values of case following the keyword **default**. It is executed if the case selector expression's value does not equal any case value of the other cases.

Switch structures are often used where a **menu** of alternatives is displayed for a user to make a selection.

Checking Bad Data

If data of the wrong data type is entered by a user, a runtime error will stop execution. If all data is read as string data, no error occurs.

A program can be designed to handle bad numerical data by reading it as a string and parsing it. The reading and parsing is preceded by the keyword **try** and, if the parsing throws a *NumberFormatException*, it can be caught by a **catch** clause. This can output an error message and allows the user to attempt to enter an appropriate data type. The **try** and **catch** are enclosed in a loop which is exited when the data is appropriate.

5.10 Exercises

1. A sequence of integers is stored in a file called "ages". Write a program to find the range of ages present, that is the difference between the oldest and the youngest.

2. Write a program to show how a mortgage on a house will be paid off (amortized) over a certain number of years given the amount of the mortgage, the proposed annual payment, and the annual interest rate charged.

   Prepare a table showing the amount of interest and capital paid in each year, and the final balance owing at the year's end. Label the columns of the table. Show also the total interest paid during the amortization.

3. Federal income tax is charged at these rates:

   17% on the first $29,590 of taxable income,

   26% on the next $29,590 of taxable income, and

   29% on any income in excess of $59,180.

   Write a program to compute the tax for any taxable income submitted by the user. Have the program work for a series of taxpayers until a negative taxable income is entered.

4. Simulated data representing exam marks out of 100 can be prepared by generating each mark as the sum of marks of 10 questions each out of 10. Generate a mark for each question as a random integer from 0 to 10. The exam marks so generated will not be uniformly distributed, as the integers generated by a single call to *random*, but will be close to a normal or Gaussian distribution (sometimes referred to as a Bell curve). Prepare a file of simulated data representing a class of 200 students and call it "examdata".

5. Write a statistical analysis program. It is to read the file "examdata" prepared in the previous exercise and determine the percentage of the class that would get various grades: A (80 or over), B (70-79), C (60-69), D (50-59), and F (below 50). Have it tabulate these statistics. Run this analysis program again using, as input, a file of simulated data of uniformly distributed exam marks. Compare the results with those that are closer to a Bell curve.

Chapter 6

Strings

In Java there are only a few primitive data types: those pertaining to numbers both integer and real, the boolean type, and two not mentioned so far: **char** and **byte**. One data type that is often primitive in other programming languages is the string data type. In Java the string is an abstract data type and a string variable is implemented as an object through the *String* class.

6.1   The String Data Type

The string data type is used for strings of characters such as names, addresses, phone numbers, and so on. For example, the string "elephant" contains eight characters. In a Java string the positions of the characters are numbered beginning at 0. In the zeroth position is the letter "e" in the first position is the letter "l", and so on. The **length** of the string is 8. This string

"148 O'Reilly St."

has 16 characters; the blanks and punctuation marks are characters. Each character is represented in Unicode which is 16 bits in length. The first 8 bits are the same as the ASCII code representation of a character.

As shown in Chapter 3, a string of characters in quotation marks (a string constant) can be output by a statement such as

c.println ("Here is a string of characters");

In an output statement it is possible to concatenate string constants and numbers using the + operator. In fact, the number is automatically converted to a string.

The conversion of objects to *String* objects is done by calling the *toString* () method of the object to be converted. Most Java class library objects support the *toString* () method. You can add a *toString* () method to your own classes to allow them to be converted to strings automatically. This is recommended because it makes debugging easier and is helpful to others using your class. Primitive data types, like **int** or **boolean** are automatically converted to strings when concatenated to other strings.

6.2   Declaring String Objects

In Java a string is an object. Declaring an object as a string requires use of the *String* class. For example, to declare a string object called *word* with the string "Charles" stored in it, these statements are required.

> *String word;*
> *word =* **new** *String* ("Charles");

This creates an object of *String* class called *word*. The string "Charles" is stored in *word*. A string constant such as "Charles" is automatically changed to a *String* object so that these can be abbreviated to the statement

> *String word =* "Charles";

The *String* class has a number of commonly-used methods. For example, the *substring* method can be used to extract a portion of a string object. There are two forms of the substring method. For the *String* object *word*

> *c.println (word.substring* (3));

produces the output

> *rles*

the substring of "Charles" starting at character position number 3 to the end of the string (the character positions start numbering at zero).

Alternatively, two actual parameters can be provided to the *substring* method. For example, the statement

> *c.println (word.substring* (2, 4));

produces the output

> *arl*

These are the characters in positions numbered 2 to 4 inclusive. The *String* class *length* method will provide the number of characters in the string. For example,

> *c.println (word.length* ());

produces the output 7, the length of the string "Charles". The *length* method has no parameters but empty parentheses must be included.

The expression

c.println (word.substring (word.length () − 1));

can be used to find the last character in a string. This character is in position *word.length* () − 1. The substring with one parameter goes from that character to the end of the string. Attempting to ask for a substring beyond the end of the string produces an **exception**. For example, the statement

c.println (word.substring (5, 8));

produces an exception since the *word* has character positions only from 0 to 6. This kind of exception need not be notified in the *main* method's header as an *IOException* must be by adding **throws** *IOException*, but it will cause execution to stop.

The *String* method *charAt* can be used to find the character at any string position. For example the statement

c.println (word.charAt (0));

produces the output C, the first character in the string.

Since a string constant such as "Charles" is automatically a *String* object, it can be used in any of the expressions where *word* is used with the same result. For example

c.println ("Charles".charAt (0));

produces the output C.

6.3   Concatenation of Strings

The concatenation operator + can be used in string expressions. Another way to concatenate two *String* objects to create a new *String* object is to use the *String* class method *concat*. For example,

```
String s1 = "sea";
String s2 = "shore";
String s3 = s1.concat(s2);
c.println (s3);
```

results in the output

seashore

Notice that string *s1* and *s2* are not changed. After a string is assigned a value it cannot be changed.

6.4   Replacing Characters in Strings

Individual characters in a string object can be replaced by other characters to create a new *String* object. For example, this program fragment

String s1 = "Mississippi";
String s2 = *s1.replace*('i', 'e');
c.println (*s2*);
c.println (*s1*);

produces the output

Messesseppe
Mississippi

Again notice that string *s1* is not changed.

Every occurrence of the character 'i' is replaced by the character 'e'. Single character constants like 'i' have single quotes around them. A single character is of primitive data type **char**. String constants like "our" have double quotes.

A special version of character replacement is obtained using the *String* class methods *toUpperCase* or *toLowerCase*. For example, if this statement were added to the previous program fragment

c.println (*s1.toLowerCase*());

the output would be

mississippi

Any upper case character is changed to a lower case one where possible. If the statement

c.println (*s1.toUpperCase* ());

were added the output would be

MISSISSIPPI

Any lower case character is changed to an upper case one where possible.

6.5   Searching for Patterns in Strings

The *String* class methods *indexOf* and *lastIndexOf* are useful in finding string patterns in other strings. For example, the program fragment

> *String vowels* = "aeiou";
> *c.println (vowels.indexOf* ((**int**) 'i'));

produces the output 2, the character position of the letter *i* in the *vowels* string. When the string pattern sought contains only one character, the character is in single quotes and must be cast as an integer. For a string pattern of more than one character, the pattern is enclosed in double quotes and is not cast as an integer. For example

> *c.println (vowels.indexOf* ("eio"));

produces the output 1, which is the position of the beginning of the substring "eio" in the string "aeiou". If the pattern is not in the string, the output is –1.

The last occurrence of the pattern in a string can be obtained using the method *lastIndexOf*.

The first occurrence of the pattern in the string starting at index *start* is found using the *indexOf* method with two parameters in this form

> *indexOf (String* pattern, **int** start)

Here is a program that reads a series of words ended by "*" and removes all the vowels in each word.

```
// The "Squish" class.
import hsa.Console;

public class Squish
{
    public static void main (java.lang.String [] args)
    {
        Console c = new Console ();
        String word, newWord;
        final String VOWELS = "aeiouAEIOU";

        c.println ("Enter a series of words, end with '*'");
        while (true)
        {
            word = c.readString ();
            if (word.equals ("*"))
                break;
            newWord = "";
            for (int i = 0 ; i < word.length () ; i++)
            {
                if (VOWELS.indexOf (word.charAt (i)) == -1)
                {
                    newWord = newWord + word.charAt (i);
                }
            }
            c.println ("Word without vowels is " + newWord);
        }
    } // main method
} /* Squish class */
```

Here is an example execution of the *Squish* class.

```
Enter a series of words, end with '*'.
elephant
lphnt
bicycle
bcycl
Extreme
xtrm
*
```

The string *newWord* has the value initialized to the null string outside the **for** loop. Inside the loop it is assigned a new value whenever the character is not a vowel. Here is a program to find the number of occurrences of a character in a string. When a character of type **char** is used instead of a string, it must be cast as an **int**.

```
// The "Occurs" class.
String word = "Mississippi";
int count = 0;
int index = 0;
int where;
char ch = 'i';
for (;;)
{
    where = word.indexOf ((int) ch, index);
    if (where != -1)
    {
        count++;
        index = where + 1;
    }
    else
        break;
}
c.println ("There are " + count + " occurrences of "
    + ch + " in the word " + word);
```

The **for** loop has null initialization, continuation, and incrementation so that a seemingly endless **for** loop would be produced. The exit occurs when the **else** clause is executed, that is, when *where* equals −1 and the **break** statement is executed. An endless **while** loop can be produced using **while (true)**.

6.6   Comparing Strings

Strings can be compared using the *String* class methods *equals,* *equalsIgnoreCase*, and *compareTo*. The boolean expression

> *s1.equals* (s2)

is true if *s1* and *s2* are strings of the same length and they have the same characters in the same sequence. Comparison of equality of strings ignoring the case of characters is obtained using the method *equalsIgnoreCase*. For example, this program fragment

> *String s1 = "Peter";*
> *String s2 = "peter";*
> *c.println (s1.equalsIgnoreCase(s2));*

produces the output *true.*

Here is a program fragment that reads words until the word "stop" is entered and outputs each word a character at a time, one to a line.

```
// The "Spelling" class.
// Output the letters of words that are input.
String word;
word = c.readLine ();
while (!(word.equals ("stop")))
{
    for (int count = 0 ; count < word.length () ; count++)
    {
        c.println (word.charAt (count));
    }
    word = c.readLine ();
}
```

Notice that the *String* class does not have a *notEquals* method so that the exclamation mark indicating the *not* unary operator is used in front of the boolean expression

> *word.equals* ("stop")

Here is a similar program fragment that reads words until the word "last" is entered and tests whether or not the word contains the letter "s".

```
// The "Ess" class.
import hsa.Console;

public class Ess
{
    public static void main (java.lang.String [] args)
    {
        Console c = new Console ();
        String word;

        c.println ("Enter a series of words, end with \"last\"");
        while (true)
        {
            c.print ("Enter word: ");
            word = c.readString ();
            if (word.equals ("last"))
                break;
            if (word.indexOf ('s') != -1)
                c.println (word + " contains an 's'");
            else
                c.println (word + " does not contain an 's'");
        }
    } // main method
} /* Ess class */
```

Notice that to include "last" in the quoted prompt each double quotation mark had to be preceded by a backslash \. We could instead have used single quotes around the sentinel in the prompt, namely as 'last'. The words must be entered one to a line since they are being read by the *readLine* method of the console.

Strings can be put into sequence, normally in alphabetic order, using the *compareTo* method. If *s1* and *s2* are string objects that have been instantiated with string values the expression

s1.compareTo (s2)

has a value 0 if the values of *s1* and *s2* are equal, is negative if *s1* is less than (comes before alphabetically) *s2*, and positive if *s1* comes after *s2*. The sequencing depends on the **Unicode** value of the characters. Capital (upper case) letters have different values than little (lower case) letters.

This program uses the *compareTo* method to find the alphabetically last of a series of names.

```
// The "LastInList" class.
// Output the alphabetically last of a series of names,
// ended by a sentinel name.
String name, sentinel, last;
c.println ("What is the sentinel name?");
sentinel = c.readLine ();
c.println ("Enter names, end with " + sentinel);
name = c.readLine ();
last = name.toLowerCase ();
while (!(name.equals (sentinel)))
{
    if (last.compareTo (name.toLowerCase ()) < 0)
    {
        last = name.toLowerCase ();
    }
    name = c.readLine ();
}
c.println ("Alphabetically last name is " + last);
```

An execution window for this program might be

```
What is the sentinel name?
Yahoo
Enter names, end with Yahoo
Dog
cat
Zebra
Lion
unicorn
Yahoo
Alphabetically last name is zebra
```

If only the sentinel is entered the final line would be

Alphabetically last name is yahoo

Notice that the sentinel itself has been converted to lower case. The method *toLowerCase* is used so that it will not matter if some names are capitalized.

6.7 The StringBuffer Class

When a *String* object has been initialized its contents cannot be altered. The *StringBuffer* class, however, can be used to create strings whose contents can be changed. For example, this fragment

```
StringBuffer s1;
s1 = new StringBuffer ("Hello");
s1.append (" there");
c.println (s1);
```

produces the output

Hello there

It is not correct to write the first two lines as

```
StringBuffer s1 = "Hello"
```

since "Hello" is a *String* object and cannot be assigned to initialize a *StringBuffer* object.

The *StringBuffer* class method *append* can be used to concatenate a string to the end of the present contents of the *StringBuffer* object.

Here is an example where a word is read in and the letters reversed to determine whether or not the string is a **palindrome** (a word or phrase that is the same backwards as forwards). It is assumed that all the letters are lower case (no capital letters).

```
// The "Palindrome1" class.
// Determines whether or not a word is a palindrome
// by reversing the letters.
String word;
c.println ("Enter a word");
```

```
word = c.readLine ();
StringBuffer reverse = new StringBuffer ();
for (int count = word.length () – 1 ; count >= 0 ; count—)
{
    reverse.append (word.charAt (count));
}
if (word.equals (reverse.toString ()))
    c.println ("The word " + word + " is a palindrome");
else
    c.println ("The word " + word + " is not a palindrome");
```

In the example it is assumed that all the letters in *word* are in lower case. A palindrome test normally should ignore the case of letters, so that a word such as *Madam* is palindrome.

The *Palindrome1* class program could be made to do this by replacing the test

if (*word.equals* (*reverse.toString* ()))

by the test

if (*word.toLowerCase* ().*equals* (*reverse.toString* ().*toLowerCase* ()))

This unusual looking boolean expression is understood by noting that the method *toLowerCase* applies to a *String* object and yields a value that is a *String* object. This is known as a **cascaded method call** and is evaluated from left to right after the part in parentheses is evaluated.

You can always use *String* objects instead of *StringBuffer* objects by repeatedly creating new *String* objects with the changed contents. This, however is slower and wastes computer memory.

There are several methods of the *StringBuffer* class besides the *append* method that are useful.

- The *charAt* (**int** *n*) method has a value that is the character of the contents at index *n*.
- The *setCharAt* (**int** *n*, **char** *ch*) method sets the character at position *n* to *ch*.
- The *setLength* (**int** *n*) method sets the length of the buffer to *n*.
- The *toString* () method converts the *StringBuffer* object to a *String* object.

- The *insert* (**int** *n*, *arg*) method converts its second argument, which can be a primitive data type or any object that has a *toString* method, and inserts it into the present string in the buffer starting at character position *n*.

For example, this program fragment

StringBuffer s = **new** *StringBuffer* ("How it is ");
s.insert (3, 7 > 6);
c.println (*s.toString* ());

would produce the output

How true it is

The boolean expression 7 > 6 has a value *true* which is converted to a string and inserted into the contents of *s* starting at position 3 which is after the first blank following *How*. Notice that there are two blanks after the word "How" in the program fragment.

6.8   The StringTokenizer Class

The *StringTokenizer* class is part of the *java.util* package. In order to use it

import *java.util.**;

must be at the beginning of the program.

This class is principally used to divide a line of text into its tokens, where a token is a series of characters separated from its neighbors by **white space** and where white space consists of blanks, end of lines, or tabs.

In this example, a line of text will be read in and its tokens output one to a line and counted. It uses several methods of the *StringTokenizer* class: *countTokens* to find the number of tokens in the line, *nextToken* to find the next token in the line, and *hasMoreTokens* to determine when the last token of the line has been processed.

```
// The "WordsInLine" class.
// Read a line of text and output tokens one to a line.
String line;
c.println ("Enter a line of text");
line = c.readLine ();
StringTokenizer words = new StringTokenizer (line);
c.println ("Number of tokens in line is " + words.countTokens ());
c.println ("The words in line are:");
while (words.hasMoreTokens ())
{
    c.println (words.nextToken ());
}
```

Here is a sample execution.

```
Enter a line of text
How now brown cow
Number of tokens in line is 4
The words in line are:
How
now
brown
cow
```

Here is a program called *Purge* that reads words from a file called "script" and outputs all of the four-letter words in the script to a file called "censor". The complete program is shown here since, as with all uses of reading from and writing to files, we must use the *java.io* and *java.util* libraries. The *main* method header must also include "**throws IOexception**".

```
// The "Purge" class.
import java.io.*;
import java.util.*;
import hsa.Console;

public class Purge
{
    public static void main (String args []) throws IOException
    {
        BufferedReader script;
```

```
PrintWriter censor;
script = new BufferedReader (new FileReader ("script"));
censor = new PrintWriter (new FileWriter ("censor"));
String word;

while (true)
{
    String line = script.readLine ();
    if (line == null)
        break;
    StringTokenizer words = new StringTokenizer (line);
    while (words.hasMoreTokens ())
    {
        word = words.nextToken ();
        if (word.length () == 4)
        {
            censor.println (word);
        }
    }
}
script.close ();
censor.close ();
} // main method.
} /* Purge class */
```

6.9   Text Processing

One of the important uses of computers is to process text. It is possible to format the text so that each line begins in a certain column and ends in a certain column. We say it is both left and right justified. Another common form is to have text left justified but leave the right side "ragged". Words are added to the line until the addition of the next word would produce a line longer than a fixed maximum.

Here is a program that reads a file named "text" and outputs a file named "ragged" with a ragged right side whose lines are as long as possible but no longer than a user-specified maximum length. The complete application program is shown here because some changes from the usual form are needed.

```
// The "Justify" class.
import java.awt.*;
import java.io.*;
import java.util.*;
import hsa.Console;

public class Justify
{
    static Console c;
    static public void main (String args []) throws IOException
    {
        c = new Console ();
        // Reformat text in file "text" in ragged right style so that the
        // number of characters in the line is limited to a given
        // maximum. Store the revised text in file "ragged".
        int maxLength;
        c.println ("What is the maximum length of line?");
        maxLength = c.readInt ();
        String inputLine;
        StringTokenizer inline;
        StringBuffer outline = new StringBuffer ();
        String infileName, outfileName;
        c.println ("What is the name of the input file?");
        infileName = c.readLine ();
        BufferedReader input;
        input = new BufferedReader (new FileReader (infileName));
        c.println ("What is the name of the output file?");
        outfileName = c.readLine ();
        PrintWriter output;
        output = new PrintWriter (new FileWriter (outfileName));
        inputLine = input.readLine ();
        int lineLength = 0;
        while (inputLine != null)
        {
            inline = new StringTokenizer (inputLine);
            while (inline.hasMoreTokens ())
            {
                String token = inline.nextToken ();
```

```
              if (lineLength + token.length () <= maxLength)
              {
                  outline.append (token + " ");
                  lineLength += token.length () + 1;
              }
              else
              {
                  output.println (outline);
                  lineLength = token.length () + 1;
                  outline = new StringBuffer (token + " ");
              }
          }
          inputLine = input.readLine ();
      }
      // Print remaining partial line and close file.
      output.println (outline);
      output.close ();
   } // main method
} /* Justify class */
```

Notice that to the standard boiler plate we have added the line

   import *java.io.*;*

and that the *main* method has

   throws *IOException*

added to the header. These changes are necessary when a program is reading from a file and writing to a file. Because the *StringTokenizer* class is to be used, the line

   import *java.util.*;*

is also added.

As a second example of text processing, here is a program that eliminates the punctuation marks in a text. This program requires the examination of the characters in each line to see if the character is a punctuation mark. If it is not, the character is appended to the output line. The same changes in the standard boiler plate are necessary as in the previous program.

```
// The "RemovePunctuation" class.
// Eliminate all the punctuation marks from the file
// "text" and store the result in "text2".
final String PUNCTUATION = ",.:;'?!()\"";
String inline;
StringBuffer outline = new StringBuffer ();
BufferedReader input;
input = new BufferedReader (new FileReader ("text"));
PrintWriter output;
output = new PrintWriter (new FileWriter ("text2"));
inline = input.readLine ();
while (inline != null)
{
    for (int index = 0 ; index < inline.length () ; index++)
    {
        if (PUNCTUATION.indexOf (inline.charAt (index)) == -1)
            outline.append (inline.charAt (index));
    }
    output.println (outline);
    outline.setLength (0); // Set outline to have no characters.
    inline = input.readLine ();
}
output.close ();
```

Computers can also be used to help to translate from one language to another. This is done all the time with computer programming languages. The Java programs that you write are translated into the bytecode language by the Java compiler. Each computer platform must then interpret the bytecode language to its own machine code. To show how computers do translations, we will look at an example program that translates English text into Pig Latin.

Pig Latin is a very simple language sometimes used by adults to baffle little children, much as parents spell words to prevent them from being understood by the young. The translation rules from English to Pig Latin are very simple: each word that begins with a vowel has *way* added to the end of it; each word that begins with a consonant has the consonant moved to the end of the word and then has *ay* added. For example, the word "it" becomes "itway" and "girl" becomes "irlgay".

Here is the translation program. The original English text is in a
file and the Pig Latin translation is written to a file. The names of
these files must be supplied by the user. (Because files are
involved we have included the complete program.)

```java
// The "PigLatin" class.
import java.io.*;
import java.util.*;
import hsa.Console;

public class PigLatin
{
    public static void main (java.lang.String [] args) throws IOException
    {
        Console c = new Console ();
        String fileName;
        BufferedReader inFile;
        PrintWriter outFile;

        c.print ("Enter the name of the file where the English is stored: ");
        fileName = c.readLine ();
        inFile = new BufferedReader (new FileReader (fileName));

        c.print ("Enter the name of the file for the Pig Latin: ");
        fileName = c.readLine ();
        outFile = new PrintWriter (new FileWriter (fileName));

        c.close ();

        String word;
        while (true)
        {
            String line = inFile.readLine ();
            if (line == null)
                break;
            StringTokenizer words = new StringTokenizer (line);
            while (words.hasMoreTokens ())
            {
                word = words.nextToken ();
                if ("aeiouAEIOU".indexOf (word.charAt (0)) != -1)
                {
                    outFile.print (word + "way ");
```

```
            }
            else
            {
                outFile.print (word.substring (1) + word.charAt (0) +
                    "ay ");
            }
        }
    }
    inFile.close ();
    outFile.close ();
} // main method
} /* PigLatin class */
```

6.10 Chapter Summary

In Java (unlike many programming languages not including C) strings are objects of a *String* class rather than being of a primitive data type.

The String Data Type

In a string the character positions are numbered from 0 to the length of the string minus 1. A string of length 8 has character positions 0, 1, 2, ..., 7. Strings can be concatenated using the + operator. In an output statement a string can consist of the concatenation of string constants, strings, and other primitive data types. If the string or string constant precedes the primitive data types they are automatically converted to strings. Objects can also be concatenated by using their *toString* methods.

A string constant is automatically created as a *String* object so that rather than declaring and initializing a string *word* by the statement

> *String word* = **new** *String* ("Charles");

the statement

> *String word* = "Charles";

is sufficient.

String Methods

There are a number of *String* class methods.

- The *length* method yields the number of characters in a string. For example,

  word.length ()

  has a value that is the length of the *String* object *word*. There are no parameters for *length* but it has empty parentheses after it.

- The *substring* method has two forms. The value of

  word.substring (5)

  is the substring of *word* from the character in position 5 to the end of the string in *word*. In the other form,

  word.substring (5, 7)

  is the substring of *word* from character position 5 to character position 7 inclusive.

- The *charAt* method is used when a substring of only one character is wanted. For example,

  word.charAt (5)

has a value that is the character of *word* at position 5.

In all these methods, using a character position outside the range of the *String* object produces an exception.

- The *concat* method is used to concatenate (join) two string objects to create a new string object. For example,

  word1.concat (*word2*)

  has a value that is a string object with the value of *word2* concatenated after the value of *word1*. This is the same as

  word + *word2*

- The *replace* method is used to replace characters or substrings in a *String* object by other characters or substrings to create a new *String* object. A string constant of a single character has single quotes.

- The *toUpperCase* method creates a *String* object that has the value with all characters changed to upper case. For example, if *word* is a *String* object whose value is *Madam*, then

  word.toUpperCase ()

  is a *String* object with value MADAM.

- The *toLowerCase* method is similar, but converts the characters in the string to lower case.

Searching for Patterns in String Objects

- The *indexOf* method is used to find a pattern in another string. For example, the statements

  String word = "even";
  c.println (word.indexOf ("ve"));

  will produce the output 1 which is the position of the first of the string "ve" in "even". If the pattern being searched for is a single character it must be cast as a type **int**. The search may also be begun at any character position. For example, these statements

  String word = "occurrences";
  c.println (word.indexOf ((**int**) 'c', 2));
  c.println (word.indexOf ((**int**) 'c', 3));

  produce the output

  2
  8

- The *lastIndexOf* method is used to find the position of the last occurrence. In these last two methods, if there is no occurrence a value −1 is returned.

Comparing Strings

A number of *String* class methods are useful in comparing the values of two *String* objects.

- The *equals* method yields a boolean value that is true for the expression

    word1.equals (word2)

    if the *String* object *word1* has the same characters in the same sequence and is the same length as has the *String* object *word2*.

- The *equalsIgnoreCase* method is the same as *equals* except that the case of the letters (upper or lower) does not matter.

- The *compareTo* method has a value for the expression

    word1.compareTo (word2)

    of 0 if the two are equal, −1 if the value of *word1* is less than that of *word2*, and +1 if the value is greater. The comparison is done on the basis of the Unicode values of characters which preserves alphabetic ordering. Upper and lower case letters have different Unicode values.

The StringBuffer Class

Once a *String* object is initialized, its value cannot be changed. The *StringBuffer* class is useful when changes are required. It is declared and instantiated by a statement such as

StringBuffer s1 = **new** *StringBuffer* ("OK");

Since "OK" is a *String* object and not a *StringBuffer* object the constructor must be used. Here are some methods of the *StringBuffer* class.

- The *length* method is similar to that for the *String* class. It has a value of the current length.

- The *append* method is used to append any *String* object to the current value of the *StringBuffer* object. If *line* is a *StringBuffer* object and *word* is a *String* object, the expression

    line.append (word)

    is the *StringBuffer* object with the word appended to it. Other primitive data types are automatically converted to *String* objects when appended.

The StringTokenizer Class

This class is useful for breaking a line of text into **tokens**, that is a sequence of characters surrounded by **white space**, where white space consists of blanks, tabs, or returns. The *StringTokenizer* methods include:

- the *countToken* method which has a value equal to the number of tokens in the line,
- the *nextToken* method which finds the next token in the line, and
- the *hasMoreTokens* method which indicates whether the line has more tokens.

These methods are useful in text processing.

6.11 Exercises

1. Write a program to read text from a given file and reformat it so that the lines are no longer than a given maximum length. Instead of having it left justified with a ragged right have it right justified with a ragged left. Store the result in a file called "right", as well as displaying it on the screen.

2. Write a program to read lines of text from a file called "right" and center each line in a space that is 80 characters wide. Display the result on the screen and store it in the file called "center".

3. Write a program to read a line of text and change the spelling of words ending in "or" to end in "our".

4. Write a program to generate the values for car licence plates that consists of three capital letters, chosen at random, followed by a space and then three digits chosen at random.

Chapter 7

Methods

As programs grow larger it is important to subdivide them into subprograms each of which is easy to create and easy to understand. In this way the complexity of larger programs is controlled.

Historically subprograms were of two basic types: **functions** and **procedures**.

- A function subprogram produced a value.

- A procedure subprogram caused one or more actions.

In a structured programming language such as Pascal or Turing, subprograms were clearly separated into these two types. In the language C, all subprograms are referred to as **functions**. In Java all subprograms are called **methods**. All Java methods must belong to a class. The methods of a class provide a way for the user of an object instantiated from the class to manipulate the instance variables of the object. This chapter examines Java methods in detail.

7.1   Kinds of Methods

One of the most important facts about methods is that, in order to use one, all that must be known about it is its **signature** and,

- if it is a function-type method, what value it produces,

- if it is a procedure-type method, what action or actions it produces.

As with C, function-type methods in Java can have **side effects**, that is, they produce actions as well as having a value.

To illustrate the two types of methods we will refer to the methods that we have used all along: the methods of the *Console* class.

The method *fillRect* will be used as an example of a procedure-type method. Its **signature** is

fillRect (**int** *x*, **int** *y*, **int** *width*, **int** *height*)

In the signature, after the method's name in parentheses, is a list of its **parameters** and their data types. The list is separated by commas. The **specification** is completed by adding that the action produced by this method is to draw a rectangle with its upper-left corner at the point with coordinates (*x*, *y*) and having the given *width* and *height*. The rectangle is to be filled with the current drawing color. The current color is set by another *Console* method called *setColor* whose signature is

> *setColor (Color clr)*;

7.2   Calling a Method in a Program

To **call** or **invoke** the use of the *fillRect* method in a program, **actual parameters** or **arguments** must be provided corresponding to the **formal parameters** of the signature. For example, this statement could be included in a program (assuming a *Console* object *c* has been instantiated first).

> *c.fillRect* (0, 0, 50, 100);

When executed, the statement would produce a filled rectangle whose upper-left corner is at the origin of coordinates (0, 0) and which is 50 pixels wide and 100 pixels high. The rectangle would be green if the rectangle-drawing statement were preceded by this statement

> -   *c.setColor (Color.green)*;

The color *green* is a constant of the *Color* class and is used as the argument of the *setColor* method.

In any call to a method the name of the object to which the method belongs precedes the method's name and is separated from it by a dot.

In the last statement, *setColor* is a method of object *c*. The call to a procedure-type method acts like a statement in the program. For example, the call to the procedure-type method *setColor* changes the current color for drawing to *green*.

In any call to a method there is always a one-to-one correspondence between the formal parameters of its signature and the actual parameters or arguments of the call to the method. For example, here is the correspondence for *fillRect*.

data type	parameter	argument
int	*x*	0
int	*y*	0
int	*width*	50
int	*height*	100

The data types of corresponding parameters and arguments must also agree.

As an example of a function-type method, we will use the *readInt* method of the *Console* class. Here is a program fragment that uses the *readInt* method to read in an integer.

```
int number
number = c.readInt ();
```

There are no parameters for the *readInt* method but parentheses are still necessary.

7.3   Defining a Method

If a method is to be used outside the class in which it is defined, it must be declared as **public** in the class. If it is a function-type method, the data type of the value returned by the function follows the keyword **public**. If it is a procedure-type method, the keyword **void** is used in this position instead. After these keywords comes the signature of the method. For example, the *fillRect* method would be defined by this **header**:

public void *fillRect* (**int** *x*, **int** *y*, **int** *width*, **int** *height*)

After this header comes the **body** of the method surrounded by curly braces.

Here is the complete definition of a function-type method called *square* that will produce a value which is the square of its single integer parameter.

```
// Method to produce the square of an integer.
static public int square (int number)
{
    return number * number;
} // square method
```

This function-type method *square* has the data type of the value returned, namely **int**, after the keyword **public**. It has one parameter called *number* which is also of data type **int**. All function-type methods have the keyword **return** followed by the value that is to be returned in their body.

Here is a program that uses this *square* method. In this case, we show the entire application program, including the boiler plate, so that the relationship between the *main* program and the *square* method of the enclosing *TableOfSquares* class is clear.

```
// The "TableOfSquares" class.
import java.awt.*;
import hsa.Console;

public class TableOfSquares
{
    static Console c;

    // Main method to compute the squares of numbers from
    // 1 to 10.
    static public void main (String args [])
    {
        c = new Console ();
        for (int value = 1 ; value <= 10 ; value++)
        {
            c.println ("Square of " + value + " = " + square (value));
        }
    } // main method

    // Method to produce the square of an integer.
    static public int square (int number)
    {
        return number * number;
    } // square method
} /* TableOfSquares class */
```

Because both *main* and *square* are methods of the *TableOfSquares* class, when *square* is called in *main*, contrary to the usual practice, the method's name is not preceded by an object or class name with a dot.

In the call to *square* in *main* the argument *value* is in correspondence with the method's parameter *number*. Both are of **int** data type.

Labelling Methods and Variables as Static

The *main* method is always declared **static** because the class in which it resides is not instantiated. For *main* to call methods contained in this class, those methods must be labelled **static**. A static method is called a **class method**.

Some classes in the Java class library, for example the *Math* class, are never instantiated. All of its methods must in fact be labelled as **static**. To call such a method, the class name, followed by a dot precedes the method's name. For example,

> **double** *sqrtOfTwo = Math.sqrt* (2);

calls the square root method *sqrt* of the *Math* class.

In most classes the methods are not labelled as **static**. (These non-static methods are called **object methods**.) Before a method of a non-static class can be used, the class must first be instantiated to create an object of the class. For example, using the *println* method of the *Console* class requires a statement such as

> *Console c* = **new** *Console* ( );

to instantiate an object of this class. Using the method *println* of this object requires the object's name followed by a dot and then the method's name. For example,

> *c.println* ("Hello there");

Variables can also be labelled as **static**. Usually, if a variable of a class is not labelled **static**, when the class is instantiated to create an object, the object has a copy of that variable. When a method of that object is then called, it uses the copy particular to that object. Such variables are called **object** or **instance variables**.

If a variable in a class is labelled **static**, it is created only once when the class is first **loaded** (assembled into the program). It is called a **class variable**. When a method of an object instantiated from that class is called, any reference to that variable is to the class variable and not to a copy in the object.

7.4   Access to Instance Variables

The idea of an object is that the data and the methods that have access to that data are encapsulated so that no outside object can have access to the data except by using the object's methods. This protects the data from unintentional interference by methods of an outside object.

Encapsulation has the advantage that the user of an object need not know how the data is being stored or the details of implementation of the methods. These details could be changed as long as the specifications of the methods remained constant.

The definition of the details is contained in the class. For example, we have *Console* class methods and *String* class methods that we know how to use but have no idea how they are implemented. To use the methods of a class we must create an **instance** of the class. The class serves as a template or pattern for creating objects of the class. The variables (data) of the object are called instance variables and the methods of the object are called object or instance methods. In general, only the instance methods of an object are available to another object. The instance variables are not; they are accessible only to the instance methods of their own object.

Because the instance variables are part of the encapsulation with the instance methods, the instance methods have direct access to them and there is no need to pass them as parameters to the methods. In a sense, the instance variables are **global variables** that are limited to a single object.

7.5   Scope of Identifiers

In Java, identifiers can only be used after they are defined. An identifier is defined by:

- declaring it in a variable declaration statement,
- declaring it as the index variable in a **for** statement,
- declaring it as the name of a method or class, or
- declaring it as the name of a parameter to a method.

The **scope** of an identifier is that part of the program where the identifier is known and can be used.

- **Scopes defined by syntactic constructs**: In general, an identifier is known from the point where it is introduced until the end of the enclosing construct.
- **Global identifiers**: Identifiers defined in the class as variables, constants, or methods are known to any contained method and are said to be local to the class.
- **Control variables for iterations**: An identifier introduced as the index of a **for** loop can be used in the body of the **for** loop but not outside. It is local to the **for** loop.
- **Structured statements**: An identifier introduced in a declaration inside the body of a structured statement, such as **for**, **while**, or **if**, can be used until the end of that body. It is local to the body.
- **Redefining is prohibited**: An identifier cannot be redefined in a scope where it is known. For example, it is not legal to write a declaration of a variable *m* in a scope where *m* is already defined, or to use the variable *i* as the index of a **for** loop in a scope where *i* is already defined.
- **Methods**: A method introduces a new scope. The name of the method is always known in the body of the method and in any other method belonging to the same class. If the method is declared as **public** it is known to any object that imports its class.
- **Reusing identifiers**: Names of parameters and local identifiers inside a method can be the same as names used in the class scope. The identifier is being reused. If it were not possible to

reuse identifiers, the programmer writing a method would need to know all of the global identifiers in the class where the method would be used. If a reused identifier appears in a statement inside the method, it is the local identifier (parameter, variable, or constant) that is meant. To use a global variable with the same name, the programmer must first use the keyword **this** followed by a dot.

- **Imported identifiers**: Identifiers used inside a method but not defined there in either the formal parameter list or in a local definition, are global to the method. These identifiers must be defined in the containing class.

- **Imported identifiers cannot be redefined**: The rule for importing and the rule prohibiting redefining taken together mean that if an identifier from the class is used in a method, that identifier cannot subsequently be redefined in the method.

Understanding the scope of identifiers is an important aspect of ensuring that your programs will actually work the way you expect them to. In the next section we will look at various ways of testing programs.

7.6   Testing of Programs

Computer programs are complicated and difficult to construct, and as a result they are often not correct. Errors in programs are traditionally called **bugs**. Most programs, especially those of any complexity, have bugs in them. Although in theory it is possible to prove programs correct, the proof process is difficult and is not usually carried out.

It is still important, though, to gain confidence in a program. Programs should therefore be tested to determine how well they conform to their specifications. It is often pointed out that testing can only show errors, not their absence. This is because any interesting program will accept many different inputs, it can go through many different states, produce many different outputs, and it can end in many different states. Testing can only examine a limited number of these situations. Nonetheless, testing is important. Given the opportunity to fly in an airplane that has had its flight control software tested, and another that has not had its software tested, a wise person will choose the one with the tested software.

Testing can be done in many ways.

In **blackbox testing** the tester has the specification of the program (often an informal description of what the program is to do) but not the text of the program itself. The program is like a black box whose internals cannot be examined. By trying out appropriate samples of data values, the tester attempts to determine if the program meets its specification.

In **whitebox testing** the tester has the specification and also the text of the program. This means that a more detailed and thorough job of testing can be done. For example, knowing how the program is constructed, the tester can ensure that each statement in the program is executed (each loop, and each branch of each selection statement). Further, by examining the text of the program the tester can see how different parts of the program depend on each other, and can ensure that each significantly different internal state of the program is entered at least once in a set of tests. It is also generally useful to test the limit conditions of programs (the ends of ranges of allowed values, lists of the minimum and maximum specified size, and so on).

One way to test a method is to write a small *main* method, called a **driver**, that provides the environment needed by the method, and that calls the method with different sets of values provided for the parameters.

7.7 Tracing of Methods

Another way to understand a method is to trace its execution. This is done by making a table that corresponds to the state of the computation, and changing the values in the table to reflect the progress of the computation. For example, here is a method to test whether the first few integers are primes.

A prime is any number that is greater than or equal to 2, and that is divided evenly only by itself and by 1. Thus, 2 is a prime number because it can be divided evenly only by itself and by 1. Since every other even number can be divided by 2, no other even number can be prime. Also, 3 is a prime number because it can be divided evenly only by itself and by 1. Similarly, 5 and 7 are prime. But 6 and 9 are not a prime because they can be divided evenly by 3.

In the *checkPrime* method the number *n* is divided by a sequence of factors going from 2 up to the integer less than the square root of *n*. If no factor up to this point divides it evenly, it is prime. We need not search for a factor larger than the square root of *n* because, if it exists, the other factor in the product must be less than the square root and we would have found it.

```
// The "TestPrime" class.
// Tests whether the integers from 2 to 10 are prime.
import hsa.Console;

public class TestPrime
{
    // Method to test whether integer is prime or not.
    static public boolean checkPrime (int n)
    {
        double sqrtr = Math.sqrt (n);
        int factor = 2;
        while (factor <= sqrtr && n % factor != 0)
        {
            factor++;
        }
        return factor > sqrtr;
    } // checkPrime method

    static public void main (String args [])
    {
        Console c = new Console ();
        for (int number = 2 ; number <= 10 ; number++)
        {
            c.println (" " + number + "," + checkPrime (number));
        }
    } // main method
} /* TestPrime class */
```

The program produces this output.

2, true
3, true
4, false
5, true
6, false
7, true
8, false
9, false
10, false

The state of the program at the beginning of the first time through the loop is

where : *main* (first time into loop)
   values :
      number = 2

The state is shown as a line indicating the point *where* in the execution that is being represented, followed by a list of variables with their values. When a method is called, the name of the method, the values of its parameters, local variables, and constants are added to the state. As soon as the method has been entered in this program, the state is

where : *main* (first time into loop)
   values :
      number = 2

where : *checkPrime* (*entry*)
   values :
      n (from *number*) = 2

The method creates a new scope so it is shown as a new *where* with its own set of variable values. Notice that the parameter *n* is explicitly tied to *number*, the variable that was passed as the corresponding actual parameter. Tracing proceeds in this manner for *number* going from 2 to 10.

A trace table like this allows programmers to manually mimic the execution of a program. It is often valuable to build such a table, especially if a program is behaving in unexpected ways.

7.8   Function Methods

The concept of a function in mathematics is that it yields a precise value for a given parameter or set of parameters. Many of the commonly-used **mathematical functions** are methods defined in the *Math* class of the Java class library. For example, *Math.cos* (*x*) and *Math.sin* (*x*) produce the cosine and sine of the angle *x* in radians.

Some mathematical functions have two parameters, for example

> *Math.min* (10.2, 9.8)

has a value 9.8, the minimum of its two parameters. The *Math* method *max* produces a value that is the maximum of its two parameters.

Some methods have no parameters. For example, the *Console* method *getWidth* has a value that is the width in pixels of the drawing area. Although there are no parameters, a call to *getWidth* must have empty parentheses following its name.

A function-type method definition is similar to that of a procedure-type method definition. Here are the main differences.

- The signature of a function-type method has the data type of the value that the method produces rather than the keyword **void** just before the name of the method. This name is followed by the parenthesized list of parameters.
- The body of the function-type method has a **return** statement at the end. The value produced by the method follows the keyword **return**.

We will now create a function-type method called *again* that will have a value that is a string with a string pattern repeated a given number of times.

```
// Method to produce a repeated string pattern n times.
static public String again (String pattern, int n)
{
    StringBuffer repeat = new StringBuffer ();
    for (int count = 1 ; count <= n ; count++)
```

```
    {
        repeat = repeat.append (pattern);
    }
    return repeat.toString ();
} // again method
```

A driver *main* method might use these statements to test this method. (Remember to add the boiler plate.)

```
// The "TestAgain" class.
for (int lineNumber = 1 ; lineNumber <= 5 ; lineNumber++)
{
    c.println (" " + lineNumber + " " + again ("*", lineNumber));
}
```

The output for this would be

```
1 *
2 **
3 ***
4 ****
5 *****
```

Here is a complete program which contains a function-type method *roundCent* that produces the value to the nearest cent of its **double** integer parameter *amount*. Notice that the parameter is first multiplied by 100 then rounded to be an integer. If, for example, the *amount* were 98.3276, the result of the multiplication would be 9832.76. This is rounded to the integer 9333. This integer value is then divided by 100.0 which would yield 93.33. This is the correct value of *amount* rounded to the nearest cent. If the integer had been divided by 100 rather than 100.0 it would have produced an incorrect answer. Because dividing an integer by an integer always results in an integer, dividing by 100 would have produced an incorrect value of 93.

In the *main* driver method to test the method *roundCent*, the values of *balance*, *interestRate*, and *interest* are all declared as **double** since numbers with decimal points will be read in. All such numbers are categorized as **double** rather than **float**.

```
// The "Interest" class.
import hsa.Console;

public class Interest
{
    public static void main (java.lang.String [] args)
    {
        Console c = new Console ();
        double balance, interestRate, interest;

        c.print ("Enter balance: ");
        balance = c.readDouble ();
        c.print ("Enter current interest rate: ");
        interestRate = c.readDouble ();
        interest = roundCent (balance * interestRate / 100);
        balance += interest;
        c.println ("New balance = " + balance);
        c.println ("Interest = " + interest);
    } // main method.

    public static double roundCent (double amount)
    {
        return Math.round (amount * 100) / 100.0;
    } // roundCent method
} /* Interest class */
```

7.9   Method Overloading

Here is another example of a function-type method. This method has a value that is the number of times a pattern occurs in a string of characters. Its header is

public int *occurrences (String pattern, String text)*

The resulting value will be the number of times the *pattern* string occurs in the *text* string. The method *occurrences* will use the *String* class method *indexOf*. In the *String* class there are several versions of the *indexOf* method. These differ from each other in that their parameter lists are different. We say the method *indexOf* is **overloaded**. One such variation of *indexOf* has this header

> **public int** *indexOf* (*String pattern*)

and a call to this particular method in the method *occurrence* would be made this way

> *text.indexOf* (*pattern*);

Its value would give the string position of the first occurrence of the *pattern* in *text*.

Another form of the *String* method *indexOf* has this header

> **public int** *indexOf* (*String pattern*, **int** *index*);

Here the value of the method *indexOf* is the position of the first occurrence of the *pattern* starting at the position *index* of the string. In either version, if the pattern is not present, the result −1 is returned. This second version of the *String* method *indexOf* will be used in the method *occurrences*.

```
// Method to find number of occurrences of pattern in text.
static public int occurrences (String pattern, String text)
{
    int count = 0, index = 0;
    while (text.indexOf (pattern, index) != -1)
    {
        count++;
        index = text.indexOf (pattern, index) + pattern.length ();
    }
    return count;
} // occurrences method
```

In a driver *main* method the statement

> // The "TestOccur" class.
> *c.println* (*occurrences* ("is", "Mississippi"));

produces the output 2.

Another example of an overloaded method is the *println* () method of the *Console* class which can take a variety of different data types as its argument.

7.10 Recursive Methods

Often a method uses other methods while computing the result required by its specification. Sometimes a method can be defined so that it uses itself on a smaller version of the problem. We say a definition is **recursive** when the thing being defined is used in the definition.

Recursive definitions are common in mathematics. Any series in which a term is defined using the values of earlier terms in the series is a recursive definition. For example, the sum of the first n integers can be defined as the value of n plus the sum of the first $n - 1$ integers. This example was used in the previous chapter.

Here is a recursive function-type method to compute this sum.

```
// Method to compute the sum of the first n integers.
static public int sum (int n)
{
    if (n <= 1)
        return n;
    else
        return n + sum (n − 1);
} // sum method
```

Notice that the method *sum* is defined with a body that uses the method *sum* on a smaller version of the problem (summing a smaller number of integers in this case). It is this use of the name *sum* inside the body of the method *sum* that makes the function recursive.

A method that has a recursive definition will result in several copies of the method's parameters and variables being used when the program is executed. Consider what happens when this statement in the *main* method uses the method *sum*.

    c.println (sum (3));

When *main* applies the method *sum* to the value 3, the result will be a chain of calls of the method. To compute the sum of the first 3 integers, the sum of the first two integers is needed, and to compute that sum it is necessary to compute the sum of the first integer. A trace table might look like this:

> *where : main* (in *println* statement)
>   values : (none)

> *where : sum* (in second **return** statement)
>   values : (none)
> $n = 3$

> *where : sum* (in second **return** statement)
>   values :
> $n = 2$

> *where : sum* (in first **return** statement)
>   values :
> $n = 1$

The third and last call is about to return the value 1, which will be used to compute the value 3 in the second call, which will be used to compute the value 6 in the first call, which will be printed by the *main* method.

Many definitions can be recast in recursive terms. Some computer scientists believe that recursion is a more natural way to think about many computations than is iteration. Other computer scientists believe that recursion is a useful way to think, but they avoid recursive programs because recursion requires more method calls. Since method calls take time and space, these people prefer to write iterative versions of algorithms so that the execution will be faster and smaller. In general, it is probably appropriate to use recursive methods when the data values being processed are most naturally and easily defined in recursive ways. Sometimes recursive algorithms are very inefficient, even if they are easy to write. Recursion is a tool that requires careful use.

Here is a recursive definition of the reverse of a string. Later in the chapter there will be another definition that is not recursive, and these two versions can be compared. An attractive feature of this one is its simplicity, but an unattractive feature of it is that for a string containing n characters it requires n method calls.

```
// Method to find reverse of string word recursively.
static public String reverse (String word)
{
    if (word.length () <= 1)
        return word;
    else
        return reverse (word.substring (1)) + (word.charAt (0));
} // reverse method
```

Here is another example of a recursive definition. The number of occurrences of a character in a string can be defined recursively: it is either 0 or 1, depending on whether the first character is the desired character or not, plus the number of occurrences in the remainder of the string. This will seem like a strange definition to many readers. It is perhaps more natural to think of this method iteratively.

7.11 An Example Using Methods

The various features of methods that have been described will now be used to determine whether a string is a palindrome. As mentioned in Chapter 6, a palindrome is a string that reads the same forwards and backwards. The string "radar" is a palindrome but "sonar" is not. Usually blanks and punctuation are ignored in palindromes, and the difference between upper case and lower case letters is also ignored. This means that the phrase "A man, a plan, a canal: Panama." is a palindrome.

A simple way to determine if a string is a palindrome is to compute the reverse of the string, and then compare it to the original string. Here is a function that computes the reverse of a string. Unlike the previous definition of the *reverse* function, this one is iterative.

```
// Iterative method to find reverse of string.
static public String reverse (String word)
{
    StringBuffer back = new StringBuffer ();
    for (int i = word.length () – 1 ; i >= 0 ; i––)
    {
        back = back.append (word.charAt (i));
    }
    return back.toString ();
} // reverse method
```

This function could be used to determine if a simple string like "radar" or "sonar" is a palindrome, but it cannot be used when a string contains blanks, punctuation, or upper case letters. To deal with the more general case it is necessary to have a function that will remove the blanks and punctuation from a string. We will call a string containing characters other than letters "dirty". This function, called *clean*, will remove all of these extra characters.

```
// Method to clean punctuation and white space out of string.
static public String clean (String s)
{
    String dirt = ",.:;()!'\\* ";
    StringBuffer t = new StringBuffer ();
    for (int i = 0 ; i < s.length () ; i++)
    {
        if (dirt.indexOf (s.charAt (i)) == –1)
            t.append (s.charAt (i));
    }
    return t.toString ();
} // clean method
```

It is still necessary to deal with upper case letters. One simple approach is to create a string that has all the upper case letters replaced by their lower case equivalents. The next method produces a string that contains only lower case letters from a string that contains both upper case and lower case letters. (Although we use it in this example, the *lowerCase* method is not actually necessary because the *String* class in Java provides a built-in method for changing the case of characters. This built-in method is called *toLowerCase*.)

```
// Method to change string so it contains only lower case letters.
static public String lowerCase (String s)
{
    StringBuffer t = new StringBuffer ();
    char ch;
    for (int i = 0 ; i < s.length () ; i++)
    {
        ch = s.charAt (i);
        t = t.append (Character.toLowerCase (ch));
    }
    return t.toString ();
} // lowerCase method
```

These three methods can now be put together to produce a method that will determine whether a string is a palindrome when punctuation and letter case are ignored.

```
// Method to use methods reverse, clean, and lowerCase to
// test palindrome.
static public boolean testPalindrome (String s)
{
    String t = lowerCase (clean (s));
    return t.equals (reverse (t));
} // testPalindrome method
```

Here is a *main* method to test these methods. It reads in three strings.

```
// The "PalindromeTest" class.
// Test method testPalindrome.
String text;
for (int count = 1 ; count <= 3 ; count++)
{
    c.println ("Enter a line of text");
    text = c.readLine ();
    c.println ("" + text + " " + testPalindrome (text));
}
```

Here is a sample execution window.

Madam, in Eden I'm Adam
   Madam, in Eden I'm Adam true
radar
   radar true
Hello
   Hello false

7.12 Function Methods with Side Effects

In mathematics a function has the property that it yields a specific value for a given parameter (or set of parameters). For example, the function that determines the square root of a number such as 16 always gives the same value when its parameter is 16.

In mathematical notation we can write $\sqrt{9}$ and be certain that this always represents the value 3. In Java we can write *Math.sqrt* (9) to compute the same value.

This unchanging nature of the value of a function, once the parameters are fixed, allows normal mathematical reasoning to be applied to functions. For example,

$$2 \times \sqrt{9} = \sqrt{9} + \sqrt{9}$$

or, more generally,

$$2 \times f(x) = f(x) + f(x)$$

If a function did not always return the same value for a given parameter, this would not be true and reasoning about functions would become very difficult.

It is possible in Java to write function-type methods that do not behave like mathematical functions. A function is not well-behaved if it makes any changes to the program in which it is called.

Changes made to the calling program by a function are called **side effects**. Side effects complicate mathematical reasoning and logic.

Here is an example of a benign side effect. Suppose a programmer wants to keep track of the number of times that a method is used. If a function contains an important part of the work to be done in a program, counting the number of times the method is called might give very helpful information to a user who is experimenting with the program.

7.13 Chapter Summary

Types of Methods

The complexity of large programs can be controlled by subdividing them into interacting objects. In turn, objects are kept simple by creating subprograms called **methods** within the object.

Methods of a class provide a way for the user of an object instantiated from the class to manipulate the instance variables of the object.

Historically subprograms have been of two types. These two types are still evident in the methods of object-oriented programs. They are:

- function-type methods that produce a value, and
- procedure-type methods that cause one or more actions.

A function-type method is called by using its name in an expression. A procedure-type method is called by using it as a statement in the program that is calling it.

Defining Methods

The **call** to a procedure-type method is like an additional statement available for writing programs in Java.

A procedure-type **declaration** has this syntax.

```
static public void method-name (formal parameter list)
{
    body of method
}
```

A **parameter list** is:

List of data type and parameter names, separated by commas

The parameters declared in the method declaration are **formal parameters**. The names of the parameters must be distinct, and different from the method's name.

A procedure-type method is called with a **call statement**.

method-name (list of actual parameters)

The actual parameters supplied in the call statement are also called **arguments**. The actual parameters are in a one-to-one correspondence with the formal parameters. The data types of the actual parameters must match, or be compatible with, the data types of the formal parameters.

Execution of a procedure-type method is from the beginning to the end of its body, unless an explicit **return** statement causes earlier termination. A **return** is seldom used in a procedure-type method but is always present at least once in a function-type method followed by the value being returned.

A function-type method is defined by

static public data-type method-name (formal parameter list)

and called by using its name, followed by the actual parameter list in parentheses, in an expression.

Local Identifiers, Global Identifiers, and Parameters

Methods can receive information from the program that calls them through their parameters or through **global identifiers**. Global identifiers are those identifiers that are declared outside of the method and are known in the class where the method is defined.

Local identifiers are those identifiers defined within the method. The names of parameters are local to the method, as are names that are introduced in the body of the method.

Testing of Programs

Testing increases confidence that a program meets its specification.

Whitebox testing takes advantage of the structure of the program. Tests should exercise every statement in the program, the limiting cases for data values, and every significantly different internal state.

Blackbox testing uses only the specification of a program and thus cannot take advantage of knowledge about how the program is built.

Tracing of Programs

A program can be traced by creating a table that shows the state at any instant, and then mimicking by hand the actions of the program as it changes the machine's state.

Recursive Methods

Sometimes a method can be defined so that it uses itself on a smaller version of the problem. A definition is **recursive** when the name being defined is used in the definition.

A method that has a recursive definition will result in several copies of the method's variables and parameters being used when the program is executed.

Many definitions can be recast in recursive terms. Some computer scientists believe that recursion is a more natural way to think about many computations than is iteration. Other computer scientists believe that recursion is a useful way to think, but they avoid recursive programs because recursion requires more method calls. Recursion is a tool that requires careful use.

Iterative and recursive methods were compared in testing whether or not a string was a **palindrome**.

A simple way to determine if a string is a palindrome is to compute the reverse of the string and then compare it to the original string.

A palindrome can also be defined in a recursive manner. A string is palindrome if the first and last characters are the same, and the remainder of the string is also a palindrome.

7.14 Exercises

1. Write a procedure-type method called *compound* that has as parameters an amount of money deposited in the bank and an annual compound interest rate, and produces a table of values of the balance after each year for 10 years. Be sure that the annual balance is kept to the nearest cent. Write a driver program and test the method.

2. Write a procedure-type method called *inputInteger* that will ask for the input of an integer and store it in the variable that is its only parameter in such a way that, if a real number or string is input, the procedure does not halt execution but simply asks the user to try again.

3. Write a function-type method called *phoneList* that accepts as a parameter a name that consists of a first and last name, and returns a value that is the last name then the first with a comma between. For example, if the value stored in *name* before calling the method was "Veena Guru" the value produced by the method would be "Guru, Veena".

4. When a person is buying a house that has a cost *c*, the money available is a combination of savings *s*, plus a mortgage loan amount *m*, that can be obtained. The financial institution from which the mortgage loan is to be obtained will establish some borrowing limit *b*, based on a consideration of the person's salary, credit history, and so on. Write a method to compute *m* in terms of *c*, *s*, and *b*. Use the *Math* methods *max* and *min*.

5. Write an implementation of the function-type method based on the recursive definition of a palindrome that accepts strings containing upper case letters, punctuation, and blanks. The upper case letters are to be converted to lower case, and the punctuation and blanks are to be ignored.

6. Write a recursive function-type method to compute the alphabetically first character in a string. For the string "recursive", the function should return the value "c".

7. Write a non-recursive function-type method to perform the same computation as in the previous exercise.

8. A string is a palindrome if the front half is a mirror image of the back half. To say this another way, a string is a palindrome if, for each character in the front half of the string, that character is the same as the character in the mirror image position in the back half of the string.

    This definition suggests another iterative way of checking if a string is a palindrome. Write a method that determines if a string is a palindrome by using a **for** statement that examines each character in the front half of the string and compares it with the character in the mirror image position in the back half of the string.

    Produce two versions of your function. In the first version, assume that the string to be checked contains only lower case letters. In the second version, assume that the string can contain upper case letters, punctuation, and blanks. The upper case letters are to be converted to lower case, and the punctuation and blanks are to be ignored.

9. Does the method *checkPrime* return the proper result for the values 2 and 3? Use tracing to explain your answer.

Chapter 8

Classes and Inheritance

In Java all programs are classes, but not all classes are programs. A standalone application program is a class that contains a *main* method, and may, or may not, contain other methods. An applet is a class that extends the class *Applet*. It contains a number of standard methods including a *paint* method. Neither one of these two classes is used as a template to create objects.

In this chapter we look at the more general idea of a class, how objects are instantiated from it and how new classes can be produced from it by inheritance.

8.1   Objects and Abstract Data Types

As programs become larger, controlling interference between parts becomes more difficult. Interference can be minimized by isolating all methods that share common variables and encapsulating them in an object, along with the shared variables. When this is done, no other part of a program needs to be concerned with how the data is stored in the object. Only those methods inside the object are involved. In this sense the data is abstracted and we speak of the whole as an **abstract data type** or **ADT**.

Of course, one object in a program must communicate with other objects or it would not be a single program, just a group of separate, smaller programs. This communication occurs when one object uses methods of another object. This is known as **message passing**. For any object to use a method encapsulated in another object, several things are necessary.

- The object using another object's method must have **imported** the other class to which the other object belongs either explicitly or implicitly.
- The method that is used must have been declared **public**.

In Java, objects are instantiated from classes which act as templates for their creation.

Whenever changes are made in the way an object stores data or the way that its methods are implemented, assuming their signatures and what they accomplish remain unchanged, other objects using objects instantiated from the class need not be altered. By this means, unwanted interference between objects in a larger program can be prevented, without having to keep each class unchanged.

8.2   Using a Class

We will begin by looking at an object instantiated from a class from the outside, as any other object or *main* method using it would, and see how it can be used. For example, consider a class called *Turtle* that can be used to instantiate objects to produce line drawings.

To visualize the object, think of a turtle that is set at a certain position on the screen and pointed in a certain direction. As the turtle moves, it traces a line on the screen. It always moves in a straight line unless its direction is changed. It can turn a certain angle to its left or to its right. It can also move without leaving a trace.

Here is the list of the public methods of the *Turtle* class with their signatures. These angles are in degrees and measured in a counterclockwise direction from a horizontal line pointing right, just as they are in mathematics.

Signature	Behavior
setColor (Color clr)	Set color of trace.
setPosition (**int** x, **int** y)	Place turtle at (x, y).
setAngle (**int** angle)	Point turtle at angle to horizontal.
move (**int** distance)	Move distance in pointing direction.
turnLeft (**int** angle)	Turn angle to turtle's left from present pointing direction.
turnRight (**int** angle)	Turn angle to turtle's right from present pointing direction.
showTrace ()	Cause trace to show.
hideTrace ()	Stop trace from showing.

If the constructor method of the Turtle class with no parameters except the *Console* name is used, the position of the turtle is initialized to be the center of the window. Its angle is set to zero, that is, pointing directly to the right side of the window. Its color is set to black and the trace is set to show.

The position and angle of the turtle are initialized to other values when the object is instantiated by the *Turtle* class constructor whose signature is

Turtle (*Console c*, **int** *x*, **int** *y*, **int** *angle*);

Here is a *main* method that uses the *Turtle* class to draw a red square of size 30 pixels with its upper-left corner at the center of the console window. (Do not forget the boiler plate.)

```
// The "RedSquare" class.
// Draw a red square of size 30 pixels with its upper–left corner
// at the center of console window.
// Instantiate object t and set color.
Turtle t;
t = new Turtle (c);
t.setColor (Color.red);
t.move (30); // Draw first side.
t.turnRight (90);
t.move (30); // Draw second side.
t.turnRight (90);
t.move (30); // Draw third side.
t.turnRight (90);
t.move (30); // Draw fourth side.
```

Classes in a class library can be grouped into packages. Since the *Turtle* class is stored as part of the package named *hsa.book* it is imported by the statement:

import *hsa.book.**;

Here is a shorter *main* method to draw a red square.

```
// The "RedSquare2" class.
// Draw a red square using repetition.
Turtle t;
t = new Turtle (c);
t.setColor (Color.red);
for (int side = 1 ; side <= 4 ; side++)
{
    t.move (30);
    t.turnRight (90);

}
```

This program leaves the turtle pointing in its original direction, to the right, whereas the previous longer program leaves it pointing up.

It is possible to create a drawing using the *Turtle* class that is the same as would be produced by the *moon* graphic created in the first chapter. Here is the *main* method to do this.

```
// The "DrawMoon" class.
// Draws a moon at center of console window
// of radius 60 pixels and color green.
Turtle t;
t = new Turtle (c);
t.setColor (Color.green);
for (int square = 1 ; square <= 36 ; square++)
{
    for (int side = 1 ; side <= 4 ; side++)
    {
        t.move (60);
        t.turnRight (90);
    }
    t.turnRight (10);
}
```

After each square is drawn the turtle is turned right an angle of 10 degrees so that the following square is tilted at an angle of 10 degrees to the one just drawn. After the 35th square is drawn, this turns the turtle so that it is pointing along the horizontal to the right side of the window. This program is simpler than the one requiring a tilted square method shown in Chapter 1.

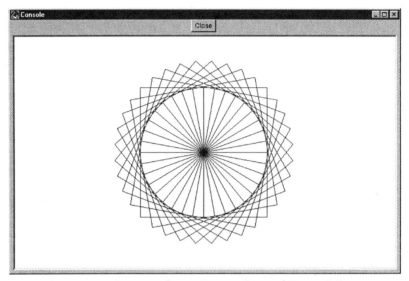

Figure 8.1 Output from Execution of DrawMoon.

8.3   Creating the Turtle Class

We will now look at how the *Turtle* class itself is implemented. Using the class requires no knowledge of its implementation. The instantiated class encapsulates both data and methods. Methods that are to be available to be used by other objects are labelled **public**. The data and methods used only by other methods of the class are labelled **protected**. The data (or instance variables) record the current position of the turtle, the direction that it is pointing, its current color, and whether or not the trace is currently showing.

Here is the *Turtle* class.

```
// The "Turtle" class.
import java.awt.*;
import hsa.Console;
```

```
public class Turtle
{
    protected Console c;
    protected int x, y, angle;
    protected boolean showing = true;
    protected Color clr = Color.black;

    // Constructor for default initial values of position and angle.
    public Turtle (Console c)
    {
        this.c = c;
        x = c.getWidth () / 2;
        y = c.getHeight () / 2;
        angle = 0;
    } // Default Turtle constructor.

    // Alternate constructor.
    public Turtle (Console c, int x, int y, int angle)
    {
        this.c = c;
        this.x = x;
        this.y = y;
        this.angle = angle;
    } // Alternate Turtle constructor.

    public void setAngle (int angle)
    {
        this.angle = angle;
    } // setAngle method

    public void setColor (Color clr)
    {
        this.clr = clr;
    } // setColor method

    public void setPosition (int x, int y)
    {
        this.x = x;
        this.y = y;
    } // setPosition method
```

```java
public void hideTrace ()
{
    showing = false;
} // hideTrace method

public void showTrace ()
{
    showing = true;
} // showTrace method

public void move (int distance)
{
    int newx, newy;
    double rAngle = (angle * Math.PI) / 180;
    newx = (int) Math.round (x + Math.cos (rAngle) * distance);
    newy = (int) Math.round (y – Math.sin (rAngle) * distance);
    if (showing)
    {
        c.setColor (clr);
        c.drawLine (x, y, newx, newy);
    }
    x = newx;
    y = newy;
} // move method

public void turnLeft (int turnAngle)
{
    angle += turnAngle;
    angle = angle % 360;
} // turnLeft method

public void turnRight (int turnAngle)
{
    angle –= turnAngle;
    angle = angle % 360;
} // turnRight method
} /* Turtle class */
```

The method *move* is slightly more complex than the other methods but is perhaps easily understood by examining Figure 8.2. Notice that

$$\sin(rAngle) = dy/distance$$
$$\cos(rAngle) = dx/distance$$

and

$$newx = x + dx$$
$$newy = y - dy$$

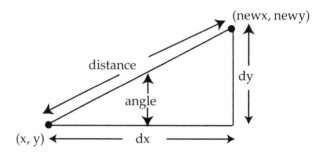

Figure 8.2 Geometry of a Move

It might be better if x, y, and $rAngle$ were maintained as real variables and rounded only when a method is called, to avoid cumulative error due to rounding at each turn.

8.4   Instantiating Two Objects from a Class

Here is a *main* method that uses two turtles to draw two spirals, one in orange and the other in cyan. Each spiral begins at the center of the screen but the orange turns to the right, and the cyan to the left.

```
// The "TwoSpirals" class.
// Instantiate two turtles from Turtle class.
// Draw spirals in opposite directions with turtle in two different colors.
Turtle turtle1, turtle2;
turtle1 = new Turtle (c);
turtle2 = new Turtle (c);
// Set turtle1 to draw in cyan.
```

```
turtle1.setColor (Color.cyan);
// Set turtle2 to draw in orange.
turtle2.setColor (Color.orange);
// Set turtle1 to start pointing to upper left.
turtle1.turnLeft (120);
// Set turtle2 to start pointing to upper right.
turtle2.turnLeft (60);
// Draw two spirals simultaneously.
for (int distance = c.getWidth () / 4 ; distance > 1 ; distance—)
{
    turtle1.move (distance);
    turtle1.turnLeft (70);
    turtle2.move (distance);
    turtle2.turnRight (70);
}
```

In each spiral, after a line is drawn, the turtle is turned by an angle of 70 degrees, to the left for the first turtle and to the right for the second. The distance moved on each leg of a spiral decreases by one pixel from the initial value of *getWidth* / 4, which is one-quarter of the window's width, down to zero.

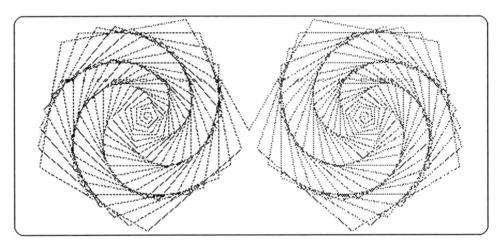

Figure 8.3 Output from Execution of Two Turtles Drawing.

8.5   Method Overloading

In the *Turtle* class definition there are two methods named *Turtle*. These are each constructor methods. When a turtle object is instantiated using the constructor with one parameter, as by *Turtle* (*Console c*), the first version is used. The turtle is set to the default position of the center of the screen, pointing to the right. The second version has, as well, parameters for the coordinates of the starting position and starting angle. This allows the user to begin drawing at another point in the window and pointing in another direction. In either case the turtle is set to showing the trace and drawing in black. In the second version of the constructor there must be a distinction between the parameters of the constructor *x*, *y*, and *angle* and the class variables *x*, *y*, and *angle*. To differentiate them, the keyword **this** identifies the variables that belong to the object itself. Thus the statement

this.x = x;

assigns to the instance variable x the value of the parameter x.

When two or more methods have the same identifier, as the two versions of the constructor method *Turtle* have here, we say the method is **overloaded**. Which version is to be used depends on the parameters provided. It is possible to have methods of a class other than the constructor method overloaded but this is not done. Many classes in the Java library provide a variety of constructor methods. No two of these can have the same number and data type of parameters or they could not be distinguished from one another. If no constructor method is provided for a class, the initial values of instance variables are automatically default values.

8.6   Creating a New Class by Inheritance

It is possible to create a new class based on an old one by modifying it in various ways. New methods can be added or existing methods changed.

We will change the class *Turtle* by allowing control of the width of the line that is traced by the turtle. This means we must add an additional class variable called *lineWidth* that can be changed from its default initialized value of 1 pixel by the operation

     setLineWidth (**int** *width*)

where *width* is the new line width. We must also change the existing method *move* to draw a line of the proper width. It, in turn, will use a new method that is added, but not made public, called *drawFatLine*. This method creates a fat line by drawing a ball of radius half the line width at points along the line, close enough together to create the effect of a solid line, somewhat like a ballpoint pen.

Here is the new class.

```java
// The "FatTurtle" class.
// For drawing graphics with a variety of line widths.
// This class extends the Turtle class.
import hsa.Console;

public class FatTurtle extends Turtle
{
    // Add a new variable.
    protected int lineWidth;
    // Only one version of constructor provided.
    public FatTurtle (Console c)
    {
        super (c);
        // Use default setting for other variables defined in Turtle class.
        lineWidth = 1;
    } // FatTurtle constructor

    // Draw a filled ball of radius and center at (x, y)
    // in the current color.
    protected void drawBall (int xc, int yc, int radius)
    {
        int diameter = radius * 2;
        int x = xc - radius;
        int y = yc - radius;
        c.fillOval (x, y, diameter, diameter);
    } // drawBall method
```

```
// Add method drawFatLine.
protected void drawFatLine (int x1, int y1, int x2, int y2)
{
    // Line drawn by moving a ball point pen whose ball
    // is half line width.
    // Line drawn at x values of ball separated by DX which
    // is half the radius.
    // Constants used in calculation.
    final double LEN = Math.sqrt (((x2 – x1) * (x2 – x1)) + ((y2 – y1)
            * (y2 – y1)));
    final double SINA = (y2 – y1) / LEN;
    final double COSA = (x2 – x1) / LEN;
    final int RADIUS = (lineWidth / 2) + 1;
    final double DX = RADIUS * COSA / 2;
    final double DY = RADIUS * SINA / 2;
    // Set position to draw first ball's center at (x1, y1).
    double xpos = x1;
    double ypos = y1;
    // Draw series of balls along line from (x1, y1) to (x2, y2).
    do
    {
        drawBall ((int) Math.round (xpos), (int) Math.round (ypos),
            RADIUS);
        xpos += DX;
        ypos += DY;

    }
    while (Math.sqrt ((x2 – xpos) * (x2 – xpos) + (y2 – ypos) * (y2 – ypos))
            >= RADIUS / 2);
} // drawFatLine method

// This method overrides the move method of the Turtle class.
public void move (int distance)
{
    double rAngle = angle * Math.PI / 180;
    final int newx = (int) Math.round (x + Math.cos (rAngle) * distance);
    final int newy = (int) Math.round (y – Math.sin (rAngle) * distance);
    if (showing)
    {
        c.setColor (clr);
        if (lineWidth == 1)
            c.drawLine (x, y, newx, newy);
        else
```

```
                drawFatLine (x, y, newx, newy);
      }
      x = newx;
      y = newy;
   } // move method

   // Add a new method to set LineWidth.
   public void setLineWidth (int newWidth)
   {
      lineWidth = newWidth;
   } // setLineWidth method
} /* FatTurtle class */
```

Notice that it is not necessary to repeat the methods of *Turtle* that are unchanged. The only new variable added is *lineWidth*. The only new method made public is *SetWidth*. The new method *move* overrides (replaces) the old version of *move*. If the width is given as 1 pixel, the *Console* method *drawLine* is used. If the width has been set at another value then the new method *drawFatLine* is used.

Using the Modified Class

Here is a *main* method that uses the *FatTurtle* class to draw concentric fat circles with centers at the center of the window. The circles will each be made up of 36 short straight lines. A yellow circle will have a radius of *getWidth* / 6 and *lineWidth* of 10 and a green circle radius *getWidth* / 4 and *lineWidth* of 20 pixels.

```
// The "FatCircles" class.
// Use FatTurtle class to draw concentric circles.
FatTurtle turtle1, turtle2;
turtle1 = new FatTurtle (c);
turtle2 = new FatTurtle (c);
turtle1.setLineWidth (10);
turtle2.setLineWidth (20);
turtle1.setColor (Color.yellow);
turtle2.setColor (Color.green);
// Set the x position of each turtle at its own radius from the center
```

```
final int XC = c.getWidth () / 2;
final int YC = c.getHeight () / 2;
final int RADIUS1 = c.getWidth () / 6;
final int RADIUS2 = c.getWidth () / 4;
final int STEPANGLE = 10;
final double STEPANGLERADIANS = STEPANGLE * 2 * Math.PI / 360;
final int DISTANCE1 = (int) Math.round (RADIUS1 *
    STEPANGLERADIANS);
final int DISTANCE2 = (int) Math.round (RADIUS2 *
    STEPANGLERADIANS);
turtle1.setPosition (XC + RADIUS1, YC + DISTANCE1 / 2);
turtle2.setPosition (XC + RADIUS2, YC + DISTANCE2 / 2);
turtle1.turnLeft (90);
turtle2.turnLeft (90);
for (int direction = 0 ; direction <= 360 ; direction += STEPANGLE)
{
    turtle1.move (DISTANCE1);
    turtle1.turnLeft (STEPANGLE);
    turtle2.move (DISTANCE2);
    turtle2.turnLeft (STEPANGLE);
}
```

Figure 8.4 Output from Execution of FatCircles

8.7   Class Hierarchy

When one class extends another class the **parent** or **base** class is called the **superclass**; the one that inherits from it is the **subclass**.

A subclass may not inherit any variables or methods of the superclass that are labelled as **private**. But it may inherit any labelled as **protected**. That is why we have labelled so many of the variables as **protected**. They cannot be used by another class outside the hierarchy in either case. An object of a subclass "**is an**" object of the superclass. But the reverse is not true. The object of a superclass is not an object of the subclass.

Structured Java data types such as strings and arrays are objects, as are those that we create such as record types or node types for a linked list. They are used by reference. All these classes are extensions of the superclass *Object*. It is thus possible, for example, to create a *List* class for maintaining a list that has data of type *Object*. Since all non-primitive data types are *Object*s the same *List* class could be used for many different structured data types.

There exist, as well, a number of classes called **type wrapper classes**, one for each of the primitive data types: *Integer* for **int**, *Float* for **float**, *Boolean* for **boolean**, and so on. In this way primitive data types can be adapted to a class written for *Objects*.

In this chapter we showed a *Turtle* class which we extended to *FatTurtle*. The *Turtle* class is the superclass, the *FatTurtle* is the subclass. Sometimes, in setting up a class hierarchy, the superclass has one or more methods which have no body. Such methods are labelled **abstract**, as is also the class itself. An abstract class cannot be used to instantiate any objects. It is used only to be the superclass of a number of different subclasses. Any object instantiated from one of the subclasses "is an" object of the superclass and thus can be referred to as such.

An abstract class can contain methods including constructors that have a body and these can be used in any subclass. Such a constructor is referred to by the keyword **super** rather than by the name of the superclass itself.

8.8   Chapter Summary

This chapter extends the ideas of classes introduced in the first chapter and shows how one class may inherit from another class.

Abstract Data Types

In programming it is common that several methods access the same variables. If one method is changed, this can affect the other methods in unexpected ways. For this reason, it is useful to encapsulate the data and methods that share the data into an **object**. This forms an **abstract data type** since other objects of the program need not be concerned with how that data is stored. Only those methods encapsulated with the data need be concerned.

Other objects may use the methods in the object provided that the signatures and behavior of the encapsulated methods are known to the user. This usage is called **message passing**. Variables that make up the encapsulated data are accessed by the object's methods as global variables and are not passed explicitly as parameters to its own methods.

Using an Object

One object, the user object, may use another object's (the used object) methods under these conditions.

- The user object must **import** the used object.
- The used object must declare the method to be used as **public**.

The Turtle Object

An example is provided of an object that is useful for making line drawings. The object is a turtle that can be placed at any point in the window, pointed in a certain direction, and moved in a straight line in that direction. It can be turned to its left or right and the next line drawn. It can be arranged that the line shows or not, so discontinuous line drawings are possible. To use the turtle, the signatures and behaviors of its methods must be known, but the mechanism of implementation need not be known.

The data that is encapsulated with these methods record: the current position, angle of pointing, color, and whether or not the trace is to show for the turtle.

Each method call in the user program must be of the form

Name-of-object.method-name (arguments);

Classes

To use a class, an object must be declared as belonging to the class by a declaration such as

class-name object-name;

This next assignment allocates space for an instance of this class.

object-name = **new** class-name (arguments);

Depending on what arguments are supplied, the appropriate constructor method of the class is executed to set initial values of the instance variables. If no arguments are provided, default values are used. Each object created from the same class must have a different identifier. If two objects from the same class are instantiated in the program the name identifies which object is referred to.

We used a *Turtle* class and instantiated two turtles and drew lines with each "simultaneously". (Actually only one turtle at a time was drawing.)

Creating a New Class by Inheritance

One of the benefits of using classes is that a class can be modified easily to:

• add new data (instance variables),
• add new methods, and
• modify existing methods.

Defining such a modified class requires an addition to the header at the beginning of the class definition of the form

> **extends** name-of-original-class

Any new instance variables are then defined and any new methods added. If an existing method is to be modified, its complete new definition must appear. This new definition will **override** the old definition which may no longer be used in the new class.

If the same identifier is used for a method's parameter as for an instance variable, in the body of the method the instance variable's name is preceded by the keyword **this** followed by a dot.

8.9   Exercises

1. Instantiate an object from the *Turtle* class and use its methods to write a method to draw a square with its upper-left corner at (*xc, yc*) and of size *size* in color *clr*. The signature of this procedure will be

    > *square* (**int** *xc*, **int** *yc*, **int** *size*, *Color clr*);

    It must, of course, be a part of a program that imports the *Turtle* class. Now write a program that uses *square* to draw 100 random-sized red squares, located with upper-left corners at random points in the window.

2. Using the Turtle class, write a method to draw a moon similar to that drawn in this chapter with a center at (*xc, yc*) made up of squares of size *size* in color *clr*. The signature of the *moon* method should be

    > *moon* (**int** *xc*, **int** *yc*, **int** *size*, *Color clr*);

    Draw 20 moons of random size at random points in the window.

3. Use an object instantiated from the *Turtle* class to draw a simple house with a peaked roof and a window as shown in Figure 8.5.

Figure 8.5 Picture of House

Make the house drawing into a method and use it in a *main* method to draw a row of houses across the bottom of the window. Modify the program to draw a series of such rows. Arrange that as the rows move from the bottom to the top of the window the houses get smaller, to create the illusion of distance.

4   Use the class *FatTurtle* to instantiate three turtles to draw in the three primary colors: blue, yellow, and red. Start each turtle at a different spot on the screen then have each make 25 moves of distance 5 pixels randomly in one of the four directions: left or right, up or down. Have them move "simultaneously", that is, the blue making one random move, then the yellow, then the red.

5.   Use the class *FatTurtle* to create a window with horizontal stripes. Have 10 stripes filling the window and alternate the colors from one stripe to the next. Make this into a method that will produce alternating stripes of any two colors with the number of stripes filling the window specified as a parameter. The signature of the method is

      stripes (**int** *number, Color clr1, Color clr2*);

6.   Use the class *FatTurtle* to instantiate two turtles, one of which will draw horizontal stripes, the other the same number of vertical stripes. Program the two turtles to draw "simultaneously", the first in red and white, the second in green and yellow.

7. Use the class *FatTurtle* to write a method to draw regular polygons of *n* sides in lines of *width* with the center at (*xc, yc*) and size (distance from center to any vertex) *size*. Its signature would be

    polygon (**int** *xc*, **int** *yc*, **int** *size*, **int** *width*, *Color clr*);

    Use the method *polygon* to approximate a circle by using as large a number of sides *n* as practical.

8. Create a class called *TurtleDash* that inherits from the *Turtle* but which draws all lines as interrupted (dashed) lines rather than continuous lines. Use the class to instantiate a turtle and draw a blue dashed square of size *getHeight* / 4.

Chapter 9

Applets and Graphical User Interfaces

An applet is a Java program that can be sent over the **Internet** and run under **World Wide Web browsers** such as **Netscape's Navigator**. Applets provide access to the **Graphical User Interface** (GUI) features of Java. Moreover, applets with a GUI can be run on many different **computer platforms**; they are **portable**. The GUI interface elements may, however, be slightly different from one platform to another

9.1   The Structure of an Applet

All applets are classes that inherit from the class *Applet* so that each must import the *Applet* class with the statement

import *java.applet.Applet;*

The *Applet* class has a number of methods and these are often overridden by new versions of the methods in the newsubclass applet.

Here are the methods.

- *init* which acts like a class constructor to initialize values of instance variables or set up GUI components. It is called automatically when the applet is run.

- *start* which initializes some of the more advanced features such as concurrent executions or complex animation. (We will not be using these.)

- *paint* which is called once, after *init* completes or again any time a *repaint* method is called. Output of text or drawings is performed in *paint* using the object *g* instantiated from the *Graphics* class.

- *stop* which is called when execution is finished to perform any termination required.

- *destroy* which cleans up after the applet is removed from memory.

The applets we will be showing will only override the *init* and *paint* methods of the Applet class. By default, the other methods listed above will be the ones inherited from the *Applet* class which, in fact, do nothing. There is one more standard Applet method.

- *action* which is perhaps the most interesting applet method. It is used so that a program can communicate with the various actions of the program's user, such as entering input, and clicking or dragging the mouse.

The three standard Applet methods *init, paint*, and *action* will be discussed in detail. Applets can contain other user-defined methods which are called by any of the standard methods.

To illustrate the structure of an applet, here is a very simple one that can be used as a template for creating other applets. It is called *AppletPlate* and can function for applets in the same way as the *BoilerPlate* class did for application programs. In other words, using it will save time.

The only method that does anything in the applet is the *paint* method. The statement

   g.drawString ("AppletPlate", 10, 20);

produces the output

   AppletPlate

starting at the point whose coordinates are (10, 20) in the *Applet Viewer* window. This statement would be replaced with the specific details of a new applet. The name *AppletPlate* would also be replaced by the new applet's name. (Note: The *g.drawString* is used in much the same way as *c.println* is used with the *Console* class except that the coordinates of the starting point are specified.)

```
// The "AppletPlate" class.
import java.applet.Applet;
import java.awt.*;

public class AppletPlate extends Applet
{
    // Instance variables.

    public boolean action (Event e, Object o)
    {
        // Body of action method.
        return true;
    } // action method
```

```
    public void init ()
    {
        // Body of init method.
    } // init method

    public void paint (Graphics g)
    {
        // Body of paint method.
        g.drawString ("AppletPlate", 10, 20);
    } // paint method
} /* AppletPlate class */
```

9.2   Applets with no Input or GUI

We will begin looking at the details of applets by restricting our attention to very simple applets. The first program outputs the first four lines of "Mary had a little lamb". (This, we believe, is not under copyright.)

Here is the applet.

```
// The "Rhyme" class.
import java.applet.Applet;
import java.awt.*;

public class Rhyme extends Applet
{
    public void paint (Graphics g)
    {
        g.drawString ("Mary had a little lamb", 20, 25);
        g.drawString ("Its fleece was white as snow", 20, 40);
        g.drawString ("And everywhere that Mary went", 20, 55);
        g.drawString ("The lamb was sure to go", 20, 70);
    } // paint method
} /* Rhyme class */
```

The *Rhyme* applet imports the *Applet* class and the *awt* package from which it is using the *Graphics* class. An object *g* of the *Graphics* class is automatically instantiated by having *g* as a standard parameter of the *paint* method.

The *drawString* method of the *Graphics* class is used to place the string constant on the screen, starting at coordinates (20, 25). Each subsequent line of the rhyme has a 15 pixels larger value of *y*. This spaces the lines of the rhyme.

Since *paint* is a procedure-type method it has the keyword **void** before its name.

After compiling the applet by saving it, it is necessary to produce a **Hypertext Markup Language (HTML)** file to place the applet in a browser for execution (browsers read text files). The *HTML* file for this applet, for example, is:

```
<html>
<applet code = "Rhyme.class" width = 300 height = 100>
</applet>
</html>
```

Classes such as *Rhyme* are compiled into files with an extension *.class* on their names. The width and height of the area of output for the applet in pixels is specified in the *HTML* file. The *HTML* file begins with the **tag** *<html>* and ends with *</html>*. The applet itself has the tag *<applet>* and is terminated by *</applet>*.

In *VisualAge for Java* the *HTML* file is prepared automatically when the program is run. To run the program in *VisualAge for Java*, click the *Run* icon. By default, *VisualAge for Java* runs the applet in a window of width 250 pixels and height 300 pixels. To change the width and height of the applet, select the applet class in the upper pane of the workbench. Next, select the *Properties* menu item from the *Selected* menu. This brings up the *Properties* window (see Figure 9.1). Change the width and the height to the appropriate values and click the *OK* button. Now whenever the program is run, the applet will appear with the specified width and height.

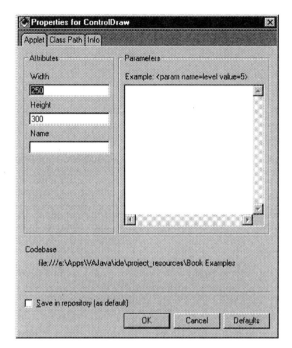

Figure 9.1 Applet Viewer Dialog Box

Figure 9.2 Output of Rhyme Applet

9.3   Applets with User Input and Output with GUI

We will now consider an example of an applet with input as well as output. This next applet program accepts input, in this case the user's age, in a box on the screen and then, when Return is pressed, outputs the bus fare that the user must pay. The fare is $2.00 for adults, $1.00 for seniors, and $.50 for children under 12 years of age.

In addition to the standard applet methods *init* and *action* a user-defined method *fare* is used to perform the actual calculation. The age of the customer is entered into a box in the window. This box is a graphical user interface (GUI) component of the class *TextField*. The box is labelled with the user prompt by a component of the *Label* class.

Here is the applet program.

```
// The "BusFare3" class.
import java.applet.Applet;
import java.awt.*;.

// Class to output bus fare given age.
public class BusFare3 extends Applet
{
    Label prompt;        // Declare user prompt.
    TextField input;     // Declare input box.
    int age;             // Declare input variable.

    // Respond to action of user's input.
    public boolean action (Event e, Object o)
    {
        age = Integer.parseInt (o.toString ());
        showStatus ("$" + fare (age)); // Show fare.
        input.setText (""); // Clear entry box.
        return true; // Shows action responded to.
    } // action method

    // Method to compute fare from age.
    public String fare (int age)
```

```
{
    if (age < 12)
        return "0.50";
    else if (age >= 65)
        return "1.00";
    else
        return "2.00";
} // fare method

// Sets up GUI components.
public void init ()
{
    prompt = new Label ("Enter age then press Return");
    input = new TextField (5);
    // Place label and text field on applet.
    add (prompt);
    add (input);
} // init method
} /* BusFare3 class */
```

Figure 9.3 shows the results of running the program.

This program uses two GUI components:

- a *Label* to indicate what is to be entered into the input box, and
- a *TextField* to hold the input.

The *Label* is given the identifier *prompt* and the *TextField* the identifier *input*.

In the *init* method the prompt *Label* is instantiated with a string constant and the input *TextField* instantiated as having spaces for up to 5 characters. The label and text field are not placed on the screen until the two *add* lines are executed.

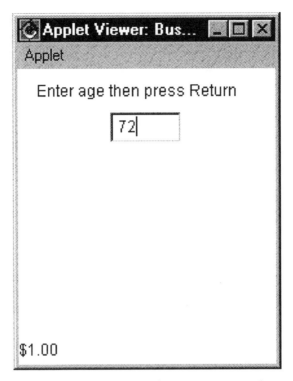

Figure 9.3 Output of BusFare3 Applet

In the *action* method there are two standard parameters: *e* of type *Event* and *o* of type *Object*. The *action* method returns a value **true** when the action has been carried out.

The *Event* argument *e* is normally used to decide what event has occurred. In this example there is only one possible event, namely the pressing of Return after entering the value for *age*, so *e* is not used explicitly in the *action* method. If a number of different actions are possible then the *e* must be examined to see which one has actually occurred.

The *Object* argument *o* will contain the contents of the text field when the Return key has been pressed. The text field input is transformed into a string using the *toString* method and must then be parsed by the *parseInt* method of the *Integer* class so that it can be assigned to *age* which is an *int* variable.

The *setText* method of the *TextField* class is used to display a null string in the field. This clears the text field so that another value of *age* can be entered.

The result of the fare calculation provided by the method *fare* is displayed in the **status bar** at the bottom of the *Applet Viewer* window. The status bar's position varies with the browser being used.

To display the result, the value of *fare*, which is a *String* type, must be shown as the argument of the *showStatus* method of the *Applet* class.

9.4   Applets with Multiple GUI Components

So far we have introduced the idea of the GUI components *TextField* and *Label*. In this section we will look at another GUI component, the **button**. A button is a box with a label in it that can be clicked by the mouse to trigger an event.

We will illustrate this with an example where there is one text field to enter an integer labelled "Input integer", two buttons one labelled "Square" the other "Cube", and a second text field labelled "Output". If an integer is entered into the input field and the button "Square" clicked, the square of the integer is displayed in the output field. If "Cube" is clicked the cube of the integer appears in the output field.

Here is the applet program.

```
// The "Powers" class.
import java.applet.Applet;
import java.awt.*;

// Class to produce either a square or cube of an integer.
public class Powers extends Applet
{
    Label enter;
    TextField input;
    int number;
    Label result;
```

```
TextField output;
Button square;
Button cube;

// Respond to action of user.
public boolean action (Event e, Object o)
{
    number = Integer.parseInt (input.getText ());
    if (e.target instanceof Button)
    {
        if (e.target == square)
            output.setText ("Square is " +
                Integer.toString (square (number)));
        else if (e.target == cube)
            ;
        output.setText ("Cube is " +
            Integer.toString (cube (number)));
        return true;
    }
    return true;
} // action method

// Method to compute cube.
public int cube (int number)
{
    return number * number * number;
} // cube method

// Set up GUI components.
public void init ()
{
    enter = new Label ("Enter an integer");
    input = new TextField (20);
    result = new Label ("Result");
    output = new TextField (20);
    square = new Button ("Square");
    cube = new Button ("Cube");
    add (enter);
    add (input);
    add (result);
    add (output);
    add (square);
```

```
        add (cube);
    } // init method

    // Method to compute square.
    public int square (int number)
    {
        return number * number;
    } // square method
} /* Powers class */
```

Figure 9.4 shows the results of running this applet.

Here, each labelled button is created by a single statement that both instantiates and labels the button. The *target* of an event is the graphical user interface component that the user activated. If *button1* is clicked, this target is equal to *button1*.

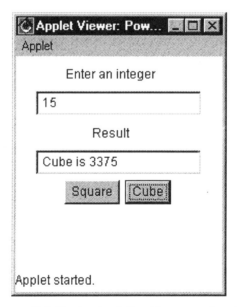

Figure 9.4 Output of the Powers Applet

9.5   Layout of GUI Components

The GUI components *Label*, *TextField*, and *Button* have, by default, been placed in the *Applet Viewer* in the order in which they are added, starting at the top left and going to the right. When no more components can be placed in the same line, the components are placed on the next line and so on. This default layout is called *FlowLayout*.

Layout can also be controlled using other **layout managers**. The programmer chooses the layout manager using the *setLayout* method of the *Container* class. A container is an area where the GUI components can be laid out. A **panel** is such a container.

There can be a number of panels in the *Applet Viewer* window and each panel is placed in the window using *FlowLayout*. In the statement that sets the layout of the panel, the space between components (horizontal gap) and the space between the component and the upper and lower edges of the panel (vertical gap) can also be set. The panel's size depends on the sizes of the components it contains and the gap sizes.

Here is an applet that has two panels. The first panel is on the top of the window. The label in that panel is left justified in accordance with the layout specified for the panel. The second panel is at the bottom of the window. The label in that panel is centered.

```
// The "PanelTest" class.
import java.applet.Applet;
import java.awt.*;

public class PanelTest extends Applet
{
    private Panel p1, p2;
    private Label label1, label2;

    public void init ()
    {
        p1 = new Panel ();
        p2 = new Panel ();
        p1.setLayout (new FlowLayout (FlowLayout.LEFT, 20, 10));
```

```
        label1 = new Label ("This label is on left");
        p1.add (label1);
        p2.setLayout (new FlowLayout (FlowLayout.CENTER, 5, 30));
        label2 = new Label ("This label is centered");
        p2.add (label2);
        p1.setBackground (Color.red);
        p2.setBackground (Color.blue);
        setLayout (new BorderLayout ());
        add ("North", p1);
        add ("South", p2);
    } // init method
} /* PanelTest class */
```

Figure 9.5 shows the result of running this program. Notice that the labels are first added to their containers (the panels) and then the panels are added to the window. In the *setLayout* method for *p1*, 20 is the horizontal gap and 10 the vertical gap. In order to see the differences in the two panels, this applet should be run in a window of width 400.

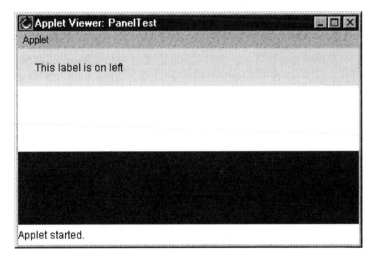

Figure 9.5 Output of the PanelTest Applet

VisualAge for Java also provides another layout manager called *BorderLayout*. In this layout, components are placed in the *Applet Viewer* window in five areas *North*, *South*, *East*, *West*, and *Center*, each area having one component in it. For example, the statement *add* ("North", *b*);

adds a button *b* in the *North* area and

setLayout (**new** *BorderLayout* ());

sets the window layout manager to *BorderLayout*.

9.6   Other GUI Components

The *Checkbox* GUI component allows the programmer to create a box on screen which can be used to elicit an "on or off" response from the user. The **check box** has only two states: checked or not checked. By default, when the box is instantiated, it is not checked. If the box is clicked at any time its state is changed from checked to unchecked, or vice versa.

For example, check boxes can be used to control type face. In this textbook some words are in italics, some in bold face, and some in italic-bold face. Others are in plain face. Since a face cannot be both plain and italic we cannot have three check boxes (plain, bold, and italic) that could be checked independently. We could, however, have two check boxes: one italic and one bold.

A *Font* object must be instantiated by a statement such as

f = **new** *Font* ("SansSerif", *Font.PLAIN*, 24);

which controls the text font. This statement sets the font name to "SansSerif" (a sans serif type), the font style to plain, and the point size of the font to 24 points. The *TextField* method *setFont* is used to set the font of a text field *name* to the font *f* with the statement

name.setFont (*f*);

Here is the applet for controlling the text style of text displayed in a text field.

```
// The "TextCheckbox" class.
import java.applet.Applet;
import java.awt.*;
```

```java
public class TextCheckbox extends Applet
{
    private TextField name;
    private Checkbox boldFont, italicFont;
    private Font f;

    public boolean action (Event e, Object o)
    {
        int box1, box2;
        if (e.target instanceof Checkbox)
        {
            // Read state of Bold box.
            if (boldFont.getState () == true)
                box1 = Font.BOLD;
            else
                box1 = Font.PLAIN;
            // Read state of Italic box.
            if (italicFont.getState () == true)
                box2 = Font.ITALIC;
            else
                box2 = Font.PLAIN;
            f = new Font ("Sansserif", box1 + box2, 24);
            name.setFont (f);
        }
        return true;
    } // action method

    public void init ()
    {
        name = new TextField ("My name", 10);
        boldFont = new Checkbox ("Bold");
        italicFont = new Checkbox ("Italic");
        f = new Font ("Sansserif", Font.PLAIN, 24);
        name.setFont (f);
        add (name);
        // Check boxes are by default initialized to unchecked.
        add (boldFont);
        add (italicFont);
    } // init method
} /* TextCheckbox class */
```

Figure 9.6 shows the result of running this program.

Figure 9.6 Output of the TextCheckbox Applet

Radio buttons are similar to check boxes except that only one of a group of buttons can be clicked at a time. Radio buttons must be grouped into a *CheckboxGroup*.

Here is an applet to demonstrate radio buttons that change the type style of printing in a text field.

```
// The "FontButtons" class.
import java.applet.Applet;
import java.awt.*;

public class FontButtons extends Applet
{
    private TextField name;
```

```
    private CheckboxGroup style;
    private Checkbox sansSerif, serif, monoSpaced;
    private Font f;

    public boolean action (Event e, Object o)
    {
        String fontName;
        if (e.target instanceof Checkbox)
        {
            if (sansSerif.getState () == true)
                fontName = "SansSerif";
            else if (serif.getState () == true)
                fontName = "Serif";
            else
                fontName = "Monospaced";
            f = new Font (fontName, Font.PLAIN, 14);
            name.setFont (f);
        }
        return true;
    } // action method

    public void init ()
    {
        name = new TextField ("My name", 15);
        f = new Font ("SansSerif", Font.PLAIN, 14);
        name.setFont (f);
        add (name);
        style = new CheckboxGroup ();

        // Check SansSerif radio button only to start.
        sansSerif = new Checkbox ("SansSerif", style, true);
        serif = new Checkbox ("Serif", style, false);
        monoSpaced = new Checkbox ("Monospaced", style, false);
        add (sansSerif);
        add (serif);
        add (monoSpaced);
    } // init method
} /* FontButtons class */
```

Figure 9.7 shows the result of running this program.

Figure 9.7 Output of the FontButtons Applet

9.7   Graphics Using Applets

So far, we have been able to draw graphics using the *hsa Console* class. Most of these same graphics methods can be used with the *Graphics* class. Graphics are drawn on a GUI component of the *Canvas* class. The size of the canvas must be set using the *setSize* method of the *Component* class. If a canvas *c* is instantiated by

Canvas c = **new** *Canvas* ();

it can be set to be 200 pixels wide and 150 pixels high by the statement

c.setSize (200, 150);

Programming Concepts in Java

Here is an applet to draw 10 blue balls of radius 20 pixels each at random locations on a canvas of width 250 pixels and height 275 pixels.

```
// The "Random" class.
import java.applet.Applet;
import java.awt.*;

public class Random extends Applet
{
    final int WIDTH = 250;
    final int HEIGHT = 275;
    final int RADIUS = 20;
    int xCenter, yCenter;

    public void drawBall (Graphics g, int x, int y, int radius, Color clr)
    {
        g.setColor (clr);
        g.fillOval (x – radius, y – radius, 2 * radius, 2 * radius);
    } // drawBall method

    public void paint (Graphics g)
    {
        Canvas c = new Canvas ();
        c.setSize (WIDTH, HEIGHT);
        for (int count = 1 ; count <= 10 ; count++)
        {
            xCenter = (int) (Math.random () * (WIDTH – 2 * RADIUS)) +
                RADIUS;
            yCenter = (int) (Math.random () * (HEIGHT – 2 * RADIUS)) +
                RADIUS;
            drawBall (g, xCenter, yCenter, RADIUS, Color.blue);
        }
    } // paint method
} /* Random class */
```

Figure 9.8 shows the result of running this program in an applet window of width 260 and height 300.

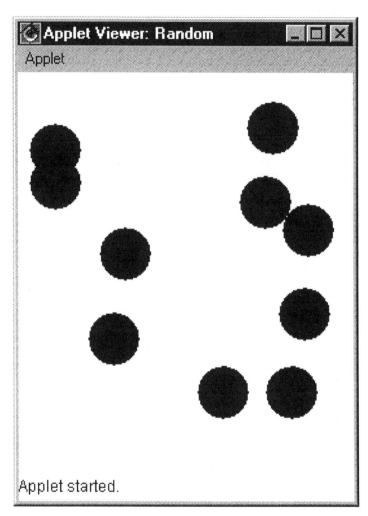

Figure 9.8 Output of the Random Applet

9.8   Simple Animation

It is possible to simulate the motion of objects by drawing an object in one position, erasing it, then redrawing it in a nearby location over and over. To demonstrate this process, we will create an applet that draws a red ball at a random position on a canvas then moves it step-by-step by a distance dx in the x-direction and dy in the y-direction. When the ball reaches the boundary of the canvas it is bounced off the border. When it reaches the top or bottom boundary the y-increment (dy) is reversed. When it reaches either side boundary its x-increment (dx) is reversed.

The drawing and redrawing is done here in the *action* method. In this method, there is no automatic instantiation of an object of the *Graphics* class as there is in the *paint* method because of its parameter.

This is done for the canvas *display* with the statements

```
Graphics displayG;
displayG = display.getGraphics ();
```

If the drawing and erasing of the ball occurs too rapidly the animation is not effective so a time wasting method called *delay* is included.

Here is the applet.

```
// The "Bounce" class.
import java.applet.Applet;
import java.awt.*;

public class Bounce extends Applet
{
    final int WIDTH = 250;
    final int HEIGHT = 275;
    Button bounce = new Button ("Bounce Ball");
    Canvas display = new Canvas ();

    public boolean action (Event e, Object o)
    {
```

```
      final int RADIUS = 20;
      Graphics displayG;
      int x, y, dx, dy;
      displayG = display.getGraphics ();
      displayG.setColor (Color.white);
      displayG.fillRect (0, 0, WIDTH, HEIGHT);
      displayG.setColor (Color.black);
      displayG.drawRect (0, 0, WIDTH, HEIGHT);
      x = (int) (Math.random () * (WIDTH – 2 * RADIUS)) + RADIUS;
      y = (int) (Math.random () * (HEIGHT – 2 * RADIUS)) + RADIUS;
      drawBall (displayG, x, y, RADIUS, Color.red);
      dx = 1;
      dy = 1;
      for (int i = 0 ; i < 1000 ; i++)
      {
          drawBall (displayG, x, y, RADIUS, getBackground ());
          x += dx;
          y += dy;
          if (x <= RADIUS || x >= WIDTH – RADIUS)
              dx = –dx;
          if (y <= RADIUS || y >= HEIGHT – RADIUS)
              dy = –dy;
          drawBall (displayG, x, y, RADIUS, Color.red);
          delay (10000); // Wastes time to produce delay.
      }
      Font f = new Font ("Serif", Font.BOLD, 72);
      displayG.setColor (Color.blue);
      displayG.setFont (f);
      displayG.drawString ("Done!", WIDTH / 2 – 80, HEIGHT / 2);
      return true;
} // action method

public void delay (int howLong)
{
    // This wastes time.
    for (int i = 1 ; i <= howLong ; i++)
    {
        double garbage = Math.PI * Math.PI;
    }
} // delay method
```

```
public void drawBall (Graphics g, int x, int y, int radius, Color clr)
{
    g.setColor (clr);
    g.fillOval (x – radius, y – radius, 2 * radius, 2 * radius);
} // drawBall method

public void init ()
{
    super.init ();
    setLayout (new BorderLayout ());
    add ("North", bounce);
    display.setSize (WIDTH, HEIGHT);
    add ("Center", display);
} // init method
} /* Bounce class */
```

The result of running the applet is difficult to show since it is a moving graphic. Once again, the applet should be run in a window of width 260 and height 300 to accommodate the size of the drawing area used by this applet.

9.9   An Example Using GUIs and Graphics

We will now look at an example that combines many of the GUI and graphic concepts presented earlier in this chapter. The *Applet Viewer* window will be divided into two main sections; one in which there are several panels containing buttons, a check box and radio buttons, and a canvas that will display graphics.

There are three buttons labelled "Draw Rectangle", "Draw Oval", and "Clear". When the "Draw Rectangle" button is clicked a rectangle will appear on the canvas. A check box labelled "Filled" controls whether the rectangle will be drawn as an outline or filled. There are three radio buttons labelled "Red", "Green", and "Blue" which control the color of the drawing.

If the "Draw Oval" button is clicked, an oval appears on the canvas, filled or not depending on the state of the "Filled" check box, and in the checked color. The "Clear" button erases the drawing on the canvas. The applet to do all this is called *ControlDraw*.

Here is the *ControlDraw* applet.

```
// The "ControlDraw" class.
import java.applet.Applet;
import java.awt.*;

public class ControlDraw extends Applet
{
    final int WIDTH = 250;
    final int HEIGHT = 275;
    Button rect = new Button ("Draw Rectangle");
    Button clear = new Button ("Clear");
    Button oval = new Button ("Draw Oval");
    CheckboxGroup colorGroup = new CheckboxGroup ();
    Checkbox red = new Checkbox ("Red", colorGroup, true);
    Checkbox green = new Checkbox ("Green", colorGroup, false);
    Checkbox blue = new Checkbox ("Blue", colorGroup, false);
    Checkbox filled = new Checkbox ("Filled", true);
    Canvas display = new Canvas ();

    public boolean action (Event e, Object o)
    {
        Graphics displayG;
        int x, y, dx, dy;
        displayG = display.getGraphics ();
        displayG.setColor (Color.black);
        if (e.target == rect)
        {
            displayG.clearRect (0, 0, WIDTH, HEIGHT);
            // Erase previous drawing.
            displayG.drawRect (5, 5, WIDTH – 10, HEIGHT – 10);
            if (red.getState ())
                displayG.setColor (Color.red);
            else if (green.getState ())
                displayG.setColor (Color.green);
            else
                displayG.setColor (Color.blue);
            if (filled.getState ())
            {
                displayG.fillRect (20, 20, WIDTH – 40, HEIGHT – 40);
            }
        }
```

```java
        else
        {
            displayG.drawRect (20, 20, WIDTH - 40, HEIGHT - 40);
        }
        return true;
    }
    else if (e.target == clear)
    {
        displayG.clearRect (0, 0, WIDTH, HEIGHT);
        displayG.drawRect (5, 5, WIDTH - 10, HEIGHT - 10);
        return true;
    }
    else if (e.target == oval)
    {
        displayG.clearRect (0, 0, WIDTH, HEIGHT);
        displayG.drawRect (5, 5, WIDTH - 10, HEIGHT - 10);
        if (red.getState ())
            displayG.setColor (Color.red);
        else if (green.getState ())
            displayG.setColor (Color.green);
        else
            displayG.setColor (Color.blue);
        if (filled.getState ())
        {
            displayG.fillOval (20, 20, WIDTH - 40, HEIGHT - 40);
        }
        else
        {
            displayG.drawOval (20, 20, WIDTH - 40, HEIGHT - 40);
        }
        return true;
    }
    return false;
} // action method

public void init ()
{
    super.init ();
    // Insert code to initialize the applet here.
    setLayout (new BorderLayout ());
    Panel radioButtonPanel = new Panel ();
    radioButtonPanel.setLayout (new BorderLayout ());
```

```
        Panel southWestPanel = new Panel ();
        southWestPanel.setLayout (new BorderLayout ());
        Panel buttonPanel = new Panel ();
        buttonPanel.setLayout (new BorderLayout ());
        Panel westPanel = new Panel ();
        westPanel.setLayout (new BorderLayout ());
        radioButtonPanel.add ("North", red);
        radioButtonPanel.add ("Center", green);
        radioButtonPanel.add ("South", blue);
        southWestPanel.add ("West", radioButtonPanel);
        southWestPanel.add ("East", filled);
        buttonPanel.add ("North", rect);
        buttonPanel.add ("Center", clear);
        buttonPanel.add ("South", oval);
        westPanel.add (buttonPanel, "North");
        westPanel.add (southWestPanel, "South");
        add ("West", westPanel);
        display.setSize (WIDTH, HEIGHT);
        add ("East", display);
    } // init method
} /* ControlDraw class */
```

The state of the radio buttons is determined using the *getState* method of the *Checkbox* class. In the *init* method the various panels are laid out using the *BorderLayout* manager.

Figure 9.9 shows the results of running the program with different boxes checked in an applet window of width 400 and height 300.

It is clear that the layout of buttons is not ideal. Chapter 15 on the *VisualAge for Java Visual Builder* shows how programmers can use the visual method of creating a graphical user interface. This visual method makes it much easier to achieve professional layouts and decreases the amount of code the programmer must write. The computer does much of this using the *VisualAge for Java Visual Composition Editor*.

Figure 9.9 Output of the ControlDraw Applet

9.10 Chapter Summary

Applets

Applets are Java programs that can be run under a **browser** and shared through the **World Wide Web**. Java applets are portable from one computer platform to another. Each applet program is a class that extends the Applet class. The Applet class has a number of standard methods that can be overridden. The standard methods used in the applets we created are:

- *init* which acts as a class constructor,

- *paint* which is used to output text and graphics, and
- *action* which is used to detect and act upon the user's actions such as the Return after input of data or the clicking of a mouse.

Other user-defined methods can be included in the applet. These are used by the standard methods which are executed automatically when the applet is run, just as the *main* method of an application program is executed. The *init* method is executed first, then the *paint* method, and then the *action* in response to the user.

Each applet must have an *HTML* file placed in the browser. This is created automatically in *VisualAge for Java* when the size of the *Applet Viewer* window is provided in the *Properties* window.

Applets with Input and Output and GUI

GUI components called *TextFields* can be labelled using the GUI component *Label*. The labels provide textual input to applets. These *TextFields* indicate to the user what is to be entered into the text field. After entry, when Return is pressed, the *action* method converts the input to a string and then parses it to yield the appropriate data type of the input. The output could be placed in a second *TextField* but is often shown in the **status bar** at the bottom of the *Applet Viewer* window.

All input and output must be a string of characters.

Applets with Multiple GUIs

In addition to actions that can be created by pressing Return after input in a text field, actions can be created using *Button* components. An example is shown which has an input text field and two buttons labelled "Square" and "Cube" that cause either the square or cube of the number in the text field to be displayed in an output text field depending on which of the buttons is clicked. The *Event* argument *e* of the action method is examined by *e.target* to determine which button was pushed. The action of pressing Return after input is ignored. Only the pressing of a button is responded to.

Layout of GUI Components

The default layout of GUI components is left to right across the top of the applet window until a line is filled. When one line is filled a new line is started. This is called *FlowLayout*.

A different **layout manager** can be selected using the *setLayout* method of the *Container* class. A window can be divided into **panels** each of which can have its own layout. The panels themselves are also laid out in the window.

BorderLayout is another layout manager which places a component in one of five areas of the container (panel or window) namely: *North, South, East, West,* and *Center*. The *add* statement identifies the component area.

Other GUI Components

Check boxes can be created as *Checkbox* components. Boxes yield a value of checked or unchecked (true or false) and their value is changed from one to the other by clicking.

A group of check boxes can be used to identify a number of mutually-compatible alternatives. Groups of boxes which are used with mutually-exclusive alternatives are called **radio buttons**. Only one of the group may be checked at a time. Check boxes used as radio buttons must be grouped explicitly into a *CheckboxGroup*.

Graphics Using Applets

All the graphics methods implemented in the *Console* class are available through the *Graphics* class which is instantiated automatically in the *paint* method. Graphics are drawn on a *Canvas* whose size is specified in the applet using the *setSize* method of the *Canvas* class.

Simple Animation

Motion of objects can be simulated by a series of still graphics where the object is placed in slightly different places on the canvas in each successive graphic. Between each, the image must be erased before it is redrawn. A **delay** between drawing and erasing can control the speed of animation.

If drawing is to be done in the *action* method rather than in the *paint* method, a *Graphics* object must be explicitly instantiated for it.

Complex Graphical User Interfaces

An example was given showing an interface with buttons, a check box, a set of radio buttons laid out in several panels, as well as a canvas for showing graphics of different kinds and in different colors depending on user input. A good layout is not easily achieved.

The *IBM VisualAge for Java Visual Composition Editor* described in Chapter 15 shows how good layouts are created and much of the code for them produced automatically.

9.11 Exercises

1. Write an applet that will produce a table showing the balance in a bank account at the end of each year if an interest rate of 10% a year is credited at the end of each year. In the table show the year, starting in 1998 when $1,000.00 is deposited, the interest for the year, and the balance at the end of the year for 10 years. You will need to display the output using the *drawString* method of the *Graphics* class.

2. Write an applet which produces the same table as Exercise 1 but asks the user to enter the starting year, the initial deposit, the interest rate, and the number of years the table is to display. You will need to create *TextFields* for each input item and a button to initialize the calculation once the data has been entered.

3. Write an applet with a panel containing two buttons, one labelled "Ball" and the other "Block", and a canvas on which either a ball or a square block is drawn depending on which button is clicked. Arrange to erase the previous drawing each time a button is clicked.

4. Modify the applet of Exercise 3 to have a second panel with radio buttons to control the color of the ball or block drawn.

5. Test the *BorderLayout* manager by adding buttons labelled "North" on the north position, one labelled "East" in the east position, and so on. Repeat the exercise using two panels, one in the north position and one in the south position.

6. Test the *FlowLayout* default manager by adding several text fields of different lengths in the applet. Change the lengths of the fields to see what happens.

7. Create an applet to show the animation of red circles radiating from the center of a canvas until they touch the border of the canvas, then starting again from the center.

8. Change the applet of Exercise 7 so that you do not erase the circle as it moves out, but when it reaches the border and starts over from the center.

9. Write an applet to show the animation of a ball starting at the center of its canvas and moving randomly in any of the four directions: north, south, east, and west by a small amount until it reaches the border of the canvas, then starting over. Try not erasing the image so as to produce a zigzag trail.

10. Modify the applet of Exercise 9 so that the color of the ball changes randomly among three different colors, each time it starts from the center. Follow the animation for 10 starts from the center.

11. Write an applet to control the type font with check boxes to indicate bold or italic, radio buttons to choose the type style, radio buttons to choose the point size, and a text field to contain the text whose font is to be controlled.

Chapter 10

Arrays

Data can also be structured so that the set of values to be used in a class or method is not just a collection of things with unique names. The relationships among data values in a computation can be made clear by organizing the values into structures. This chapter introduces arrays as one of the mechanisms that Java provides for structuring data values.

10.1 Lists as Arrays

Related data values can be grouped together and isolated from other data values in a program in several different ways.

One way is to make an **array** of variables of the same type. This array has a single name, and an individual **element** of the array is selected by giving an **index** value that uniquely identifies it.

This is a familiar idea from mathematics. A sequence of terms can be represented by a variable t. A particular term in the sequence can be represented by an expression such as t_i where i is the index value of the term. Values of the sequence can be defined and used in expressions like this.

$$t_{n+1} = k \times t_n$$

An array in Java is a group of variables that are all of the same type, and that can be referenced using a single name together with an index. The array must be declared. The declaration gives the array's name, the data type of the elements of the array, as well as the range of values to be used as its index. Here is an array declaration.

> int a [] = **new int** [10];

The declaration makes a the name of an array of integers. The array contains 10 elements, which can be accessed using the index values 0 through 9 inclusive. The individual element in array a with index i is written as $a[i]$ rather than in the mathematical form a_i. The index of an array element is sometimes referred to as a **subscript** because of the mathematical notation.

The array declaration can also be written in a slightly different form namely

    int [] *a* = **new int** [10];

One of the simplest uses of an array is for storing a **list** of values. As an example, we will look at a problem where a random list of ten positive integers between 1 and 1000 is to be generated, and then printed with each value expressed as a fraction of the largest value in the list. Our program to solve this problem will have three parts. First the values are generated and stored in an array. Second the array is searched to find the largest value. Third the values in the array are output, with their values divided by the largest value.

Here is the program. As usual the boiler plate is omitted.

```
// The "Normalize" class.
// Normalize each element in list of 10 random integers
// dividing it by the largest integer in the list.
final int SIZE = 9;
int list [] = new int [SIZE + 1];
// Generate random value for list.
for (int i = 0 ; i <= SIZE ; i++)
{
    list [i] = (int) (Math.random () * 1000) + 1;
}
// Find largest value in list.
int largest = list [0];
for (int i = 1 ; i <= SIZE ; i++)
{
    if (list [i] > largest)
        largest = list [i];
}
// Output normalized values.
for (int i = 0 ; i <= SIZE ; i++)
{
    c.print (i, 3);
    c.println ((double) list [i] / largest, 7, 2);
}
```

The program will produce output of this nature.

0	0.98
1	0.76
2	0.90
3	0.68
4	0.74
5	0.31
6	1.00
7	0.50
8	0.29
9	0.42

Notice that the array declaration uses a named constant *SIZE* rather than the integer 9. This name is used to control each of the three iterations in the program. It is good style to use named constants so that readers can see the meaning of the bounds for iterations. More important, the program can be easily changed to work with a different size of array. Only the definition of the constant *SIZE* need be changed.

Frequency Distribution

As a second example that uses arrays, consider the problem of determining how many times each value occurs in 1000 throws of two dice, and printing a table of the accumulated results. This is called a **frequency distribution**. An array can be declared to store the counters for all the possible throws.

Since the array elements here are to be counters, each one must be initialized to zero. This happens automatically when an array of integers or reals is declared.

Here is the *DiceTest* class.

```
// The "DiceTest" program.
// Count the frequency of the 11 different values of the
// throw of two dice 1000 times.
int freq [] = new int [11];
// Note freq [0] contains the number of throws with value 2.
int die1, die2, roll;
```

```
for (int times = 1 ; times <= 1000 ; times++)
{
    die1 = (int) (Math.random () * 6) + 1;
    die2 = (int) (Math.random () * 6) + 1;
    roll = die1 + die2;
    freq [roll – 2]++;
}
// Frequency distribution.
for (int i = 0 ; i < 11 ; i++)
{
    c.println ("Throw of " + (i + 2) + " occurred " + freq [i] + " times");
}
```

Perhaps the program would be easier to understand if the array *freq* had been declared to have 13 elements and *freq* [2] contained the number of times a 2 was rolled and so on. This means *freq* [0] and *freq* [1] would not be used.

A Class for Maintaining a List of Names

A class can be particularly useful for maintaining data structures such as a list of names. By implementing a list as a class called *NameList*, a name can be added to the list, a name can be deleted from the list, or the list can be printed.

The list of names encapsulated in the class is stored in an array. Each of the operations of the class is written as a method that manipulates the array.

When a value is added, it goes at the end of the list. A value can appear more than once in the list.

Before a value is deleted, its position in the list must be determined. This is done by moving along the list from the first element and examining each element until the value is found. Once the value to be deleted has been found, the last value in the list can be stored in the position of the value to be deleted and the list can be shortened. Because the last value in the list moves forward into the position of the value being deleted, the values in the list do not maintain their order as deletions occur. Only the first occurrence of a repeated name is deleted.

Here is the *NameList* class which implements a list of names. This class must be instantiated to create a list.

```java
// The "NameList" class.
import hsa.Console;

public class NameList
{
    final int MAX = 10;
    // Declare variables.
    String list [] = new String [MAX];
    int size = 0;
    Console c;

    // Constructor.
    public NameList (Console c)
    {
        // All elements of integer list set to zero automatically.
        this.c = c;
    } // NameList constructor

    // Delete a name from list.
    public void delete (String name)
    {
        int i = 0;
        while (!name.equals (list [i]))
        {
            i++;
        }
        // Place last name in list at the deletion point.
        list [i] = list [size – 1];
        size—;
    } // delete method

    // Add a name to list.
    public void insert (String name)
    {
        size++;
        list [size – 1] = name;
    } // insert method
```

```
    // Output list of names.
    public void printList ()
    {
        c.print ("[");
        for (int i = 0 ; i < size – 1 ; i++)
        {
            c.print (list [i]);
            c.print (", ");
        }
        if (size > 0)
            c.print (list [size – 1]);
        c.println ("]");
    } // printList method
} /* NameList class */
```

Here is a client application program that uses an object of this class, reads commands from a user, and manipulates the object using the object's methods.

```
// The "UseNameList" class.
// This is a main method to test the class NameList.
// Instantiate an object of NameList class.
NameList names = new NameList (c);
c.println ("Commands you can give after the prompt");
c.println ("i to insert a name");
c.println ("d to delete a name");
c.println ("p to print the list");
c.println ("q to quit");
while (true)
{
    char command;
    c.print ("> "); // Prompt for command.
    command = c.readLine ().charAt (0);
    if (command == 'q')
        break;
    switch (command)
    {
        case 'i':
            String newName;
            c.print ("Enter name to insert: ");
            newName = c.readLine ();
```

```
            names.insert (newName);
            break;
       case 'd':
            String oldName;
            c.print ("Enter name to delete: ");
            oldName = c.readLine ();
            names.delete (oldName);
            break;
       case 'p':
            names.printList ();
            break;
       default:
            c.println ("This is an incorrect command try again");
            break;
       }
    }
}
```

Here is a sample output.

```
Commands you can give after the prompt >
  i to insert a name
  d to delete a name
  p to print the list
  q to quit
>i
Enter name to insert: Hercule Poirot
>i
Enter name to insert: Jane Marple
>i
Enter name to insert: Hercule Poirot
>i
Enter name to insert: Nero Wolfe
>p
[Hercule Poirot, Jane Marple, Hercule Poirot, Nero Wolfe]
>d
Enter name to delete: Hercule Poirot
>p
[Nero Wolfe, Jane Marple, Hercule Poirot]
>q
```

Computing Prime Numbers

With arrays it is possible to write very interesting and subtle programs. For example, an array can be used to determine a list of all the prime numbers up to some given value.

The general idea for this algorithm originated with a Greek mathematician named Eratosthenes who developed an algorithm now called the **sieve of Eratosthenes**. It works like this. First, make a list of all the integers from 2 up to some limit, such as 20.

$$2,3,4,5,6,7,8,9,10,11,12,13,14,15,16,17,18,19,20$$

Values in the list can be marked, meaning that they are not prime. In the beginning, no values are marked.

Starting at the left end of the list, find the next value that is not marked. It is a prime number. But all multiples of it are not prime, so they can be marked. Since the first value in the list is 2, it is considered to be prime. All multiples of 2 are not prime, and are marked.

$$2,3,\overline{4},5,\overline{6},7,\overline{8},9,\overline{10},11,\overline{12},13,\overline{14},15,\overline{16},17,\overline{18},19,\overline{20}$$

The next unmarked value after 2 is 3, so it too is prime. All multiples of 3 can then be marked. Some of them, such as 6, have already been marked.

$$2,3,\overline{4},5,\overline{6},7,\overline{8},\overline{9},\overline{10},11,\overline{12},13,\overline{14},\overline{15},\overline{16},17,\overline{18},19,\overline{20}$$

The value 4 is skipped over now, because it has been marked. The next unmarked value 5 is a prime. All of the multiples of 5 need to be marked. As it turns out, all of them have been marked so the list remains the same. The value 6 is skipped (it is marked). The value 7 is prime but all its multiples have been marked. In fact, there are no more marks to be added to the list. All of the values that are unmarked are primes.

Eratosthenes' algorithm can be implemented in a direct way using an array. It is not necessary to store the integers themselves, because they are determined by their index in the list. Instead, it is only necessary to store an indication of whether a value has been marked. The boolean data type is sufficient for this purpose. The array *isPrime* contains a boolean value for each integer. If the boolean value ends up being true, the integer corresponding to the index is prime, otherwise the integer is not prime (it is a multiple of some smaller integer). We will not use the two elements of *isPrime* with indexes 0 and 1 so that the array index is the actual integer being tested.

Here is the *FindPrimes* class.

```
// The "FindPrimes" program.
// Find prime numbers using Erastosthenes' sieve.
int size;
c.println ("Enter maximum value to test");
size = c.readInt ();
// Declare array isPrime.
boolean isPrime [];
isPrime = new boolean [size + 1];
// A boolean array is automatically initialized to false.
// Initialize array elements as true.
for (int i = 2 ; i <= size ; i++)
{
    isPrime [i] = true;
}
// Multiples of a prime are not prime.
for (int i = 2 ; i <= size ; i++)
{
    if (isPrime [i]) // This value is prime.
    {
        for (int j = 2 * i ; j <= size ; j += i)
        {
            isPrime [j] = false;
        }
    }
}
c.println ("Between 2 and " + size + " the primes are");
final int valuesPerLine = 10;
int valuesPrinted = 0;
for (int i = 2 ; i <= size ; i++)
{
    if (isPrime [i])
    {
        c.print (i, 5);
        valuesPrinted++;
        if (valuesPrinted % valuesPerLine == 0)
```

```
          c.println ("");
    }
}
if ((valuesPrinted % valuesPerLine) != 0)
    c.println ("");
```

The program produces this output for an input value of 500.

```
Enter maximum value to test: 500
Between 2 and 500 the primes are:
    2     3     5     7    11    13    17    19    23    29
   31    37    41    43    47    53    59    61    67    71
   73    79    83    89    97   101   103   107   109   113
  127   131   137   139   149   151   157   163   167   173
  179   181   191   193   197   199   211   223   227   229
  233   239   241   251   257   263   269   271   277   281
  283   293   307   311   313   317   331   337   347   349
  353   359   367   373   379   383   389   397   401   409
  419   421   431   433   439   443   449   457   461   463
  467   479   487   491   499
```

10.2 Related Lists

Sometimes several kinds of values need to be kept together. For example, to keep a list of books in a library it may be necessary to record the author and title of each book. There are many other pieces of information that could be kept as well.

This can be done by keeping arrays that are conceptually related to each other: the first entry in the author list corresponds to the first entry in the title list, and so on. Although there is nothing explicit in the declarations to show that the lists are related, the program treats them as related; every time an author is used, the corresponding title is also used.

A book list can be maintained using the same algorithms as were used earlier for maintaining a list of names. Notice that when a book is inserted in the list, both the author and title values are inserted. Similarly, when a book is deleted from the list, both an author and a title are deleted. The class *BookList* is very similar to the class *NameList*.

Here is the *BookList* class which implements a l.ist of up to 10 authors and titles. This class must be instantiated to create a list.

```
// The "BookList" class.
// A class to maintain a list of authors and titles.
import hsa.Console;

public class BookList
{
    // Declare variables.
    final int MAX = 10;
    String author [] = new String [MAX];
    String title [] = new String [MAX];
    int size = 0;
    Console c;

    // Constructor.
    public BookList (Console c)
    {
        // All elements of author and title array set to null automatically.
        this.c = c;
    } // BookList constructor

    // Delete a book from the list.
    public void delete (String name, String book)
    {
        int where = 0;
        while (true)
        {
            if (author [where].equals (name) && title [where].equals (book))
                break;
            where++;
        }
        // Put the last item in bookList in position where.
        author [where] = author [size - 1];
        title [where] = title [size - 1];
        size—;
    } // delete method
```

```
// Add a book to the list.
public void insert (String name, String book)
{
    size++;
    author [size – 1] = name;
    title [size – 1] = book;
} // insert method

// Print list of books.
public void printList ()
{
    for (int i = 0 ; i < size ; i++)
    {
        c.println ("  " + author [i] + "/ " + title [i]);
    }
} // printList method
} /* BookList class */
```

Here is the driver application program that manipulates the class. It is similar to the driver for *NameList*.

```
// The "UseBookList" program.
// A main method to test the class BookList.
// Instantiate an object of BookList class.
BookList books = new BookList (c);
c.println ("Commands you can give after the prompt >");
c.println ("i insert a book into the list");
c.println ("d delete a book from the list");
c.println ("p print the list of books");
c.println ("q quit");
while (true)
{
    char command;
    c.print ("> "); // Prompt for command.
    command = c.readLine ().charAt (0);
    if (command == 'q')
        break;
    switch (command)
    {
```

```
        case 'i':
            String newAuthor, newTitle;
            c.print ("Enter author to insert: ");
            newAuthor = c.readLine ();
            c.print ("Enter title to insert ");
            newTitle = c.readLine ();
            books.insert (newAuthor, newTitle);
            break;
        case 'd':
            String oldAuthor, oldTitle;
            c.print ("Enter author to delete: ");
            oldAuthor = c.readLine ();
            c.print ("Enter title to delete: ");
            oldTitle = c.readLine ();
            books.delete (oldAuthor, oldTitle);
            break;
        case 'p':
            books.printList ();
            break;
    }
}
```

Here is a sample output from this program.

```
    Commands you can give after the prompt >
    i  insert a book into the list
    d  delete a book from the list
    p  print the list of books
    q  quit
    >i
    Enter author to insert: Elizabeth George
    Enter title to insert: A Great Deliverance
    >i
    Enter author to insert: Minette Walters
    Enter title to insert: The Ice House
    >i
    Enter author to insert: Elizabeth George
    Enter title to insert: Playing For the Ashes
    >p
      Elizabeth George / A Great Deliverance
      Minette Walters / The Ice House
      Elizabeth George / Playing For the Ashes
    >q
```

10.3 Declaration of Arrays

In Java a one-dimension array is declared by placing empty square brackets after the array's name. The declaration

> **int** *marks* [];

indicates that *marks* is to be an array of integers. An alternative declaration is

> **int** [] *marks*;

In Java, an array is an object and must be instantiated. The statement

> *marks* = **new int** [12];

instantiates the array *marks* to be an array of 12 elements. The individual elements are named *marks* [0], *marks* [1], *marks* [2] ... *marks* [11].

All arrays know their own length. The integer expression

> *marks.length*

gives the length for the array *marks*. Notice that there are no empty parentheses after *length*.

The size of the array can be read in when the program is executed. When this happens, the array is dynamic. Here is an example of a dynamic array.

> *c.println* ("Enter size of array");
> **int** *size*;
> *size* = *c.readInt* ();
> **int** *marks* [];
> *marks* = **new int** [*size*];

Initial values are automatically assigned to arrays. Elements of numeric arrays are all set to zero. Boolean arrays are set to **false**. Arrays of objects, such as strings, are set to **null**.

Initial values can be assigned at the time of declaration. For example, the single statement

> **int** [] *number* = {1, 3, 5, 7, 9};

establishes an array of 5 elements where *number* [0] has the value 1, *number* [1] has the value 3, and so on. The array is fully created and initialized.

10.4 Two-Dimensional Arrays

Arrays can have more than one dimension. The two-dimensional array is useful for storing tables of information. A table contains rows and columns of entries. Each entry is of the same data type. To declare a two-dimensional array of integers called *table* we use the statement

int *table* [] [];

This integer array can be instantiated to have 10 rows and 5 columns by the statement

table = **new int** [10] [5];

Here is a program segment that will compute a table of powers of the integers from 1 to 10. The columns will correspond to powers 1, 2, 3, 4, and 5. This means the integers 1 to 10 will be in column 1, their squares in column 2, their cubes in column 3, and so on.

```
// The "Powers2" class.
// Compute a table of powers of integers from 1 to 10.
int table [] [];
table = new int [10] [5];
for (int i = 0 ; i < 10 ; i++)
{
    table [i] [0] = i + 1;
    for (int j = 1 ; j < 5 ; j++)
    {
        table [i] [j] = table [i] [j – 1] * (i + 1);
    }
}
// Print table.
for (int i = 0 ; i < 10 ; i++)
{
    for (int j = 0 ; j < 5 ; j++)
```

```
    {
        c.print (table [i] [j], 7);
    }
    c.println ();
}
```

This is the output of the program.

1	1	1	1	1
2	4	8	16	32
3	9	27	81	243
4	16	64	256	1024
5	25	125	625	3125
6	36	216	1296	7776
7	49	343	2401	16807
8	64	512	4096	32768
9	81	729	6561	59049
10	100	1000	10000	100000

10.5 Methods With Array Parameters

An element of an array can be passed as a parameter to a method in the same way that a primitive variable can be passed.

Entire arrays can also be passed as parameters. Since the array is an object, the parameter is a **reference** to the array. The signature of the subprogram must contain a specification of the array type.

Here is an example where an array is passed to a method to be initialized. This method initializes an array of *size* elements to random integers between 1 and 10.

```
// A method to initialize the first size elements of an array
// to random integers between 1 and 10.
static public void initialize (int a [], int size)
{
    for (int i = 0 ; i < size ; i++)
    {
        a [i] = (int) (Math.random () * 10) + 1;
    }
```

```
} // initialize method

// This method prints the first n elements of an array of integers.
static public void printArray (int a [], int n)
{
    for (int i = 0 ; i < n ; i++)
    {
        c.println (a [i]);
    }
} // printArray method
```

Here is a driver program to test these methods.

```
// The "RandTest" class.
// A main method to test the methods initialize and printArray.
int howBig;
c.print ("Enter size of array ");
howBig = c.readInt ();
int array [];
array = new int [howBig];
initialize (array, howBig);
printArray (array, 5);
```

In the method *initialize*, all the elements of the array are initialized. Sometimes only part of the array whose size is declared in the *main* method is to be used in a method. When this is true, an additional parameter must be passed to the method to indicate how much of the array is to be used. The call to the *printArray* method prints only the first 5 elements of the array. The entire array can be printed by making the second parameter have the value *howBig*.

The number of elements in an array that are to be processed in a method need only be given as a parameter if that number is different from the size of the array declared. If it is the same, within the body of the method the array method *length* can be used to find the actual value of the number of elements in the array. This is similar to the method *length* for the *String* class except that here no parentheses are needed.

Here is part of a class that sums the values of an array.

```
// A method to compute the sum of all the values of an integer array.
static public int sumArray (int a [])
{
    int sum = 0;
    for (int i = 0 ; i < a.length ; i++)
    {
        sum += a [i];
    }
    return sum;
}
```

Here is driver *main* method to test this method.

```
// The "TestSumArray" program.
// A main method to test the method sumArray.
int list [];
list = new int [10];
for (int i = 0 ; i < 10 ; i++)
{
    list [i] = i + 1;
}
c.println ("Sum of elements of list = " + sumArray (list));
```

Here is another example of a method with an array parameter shown together with the *main* driver method to test the method. The method *maxArray* is a function-type method whose value is the largest element in the array that is its parameter. Again, the *length* method is used to find the length of the array. This is possible because the number of elements in the array is the same as the length declared when it is instantiated, namely 5.

```
// The "Best" class.
import hsa.Console;

public class Best
{
    public static void main (String args [])
    {
```

```
Console c = new Console ();
int [] mark = new int [5];

c.println ("Enter five marks");
for (int i = 0 ; i < 5 ; i++)
    mark [i] = c.readInt ();
c.println ("The best mark is " + maxArray (mark));
} // main method

public static int maxArray (int [] list)
{
    int biggest = list [0];

    for (int i = 1 ; i < list.length ; i++)
    {
        // The following two lines could be replaced by:
        //     biggest = Math.max (biggest, line [i]);
        if (list [i] > biggest)
            biggest = list [i];

    }
    return biggest;
} // maxArray method
} /* Best class */
```

10.6 Searching

Arrays are often used to store information that will be used many times. Sometimes it is important to know whether a value is in a list, for example checking to see if a person is authorized to use some service (such as gain entry to a secure area). Sometimes it is important to find information associated with a key, as in looking up a name in a telephone directory in order to retrieve the associated telephone number.

The search program earlier in the chapter worked with a list of names in arbitrary order. Often, however, it is more useful to maintain lists that are sorted. A list is sorted in ascending order if each value in the list is no larger than the one that comes after it in the list.

When a list is sorted there is more work involved when inserting or deleting values if the order is to be maintained. Think of the list as being laid out from left to right. Before a value can be inserted, the appropriate location for it must be found in the list; then the value in that location, together with all the values to the right of that location, must be shifted to the right to make room for the new value. Before a value can be deleted, its location must be found in the list; then all the values to the right of that location must be shifted to the left.

Only one element of an array can be manipulated at a time. To shift a part of a list left or right, the values must be shifted one at a time. To shift to the right, the last element must be moved to the right and the previous element must then be moved into the vacated position, and so on. To move to the left, the first element must be moved to the left and the second element must then be moved into the vacated position, and so on.

The methods that maintain a sorted list can be used to override the previously-written methods in the *NameList* class. Here are the *insert* and *delete* methods that maintain a sorted list, as part of a new class called *SortedList*.

```
// A class that keeps list sorted called SortedList.
import hsa.Console;

public class SortedList extends NameList
{
    // Constructor for SortedList.
    public SortedList (Console c)
    {
        super (c);  // Call NameList's constructor.
    } // SortedList constructor

    // Override delete method of NameList.
    public void delete (String name)
    {
        int i = 0;
        while (!name.equals (list [i]))
        {
            i++;
        }
```

```
    // Shift remaining items down.
    for (int j = i ; j < size – 1 ; j++)
    {
        list [j] = list [j + 1];
    }
    size—;
} // delete method

// Override insert method of NameList.
public void insert (String name)
{
    int i = 0;
    while (i < size && (name.compareTo (list [i]) > 0))
    {
        i++;
    }
    // Shift the remaining items to make room.
    for (int j = size ; j >= i + 1 ; j—)
    {
        list [j] = list [j – 1];
    }
    size++;
    list [i] = name;
} // insert method
} /* SortedList class */
```

Because the list of values is now maintained in sorted order, the output from the driver program will look like this.

```
Commands you can give after the prompt >
    i  insert a name into the list
    d  delete a name from the list
    p  print the list of names
    q  quit
>i
Enter name to insert: Hercule Poirot
>i
Enter name to insert: Jane Marple
>i
Enter name to insert: Hercule Poirot
>i
Enter name to insert: Nero Wolfe
```

```
>p
[Hercule Poirot, Hercule Poirot, Jane Marple, Nero Wolfe]
>d
Enter name to delete: Hercule Poirot
>p
[Hercule Poirot, Jane Marple, Nero Wolfe]
>q
```

Notice that the names are sorted by their first letters, so *Hercule* Poirot comes alphabetically before *Jane* Marple.

Each of the two methods *insert* and *delete* must first search in the list: either to find a location where a new value is to be placed, or to find a location from where a value is to be deleted. The searching can be separated out into a method that both other methods can use.

Here is another class that implements a sorted list.

```java
// The "SortedList2" class.
// A class to keep list sorted that uses a separate find method.
import hsa.Console;

public class SortedList2 extends NameList
{
    // Constructor for SortedList2.
    public SortedList2 (Console c)
    {
        super (c);  // Call NameList's constructor.
    } // SortedList2 constructor

    // Override delete method of NameList.
    public void delete (String name)
    {
        int location = find (name);
        if (location < size && list [location].equals (name))
        {
            // Shift remaining items down.
            for (int j = location ; j < size - 1 ; j++)
            {
                list [j] = list [j + 1];
            }
            size--;
```

```
        }
    else
    {
            c.println ("Name " + name + " is not in list");
    }
} // delete method

// A new method find used by insert and delete methods.
protected int find (String name)
{
    int where = 0;
    while (where < size && list [where].compareTo (name) < 0)
    {
            where++;
    }
    return where;
} // find method

// Override insert method of NameList.
public void insert (String name)
{
    int locationToInsert = find (name);
    // Shift the remaining items over to make room.
    for (int j = size ; j >= locationToInsert + 1 ; j—)
    {
            list [j] = list [j – 1];
    }
    size++;
    list [locationToInsert] = name;
} // insert method
} /* SortedList2 class */
```

The search method used here is called **sequential search** because it examines the locations one after the other sequentially. The *insert* and *delete* methods have been changed to use this common method.

While sequential search is effective, it is not efficient. The fact that the values are sorted can be exploited to make searching faster. The **binary search** technique works by dividing a sorted list of values in two parts (hence binary) at each step, and retaining only half of the values for further consideration. The search algorithm is given a list of sorted values, together with a value to be found (or a location in which the value will be placed, if the value is to be inserted).

At each step the search proceeds like this: examine the value in the middle of the list; if it is larger than the value being searched for, discard the right half of the list, but if the value in the middle is smaller, discard the left half of the list. When the list being searched is reduced to a single entry, either the value has been found, or the place where it is to be inserted has been found.

The class *FastSortedList* includes an implementation of the binary search algorithm.

```
// The "FastSortedList" class.
// An extension of SortedList2 with a binary search method for find.
import hsa.Console;

public class FastSortedList extends SortedList2
{
    // Constructor for FastSortedList.
    public FastSortedList (Console c)
    {
        super (c); // Call SortedList2's (and thus NameList's) constructor.
    } // FastSortedList constructor

    // This method overrides the find method SortedList2.
    protected int find (String name)
    {
        int first = 0;
        int last = size - 1;
        while (first != last && last > 0)
        {
            int middle = (first + last) / 2;
            if (name.compareTo (list [middle]) <= 0)
            {
                // Name lies in first half or not in list.
                last = middle;
            }
            else
            {
                // Discard first half (including middle)
                first = middle + 1;
```

```
                }
            }
        int where = first;
        if (where < size && name.compareTo (list [where]) > 0)
            where++;
        System.out.println (where + " " + name);
        return where;
    } // find method
} /* FastSortedList class */
```

10.7 Efficiency of Algorithms

Some algorithms run much faster than others. The speed of an algorithm depends upon many factors including the speed of the underlying computer, the quality of the compiler that translates it to machine language, and the skill of the programmer. Beyond these factors, in many cases there is a fundamental reason why one program will always run faster than another. This reason has to do with how many times the parts of the algorithm are executed as a function of the size of the input to the algorithm.

We will show that the time required for a binary search is essentially a constant k_1 times the *log* of the number n of items to be searched.

Time for binary search = $k_1 \log n$

We will also show that the time required for a sequential search of the same list is essentially a constant k_2 times n.

Time for sequential search = $k_2 n$

The sizes of the constants k_1 and k_2 depend on the things we have mentioned, such as the computer, the compiler, and the programmer. However, as n increases, *log* n grows much more slowly than n, so for large enough n, eventually it will be true that

$k_1 \log n < k_2 n$

This implies that for long lists, the time for a binary search will be less than the time for a sequential search, no matter what values we have for constants k_1 and k_2.

Running Time for Sequential Search

We will now analyze the time taken for a sequential search. This algorithm inspects each item in a list to see if the item matches the input key (see Figure 10.1). If the key matches the item, the inspection loop terminates.

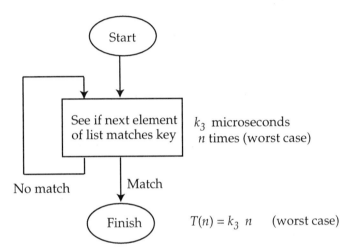

Figure 10.1 Timing Analysis for Sequential Search

There are a fixed number of things to be done in each loop iteration so we can conclude that each iteration takes a fixed amount of time, which we will take to be k_3 microseconds. (We have used microseconds as our unit for time. Other units, such as seconds, can be used as well.) The number of iterations of the loop will vary from 1 iteration, when the first element matches the key, to n iterations, when no elements in the list match the key. On average, if the key is randomly chosen from a set of n distinct elements and the list contains these same elements in a random order, there will be $n/2$ iterations. From this we can conclude that the best, average, and worst times to execute a sequential search are:

$$T_{best}\ (n) = k_3 \qquad \text{Best time}$$
$$T_{avg}\ (n) = k_3\ n/2 \qquad \text{Average time}$$
$$T_{worst}\ (n) = k_3\ n \qquad \text{Worst time}$$

We ignore the time taken to start up (or to finish) the algorithm, on the grounds that this time will be small compared to the total time of the algorithm when n is large.

The average time can be useful for predicting the time for the search. (Note that our assumptions regarding randomness that we made in determining T_{avg} are often not true in practice.) We usually concentrate on the worst time for two reasons. First, it is often easier to determine the worst time. Second, the worst time is useful if we need to put a bound on the time a program will take. From now on, we will write $T(n)$ to mean $T_{worst}(n)$.

Running Time for Binary Search

A binary search repeatedly discards halves (and sub-halves and so on) of a list until only one element remains. This is illustrated in Figure 10.2.

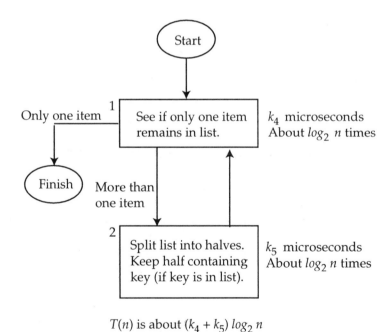

$T(n)$ is about $(k_4 + k_5) \log_2 n$

Figure 10.2 Analysis of Running Time for Binary Search

Each test to see if the list has been reduced to a single element consumes a fixed amount of time, which we will take to be k_4 microseconds (see Figure 10.2). Each split, together with discarding half of the list, consumes a fixed amount of time, which we take to be k_5 microseconds. If the original list is 8 long, we will have to split 3 times:

        Split down to size 4
        Split down to size 2
        Split down to size 1

The number of splits is equal to $log_2 8$ because, if n is a power of 2,

$$log_2 n = \text{number of times to divide } n \text{ by 2 until } n \text{ is 1}$$

Table of Powers of 2

n	2^n		n	2^n
0	1		10	1024 = 1K
1	2		11	2K
2	4		12	4K
3	8		13	8K
4	16		14	16K
5	32		15	32K
6	64		16	64K
7	128		17	128K
8	256		18	256K
9	512		19	512K
10	1024 = 1K		20	1024K = 1M
$log_2 n$	n		$log_2 n$	n

Table of Logarithms Base 2 of n

Figure 10.3 Powers of 2 and Logarithms Base 2

Figure 10.3 is both a table of powers of 2 and a table of logarithms of 2. For example, reading the fourth line of the table from left to right, we get $2^3 = 8$. Reading that same line from right to left, we get $log_2 8 = 3$. The value of $2^{10} = 1024$ is often written in computer literature as K for kilo, because it is very close to the value 1000. Similarly, 2^{20} is often written as M for mega.

Returning to our analysis of binary search, if n is a power of 2, that is, if n is one of 1, 2, 4, 8, 16, 32, etc., the number of times to execute each of boxes 1 and 2 in Figure 10.3 will be $log_2 n$. If n is not a power of 2, the number of splits will be the ceiling of $log_2 n$, which is the next integer above $log_2 n$. For our purposes, the difference between $log_2 n$ and the ceiling of $log_2 n$ is not significant so we ignore it. Adding the total times for boxes 1 and 2 in Figure 10.2, we can determine that the running time for binary search is

$$T(n) = (k_4 + k_5) \, log_2 n$$

Since $k_4 + k_5$ is a constant, we can write this as

$$T(n) = k_6 \, log_2 n$$

It turns out that the base of the logarithm, 2 in this case, is not important because changing the base only changes the size of the constant preceding it. For example,

$$k_6 \, log_2 n = 3.322 \, k_6 \, log_{10} n$$

Because of this, we will drop the 2 and write the running time of binary search as simply

$$T(n) = k_6 \, log \, n$$

(To be precise here, we should really have changed the name of constant k_6, for example to k_7, to reflect the scaling of its value.)

Big O Notation

It may seem that we have not paid sufficient attention to details in computing the running times of the sequential and binary searches. For example, we ignored the time required in a binary search to initialize the variables (*first* and *last*) that keep track of the ends of the remaining list. We have ignored these details in order to concentrate only on those aspects of algorithms that fundamentally contribute to their running time.

We will now introduce a notation, called **big O**, which makes precise this idea of ignoring unimportant details. The basic idea of big O notation is that it concentrates on the fundamental part of a function $T(n)$ that causes $T(n)$ to grow large as n grows large.

In the examples we have seen so far, $T(n)$ was proportional to n or to $log\ n$. For these examples, we write

$T(k_3\ n/2)$ is $O(n)$ Timing function $k_3\ n/2$ is order n.
$T(k_6\ log\ n)$ is $O(log\ n)$ Timing function $k_6\ log\ n$ is order $log\ n$.

As these examples illustrate, big O notation ignores constant factors such as k_5 and k_6, but this is not all that it ignores.

The definition of $O(f\ (n))$ is

$T(n)$ is $O(f\ (n))$ if $T(n)$ is always at most a constant k times $f\ (n)$, except for some small values of n.

We can state this formally as

$T(n)$ is $O(f\ (n))$ if there exists an integer n_0 and a constant $k > 0$ such that for all $n \geq n_0$, $T(n) \leq kf\ (n)$.

It follows from this definition that:

- **Constant factors are immaterial**. For example, both $20n$ and $400n$ are $O(n)$.
- **Low-order terms are immaterial**. For example, $20\ n^3 + 500\ n^2 + 800\ n$ is $O(n^3)$. Similarly $k_1\ n + k_2$ is $O(n)$.

When we determined $T(n)$ for sequential and binary searches, we ignored details such as the constant time that should in principle be part of $T(n)$, because our purpose was to determine the corresponding big O class.

If $T(n)$ is independent of n, we say it is $O(1)$. For example, the time to compare a key to an element in sequential search is $O(1)$.

Concentrating on Loops and Recursion

Since constant factors and low order terms are immaterial for big O times, it follows that when we are determining the big O time of an algorithm, the only parts we need to consider are the loops, including nested loops, and the recursive method calls. This is because these are the only constructs whose time depends on n (the size of the input). For example, suppose a program has this structure.

```
for (int i = 1; i <= n; i ++)
{
    for (int j = 1; j <= n; j ++)
    {
        ....calculation whose time is independent of n...
    }
}
```

By inspection, we can tell that this program has running time $O(n^2)$. We observe that it consists of an $O(1)$ loop body, within an inner loop whose range $1 .. n$ is proportional in size to n, and an outer loop whose range is also proportional to n. This implies that the inner loop body is executed on the order of n^2 times so $T(n)$ is $O(n^2)$.

10.8 Chapter Summary

Lists as Arrays

A list of data values of the same type can be stored in an array. The values are accessed using a single name together with an integer-valued **index**.

The **sieve of Eratosthenes** is an algorithm that uses a list of boolean values to determine which integers are **prime numbers**.

Related Lists

Sometimes values of different data types need to be kept together. This can be done by keeping related values in arrays that are conceptually in parallel. For example, a list of books can be kept as two related lists: an array of authors and an array of titles.

Declaration of Arrays

A **one-dimensional array** declaration indicates the type of the elements of the array, as well as the acceptable values for the index used with the array name. These statements instantiate an integer array of 12 elements.

int *a* [];
a = **new int** [12];

The elements of the array have indexes running from 0 to the length of the array minus 1. The length of the array is available from the expression *a.length*. The element of an array *a* with index value *i* is referred to as *a* [*i*]. Arrays can have their sizes determined at the time that the program is run. These are called **dynamic arrays**.

Tables as Arrays

Arrays with two dimensions can be used to represent tables. A **two-dimensional array** integer *b* is defined by a declaration of the form

int *b* [] []

The element of array *b* whose first index is *i* and second *j* is referred to as *b*[*i*][*j*].

Methods With Array Parameters

Arrays can be passed as parameters to methods. The signature of the method must contain a specification of the array type.

Searching

Sequential searching examines the values in a list from first element to last to find a value being searched for, or a place to insert a new value if the list is sorted. **Binary searching** examines the middle value of a sorted list, discarding either the part of the list before the middle value, or the part after the middle value, at each step. The process continues until a single element remains. Either this is the sought value or the value is not in the list.

Efficiency of Algorithms

An algorithm that takes input, such as a list, of size n is said to run in time $T(n)$, that is, the running time depends in some way on the number of elements n. Usually the worst case time is of interest and $T(n)$ is taken to mean $T_{worst}(n)$. **Big O** notation is used to concentrate on fundamental effects, and to ignore constants and low-order terms. For example, if $T(n) = 4n^2 + 16n$, it is $O(n^2)$. The running time of linear search is $O(n)$ and binary search is $O(\log n)$.

10.9 Exercises

1. Modify the "Normalize" program that generates the random numbers so that the largest value is found in the same loop that generates the list of random values.

2. The program to find primes can be improved in several ways. One improvement results from using an array to store a boolean value only for the odd integers (since every even integer larger than 2 is not prime) and to treat 2 as a special case. This means that the ith array entry corresponds to the integer $2i+1$. A program that incorporates this improvement could look for primes over twice as large a range with a given amount of memory. Modify the program to store a boolean value only for odd integers.

3. Make the prime number program more efficient by combining the iteration that marks values with the iteration that prints unmarked values.

4. Write a program that reads a list of names from a file and outputs the list with any duplicates removed.

5. Write a program to read an unordered list of integers. The list is to be printed in ascending order. Keep an associated list that marks those values that have been printed. The program should use an iteration to find the smallest unmarked value, print it, and mark it.

6. Extend the class definition for *BookList* to include a method
    called *printAuthors* that prints the list with each author being
    listed once, and all of the books by that author indented under
    the author's name.

7. A two-dimensional array of characters can be used to store a
    picture if the blank is used for background and an asterisk is
    used for non-blank parts. Write a class for pictures that has two
    methods. The first method should put a horizontal line into the
    picture; the method will have the coordinates of the endpoints
    as parameters. The second method will output a picture.

8. Extend the class from the previous exercise to allow a rectangle
    to be inserted into a picture.

9. Extend the class from the previous exercise to allow a circle to
    be inserted into a picture.

Chapter 11

Records in Java

In the chapter on arrays we introduced the idea of a structured data type. An array is a sequence of items that are all of the same data type. The arrays we have shown so far are sequences of fairly primitive data types or *String* objects. The sequence of the items is determined by an index. In this chapter we will present the way that records are represented in Java.

11.1 Records

In Java objects consist of instance variables and methods that operate on these variables. The instance variables are the fields of the object. The object is the obvious way to represent a data type called **record** that consists of a number of fields which may be of primitive data types or may be structured data types such as other objects.

Here is a definition of a class that might be suitable for recording the name and phone number of a person.

```
// The "PhoneRecord" class.
public class PhoneRecord
{
    protected String name, phone;
    // Constructor.
    public PhoneRecord (String name, String phone)
    {
        this.name = name;
        this.phone = phone;
    } // PhoneRecord constructor

    // Method to get name.
    public String getName ()
    {
        return name;
    } // getName method

    // Method to get phone.
    public String getPhone ()
    {
```

```
        return phone;
    } // getPhone method

    // Method to change name.
    public void setName (String newName)
    {
        name = newName;
    } // setName method

    // Method to change phone.
    public void setPhone (String newPhone)
    {
        phone = newPhone;
    } // setPhone method
} /* PhoneRecord class */
```

The fields *name* and *phone* of the record are the instance variables and are labelled **protected**. Their values can be set by the *PhoneRecord* class methods *setName* and *setPhone,* or retrieved by the methods *getName* and *getPhone.*

To instantiate an object called *person* of type *PhoneRecord* and initialize it to the name "Maria Sanchez" and phone "(407)716-2780" would require the statement

PhoneRecord person = **new** PhoneRecord ("Maria Sanchez",
"(407)716-2780");

To output the record's fields would require a statement of this sort

c.println (person.getName () + " " + person.getPhone ());

which would produce the result

Maria Sanchez (407)716-2780

On the surface this seems to be a rather round about way of setting and getting values of the instance variables. If they were labelled **public** in the first place then the same output result could be obtained by the statement

c.println (person.name + " " + person.phone);

This however is out of the spirit of object-oriented programming since one of the main points is to protect instance variables from being interfered with by other objects in any way except by the methods of the class.

Frequently the *set* and *get* methods check to see that what is being done is appropriate. In the *PhoneRecord* class there is no checking going on.

As well as *set* and *get* methods a class that is used for records can have other methods, for example, to read or write the record.

11.2 Arrays of Records

We can combine the *PhoneRecord* structured data type with the structured type **array** and have an array of such records. To declare an array of phone records for a list of 50 friends we would use

   PhoneRecord friend [] = **new** *PhoneRecord* [50];

The phone number of the 6th friend in the array could be output by the statement

   c.println (friend [5].*getPhone* ());

One of the most important operations on an array of records is to search for a particular record.

Searching an array of records for a particular record is very similar to searching related arrays. One of the fields of the record is designated as the **key**. The other field or fields can be retrieved once the index for the record, whose key field matches the key value for the record being sought, is found. If the key values of the array of records are not in sorted order, a **sequential search** must be done. If they are sorted, the much more efficient **binary search** may be used; so it is important to be able to sort arrays of records.

One advantage of the record object is that an entire record can be moved (copied) from one memory location to another. Many sorting methods involve swapping two records in the array.

Here is a method for swapping the record with index *i* with the record with index *j* in an array *list* whose records are objects of *PhoneRecord* class. (This method assumes that the *PhoneRecord* has already been defined.)

```
// Method to swap i and jth record in list.
public void swap (PhoneRecord list [], int i, int j)
{
    PhoneRecord temp = list [i];
    list [i] = list [j];
    list [j] = temp;
} // swap method
```

As an example of an array of records we will look at a class called *CardDeck* that has methods to generate and shuffle a deck of playing cards, as well as to print the deck.

There are 52 cards in the deck consisting of equal numbers of 4 suits: spades, hearts, diamonds, and clubs which we will represent by their first letters "S", "H", "D", and "C". In each suit there are 13 cards: namely a 2, 3, 4, 5, 6, 7, 8, 9, 10, Jack, Queen, King, and Ace. To the face cards: Jack, Queen, King, and Ace we assign the values 11, 12, 13, and 14. Each card can be represented by a record with two fields; one for the suit and one for the value. Here is the definition for the class *CardType*. We will not define any *set* methods as the deck of cards will not be changed once it is instantiated.

```
// The "CardType" class.
public class CardType
{
    protected int value;
    protected String suit;

    // Constructor.
    public CardType (int value, String suit)
    {
        this.value = value;
        this.suit = suit;
    } // CardType constructor

    // Method to get suit of card.
    public String getSuit ()
    {
        return suit;
    } // suitMethod
```

```
      // Method to get value of card.
      public int getValue ()
      {
          return value;
      } // getValue method
} /* CardType class */
```

The deck of cards will be represented by the class *CardDeck*.

```
// The "CardDeck" class.
import hsa.Console;

public class CardDeck
{
    final int CARDS_IN_DECK = 52;
    final int NUMBER_OF_SUITS = 4;
    final int CARDS_IN_SUIT = 13;
    final String [] suit = {"S", "H", "D", "C"};
    CardType [] deck = new CardType [CARDS_IN_DECK + 1];

    // Constructor for deck.
    public CardDeck ()
    {
        int card = 1;   // Note: deck [0] not used.
        for (int whichSuit = 0 ; whichSuit < NUMBER_OF_SUITS ;
            whichSuit++)
        {
            for (int whichValue = 2 ; whichValue <= 14 ; whichValue++)
            {
                deck [card] = new CardType (whichValue, suit [whichSuit]);
                card++;
            }

        }
    } // CardDeck constructor

    // Method to print deck.
    public void printDeck (Console c)
    {
        for (int card = 1 ; card <= CARDS_IN_DECK ; card++)
```

```
        {
            c.println (deck [card].getSuit () + " " +
                deck [card].getValue ());
        }
    } // printDeck method

    // Method to shuffle deck.
    public void shuffleDeck ()
    {
        for (int whichCard = 1 ; whichCard <= CARDS_IN_DECK ;
            whichCard++)
        {
            // Generate random integer between 1 and CARDS_IN_DECK.
            int where = (int) (Math.random () * CARDS_IN_DECK) + 1;
            swap (whichCard, where);
        }
    } // shuffleDeck method

    // Method to swap ith and jth card.
    protected void swap (int i, int j)
    {
        CardType temp = deck [i];
        deck [i] = deck [j];
        deck [j] = temp;
    } // swap method
} /* CardDeck class */
```

Here is a driver program to test the class *cardDeck*.

```
// The "CardDeckTest" class.
import java.awt.*;
import hsa.Console;

public class CardDeckTest
{
    static public void main (String [] args)
    {
        Console c = new Console ();
        CardDeck deck = new CardDeck ();
        deck.printDeck (c);
```

```
            deck.shuffleDeck ();
            deck.printDeck (c);
        } // main method
    } /* CardDeckTest class */
```

The deck as it is first constructed is sorted like a freshly-opened deck of cards, with the suits in order from spades to clubs and within each suit the values in order from 2, 3 ... to King, and Ace. Here is the algorithm used to shuffle the deck in the *shuffleDeck* method.

For each card in deck in turn:

• generate a random number between 1 and *CARDS_IN_DECK*, and

• swap the card with the card that the random number locates.

Two-Dimensional Arrays of Records

A two-dimensional array of records can be used to deal four hands of 13 cards each suitable for a game of bridge. The class *CardDeck* will be extended to deal hands and list the hands. The class will be called *PlayBridge*.

```
// The "PlayBridge" class.
import hsa.Console;

public class PlayBridge extends CardDeck
{
    // Additional constants and variables.
    final int NUMBER_OF_HANDS = 4;
    final int CARDS_IN_HAND = 13;
    CardType hand [] [] = new CardType [NUMBER_OF_HANDS + 1]
        [CARDS_IN_HAND + 1];

    // Constructor.
    public PlayBridge ()
    {
        // Calls constructor of CardDeck to generate deck.
```

```
        super ();
    } // PlayBridge constructor

    // Method for dealing hands from deck.
    public void dealHands ()
    {
        // Deal one card to each hand in turn repeatedly.
        int card = 1;
        for (int cardCount = 1 ; cardCount <= CARDS_IN_HAND ;
            cardCount++)
        {
            for (int handCount = 1 ; handCount <= NUMBER_OF_HANDS ;
                handCount++)
            {
                hand [handCount] [cardCount] = deck [card];
                // Move to deal next card.
                card++;
            }
        }
    } // dealHands method

    // Method for listing hands.
    public void listHands (Console c)
    {
        // Hands are listed one card to a line unsorted.
        for (int whichHand = 1 ; whichHand <= NUMBER_OF_HANDS ;
            whichHand++)
        {
            c.println ("Here are the cards for hand " + whichHand);
            for (int whichCard = 1 ; whichCard <= CARDS_IN_HAND ;
                whichCard++)
            {
                c.println (hand [whichHand] [whichCard].suit + hand
                    [whichHand] [whichCard].value);
            }
        }
    } // listHands method
} /* PlayBridge class */
```

Here is a test program to see the result of shuffling and dealing a deck.

```
// The "PlayBridgeTest" class.
import hsa.Console;

public class PlayBridgeTest
{
    static public void main (String args [])
    {
        Console c = new Console ();
        PlayBridge deck = new PlayBridge ();
        deck.shuffleDeck ();
        deck.dealHands ();
        deck.listHands (c);
    } // main method
} /* PlayBridgeTest class */
```

11.3 Storing Records in Binary Files

Arrays of records are often stored in a file to save them from one use to another. The records must be stored or retrieved field-by-field. One way to store these is in the form of a text file. To do this each field is stored by a *println* statement and retrieved by a *readLine* statement. Storing data in text files was discussed in Chapter 4.

Records stored in text form must be read **sequentially**. A more common and useful form of storage of records is in **binary form**. This permits the user to access any one record as easily as any other; it permits **random access** to the records. In text form records take up different amounts of space, and require different numbers of bytes to store them since, for example in phone records, some names are longer than others.

In binary form all records are of equal length, that is, they require the same number of bytes. This means that the position of the beginning of the fourth record in the file will be at a point that is three times the length of a single record in bytes.

To achieve a fixed record length, all *String* fields must be stored as character arrays of fixed length. For example, in a phone record the phone number requires 13 characters. This is stored as 26 bytes. In Java, each character is represented in Unicode by two bytes. Java uses Unicode representation so that characters from all languages can be represented.

As an example of storing records in binary form we will look at the storage of student records. For each student we will store a name, address, year, and average mark. This will illustrate how integers and real numbers are handled as well as strings. Here is the definition of the class *StudentRecord*.

```
// The "StudentRecord" class.
import java.io.*;

public class StudentRecord
{
    protected static final int MAX_NAME_SIZE = 30;
    protected static final int MAX_ADDR_SIZE = 40;
    protected static final int RECORD_SIZE = 160;

    protected String name;       // Allow MAX_NAME_SIZE chars.
    protected String address;    // Allow MAX_ADDR_SIZE chars.
    protected int year;          // Needs 4 bytes.
    protected double average;    // Needs 8 bytes.
    // RECORD_SIZE = 4 [size of name's length] + 60 [size of name] +
    //          4 [size of address' length] + 80 [size of address] +
    //          4 [size of year] + 8 [size of average] = 160

    // Constructor reads record from file.
    public StudentRecord (RandomAccessFile input) throws IOException
    {
        // Read in the name. Read in the number of characters in the
        // name, the array of chars and convert the array into a String.
        int nameSize = input.readInt ();
        char [] nameChars = new char [MAX_NAME_SIZE];
        for (int i = 0 ; i < MAX_NAME_SIZE ; i++)
            nameChars [i] = input.readChar ();
        name = new String (nameChars, 0, nameSize);
```

```
// Read in the address. Read in the number of characters in the
// address, the array of chars and convert the array into a String.
int addressSize = input.readInt ();
char [] addressChars = new char [MAX_ADDR_SIZE];
for (int i = 0 ; i < MAX_ADDR_SIZE ; i++)
    addressChars [i] = input.readChar ();
address = new String (addressChars, 0, addressSize);

// Read in the year and average.
year = input.readInt ();
average = input.readDouble ();
} // StudentRecord constructor

// Constructor uses data from keyboard.
public StudentRecord (String name, String address, int year,
    double average)
{
    this.name = name;
    this.address = address;
    this.year = year;
    this.average = average;
} // StudentRecord constructor

// Method to get address.
public String getAddress ()
{
    return address;
} // getAddress method

// Method to get average.
public double getAverage ()
{
    return average;
} // getAverage method

// Method to get year.
public int getYear ()
{
    return year;
} // getYear method
```

```
    // Method to get record size.
    public static int recordSize ()
    {
        return RECORD_SIZE;
    } // recordSize method

    // Method to write a record to file.
    public void write (RandomAccessFile output) throws IOException
    {
        // Write out the name. Write out the number of characters in the
        // name, convert the String into an array, and write out the array
        // of chars.
        int nameSize = Math.min (name.length (), MAX_NAME_SIZE);
        output.writeInt (nameSize);
        char [] nameChars = new char [MAX_NAME_SIZE];
        name.getChars (0, nameSize, nameChars, 0);
        for (int i = 0 ; i < MAX_NAME_SIZE ; i++)
            output.writeChar (nameChars [i]);

        // Write out the address. Write out the number of characters in
        // the address, convert the String into an array, and write out the
        // array of chars.
        int addressSize = Math.min (address.length (), MAX_ADDR_SIZE);
        output.writeInt (addressSize);
        char [] addressChars = new char [MAX_ADDR_SIZE];
        address.getChars (0, addressSize, addressChars, 0);
        for (int i = 0 ; i < MAX_ADDR_SIZE ; i++)
            output.writeChar (addressChars [i]);

        // Write out the year and average.
        output.writeInt (year);
        output.writeDouble (average);
    } // write method
} /* StudentRecord class */
```

The *StudentRecord* class has a method for constructing a record by reading from the file and a method for writing a record to the file. For the name, an array of chars called *nameChars* is set up of length 30. In the *read* of the constructor, the size of the name (in characters) is read and then 30 characters are read from the file and stored in *nameChars*. The *nameChars* array is then converted to a *String* and stored in *name*. The constructor

  String (*nameChars*, 0, *nameSize*)

assigns the first *nameSize* characters of the *nameChars* array to the String.

In the *write* method of *StudentRecord*, the size of the name is set with a maximum length of 30. The *String* class method *getChars* copies the characters of the string into a char array starting at the character in position 0 (the first argument of *getChars*). The second argument is the position just past the last character (given by *nameSize*). The third argument gives the name of the character array starting at 0 (the fourth argument). Each character is in Unicode and takes two bytes.

For binary files, the primitive data types are written by *writeInt* (), *writeDouble* (), *writeBoolean* (), and so on. They are read by *readInt* (), *readDouble* (), *readBoolean* (), and so on.

The size of the *StudentRecord* is 160 bytes: 4 for the size of the name, 60 for the name, 4 for the size of the address, 80 for the address, 4 for the year, and 8 for the average. This is available from the *recordSize* method of the *StudentRecord* class.

A binary file called "school" is opened for reading and writing by a statement of the form

  RandomAccessFile schoolFile = **new** *RandomAccessFile* ("school", "rw");

If the file is just for reading use "r". To position the file for reading or writing the *seek* method is used. The form for reading or writing records called *student* of *StudentRecord* class is

  schoolFile.seek ((**long**) *recordNumber* * *student.recordSize* ());

The *seek* method requires a **long** argument and sets the file position. The file position is the number of bytes from the beginning of the file, the zero position. The *recordNumber* must start at record zero.

At any stage the file position can be determined by the function-type method *getFilePointer* (), which is a method of the *RandomAccessFile* class.

11.4 Example of Using a Binary File

We will now examine a program that reads in student records of the class *StudentRecord* and stores them in a file in binary form called "school". As each record is stored its whereabouts are recorded in an array called *directory*. This is an array of records of the class called *WhereAbouts*.

```java
// The "WhereAbouts" class.
public class WhereAbouts
{
    // This is the directory record.
    protected String name;
    protected int where;    // Location in file.

    // Constructor.
    public WhereAbouts (String name, int where)
    {
        this.name = name;
        this.where = where;
    } // WhereAbouts constructor

    // Method to find file location of name from directory.
    public int getLocationIfMatch (String name)
    {
        if (name.equals (this.name))
        {
            return where;
        }
        else
        {
            return - 1;
        }
    } // getLocationIfMatch method
} /* WhereAbouts class */
```

Here is the *Students* class application program to read student records from the keyboard, store them in the binary file "school", and prepare a directory entry for each. The program allows the user to look up individual records randomly.

```java
// The "Students" class.
import java.io.*;
import hsa.Console;

public class Students
{
    static int recordNumber = 0;
    static WhereAbouts directory [] = new WhereAbouts [100];

    public static int find (String name)
    {
        int count = 0;
        int location = -1;
        while (count < recordNumber && location == -1)
        {
            location = directory [count].getLocationIfMatch (name);
            count++;
        }
        return location;
    } // find method

    // Main method to find name in directory.
    public static void main (String args []) throws IOException
    {
        Console c = new Console ();
        String choice;
        String name, address;
        int year;
        double average;
        // Open school file to read and write.
        RandomAccessFile schoolFile =
            new RandomAccessFile ("school", "rw");
        StudentRecord student;
        while (true)
        {
            c.println ("Enter");
            c.println (" e to enter a new record");
            c.println (" f to find student information");
```

```
                    c.println (" q to quit");
                    c.print ("Choice: ");
                    choice = c.readLine ();
                    if (choice.equals ("e"))
                    {
                        c.print ("Enter name: ");
                        name = c.readLine ();
                        c.print ("Enter address: ");
                        address = c.readLine ();
                        c.print ("Enter year: ");
                        year = c.readInt ();
                        c.print ("Enter average: ");
                        average = c.readDouble ();
                        student = new StudentRecord (name, address, year, average);
                        // Set the file position to the end of file.
                        schoolFile.seek ((long) recordNumber *
                            StudentRecord.recordSize ());
                        // Store record in file.
                        student.write (schoolFile);
                        directory [recordNumber] =
                            new WhereAbouts (name, recordNumber);
                        recordNumber++;
                    }
                    else if (choice.equals ("f"))
                    {
                        c.println ("Enter the name of the student: ");
                        name = c.readLine ();
                        int location = find (name);
                        if (location == -1)
                        {
                            c.println (name + " not found");
                        }
                        else
                        {
                            schoolFile.seek ((long) location *
                                StudentRecord.recordSize ());
                            student = new StudentRecord (schoolFile);
                            c.println ("Name = " + name);
                            c.println ("Address = " + student.getAddress ());
                            c.println ("Year = " + student.getYear ());
                            c.println ("Average = " + student.getAverage ());
                        }
```

```
            }
        else if (choice.equals ("q"))
            {
                break;
            }
        }
    } // main method
} /* Students class */
```

If the directory list is to be kept sorted so that a binary search is possible, as insertions occur they must be placed in their proper place in the directory. Maintaining a sorted list with insertions and deletions is described in the next chapter.

11.5   Records with Alternative Sets of Fields

Often it is required that a file be maintained in which records do not all have the same set of fields. For example, a file might be required to store information by the motor vehicle department for licensing purposes. Each record would have common fields, for example, license plate, name, and address, but there might be three different record types: one for passenger vehicles, one for commercial vehicles, and one for recreational vehicles.

A class would be set up called *Vehicle* with the common fields, then the three classes *Passenger*, *Commercial*, and *Recreational* would be defined as extending the *Vehicle* class.

Each would have its own additional fields. If a binary file is to be kept of the different vehicle types the record size must be the number of bytes required to store the longest of the three types.

If an array of such records were maintained in memory called *vehicle* it would be defined by

Vehicle vehicles [] = **new** Vehicle [100];

Any *Vehicle* class record can be tested to see which type it belongs to using the comparison operator **instanceof**. For example, we could test the *i*th record of the *vehicles* array to see if it is for a passenger vehicle by the statement

```
if (vehicle [i] instanceOf Passenger)
{
     Passenger p = (Passenger) vehicles [i];
     p.setMake ("GM");
     p.setColor (Color.green);
          and so on
}
```

In this the methods *setMake* and *setColor* belong to the *Passenger* class. This is an example of **polymorphism**, the inclusion of a number of different forms of the base class *Vehicle*. In other programming languages this problem is solved by having **variant records**.

11.6 Chapter Summary

Records as Objects

In Java objects are the natural way to represent records; the instance variables are the **fields** of the record. Since in object-oriented programming direct access to the instance variables by other objects is not desired, the record object must contain *set* and *get* methods to permit the user to manipulated the variables.

The *set* and *get* methods should, in principle, provide protection against improper interference.

As well, the class that is used to instantiate records could contain other methods such as those to read and write records to files.

Array of Records

An array of records is essentially an array of objects. If the array is to be used for the retrieval of information then one field is designated as the key field. If the array is arranged so that the key fields are in random order then a linear search is needed to locate the record with the required key.

If the array is in sorted order according to the key fields the much more efficient binary search can be used. This means that for efficiency arrays of records should be kept in sorted order. Most sorting algorithms require the movement of records from one place in the array to another, an operation that is very simple since the records are objects and are passed by reference.

Example of Using Records

As an example of using records in both one and two dimensional arrays a program was developed to shuffle and deal a deck of cards into hands suitable for the game of bridge. A *CardType* class represented the individual cards. A class called *CardDeck* represented an array of 52 of such records. Methods were included in *CardDeck* to initialize the deck, shuffle the cards, and output the card records in the deck.

A class called *PlayBridge* extended the *CardDeck* class defining additional constants and instance variables to represent four bridge hands of 13 cards each. The hands were represented by a two-dimensional array of card records. The *PlayBridge* class had methods for dealing the hands from the deck and listing the contents of each hand.

Storing Records in Binary Files

Records written as text files field-by-field must be accessed sequentially. Records written in binary form can be accessed randomly, as well as sequentially. In binary form all records must be the same length so individual records can be replaced in the file. Fields that are of primitive data types require a fixed number of bytes given by the data type. Strings can be of various lengths but must be stored as a fixed number of characters. This size must be determined for each string field.

Reading of strings is by a fixed number of bytes using the *readFully* method of the *RandomAccessFile* class. Writing strings to files uses the *getBytes* method of the *RandomAccessFile* class. Primitive data types are read by *readInt* (), *readDouble* (), *readBoolean* (), and so on. They are written by the corresponding *writeInt*, *writeDouble*, *writeBoolean*, and so on.

To open a binary file of class *RandomAccessFile* called *file* for reading and writing we use

RandomAccessFile file = **new** *RandomAccessFile* ("file name", "rw");

where "file name" is the external name of the file and is placed in quotes.

Searching a Random Access File

The file position of an individual record in a random access binary file is its record index multiplied by the length of each record. The file position must be given as a **long** integer. To position the reading or writing pointer at the beginning of a record in *file* at *filePosition* the statement is

file.seek ((**long**) *filePosition*);

To find the file position of the pointer at any time the *getFilePointer* () method of the *RandomAccessFile* class is used.

Records with Alternative Sets of Fields

If a single file is kept of records that have variations in the fields that they require then a base record class is defined and variant classes created as extensions of the base class.

The common fields are instance variables in the base class and the variations are fields in the extended class or classes. Such records all belong to the base class and can be manipulated in an array or file as objects of this same class. To determine their particular or actual class the comparison operator **instanceof** is used.

11.7 Exercises

1. A *StudentRecords* class is to be defined with these instance variables definition

String name; // Allow 40 characters.
int *mark* [] = **new int** [4];
double *average*;

Create an array of 26 such records and initialize them with simulated data giving names A, B, C, D and so on to the students. Fill in marks for each records as random numbers between 0 and 100. Give all the averages a temporary value of −1. Store the array as a file in binary form.

2. Read the binary file created in Exercise 1, computing the average mark for the student and recording it in *average*. Read each record, process it, and return it as an updated record to the binary file.

   At the same time compute the class average for each of the four subjects and the overall average mark outputting them in a summary.

3. Devise a program so that individual students could request information from the file with the proper averages. Be sure to have a directory created.

4. Modify the *find* method used in the *Students* class of this chapter to use the binary method of search on the file created in Exercise 2 which is possible since the records will be sorted by name, that is, A first, B second, and so on.

5. In the game of bridge the high-card point value of a hand can be calculated by assigning a 4 to an ace, 3 to a king, 2 to a queen, and 1 to a jack. Extend the *PlayBridge* class so that the number of points of each hand is displayed along with the hand itself.

6. In a bridge game players are in pairs that cooperate with each other: player 1 is a partner of player 3, player 2 is a partner of player 4. If a team has 25 high-card points between them they can score a "game in one hand". Write a program that counts the number of times each of the two teams of players could get a game in one hand in a fixed number of deals. What is the percentage of the deals that produces a "game in one hand" situation. Try dealing 10 hands to begin, then try dealing 100 hands.

Chapter 12

Algorithms for Sorting Lists

In the last chapter we examined the record data type. Records are convenient data structures for keeping lists of data where several items of information are to be kept together. In many situations a list must be kept up-to-date; it must be maintained. New items are added, items are changed, and items are deleted. The purpose of keeping this list is to be able to retrieve information.

The binary search technique is vastly superior to the linear (or sequential) search for a large sized list. To obtain this efficiency, the list must be maintained in sorted order. In this chapter we will examine algorithms for sorting an unsorted list.

12.1 What is Sorting?

For a list such as a list of names to be sorted, the values in the list must be placed in ascending (non-decreasing) or descending (non-increasing) order. Most often lists are sorted in ascending (non-decreasing) order. For example, the names in a telephone book are sorted this way. We say non-decreasing because names could be identical. When sorting is complete the final list must be a rearrangement of the original list. It must be a **permutation** of the original values.

If a list to be sorted contains composites, like records that contain several data components, then one field is designated as the **key** to the sorting. The list is sorted in ascending or descending values of the key field.

There are a large number of different basic methods for sorting lists and these vary widely in their efficiencies. In this chapter we will examine a number of the best known sorting algorithms and compare their **time complexities**. For shorter lists, all methods are about equal in efficiency. For long lists the difference can be striking.

Before we begin looking at specific algorithms we will examine two fundamental manipulations called **swapping** and **shifting** which are the basis of many different kinds of sorts.

Many of the simple methods of sorting involve repeatedly exchanging two values in the list. This is called swapping.

Here is a useful method which swaps elements in a list of string values such as a list of names. We will be incorporating this method into a class that has the size of the list *listSize* and the declaration of *list* as an array of strings as instance variables.

```
// Method to swap the ith and jth elements of list of strings.
protected void swap (int i, int j)
{
    String temp = list [i];
    list [i]= list [j];
    list [j] = temp;
} // swap method
```

The *swap* action is shown in Figure 12.1.

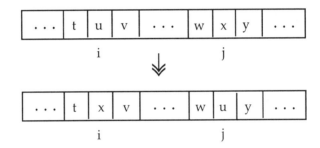

Figure 12.1 The Swap Operation

Shifting is another useful operation for sorting arrays. In a shift operation the *j*th item in the list is moved to the *i*th position (where $i < j$) and the *i+1*th to *j*th items each moved one position to the right. The list here is written horizontally with the smallest values of the array index on the left.

Figure 12.2 shows the *shift* action.

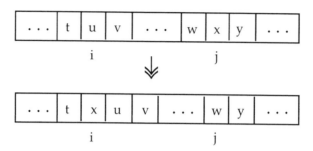

Fig. 12.2 The Shift Operation

Here is a method for shifting. Again it is to be part of a class that has *list* declared.

```
// Method for shifting.
protected void shift (int i, int j)
{
    String temp = list [j];
    for (int k = j; k < i; k --)
    {
        list [k] = list [k – 1];
    }
    list [i] = temp;
} // shift method
```

The *swap* and *shift* methods will be used in a number of algorithms.

These two methods, along with two others called *fakeData* and *printList*, are going to be incorporated into an abstract class called *Sort* which can be extended to use the various sorting algorithms. The reason the class is abstract, and therefore cannot be instantiated, is that it has a method called *sort* that has no body. When *Sort* is extended the *sort* method will be overridden by the actual sorting algorithm being implemented. We will have a different *sort* method for each algorithm. Each one of the sorting classes will be an extension of the abstract class *Sort*.

Here is the *Sort* class.

```
// The "Sort" class.
import hsa.Console;

public abstract class Sort
{
    Console c;
    int listSize;
    String list [];

    // Constructor.
    public Sort (Console c, int listSize)
    {
        this.c = c;
        list = new String [listSize + 1];
        this.listSize = listSize;
        fakeData ();
    } // Sort constructor

    // Method to generate simulated data.
    protected void fakeData ()
    {
        for (int i = 1 ; i <= listSize ; i++)
        {
            String alphabet = "abcdefghijklmnopqrstuvwxyz";
            StringBuffer temp = new StringBuffer ();
            for (int letter = 0 ; letter < 4 ; letter++)
            {
                // Generate a random integer between 0 and 25.
                int where = (int) (Math.random () * 26);
                temp.append (alphabet.charAt (where));
            }
            list [i] = temp.toString ();
        }
    } // fakeData method

    // Method to output list of strings.
    public void printList ()
    {
        for (int i = 1 ; i <= listSize ; i++)
        {
```

```
            c.print (list [i] + " ");
        }
        c.println ("");
    } // printList method

    // Method to shift elements in list.
    protected void shift (int i, int j)
    {
        String temp = list [j];
        for (int k = j ; k >= i + 1 ; k--)
        {
            list [k] = list [k – 1];
        }
        list [i] = temp;
    } // shift method

    // Abstract method to sort list.
    public abstract void sort ();
    // Method to swap the ith and jth elements of list of strings.
    public void swap (int i, int j)
    {
        String temp = list [i];
        list [i] = list [j];
        list [j] = temp;
    } // swap method
} /* Sort class */
```

Notice that the *Sort* class is labelled as **abstract**, as is the method *sort* which has no body. The instance variables *c*, *listSize*, and *list* are declared, and in the constructor the *listSize* is provided. We will not be using the array element *list* [0] so that the *list* must be stored in an array of length *listSize* + 1. The constructor calls on the **protected** method *fakeData* to compile an array of random four-letter words. The method *printList* can be used to output the elements in *list* from *list* [1] to *list* [*listSize*]. We are now ready to look at the different sorting algorithms.

12.2 Insertion Sort

Insertion sorting is an algorithm which might be used, for example, to sort the cards of a bridge hand as they are picked up one by one. In this method there is a sorted part (the cards already picked up) and an unsorted part (the cards still on the table). As each card is picked up and inserted in its proper position in the hand, the sorted part gets longer and the unsorted part shorter.

Figure 12.3 shows a sequence of four steps (*a*, *b*, *c*, and *d*) in this sorting method. Step *a* shows the two parts of the list at any stage: the part that is sorted and the part still unsorted. In step *b* the first value *u* of the unsorted sequence is examined. In step *c* the position where this value should be inserted is found in the sorted sequence; this is the position that contains *v*, the smallest value larger than *u* in the sorted sequence. The value *u* is inserted ahead of *v*, making the sorted sequence longer by one entry, as shown in *d*. This is accomplished by shifting all elements from *v* to the end of the list to the right thus leaving the space for *u*.

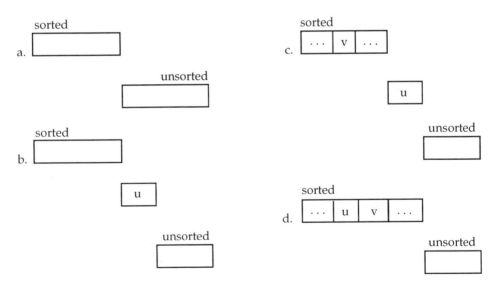

Figure 12.3 Insertion Sorting

If all the items are to be kept in a single array, the boundary between the sorted and the unsorted items must be identified. The

sorting is done by moving the element at the boundary in the
unsorted part into its proper place in the sorted part.

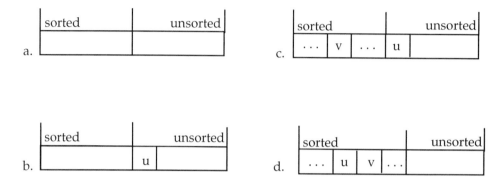

Figure 12.4 Insertion of Next Element

Figure 12.4 shows the moves that are made as *u* is inserted.
Notice that when the insertion is made, a shift operation occurs so
the *shift* method can be used.

The insertion sorting algorithm will be placed in a class called
InsertSort which extends the *Sort* class, providing a *sort* method to
override the abstract *sort* method of *Sort*. A driver program of the
InsertSortTest class instantiates an object *sortList* of the class
InsertSort with a *listSize* of 10 and calls the *sort* method of *InsertSort*.
It prints the list before and after sorting using the *printList* method
of *InsertSort*.

Here is the *InsertSortTest* class.

```
// The "InsertSortTest" class.
import java.awt.*;
import hsa.Console;

public class InsertSortTest
{
    static public void main (String args [])
    {
        Console c = new Console ();
        InsertSort sortList = new InsertSort (c, 10);
```

```
        sortList.printList ();
        sortList.sort ();
        sortList.printList ();
    } // main method
} /* InsertSortTest */
```

In the *sort* method itself there are *print* statements that output the values of *i* and *j* and the current elements of *list* at each stage of sorting.

In the constructor of *InsertSort* the constructor of *Sort* is invoked by the keyword **super**.

Here is a listing of the *InsertSort* class.

```
// The "InsertSort" class.
import java.awt.*;
import hsa.Console;

public class InsertSort extends Sort
{
    // Constructor.
    public InsertSort (Console c, int listSize)
    {
        super (c, listSize);
    } // InsertSort constructor

    //Method to sort list of strings by insertion.
    public void sort ()
    {
        for (int j = 2 ; j <= listSize ; j++)
        {
            // Find where to insert jth element.
            int i = 1;
            while (i != j && list [i].compareTo (list [j]) < 0)
            {
                i++;
            }
            shift (i, j);
            // Temporary statements to trace execution.
            c.print (i, 3);
            c.print (j, 3);
```

```
        c.print (" ");
        printList ();
    }
  } // sort method
} /* InsertSort */
```

Here is a typical output from running the driver program.

```
ppnq rbzh bvkf bdpi zzbg jksg ekfi ykav xkfa bsbp
 2  2 ppnq rbzh bvkf bdpi zzbg jksg ekfi ykav xkfa bsbp
 3  1 bvkf ppnq rbzh bdpi zzbg jksg ekfi ykav xkfa bsbp
 4  1 bdpi bvkf ppnq rbzh zzbg jksg ekfi ykav xkfa bsbp
 5  5 bdpi bvkf ppnq rbzh zzbg jksg ekfi ykav xkfa bsbp
 6  3 bdpi bvkf jksg ppnq rbzh zzbg ekfi ykav xkfa bsbp
 7  3 bdpi bvkf ekfi jksg ppnq rbzh zzbg ykav xkfa bsbp
 8  7 bdpi bvkf ekfi jksg ppnq rbzh ykav zzbg xkfa bsbp
 9  7 bdpi bvkf ekfi jksg ppnq rbzh xkfa ykav zzbg bsbp
10  2 bdpi bsbp bvkf ekfi jksg ppnq rbzh xkfa ykav zzbg
bdpi bsbp bvkf ekfi jksg ppnq rbzh xkfa ykav zzbg
```

One line of output is produced as each value is inserted into the sorted part of the list. The first two entries on the line give the number of values now sorted and the position to which the inserted value has been moved. The next entries show the list with this item inserted. By examining the output, it is possible to see how the process progresses. At each line the sorted part of the list becomes one element longer until, in the last line, the entire list is sorted.

12.3 Selection Sort

The **selection sort** is a sorting algorithm where each item in the list is examined to find the item that should be first. For a list of numbers this would be the smallest. For strings, it would be the alphabetically least. When the smallest item is found it is moved to the beginning of the list. Then the list from the 2nd entry to the last is examined to select the smallest (least) item, which is then moved to the second position. As before, the part of the list that is sorted grows and the part that is still unsorted shrinks. The smallest item just selected is swapped with the first item in the unsorted part of the list.

Figure 12.5 shows how the process proceeds.

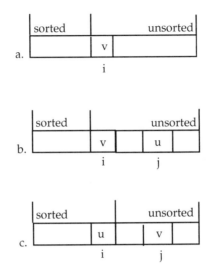

Figure 12.5 Selection Sorting

The first item v in the unsorted part is in position i. The first $i - 1$ values are sorted. The smallest value u of the unsorted part is in position *locationOfSmallest*. The items in position i and *locationOfSmallest* are then swapped.

Here is the class *SelectSort* that extends the *Sort* class and provides the *sort* method incorporating the selection method.

A driver program for this sort algorithm is the same as *InsertSortTest* except that the *sortList* object is instantiated from the *SelectSort* class. The driver is called *SelectSortTest*.

Here is the *SelectSort* class.

```
// The "SelectSort" class.
import java.awt.*;
import hsa.Console;

public class SelectSort extends Sort
{
    // Constructor.
    public SelectSort (Console c, int listSize)
```

```
{
    super (c, listSize);
} // SelectSort constructor

// Method to sort list of strings by selection.
public void sort ()
{
    for (int i = 1 ; i <= listSize ; i++)
    {
        // Select smallest element.
        int whereSmall = i;
        for (int j = i + 1 ; j <= listSize ; j++)
        {
            if (list [j].compareTo (list [whereSmall]) < 0)
            {
                whereSmall = j;
            }
        }
        swap (i, whereSmall);
        // Temporary statements to trace execution.
        c.print (i, 3);
        c.print (whereSmall, 3);
        c.print (" ");
        printList ();
    }
} // sort method
} /* SelectSort class */
```

Execution of *SelectSortTest* might give these results.

```
nrbk favg jbgi jddo lezm efsl ngzl btfu xrot ejgb
  1  8 btfu favg jbgi jddo lezm efsl ngzl nrbk xrot ejgb
  2  6 btfu efsl jbgi jddo lezm favg ngzl nrbk xrot ejgb
  3 10 btfu efsl ejgb jddo lezm favg ngzl nrbk xrot jbgi
  4  6 btfu efsl ejgb favg lezm jddo ngzl nrbk xrot jbgi
  5 10 btfu efsl ejgb favg jbgi jddo ngzl nrbk xrot lezm
  6  6 btfu efsl ejgb favg jbgi jddo ngzl nrbk xrot lezm
  7 10 btfu efsl ejgb favg jbgi jddo lezm nrbk xrot ngzl
  8 10 btfu efsl ejgb favg jbgi jddo lezm ngzl xrot nrbk
  9 10 btfu efsl ejgb favg jbgi jddo lezm ngzl nrbk xrot
btfu efsl ejgb favg jbgi jddo lezm ngzl nrbk xrot
```

Here each line of the trace shows first how many values have been sorted, then the position from which the smallest was selected.

12.4 Bubble Sort

The next sorting algorithm we will examine is called **bubble sort**. The bubble sort algorithm works by swapping adjacent pairs in the list until all adjacent pairs are in order, at which time the entire list is sorted. It does this by making repeated **passes** through the array. The first pass compares element 1 to element 2 and swaps them if they are out of order, then compares element 2 to element 3 and swaps them if they are out of order, and so on.

In Figure 12.6, the original list to sort is (D, B, E, C, A). This is shown in the top left line of the figure. Eventually this list should be rearranged to be sorted as (A, B, C, D, E). This is shown in the bottom right line.

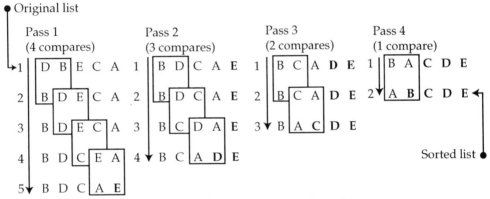

Each box does a compare, and possibly a swap.
Boldface items have reached their final positions.

Figure 12.6 Passes of a Bubble Sort

In this example the algorithm makes four passes through the array. These passes are represented by the downward pointing arrows. For a list of length n (5 in this example), there are $n - 1$ passes (4 in this example). Each pass moves from left to right across the list, comparing the two elements in each pair and swapping the elements if they are out of order.

Pass 1 begins in line 1, comparing the first pair of items, D and B. Since D and B are out of order, they are swapped, as shown in line 2. Next, the second pair, *D* and *E*, are compared in line 2. Since they are found to be in order, they are not swapped, as shown in line 3. Pass 1 continues in this way, comparing each pair, with swapping if necessary to put them into order.

At the completion of pass 1, the swapping will have caused the largest element (*E* in this example) to be moved into the right-most position of the list (see line 5). The next pass can then stop before inspecting the right-most position. Pass 2 is just like pass 1, scanning from left to right, swapping out-of-order pairs, but it stops before reaching the right-most position. Each successive pass is similar, but each stops one position earlier, until the final pass, pass 4 in this example, handles only the left-most pair.

The term **bubble sort** comes from the idea that large elements are moved (bubbled) to the right. If we visualize the list with the first element on the bottom and the last element on the top, we can think of the bubbles (the large elements) as drifting toward the top of the list.

Top Down Design of Bubble Sort

It is also possible to develop a bubble sort method using successive refinement. In successive refinement we move step-by-step from a statement of what we hope to accomplish (the specification of the problem) to the algorithm for doing it. The specification of the problem in English is step-by-step transformed into the algorithm in Java.

In Figure 12.7 the top node gives the informal specification for sorting the list.

The first refinement, from node 1 to node 2, creates a loop whose iterations implement the passes of bubble sort. This creates the new requirement to

Swap elements in *list* [1] .. [*last*] so largest is in *list* [*last*].

This problem is solved in the next node, node 3, by an inner loop that bubbles the largest element into *list* [*last*]. The next refinement, from node 3 to node 4, introduces an **if** statement that checks to see if a pair is in order.

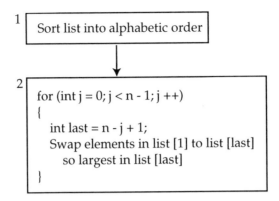

Figure 12.7 Successive Refinement for Bubble Sort

We require one final refinement, in node 4, to implement the swap of two array elements in Java, thereby completing all the refinements.

The class *BubbleSort* incorporates the *sort* which is a bubble sort. Again a driver program *BubbleSortTest* would be required.

```
// The "BubbleSort" class.
import java.awt.*;
import hsa.Console;

public class BubbleSort extends Sort
{
    // Constructor.
    public BubbleSort (Console c, int listSize)
    {
        super (c, listSize);
    } // BubbleSort constructor

    // Method to sort list of strings by bubble sort.
    public void sort ()
    {
        for (int j = 1 ; j < listSize ; j++)
        {
            int last = listSize − j + 1;
            // Swap elements in list 1 to last so largest is in list [last].
```

```
            for (int k = 1 ; k < last ; k++)
            {
                    // Swap pair (k, k + 1) if out of order.
                    if (list [k].compareTo (list [k + 1]) > 0)
                        swap (k, k + 1);
                    // Temporary statements to trace execution.
                    c.print (k, 3);
                    c.print (k + 1, 3);
                    c.print (" ");
                    printList ();
            }
    }
  } // sort method
} /* BubbleSort class */
```

A word of caution is in order regarding top down programming. In principle, a programmer starts with a specification and refines it, step-by-step, into a program. In actual practice, the programmer more often works partly top down and partly bottom up, with various detours along the way. Even though the program has not been developed in a top down order, it should be possible to give a top down description of its structure. This is possible because the parts of the program should each correspond to specifications given at a high level in the description.

Improving Bubble Sort

In the example of bubble sort provided in Figure 12.6, each pass swaps at least one pair. If, however, a pass does no swapping, it would indicate that all of the pairs are in order, which implies that the entire list is already in order. We can therefore improve the algorithm by adding a flag (a boolean variable) that keeps track of whether a pass has done any swaps. If it has not, the algorithm should terminate without doing any further passes.

This improvement is particularly important if the list to be sorted is "almost" in order. This would be the case if we had a previously-sorted list with a few new names added.

12.5 Running Time for Sorting Algorithms

Because sorting is an operation that is frequently required in processing data, it is important to have it performed as efficiently as possible. One way to determine efficiency is to compare the running time of various algorithms. We will do an analysis to show that the running time of the bubble sort algorithm depends on the square of the number of items being sorted.

Running Time for Bubble Sort

The analysis of the running time of bubble sort is significantly more complex than that for the sequential and binary searches in Chapter 10. This complexity arises because the bubble sort contains a loop within a loop. Figure 12.8 illustrates the structure of bubble sort.

The set up for each pass (box 1 in Figure 12.8) takes a fixed amount of time, which we will call k_8 microseconds. Since there are $n - 1$ passes, this part of the algorithm uses $k_8(n - 1)$ microseconds.

Similarly, the set up for the inner loop (box 2) takes a fixed amount of time (k_9 microseconds). This set up is done $n - 1$ times for the first pass, $n - 2$ times for the second pass, and so on down to 1 time for the final pass. The total time to execute this box is

$$k_9 \left((n - 1) + (n - 2) + \ldots + 2 + 1 \right) = \frac{k_9\, n\, (n - 1)}{2}$$

The sum of the first n integers is $n(n + 1)/2$. In this case, the first $n - 1$ integers are summed, so the sum is $n(n - 1)/2$. By a similar argument, the total time used by box 3 is $k_{10}\, n(n - 1)/2$.

The time spent in box 4 is not so clear because that box is entered only when a pair is out of order. The letter p stands for the fraction of inspected pairs that are found out of order and are actually swapped; p is at least 0 and at most 1. In the worst case, p is 1. The total time in box 4 is

$$p\, k_{11}\, n\, (n - 1)\, /\, 2$$

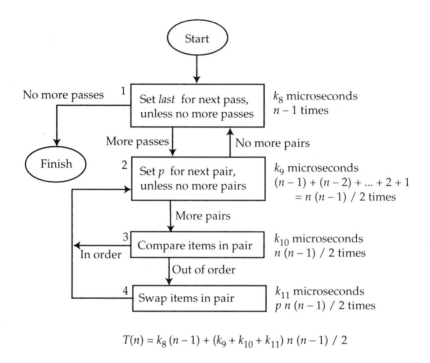

$$T(n) = k_8 (n - 1) + (k_9 + k_{10} + k_{11}) \, n \, (n - 1) / 2$$

Figure 12.8 Bubble Sort Timing

In the worst case, p is 1 and this becomes

$k_{11} \, n(n - 1) / 2$

Adding up the times for all the boxes produces

$$T(n) = k_8(n - 1) + (k_9 + k_{10} + p \, k_{11}) \, n \, (n - 1) / 2$$
$$= k_{12} \, n^2 + k_{13} \, n + k_{14}$$

Since constants and low-order terms are immaterial for big O notation

$T(n)$ is $O(n^2)$

Many simple sorting algorithms including insertion, selection, and bubble sort are $O(n^2)$. There are also many sorting algorithms that are $O(n \log n)$; these are much faster (for large n) than those that are $O(n^2)$. One of the simplest of the $O(n \log n)$ sorts is merge sort, which is presented next.

Running Time of Insert and Selection Sort

For insertions, the nested loop is executed at most $i - 1$ times, where i is the current value of the index of the **for** loop which goes from 2 to n. This means that the timing is proportional to

$$\sum_{i=2}^{n}(i-1)$$

which is the same as

$$\sum_{i=1}^{n-1}i$$

which we know is

$$\frac{n(n-1)}{2} = \frac{1}{2}n^2 - \frac{1}{2}n$$

Ignoring the lower order term, the expression is $O(n^2)$. The shift operation following the inner loop will take time proportional to the time of the body of the loop which will not change the big O result.

Selection can be shown to be $O(n^2)$ also.

12.6 Merge Sort

Merging is a process whereby two (or more) sorted lists are combined to produce a single sorted list. Suppose we have an array of strings arranged so that the items from *first* to *middle* are sorted in ascending order. The other half of the array from *middle* + 1 to *last* is similarly sorted.

The merging of these two halves requires a temporary storage array called *temp* that is large enough to hold both halves. There are three index variables: *point1* that points to successive elements of the first half, *point2* that points into the second half, and *point3* that points into the merged array that is formed in *temp*.

Here is a *merge* method that will be used in the *MergeSort* class.

```
public void merge (int first, int middle, int last)
{
    // List going from first to middle is sorted.
    // List going from middle + 1 to last is sorted.
    String temp [] = new String [last + 1];
    int point1 = first;
    int point2 = middle + 1;
    int point3 = first;
    while (point3 <= last)
    {
        // Point 3 locates item in merged list.
        if (point1 < middle + 1 && (point2 > last ||
                list [point1].compareTo (list [point2]) < 0))
        {
            temp [point3] = list [point1];
            point1++;
        }
        else
        {
            temp [point3] = list [point2];
            point2++;
        }
        point3++;
    }
    // Copy merged array back to original place.
    for (int i = first ; i <= last ; i++)
    {
        list [i] = temp [i];
    }
    // Temporary statements to trace execution.
    c.print (first, 3);
    c.print (last, 3);
    c.print (" ");
    printList ();
} // merge method
```

With a list of n strings divided into two sorted lists of $n/2$ strings each, the time to merge the two lists into a single sorted list is $O(n)$, since every comparison results in one item being placed in the sorted list.

Producing a completely sorted list using the merge sort also requires a method for sorting each half of a list of strings. In the case of a bubble sort, the time $T(n)$ to sort a list of n items is

$$T(n) = k'n(n-1)/2 = kn^2 - kn$$

The time to sort two lists of $n/2$ items each by the bubble sort would be

$$T(n) = 2\left[k\left(\frac{n}{2}\right)^2 - k\frac{n}{2} \right] = k\frac{n^2}{2} - kn$$

The total time for a hybrid method of sorting that consisted of:

- dividing the unsorted list of n items into two halves,
- sorting each half by the bubble sort, and
- merging the two sorted halves

would be

$$T(n) = k\frac{n^2}{2} - kn + jn$$

where jn is the time for the merging. The time complexity of both these methods: the straight bubble sort and the hybrid method, is $O(n^2)$ since the items in n can be neglected and the constants ignored. If the constants were maintained, the bubble sort would require time proportional to kn^2, whereas the hybrid sort would require time proportional to $kn^2/2$. The time would grow in the same way but the hybrid method takes half the time of the straight bubble sort.

It seems possible to improve the time to do a sort by dividing the list in two, sorting each half, and then merging the two sorted halves. If this is such a great method, why not use it as the method for sorting each half instead of using the bubble sort? Each half of the original list could be subdivided, these quarters in turn could be subdivided, and so on until only one item is left in each part. It would not be necessary to sort the parts because they contain only one element; they are sorted already, eliminating the need for the bubble sort, or any other method for that matter. And what is more, each subdivision of a part improves the efficiency over a straight bubble sort of that part.

An analysis of the time complexity of this new sorting method shows that it is

$$O(n \log n)$$

which is a great improvement over $O(n^2)$ for the bubble sort. To see that this is so, recall that the original list of n items is subdivided until each part contains only one item. This subdivision takes $\log_2 n$ stages. Merging must take place at each stage, as it progresses back to the single sorted list. At each stage there are n items merged, so that each stage (of the merging process) is $O(n)$. This means that the whole process of merging n items $\log_2 n$ times is $O(n \log_2 n)$.

Here is the method *mergeSort* that uses the *merge* method to sort the list.

```
// Recursive method that uses itself and the merge method to sort.
public void mergeSort (int first, int last)
{
    if (last > first)
    {
        int middle = (first + last) / 2;
        mergeSort (first, middle);
        mergeSort (middle + 1, last);
        merge (first, middle, last);
    }
} // mergeSort method
```

This method is a **recursive** method in that it calls itself. In the *sort* method, the call to *mergeSort* will give the value of *first* as 1 and *last* as *listSize*. Each time *mergeSort* is called, an activation record is set up containing the values of *first, last,* and *middle* for that particular call. If the *last* of list is the same as the *first* then the list contains only one element. No sorting is necessary and it returns from the method *mergeSort* to the method that called it, or to the *main* method when the whole list is sorted.

The stack of activation records for the recursive calls increases in size with each call to a method and shrinks when a method returns to its point of call. The depth of the activation record stack does not exceed $log_2 n$ at any time. Following what happens as the process proceeds is not a simple matter, but Java handles all of the growing and shrinking of the stack automatically so this need not concern the user.

The Nature of Recursion

The merge sort provides an excellent example of how recursion works in sorting. It is more efficient to sort two lists of half the size of the original then merge the two halves, than to sort the list as a whole. We use the same method to sort each half of the list: divide it in half and then merge the two halves. This subdivision continues until each half contains only one item. At this point there is no need for sorting and the process ends.

The nature of recursion is that it constantly moves, on each recursive call, to a smaller problem until the problem vanishes, as it does here, or it becomes very simple. This is the **base** (or **degenerate**) **case**, for which the answer is known.

The solutions to the subproblems are then combined to produce the solution to the problem itself.

To summarize, using a recursive approach requires:

- a way to make the problem smaller,
- a way of dealing with the base (or degenerate) case, and
- a way of building up the larger result from partial results.

These requirements are satisfied for the merge sort.

- The problem is made smaller by splitting the list in two.
- The base case is a list containing a single item, which is obviously sorted.
- The large result is produced by merging two smaller results.

Here is the class *MergeSort* that uses the recursive merge sort.

```
// The "MergeSort" class.
import hsa.Console;
```

```java
public class MergeSort extends Sort
{
    // Constructor.
    public MergeSort (Console c, int listSize)
    {
        super (c, listSize);
    } // MergeSort constructor

    public void merge (int first, int middle, int last)
    {
        // List going from first to middle is sorted.
        // List going from middle + 1 to last is sorted.
        String temp [] = new String [last + 1];
        int point1 = first;
        int point2 = middle + 1;
        int point3 = first;
        while (point3 <= last)
        {
            // Point 3 locates item in merged list.
            if (point1 < middle + 1 && (point2 > last ||
                        list [point1].compareTo (list [point2]) < 0))
            {
                temp [point3] = list [point1];
                point1++;
            }
            else
            {
                temp [point3] = list [point2];
                point2++;
            }
            point3++;
        }
        // Copy merged array back to original place.
        for (int i = first ; i <= last ; i++)
        {
            list [i] = temp [i];
        }
        // Temporary statements to trace execution.
        c.print (first, 3);
        c.print (last, 3);
        c.print (" ");
        printList ();
```

```
} // merge method

// Recursive method that uses itself and the merge method to sort.
public void mergeSort (int first, int last)
{
    if (last > first)
    {
        int middle = (first + last) / 2;
        mergeSort (first, middle);
        mergeSort (middle + 1, last);
        merge (first, middle, last);
    }
} // mergeSort method

// The sort method.
public void sort ()
{
    mergeSort (1, listSize);
} // sort method
} /* MergeSort class */
```

12.7 Quicksort

Another sorting algorithm that has a simple recursive form is the **Quicksort** algorithm. In this algorithm the list of items to be sorted is divided into two parts by choosing a **pivot** item. All entries less than the pivot are placed in the first part; those greater than the pivot are in the second part. The ideal would be to have the two parts of roughly equal length but it is hard to choose a pivot element to achieve this. For simplicity we will take as the pivot element the one in the middle of the list. First, the pivot is moved out of the way by swapping it with the first element in the list. A sweep is then made across the remainder of the list. When a value examined is larger than the pivot (that is, less than or equal to the pivot), it is swapped with the value just to the right of the boundary between the two sets of values. This makes the part containing values not larger than the pivot bigger by one element. Figure 12.9 illustrates the behavior of the algorithm.

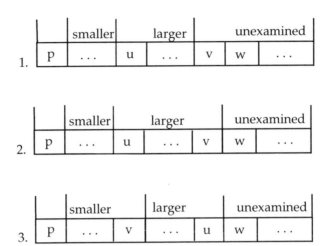

Figure 12.9 Quicksort Algorithm

In part 1 the first element v of the unexamined part is examined. If it is larger than the pivot value p, it is left where it is, as shown in part 2 of the figure. The region of smaller values stays the same, the region of larger values increases in size, and the unexamined region shrinks. If, on the other hand, v is not larger than the pivot p, it is swapped with the value u just to the right of the boundary between the small and large regions as in part 3 of the figure. Here the region of smaller values increases in size, the region of larger values stays the same size (although the value formerly at its left end is now at its right end), and the unexamined region has shrunk.

Once the pass across the sequence is complete, the pivot value is swapped to the boundary between the large and small regions. If the pivot choice was ideal, this should be near the middle of the list.

To implement *Quicksort* the process just described must be executed recursively. Each part is in turn split into two parts, and so on until each part contains only one element. This was also the case with the recursive merge sort. The difference here is that when the final split has taken place the list will be sorted, whereas with *mergeSort* the parts had to be merged.

Here is the recursive *quickSort* method which copes with an array between the indexes *left* and *right*.

```
// Recursive method QuickSort to sort list of strings between
// index left and index right.
public void quickSort (int left, int right)
{
    int pivotPlace;
    // Place pivot at left side of list.
    swap (left, (left + right) / 2);
    int lastSmall = left;
    for (int i = left + 1 ; i <= right ; i++)
    {
        if (list [i].compareTo (list [left]) <= 0)
        {
            lastSmall++;
            swap (lastSmall, i);
        }
    }
    // Place pivot at boundary.
    swap (left, lastSmall);
    pivotPlace = lastSmall;
    // Sort left part.
    if (left < pivotPlace – 1)
    {
        quickSort (left, pivotPlace – 1);
    }
    // Sort right part.
    if (pivotPlace + 1 < right)
    {
        quickSort (pivotPlace + 1, right);
    }
} // quickSort method
```

In the program that uses the recursive *quickSort* method the call to *quickSort* is:

```
quickSort (1, size);
```

Here is the complete *QuickSort* class.

```
// The "QuickSort" class.
import hsa.Console;

public class QuickSort extends Sort
{
    // Constructor.
    public QuickSort (Console c, int listSize)
    {
        super (c, listSize);
    } // QuickSort constructor

    // Recursive method QuickSort to sort list of strings between
    // index left and index right.
    public void quickSort (int left, int right)
    {
        int pivotPlace;
        // Place pivot at left side of list.
        swap (left, (left + right) / 2);
        int lastSmall = left;
        for (int i = left + 1 ; i <= right ; i++)
        {
            if (list [i].compareTo (list [left]) <= 0)
            {
                lastSmall++;
                swap (lastSmall, i);
            }
        }
        // Place pivot at boundary.
        swap (left, lastSmall);
        pivotPlace = lastSmall;
        // Sort left part.
        if (left < pivotPlace - 1)
        {
            quickSort (left, pivotPlace - 1);
        }
        // Sort right part.
        if (pivotPlace + 1 < right)
        {
            quickSort (pivotPlace + 1, right);
        }
```

```
        } // quickSort method

        // The sort method.
        public void sort ()
        {
            quickSort (1, listSize);
        } // sort method
} /* QuickSort class */
```

***

12.8 Chapter Summary

A sorting algorithm for a list must produce a permutation of the original list arranged so that the smallest (least) value comes first, the second smallest next, and so on. There are many different sorting algorithms. We examined three that involve interchanging elements in the list.

Insertion Sort

In this algorithm the sorting proceeds from left to right. The elements on the left are sorted but the remainder is unsorted. The value at the boundary is examined and its proper position in the sorted part is determined. The values to the right are then moved to make room for it. The worst case execution time is $O(n^2)$.

Selection Sort

As with the insertion sort at any stage, the elements in the left part are sorted; those in the right are not. The sorted part is extended by selecting from the unsorted part its smallest element and swapping it with the element in the unsorted part just past the boundary. This algorithm is also $O(n^2)$ in its worst case.

Bubble Sort

Here the sorted part of the list is extended by passing from the right to the left in the unsorted part, comparing adjacent elements, and exchanging them whenever they are out of order. This results in the smallest remaining value "bubbling" to the boundary. The worst case execution time is $O(n^2)$.

Recursive Sorts

In these sorts the list is split into two parts, each part is sorted, using the same method, and the parts are recombined to give a complete sorted list. The recursive splitting stops when every part contains only one element.

Merge Sort

In this sort the list is split in the middle each time. Merging is required to recombine the parts.

Quicksort

In this method the splitting into parts is more complex. The element in the middle is taken as a **pivot** and the rest of the elements divided into two parts; those with values less than or equal to the pivot value, and those with values greater than the pivot. Unlike the merge sort, these two parts are not necessarily the same size. When the Quicksort is applied recursively, the elements will have been moved into sequence.

Timing of Recursive Sorts

The merge sort has a time complexity $O(n \ log \ n)$ which is considerably faster than the $O(n^2)$ of the exchange sorts. The timing of the Quicksort is more complicated. In the worst case, if the pivot is badly chosen the requirement is $O(n^2)$. On the average, however, it is like the merge sort and so runs in time closer to $O(n \ log \ n)$.

12.9 Exercises

1. Write a method that determines the median of a list of n marks. The median is the mark that divides the list (if sorted) into two equal halves. If the list contains an even number of items, the halves are different by one item. Use it to find the median of a list of 100 simulated exam marks.

2. Adapt the insertion sorting method of this chapter to work for a list of student records with fields for name, address, and year. The *swap* and *shift* methods will also have to be modified. Test the new sort method.

3 Two strings of n characters are to be compared to see whether the second string could be formed by permuting the characters in the first string. Analyze the efficiency of three possible algorithms for doing this.

   a. Scan the first string one character at a time and see if each character has a corresponding character in the second. Be sure to erase a character in the second string once it has been "used".

   b. Sort the two strings and compare them character-by-character.

   c. Prepare a frequency count of each character in each string and compare the counts.

4. A variation of the selection sort is called **quadratic selection**. In this sort the list of n items to be sorted is divided into 4 equal sized groups of $n/4$ each. The smallest element in each group is selected and placed in a temporary array of 4 elements. From these the smallest is selected. It is then replaced by the next smallest elements from its original group until sorting is complete. Program this algorithm. Analyze its performance. How does it compare with selection sorting?

Chapter 13

Self-Referential Classes and Linked Lists

In the last chapter we looked at a number of algorithms for sorting lists of strings such as the insertion, selection, bubble, and merge sorts. As well, we examined the complexity of these various algorithms in order to get an estimate of their relative efficiencies. The lists that were being sorted were stored as arrays. When sorted, the strings were stored in the array so that they were either non-decreasing or non-increasing.

Lists of records stored in an array can be sorted by the same methods. One field of the record acts as the key field in the sorting. This chapter will look at an entirely different way of storing records in memory, in which an additional field of each record indicates where the next record in the sequence is stored in memory. The field acts as a **reference** to the next record's location. It provides a **link** to the next record in the sequence.

13.1 Links

Links are frequently used when a number of records form a data structure. In an array of records, there is an implicit structure in the way that the records are stored in the array. The index of the array is used to find the next element in a list. When links are used, however, the individual elements have no such spatial relationship but each record contains a field that provides a **link** to the next record in the list.

For example, consider a list of names that are linked together. Each record in the list could be an object of a *LinkRecord* class defined this way.

```
// The "LinkListRecord" class.
// A class for creating self-referential records.
public class LinkListRecord
{
    protected String data;
    protected LinkListRecord next;

    // Constructor that initializes name but sets next to null.
    public LinkListRecord (String name)
    {
```

```
        data = name;
        next = null;
    } // LinkListRecord constructor

    // Constructor that initializes name and nextNode.
    public LinkListRecord (String name, LinkListRecord nextNode)
    {
        data = name;
        next = nextNode;
    } // LinkListRecord constructor

    // Method to get data in node.
    public String getData ()
    {
        return data;
    } // getData method

    // Method to get next in node.
    public LinkListRecord getNext ()
    {
        return next;
    } // getNext method

    // Method to set data in node.
    public void setData (String data)
    {
        this.data = data;
    } // setData method

    // Method to set next in node.
    public void setNext (LinkListRecord next)
    {
        this.next = next;
    } // setNext method
} /* LinkListRecord class */
```

This definition is a recursive definition, since the definition of the record type *LinkListRecord* defines the link as a reference to the record type *LinkListRecord*. It is **self-referential.**

We will now set up a simple linked list with only two records in the list. The first record of the list stores the name "alpha" and the second record stores the name "beta". To find the first record there must be a link outside the list itself to point to the first record. The first record must also have a link to the second record. Because there are only two records, the second record has a link that points to no other record. This requires a special value called **null**. Figure 13.1 shows the arrangement of this linked list.

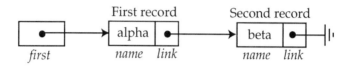

Figure 13.1 Linked List of Two Records

Here are the statements that set up this linked list.

first = **new** *LinkListRecord* ("alpha");
second = **new** *LinkListRecord* ("beta");
first.setNext (*second*);
second.setNext (**null**);

This shows how the self-referential class *LinkListRecord* is used to create a linked list

13.2 Singly Linked Lists

In a simple linked list each record contains a link to the next element in the list. The last element contains a **null** value link. Other lists, however, can contain more than a single link in each record. For this reason we refer to this structure as a **singly linked list**.

A more realistic example of storing names in a linked list involves inputting a list of names, and then modifying the program to output the list in reverse order. As each name is added, it is placed at the beginning of the list. The link to the list is called *last*, since it always points to the name added last. Figure 13.2 shows the growth of the list as the names *Bob, Anna*, and *Lee* are input.

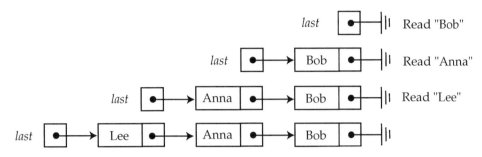

Figure 13.2 Growth of List of Names

Here is the *main* method that reads in the names and uses the class *LinkListRecord*.

```
// The "TestLinkListRecord" class.
// Show names inserted in linked list
// then print them in reverse order.
String name;
// Start with an empty list.
LinkListRecord last = null;
c.println ("Enter names one to a line");
while (true)
{
    String newName;
    c.println ("Enter new name, end with q");
    newName = c.readLine ();
    if (newName.equals ("q"))
        break;
    LinkListRecord p;
    p = new LinkListRecord (newName, last);     // Allocate new record.
    last = p;       // Set last to point to new record.
}
// Print list is reverse order.
c.println ("Here is the list in reverse order");
while (last != null)
{
    c.println (last.getData ());
    LinkListRecord p; // Declare a link.
    p = last; // Locate record to remove from list.
    last = p.getNext (); // Change last to point to next record.
}
```

In the loop, the program has a local link variable *p* which is used to allocate each new record. When the record has been allocated, its *link* field is set to *last* which currently points to the beginning of the existing list. Once the *link* field is set, the value of the link *last* is changed to point to the new record which is located by *p*.

A list that is, as this one, stored in a **last-in-first-out** basis is called a **stack**.

13.3 A List Class

We will now develop a list class to store items that are pairs of string information, such as names and phone numbers or names and addresses. It will permit new items to be entered and old items deleted. The items will be records where the first field of the record will act as the **key field** of the record and the second field will be the **information field**. We will be able to look up the information corresponding to any key, presuming that the key is in the list, and change the information field of any record whose key is specified. We will also be able to output the entire list.

Here is a summary of the methods that are to be provided for the list which is an abstract data type (ADT).

List: An Abstract Data Type

The list containing a set of data elements that each contain a key and information. Elements can be entered into the list. Using the key, an element can be looked up, have its information changed, or be deleted. The list can also be output.

Methods

void enter (key, info)	Add new record.
void delete (key)	Delete record.
void change (key, info)	Change information in record.
String lookUp (key)	Find info for given key.
void display	Display all records in list.

This definition of the ADT *List* is kept simple by requiring that it be used in a particular way. For example, the user must not try to delete or change an item not already in the list. If there is any doubt, the *lookUp* operation should be used before doing either of the other two operations. We will implement *List* as a class. It will use the *LinkRecord* class.

Here is the definition of the *LinkRecord* class.

```
// The "LinkRecord" class.
class LinkRecord
{
    protected String key;
    protected String info;
    protected LinkRecord next;

    // Constructor to create a LinkRecord with key and info, link null.
    public LinkRecord (String key, String info)
    {
        this.key = key;
        this.info = info;
        next = null;
    } // LinkRecord constructor

    // Constructor to create a LinkRecord with key, info, and next.
    public LinkRecord (String key, String info, LinkRecord next)
    {
        this.key = key;
        this.info = info;
        this.next = next;
    } // LinkRecord constructor

    // Get info in LinkRecord.
    public String getInfo ()
    {
        return info;
    } // getInfo method

    // Get key in LinkRecord.
    public String getKey ()
```

```
        {
            return key;
        } // getKey method

        // Get next in LinkRecord.
        public LinkRecord getNext ()
        {
            return next;
        } // getNext method

        // Set info in this LinkRecord.
        public void setInfo (String info)
        {
            this.info = info;
        } // setInfo method

        // Set next in LinkRecord.
        public void setNext (LinkRecord next)
        {
            this.next = next;
        } // setNext method
    } /* LinkRecord class */
```

Here is the driver program to test the *List* class.

```
// The "TestList" class.
// Program to test List class.
// This assumes a class LinkRecord defined.
List p;
p = new List (); // Instantiate a list.
String name, phone, info;
String command;
c.println ("Phone list program");
c.println ("You must give a command and supply requested information");
c.println ("Enter(e), Delete(d), Change(c), LookUp(l), Print(p), or Quit(q)");
// Read and handle each command.
while (true)
{
    c.print ("Command: ");
    command = c.readLine ();
```

```
if (command.charAt (0) == 'q')
    break;
switch (command.charAt (0))
{
    case 'e':  // Enter.
        c.print ("Give name: ");
        name = c.readLine ();
        c.print ("Give phone number: ");
        phone = c.readLine ();
        // Look to see if already in list.
        info = p.lookUp (name);
        if (info == null)
            p.enter (name, phone);
        else
            c.println ("Item already in list");
        break;
    case 'd':  // Delete.
        c.print ("Give name: ");
        name = c.readLine ();
        info = p.lookUp (name);
        if (info != null)
        {
            p.delete (name);
            c.println ("Entry is deleted");
        }
        else
            c.println ("Item is not in list");
        break;
    case 'c':  // Change.
        c.print ("Give name: ");
        name = c.readLine ();
        info = p.lookUp (name);
        if (info != null)
        {
            c.print ("Give new phone number: ");
            phone = c.readLine ();
            p.change (name, phone);
        }
        else
            c.println ("Name not in book");
        break;
    case 'l':      // Lookup.
```

```
                    c.print ("Give name: ");
                    name = c.readLine ();
                    phone = p.lookUp (name);
                    if (phone != null)
                        c.println ("Phone number is " + phone);
                    else
                        c.println ("Name not in book");
                    break;
                case 'p':  // Print.
                    p.display (c);
                    break;
                default:
                    c.println ("Command \"" + command + "\" not available");
        }
    }
    c.println ("Quitting list not saved");
```

Sample Execution of Demonstration Program

Here is the output for an execution of the program.

```
Phone list program
You must give a command and supply requested information
Enter(e), Delete(d), Change(c), LookUp(l), Print(p), or Quit(q)
Command: e
Give name: Graeme Hirst
Give phone number: (416) 555-4521
Command: e
Give name: Pam Linnemann
Give phone number: (519) 555-8372
Command: e
Give name: Inge Weber
Give phone number: (905) 555-8009
Command: l
Give name: Graeme Hirst
Phone number is: (416) 555-4521
Command: d
Give name: Pam Linnemann
Entry is deleted
Command: c
Give name: Inge Weber
```

Give new phone number: (905) 555-6338
Command: l
Give name: Pam Linnemann
Name not in list
Command: p
Inge Weber   (905) 555-6338
Graeme Hirst   (416) 555-4521
Command: q
Quitting, list not saved.

The order of entries in the list will depend on the implementation.
Changing an entry does not alter its position in the list.

13.4 Implementation of List Class

Since *List* is an abstract data type, the programmer does not
need to be concerned with the details of implementation. This
section, however, will illustrate how to implement the *List* class,
with the list as a linked list using a self-referential class.

```
// The "List" class.
import hsa.Console;

class List
{
    protected LinkRecord first;

    // Constructor to produce empty list.
    public List ()
    {
        first = null;
    } // List constructor

    // Change info for item assumed in list.
    public void change (String key, String info)
    {
        LinkRecord where = find (key);
        if (where != null)
            where.setInfo (info);
    } // change method
```

```
// Delete item assumed already in list.
public void delete (String key)
{
    LinkRecord where;
    if (first.getKey ().equals (key))
    {
        where = first;
        first = where.getNext ();
    }
    else
    {
        LinkRecord prev = first;
        where = prev.getNext ();
        while (!where.getKey ().equals (key))
        {
            prev = where;
            where = prev.getNext ();
        }
        prev.next = where.getNext ();
    }
} // delete method

// Print all items in list.
public void display (Console c)
{
    LinkRecord p = first;
    if (p != null)
    {
        do
        {
            c.println (p.getKey () + "   " + p.getInfo ());
            p = p.next;
        }
        while (p != null);
    }
    else
        c.println ("There are no items in list");
} // display method

// Add a new item assumed not already present.
// Add to head of list.
```

```
public void enter (String key, String info)
{
    LinkRecord p = new LinkRecord (key, info, first);
    first = p;
} // enter method

// This method used internally not exported.
protected LinkRecord find (String key)
{
    LinkRecord where = first;
    while (where != null && !where.getKey ().equals (key))
    {
        where = where.getNext ();
    }
    return where;
} // find method

public String lookUp (String key)
{
    String info;
    LinkRecord where = find (key);
    if (where != null)
        info = where.getInfo ();
    else
        info = null;
    return info;
} // lookUp method
} /* List class */
```

We were able to use the *find* method in the *change* and *lookUp* methods, but not in the *delete* method. The *delete* method requires both a reference to the item preceding the item to be deleted, and the reference to the item to be deleted itself.

Although we have implemented the *List* class using a linked list it could also have been implemented using an array. The important point of using an abstract data type like *List* is that the details of implementation do not concern its user and can be changed without affecting its use.

13.5 Ordered Lists

Another kind of list, called the **ordered list**, is useful when the user requires printouts that are in sorted order. In this kind of list, the items are to be kept so that they are at all times sorted by key. The programmer can create a *SortedLinkedList* class from the *List* class using inheritance. The only thing that the programmer needs to do is change the *enter* method so that, instead of placing a new entry at the start of the list, it is placed in its proper sorted location.

Here is an implementation of the *SortedLinkedList* class.

```java
// The "SortedLinkedList" class.
class SortedLinkedList extends List
{
    // Override method of List to maintain sorted order.
    public void enter (String key, String info)
    {
        LinkRecord p = new LinkRecord (key, info);
        // See if item goes first in list.
        if (first == null || first.getKey ().compareTo (key) >= 0)
        {
            p.setNext (first);
            first = p;
        }
        else
        {
            // Find location to insert new entry.
            LinkRecord prev = first;
            LinkRecord follow = first.getNext ();
            while (follow != null && follow.getKey ().compareTo (key) < 0)
            {
                prev = follow;
                follow = follow.getNext ();
            }
            // Adjust links to make insertion.
            prev.setNext (p);
            p.setNext (follow);
        }
    } // enter method
} /* SortedLinkedList class */
```

The result of using this *SortedList* class with the demonstration program would be that the list output would be sorted.

Sample Execution of Demonstration Program

Here is the output for an execution of the program.

```
Phone list program
You must give a command and supply requested information
Enter(e), Delete(d), Change(c), LookUp(l), Print(p), or Quit(q)
Command: e
Give name: Pam Linnemann
Give phone number: (519) 555-8372
Command: e
Give name: Inge Weber
Give phone number: (905) 555-8009
Command: e
Give name: Graeme Hirst
Give phone number: (416) 555-4521
Command: p
Graeme Hirst    (416) 555-4521
Pam Linnemann  (519) 555-8372
Inge Weber       (905) 555-8009
Command: l
Give name: Graeme Hirst
Phone number is: (416) 555-4521
Command: d
Give name: Pam Linnemann
Entry is deleted
Command: c
Give name: Inge Weber
Give new phone number: (905) 555-6338
Command: l
Give name: Pam Linnemann
Name not in list
Command: p
Graeme Hirst    (416) 555-4521
Inge Weber       (905) 555-6338
Command: q
Quitting, list not saved.
```

13.6 Chapter Summary

This chapter has explored self-referential classes to implement **linked lists**.

Links

Multiple records are usually maintained in a data structure. A list is such a structure. A list of records would have a sequence; there would be a first item in the list, a second, a third, and so on. The array index indicates the sequence in an array. The first item has an index 0, the next an index 1, and so on. In an array, the list is stored in sequential memory locations and this provides the list item sequence.

When memory is allocated using self-referential classes one of the fields of each record, called a **link**, points to the next record in the list's sequence.

A list of records containing a **key** field and one or more information fields can be kept as a **stack** according to a last-in-first-out discipline.

List Class

A *List* class can be used to instantiate a *List* object. This object can be defined in terms of the operations *enter, delete, change, lookUp,* and *display*. A demonstration program was presented to use an instance of the *List* class to maintain a list of names and corresponding phone numbers. The name field was used as a **key** to the records for purposes of deletion, changing, and lookup.

Linked List Implementation of List Class

The implementation of the *List* class was shown as a linked list of the data items.

Ordered Lists

Usually an ordered list is one in which the keys of successive records are in a non-decreasing (ascending) or non-increasing (descending) order. We say the list is sorted on the key.

The *List* class can be modified to produce a *SortedList* class by inheritance. The *enter* method of *List* must be overridden with a new method to maintain the list in sorted order as each new item is entered. In this way one class can be used to create a new class, thus saving considerable effort.

13.7 Exercises

1. A stack is a list in which new entries go at the head (or top) of the list and are said to be pushed onto the stack. Entries are removed from the top of this list and are said to be popped from the stack. Define these operations for an ADT *Stack*.

    push, pop, display

    Write a demonstration program to push names onto the stack and pop them off the stack. Implement a *Stack* class using links.

2. A queue is a list in which new entries are placed at the end (or tail) of the queue and removed from the first (or head) of the queue. This is a first-in-first-out (FIFO) discipline. Write a linked implementation of a *Queue* class with operations

    enter, leave, print

    Write a program to test this class.

3. It is often useful to save a list in memory between one use and the next. Modify the *List* class so that the operations *load* and *save* are added. These are used to initialize the list by reading it from a file rather than initializing it as being empty. If a *save* operation is given before leaving any program that uses the list, the list can be read from the file by a *load* operation the next time the program is used.

Chapter 14

Trees

In the previous chapter we showed how the maintenance of an ordered list can be implemented using a linked list. Although the insertion and deletion of entries in the list was in itself simple (it was an operation of O(1)) finding where the insertion was to be made, or where the element to be deleted was located, required operations of O(n) since a linear search had to be used.

For the array implementation, finding the place to insert or delete in the list could be done efficiently by a binary search with O(*log n*), but the actual insertion and deletion were O(n) since elements in the array had to be moved to make room for the insertion or fill up the space no longer required due to the deletion.

In this chapter we will show how using a **binary tree** structure to store data makes it possible to combine the efficiency of the binary search with the efficiency of the actual insertion and deletion operations of a linked list implementation.

14.1 Binary Search Trees

Binary search trees provide an important means of improving searching efficiency.

In order to understand how data is stored in a binary search tree it is best to look at an example. Figure 14.1 shows a binary tree in which names are stored. The names are the keys to the ordering although there can be other information. Each element of the tree is called a **node** and consists of the data (key and information) and two links, one pointing to the **left subtree**, the other to the **right subtree**. The element with the key *Inge* is the **root** of the tree and a reference called *root* points to it. When there is no subtree from a particular node, the corresponding link is set to **null**.

The definition of an **ordered binary tree** or **binary search tree** is that there are at most two subtrees of each node and that the keys of items in the left subtree come before the key in the root, and all those in the right subtree come after the root. This is true for each node in turn.

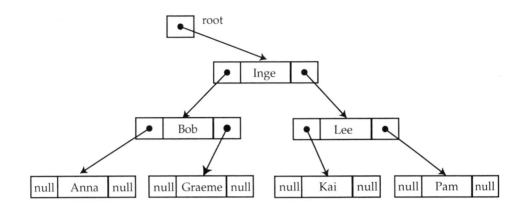

Figure 14.1 An Ordered Binary Tree

When we search for an item, we start by comparing its value with that in the root. If it is less, then it must, if it is there, be in the left subtree and one comparison eliminates all the items in the right subtree. For a **balanced** tree, the **search space** is thereby cut in half, just as in a binary search. The search process continues by comparing the root of the left subtree with the item and eliminating either its left subtree or its right subtree. The process continues until either the data is found or a **null** link indicates that a dead end is reached. The **null** link indicates that the item is not in the tree and shows where an item to be inserted should be placed. A node with two **null** links is called a **leaf node**.

14.2 An Implementation of the Ordered List Using a Tree

This section illustrates how a tree can be used to implement an ordered list by producing a partial implementation equivalent to the *SortedList* class of the previous chapter, where only the *enter* and *print* are included and the operations *delete, change,* and *lookUp* are not present. These operations can be added later by inheritance. The *enter* operation requires careful study to see how it is accomplished. A *delete* operation would be similarly complex.

To begin, we define a class called *TreeNode* from which the individual nodes in the tree can be instantiated. This is a self-referential class.

```
// The "TreeNode" class.
public class TreeNode
{
    protected String key, info;
    protected TreeNode left, right;

    // Alternate constructor.
    public TreeNode (String key, String info)
    {
        this.key = key;
        this.info = info;
        left = null;
        right = null;
    } // TreeNode constructor

    public String getInfo ()
    {
        return info;
    } // getInfo method

    public String getKey ()
    {
        return key;
    } // getKey method

    public TreeNode getLeft ()
    {
        return left;
    } // getLeft method

    public TreeNode getRight ()
    {
        return right;
    } // getRight method

    public void setLeft (TreeNode newLeft)
    {
```

```
        left = newLeft;
    } // setLeft method

    public void setRight (TreeNode newRight)
    {
        right = newRight;
    } // setRight method
} /* TreeNode class */
```

Here is the implementation of *SortedListTree* with just *enter* and *print*. It uses the class *TreeNode*.

```
// The "SortedListTree" class.
// An implementation of SortedListTree using a binary tree where each
// node contains a key, information, and two links.
// New entries can be entered and the list displayed.
import hsa.Console;

public class SortedListTree
{
    TreeNode root = null;

    public void enter (String key, String info)
    {
        TreeNode p = new TreeNode (key, info);
        // Find location to insert new entry.
        if (root == null)
        { // Entry goes at root of tree.
            root = p;
        }
        else
        {
            TreeNode where = root;
            while (true)
            {
                // The link "where" locates non-empty subtree
                // where new node is to be entered.
                if (p.getKey ().compareTo (where.getKey ()) < 0)
                {
                    if (where.getLeft () == null)
```

```
            {
                // Attach new node here.
                where.setLeft (p);
                break;
            }
            else
            {
                // Search left subtree.
                where = where.getLeft ();
            }
        }
        else
        {
            if (where.getRight () == null)
            {
                // Attach new node here.
                where.setRight (p);
                break;
            }
            else
            {
                // Search right subtree.
                where = where.getRight ();
            }
        }
    }
} // enter method

// Output subtree pointed to by where.
// Recursive printing.
public void recursivePrint (TreeNode where, Console c)
{
    if (where != null)
    {
        recursivePrint (where.getLeft (), c);
        c.println (where.getKey () + " " + where.getInfo ());
        recursivePrint (where.getRight (), c);
    }
} // recursivePrint method
```

```
    // Uses method recursivePrint.
    public void print (Console c)
    {
        recursivePrint (root, c);
    } // print method
} /* SortedListTree class */
```

The *print* operation uses the recursive method *recursivePrint* which recursively outputs the left subtree then outputs the root and recursively outputs the right subtree. As the recursive calls are made, the value of the parameter *where* changes.

This example demonstrates that a list can be sorted by entering the items one at a time into the binary search tree and then printing the tree.

14.3 Deleting a Node from a Tree

We will now expand our discussion of trees to consider the *lookUp*, *delete* and *change* methods that were not included in the *SortedListTree* class.

The *lookUp* method is similar to *enter* except that in this case we are looking for a match between the key being sought and the key stored in the tree node. When a match occurs, the value of the corresponding *info* field is returned. If a **null** link is encountered no such entry exists in the tree. The *change* operation is similar except that the *info* field is changed to the value provided.

The *delete* operation for a tree is perhaps the most complicated operation. First the node containing the item to be deleted must be found. If it is a leaf node, that is, if both its left and right links are **null**, it can be chopped off and the link in its parent node changed to **null**. This means that at each stage of *lookUp* the parent node's location must be "remembered".

If the node to be deleted has one **null** link the deletion process is similar to deletion from a singly-linked list.

If the node to be deleted has no **null** links then it must be replaced to keep the tree linked up. As a replacement, we can promote the node with the largest key in the left subtree or the node with the smallest key in the right subtree. This will guarantee that the binary tree property will be maintained, that is, that the root will be greater than or equal to any in the left subtree and less than or equal to any in the right subtree. The node promoted is bound to be a leaf node and can easily be deleted from its present position.

The *change* method uses the *lookUp* method to locate the node to be changed. It then makes the change.

The *SortedListTree* class can be extended by adding the *lookUp*, *delete*, and *change* methods. This allows the programmer to use inheritance to extend the capabilities of the original class.

14.4 Using a Binary Tree to Sort: Heap Sort

We will now look at another kind of binary tree called a **heap**. The definition of a heap is that each node n is greater than or equal to all the nodes that descend from that node. If a node descends from another node, it is called a **child** of the **parent** node. In a heap, each parent is greater than, or equal to, each of its children.

Figure 14.2 shows two alternative ways in which the integers 1, 2, 3, 7, 8, and 9 could be arranged in a heap.

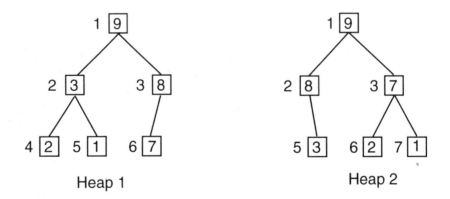

Heap 1   Heap 2

Figure 14.2 Two Alternative Heaps of Same Integers

We have shown how trees can be implemented using links. We will now show how an array can be used to represent the tree as a heap. In Figure 14.2 the nodes of the two alternative heaps are numbered. We will not use element 0 in the array to simplify the program. The root has been numbered 1. Its descendants (children) are numbered from left to right 2 and 3. Their children are numbered 4, 5, and 6 for Heap 1 and 5, 6, and 7 for Heap 2. In a heap, a node in position i will have children in $2*i$ and $2*i + 1$. For example, the children of node 2 are in 4 and 5. This means that the parent of node i is in position $i / 2$. The parent of nodes 6 and 7 is 3. The arrays corresponding to the heap arrangements in Figure 14.2 are shown in Figure 14.3.

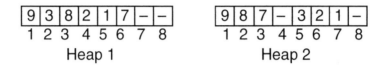

Heap 1   Heap 2

Figure 14.3 Location of Nodes in Array

The arrangement of Heap 2 leaves a gap in the array at position 4. Building a heap with no gaps like Heap 1 requires that as new items are added to the heap they be placed as far left as possible in the tree. To insert a new item we place it in the first available location in the array. This may not preserve the heap property so the item must be moved up the tree until the property is preserved. It is "sifted up". If the new item is greater than its parent (as located using $i / 2$) the two are interchanged; if then as a child of another parent it is still greater, a second interchange occurs, and so on until the heap property is restored.

Suppose that we have a heap that fills array locations 1, 2, up to $i - 1$ and we want to add a new item. We place it in location i. Its parent will be in $i / 2$.

Here is the method for inserting elements into a heap. The *HeapSort* class will be inheriting from the *Sort* class in Chapter 12. The array to be sorted is called *list* and it has *listSize* elements. Each element is a *String* object.

```
// Insert an item into the heap so as to preserve heap property.
public void insertHeap (int i, String item)
{
    int child = i;
    list [i] = item;
```

```
    while (true)
    {
        // Sift up as required.
        int parent = child / 2;
        if (child == 1 || list [parent].compareTo (list [child]) >= 0)
        {
            break;
        }
        // Interchange parent and child.
        swap (parent, child);
        child = parent;
    }
} // insertHeap method
```

This method assumes that the array is large enough that no heap overflow occurs. The maximum number of times that the loop has to be repeated is $\log_2 i$, since *child* is divided by 2 each time and the loop exits when *child* is equal to 1, that is, when it is at the top of the heap.

Using the heap data structure as a means of sorting an array of items requires the procedure *insertHeap* to rearrange the items to form a heap. The largest element will then be in *heap* [1]. (Remember, for simplicity we are not using *heap* [0].) The largest element is removed to a temporary location and the last element of the array put in its place in *heap*[1]. If there were *n* items in the array, the last would be in *heap*[*n*]. The heap property is then restored by "sifting down". If the element is smaller than either of its two children, it is exchanged with the larger one and the process repeated. If the parent is in *heap* [*parent*], its children, if any, will be in *heap* [2 * *parent*] and *heap* [2 * *parent* + 1].

Here is the method that removes the largest element from the heap and then restores the heap property by sifting down.

```
// Find largest item, remove it, and restore heap.
public String removeLargest (int n)
{
    String largest = list [1];
    list [1] = list [n];
    int parent = 1;
    while (true)
```

```
        {
            int child = 2 * parent;  // Left child.
            if (child > n)
                break;
            if (child < n && list [child + 1].compareTo (list [child]) > 0)
            {
                child++;   // Right child.
            }
            // Child is now the left child.
            if (list [parent].compareTo (list [child]) >= 0)
            {
                break;
            }
            // Interchange parent and large child.
            swap (parent, child);
            parent = child;

        }
    return largest;
} // removeLargest method
```

This is an example of a method that is both a function-type: it returns a value, and procedure-type: it restores the heap property of the remainder. This restoration of the heap property is one example of a beneficial side effect.

Using these methods to sort a list does not require more than a single array, since elements are inserted into the heap starting at the first element of the array that is unsorted. This releases the space for storing the first node of the heap. The original array is thus transformed into a heap. Once the heap is formed, the largest nodes are removed one at a time, to produce the final sorted array. As the nodes are removed from the heap, they are stored starting at the end of the array, and take up the space vacated by the shrinking heap.

Here is the rest of the *HeapSort* class including the *sort* method. To show the action of the heap sort, we have included additional *print* statements to provide the current state of the array after every insertion and removal.

```
// The "HeapSort" class.
import java.awt.*;
import hsa.Console;

public class HeapSort extends Sort
{
    // Constructor
    public HeapSort (Console c, int listSize)
    {
        super (c, listSize);
    } // HeapSort constructor

    // Sort array elements 1 to n using heap sort.
    public void sort ()
    {
        // Make array into heap starting at element 2.
        // Element 1 is already a heap.
        for (int i = 2 ; i <= listSize ; i++)
        {
            insertHeap (i, list [i]);
            c.print ("Added ");
            c.print (i, 3);
            c.print (" ");
            printList ();
        }
        // Remove elements from heap and put in array.
        for (int i = listSize ; i > 1 ; i—)
        {
            list [i] = removeLargest (i);
            c.print ("Removed ");
            c.print (i, 3);
            c.print (" ");
            printList ();
        }
    } // heapSort method
} /* HeapSort class */
```

Both *insertHeap* and *removeLargest* take time that is proportional to *log n* and each is called $n - 1$ times so *heapSort* is O($n \log n$).

A heap sort could be implemented using links but the word "heap" usually refers to a tree stored in an array.

Here is the driver program for testing the *HeapSort* class.

```
HeapSort sortList = new HeapSort (c, 10);
sortList.printList ();
sortList.sort ();
sortList.printList ();
```

Here is a typical output from running the driver program.

```
ppcy pipj umen eisa btwm xcdb oqnq aple fnad vksq
Added  2 ppcy pipj umen eisa btwm xcdb oqnq aple fnad vksq
Added  3 umen pipj ppcy eisa btwm xcdb oqnq aple fnad vksq
Added  4 umen pipj ppcy eisa btwm xcdb oqnq aple fnad vksq
Added  5 umen pipj ppcy eisa btwm xcdb oqnq aple fnad vksq
Added  6 xcdb pipj umen eisa btwm ppcy oqnq aple fnad vksq
Added  7 xcdb pipj umen eisa btwm ppcy oqnq aple fnad vksq
Added  8 xcdb pipj umen eisa btwm ppcy oqnq aple fnad vksq
Added  9 xcdb pipj umen fnad btwm ppcy oqnq aple eisa vksq
Added 10 xcdb vksq umen fnad pipj ppcy oqnq aple eisa btwm
Removed 10 vksq pipj umen fnad btwm ppcy oqnq aple eisa xcdb
Removed  9 umen pipj ppcy fnad btwm eisa oqnq aple vksq xcdb
Removed  8 ppcy pipj oqnq fnad btwm eisa aple umen vksq xcdb
Removed  7 pipj fnad oqnq aple btwm eisa ppcy umen vksq xcdb
Removed  6 oqnq fnad eisa aple btwm pipj ppcy umen vksq xcdb
Removed  5 fnad btwm eisa aple oqnq pipj ppcy umen vksq xcdb
Removed  4 eisa btwm aple fnad oqnq pipj ppcy umen vksq xcdb
Removed  3 btwm aple eisa fnad oqnq pipj ppcy umen vksq xcdb
Removed  2 aple btwm eisa fnad oqnq pipj ppcy umen vksq xcdb
aple btwm eisa fnad oqnq pipj ppcy umen vksq xcdb
```

The first line is an array of 10 random four-letter words. The array is transformed into a heap by adding the elements one at a time. As the second element is added, the first two form a heap. As the third element is added, the first three form a heap and so on. The elements are then removed one at a time.

14.5 Chapter Summary

The linked list and the array implementations of an ordered list as described in the Chapter 13 have advantages and disadvantages.

The array implementation permits the efficiency of a binary search for retrieving information or finding the location of items to be deleted or new entries to be inserted. This operation is O(*log n*). However, the insertion or deletion operation requires time O(*n*) since a search is required to find the proper location. With a linked list, all searches are O(*n*) and the actual deletion or insertion are O(*1*).

The **binary search tree** was introduced as a way of obtaining the combined efficiency of binary search for locating elements, and deletion and insertion of the linked list once the location is found.

Binary Search Trees

A binary search tree consists of nodes with information containing a **key** and two pointers: one to a **left subtree** of nodes and one to a **right subtree**. All elements in the left subtree of node *n* have keys that are less than that of **node** *n*; those in the right subtree have larger keys.

A search for a particular key begins at the root node of the tree as a whole. By comparing the key sought with the root node's key, a decision is made as to which subtree to search next. On each comparison, if the tree is balanced, one half of the tree is eliminated from the search – the **search space** is cut in half. The average number of comparisons to find an element is log_2n if *n* is the number of nodes in the tree. If a link locates no subtree, it is set to **null**. Items to be inserted are placed in the location where a **null** link is encountered.

Sorting Using a Binary Search Tree

A class called *SortedListTree* was developed which would allow insertion and listing. A sorted list is obtained by inserting elements from an unsorted list one at a time into a binary search tree using a *SortedListTree* and then listing it. The tree is printed by a recursive method whose actions, if the tree is not empty, are:

- output the left subtree,
- output the root, and
- output the right subtree.

Heaps

Another kind of binary tree used in sorting is the **heap**. In a heap, each **parent** node is larger than or equal to either of its two **child** nodes.

The heap sort forms a heap from an unsorted list by rearranging the nodes in a heap to restore its heap nature as each element is added.

Implementing a Heap Using an Array

One of the easiest ways to implement a heap is to use an array. The array lengthens as each element is added at its end. The elements are arranged in the array such that, if an element is in location i of the array, its parent is in location $i / 2$, and its children are in $2 * i$ and $2 * i + 1$.

Sorting Using a Heap

A heap sort begins by removing the root of the heap. Because it is the largest element, it will be last in the sorted list. The array is then adjusted to restore its heap character and the process is repeated to pick off the largest element remaining, which will be the second largest element of the final sorted list, and so on.

14.6 Exercises

1. Write a method called *treeSort* that uses a binary tree with links to sort an array *A* with elements of type **int**. Place the sorted array in the same memory space as the original array. Test the method in an application program by generating an array of 25 integers randomly between 0 and 100 and then sorting them.

    Analyze the *treeSort* algorithm and show that it is O(*n log n*) on average for a randomly ordered list. What is the result if the original list is already ordered? What if the list is exactly in reverse order?

2. Write a program that reads lines of a file, sorts them, and outputs them in order, deleting duplicates. Use the *SortedListTree* class, modifying the *enter* operation to create a new class that omits duplicates.

3. Write a recursive method that displays a binary tree with one value per line and the indentation of the line corresponding to the depth of the node in the tree. Use the method in a program to see how well-balanced the tree is that is formed if random integers are entered into the tree.

4. A tree can be traversed in several systematic ways, including:
    *   output the left subtree,
    *   output the root, and
    *   output the right subtree.

    This is called **inorder traversal** of the tree. Modify the *recursivePrint* method of this chapter to output a tree in **preorder traversal** which is defined by:
    *   output the root,
    *   output the left subtree, and
    *   output the right subtree.

5. The method *countDepth* computes the maximum depth of a binary search tree using post order traversal. To compute the height below a given node, we need to know the heights below its two subtrees, and then take the maximum. Each node is of type *node* with *left* and *right* links.

```
public int countDepth (TreeNode t)
{
    if (t == null)
        return 0
    else
        return 1 + Math.max (countDepth (t.left), countDepth (t.right))
}
```

Use this method to determine the depth of trees created by generating of groups of 20 random integers between 0 and 100. What is their average depth?

Chapter 15

VisualAge for Java Visual Builder

In Chapter 9 it was apparent that designing good interfaces between users and applets is a complex task. To make this task much easier, the *VisualAge for Java, Professional Edition for Windows, Version 2.0* environment provides programmers with a **Visual Builder** called the **Visual Composition Editor**. This Visual Builder has visual programming tools which allow a programmer to develop applets or applications quickly by clicking and dragging from a palette of GUI components. With these components, the programmer can design the user interface, specify the behavior of the components, make the connections between the components, and define the relationship between the interface and the rest of the program. *VisualAge for Java* generates the Java code to meet these specifications.

15.1 JavaBeans

One of the prime benefits of the Java language is that it supports the reuse of parts or components of systems. The graphical user interface components are examples of reusable parts.

JavaBeans is the standard GUI component model for Java and is the basis of *VisualAge for Java*. The *Visual Composition Editor* allows programmers to create program interfaces from existing *JavaBeans*. For brevity, *JavaBeans* will be referred to simply as **beans**.

Although the *Visual Composition Editor* provides a standard **palette** of possible beans from which users can choose, programmers can also create and add their own beans to the palette.

The easiest way to understand how to use the *Visual Composition Editor* is to see how an applet is created step-by-step. To do this, we will create an applet that is to be used in the ticket wicket of a movie theater. Figure 15.1 shows what the user interface for this applet should look like.

There are four buttons on the left-hand side that can be clicked and a fifth on the right-hand side. The cashier has to click the *Adult* button for each adult, the *Senior* button for each senior, and the *Child* button for each child. As this happens, a running total of admission charges is displayed and when the *Print Ticket* button is clicked, the details of the ticket appear in the window labelled "Total". The *Clear* button allows the cashier to start over if a mistake is made. After *Total* is displayed, the next click of any of the left-hand buttons results in the clearing of the *Total* window to start another customer's requests.

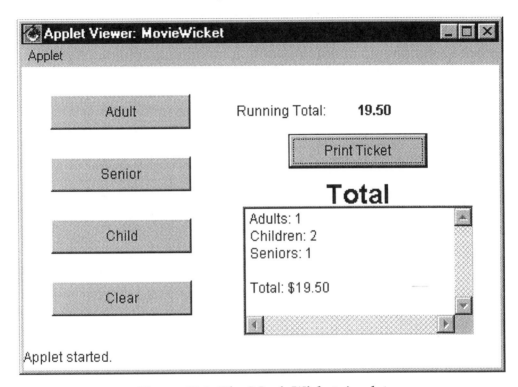

Figure 15.1 The MovieWicket Applet

It is important for users to be able to specify what they want to accomplish in an applet and to decide what its graphical user interface will be like before they start to create it. In the next section we will describe step-by-step the process of creating an applet named "MovieWicket" with this interface. We highly recommend that you follow this process on the computer to make sure that you understand each step.

15.2 Beginning to Use the Visual Builder

Now we will begin building the example applet.

In the *Workbench*, select the default package for the project in the upper pane and click the *Create Applet* icon. In the resulting dialog box, enter the name "MovieWicket", click the *Compose the class visually* check box, and click the *Finish* button. At this point the class window (indicated with a Class icon in the title bar) for *MovieWicket* appears with the *Visual Composition* tab selected.

Figure 15.2 shows the *Visual Composition Editor* with the name of the new class. If it becomes necessary to return to the *Visual Composition Editor*, double click on the *MovieWicket* class in the *Workbench* to bring up the class window and then click the *Visual Composition* tab.

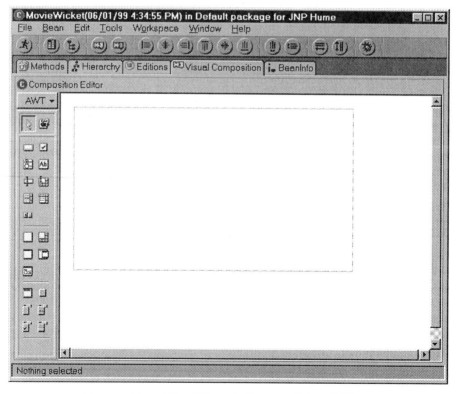

Figure 15.2 The Visual Composition Editor

The **beans palette** is along the left, the **status area** along the bottom, the **tool bar** along the top, and the **free-form surface**, where you lay out the beans, on the right. The dotted rectangle will be the Applet Viewer window.

The beans palette is organized into groups of beans. We will be using only the first group which consists of (listed left to right, top to bottom): Button, Checkbox, CheckboxGroup, Label, TextField, TextArea, List, Choice, and Scrollbar.

The tool bar provides the tools used for manipulating beans: positioning them, sizing them, and showing or hiding connections between beans. The status area shows which bean is currently selected. Placing the mouse over any bean causes a description of its function to appear.

Figure 15.3 shows four buttons in the free-form surface.

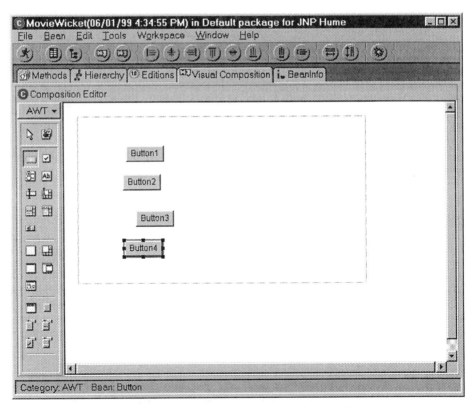

Figure 15.3 Four Buttons Created

Create a button by clicking the *Button* icon in the bean palette. Once the *Button* bean icon has been selected, the mouse cursor is then said to be "loaded" with a button. The mouse cursor changes to a cross-hair when it is loaded. Move the mouse so that it is over the free-form surface and place the cross-hair where you want the top-left corner of the button to be placed and click. The button is temporarily labelled "Button1".

Create the second button by again clicking the Button bean (which again loads the mouse cursor), moving to the free-form surface underneath the first button, and clicking. When four buttons have been created, replace their temporary labels. To change the label from "Button1" (the "Button1" label was provided automatically) to an appropriate label, double click on the button in the free-form surface. Figure 15.4 shows the *Properties* dialog box that will appear as a result of this action.

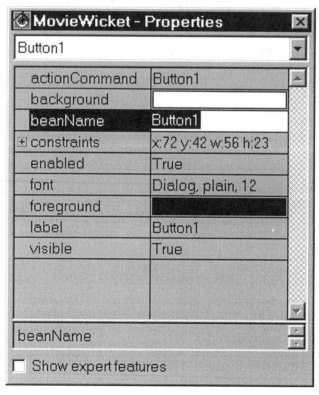

Figure 15.4 Button *Properties* Dialog Box

The **properties** of the bean are the characteristics that can be specified. Default values are provided in the dialog box but these can be changed. Change both the *beanName* and the *label* to "Adult" by clicking on the property name, which highlights the current value, and typing a new value.

Next, pull down the pop-up menu beneath the title bar of the *Properties* dialog box. This menu contains a list of all the beans that have already been placed. From the menu select the button labelled "Button2". Change its *beanName* and *label* to "Senior", and so on for "Button3" and "Button4". Figure 15.5 shows what the interface now looks like.

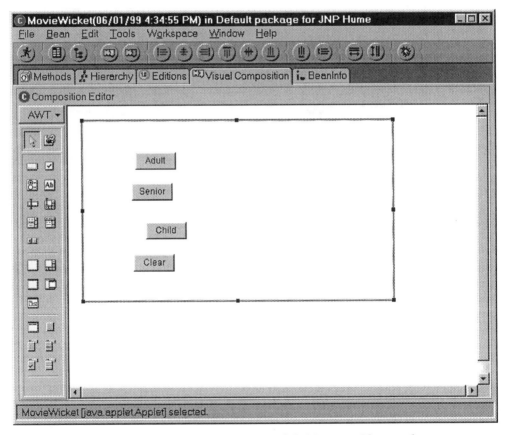

Figure 15.5 Four Buttons with Names Changed

15.3 Positioning, Sizing, and Aligning Beans

You can move beans around by selecting the bean in the free-form surface by clicking on it, and then holding the mouse button down, dragging it to the new location and releasing it. You can also change the size of the bean by dragging any one of the **selection handles** that appear when the bean is clicked.

In our example, we want all four buttons to be the same size and to be aligned. To do this, select the beans of the group you want to align, by clicking on one of the beans, then, holding down the *Control* key and clicking on the other beans you want to select. The last bean selected is the **anchor** around which aligning and sizing takes place. It has solid selection handles; the others have hollow handles. Figure 15.6 shows the selected beans.

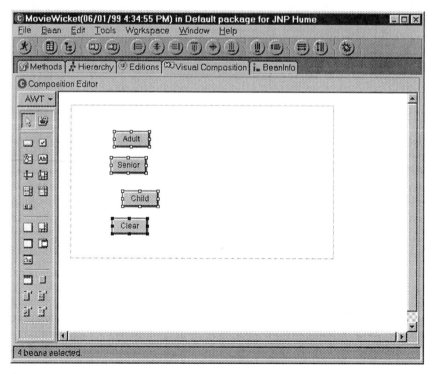

Figure 15.6 Four Buttons Selected with *Clear* Button as Anchor

You align the beans by clicking one of the **alignment tools** from the tool bar. These are the 6th to 11th icon buttons. They produce alignment respectively to the left, center, right, top, middle, and bottom of the anchor bean.

There are various other ways to manipulate beans.

- Beans can be distributed evenly horizontally or vertically over the free-form surface using the *Distribute-Horizontally* and *Distribute-Vertically* icon buttons (the 4th and 5th from the right).
- Beans can be made to have the same horizontal and vertical size by using the *Match-Width* or *Match-Height* icon buttons (the 2nd and 3rd from the right).
- Beans can be deleted by selecting them and pressing the *Delete* key.
- Beans can be copied by holding down the *Control* key, selecting the bean to be copied, then dragging the mouse so that it is pointing to where the copy is to be placed, and releasing both it and the *Control* key.
- Beans can be deselected by clicking on another bean (without holding down the *Control* key).

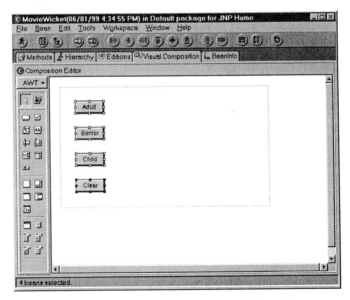

Figure 15.7 Four Buttons Aligned

Figure 15.7 shows the result of aligning and distributing the four buttons by first selecting the top button (*Adult*), *Control*-clicking the other three buttons, clicking the *Align-Left* icon button, and then the *Distribute-Vertically* icon button. To prevent the beans from being accidentally copied be sure to release the *Control* key before manipulating the bean.

15.4 Adding More Beans

The next step in creating the *MovieWicket* interface is to add a labelled text field by first selecting *Label* bean (the icon with the Ab). The mouse cursor is now loaded with a *Label* bean.

By clicking in the free-form surface, place the label to the right of the *Adult* button. It appears as selection handles with "Label1" inside them. There is no box around the word "Label1".

Double click on the label to get its *Properties* dialog box and change *beanName* to "RunningTotalLabel" and *text* to "Running Total:". Adjust the size of the *Label* bean to just fit the actual label by clicking on the lower-right selection handle and dragging it. Figure 15.8 shows the renamed bean.

Next, place a text field just to the right of the label by first clicking the *TextField* icon. Now, double click on the *TextField* after it is placed and, in its *Properties* dialog box, change its *beanName* to "RunningTotal", its *editable* property to **false**, and its *text* to "0.00". Figure 15.9 shows the *TextField Properties* dialog box.

Now click *font* in the *Properties* dialog box and click the small box that appears to the right of the font description. A second dialog box labelled *Font* appears. Change *Style* to "bold" and click *OK*. Figure 15.34 at the end of the chapter shows the *Font* dialog box.

To size the *TextField* bean, drag a selection handle so that it can fit as big a total as 999.99 and slide it to the left beside the *RunningTotal* label. Select both the label and the text field and click the *Align-Middle* icon. Figure 15.10 shows the centered beans.

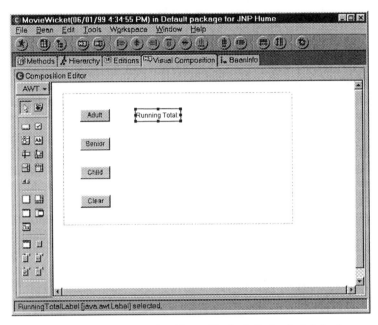

Figure 15.8 *RunningTotalLabel* Label Added

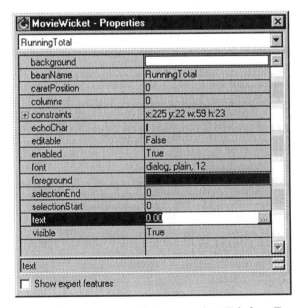

Figure 15.9 TextField Properties Dialog Box

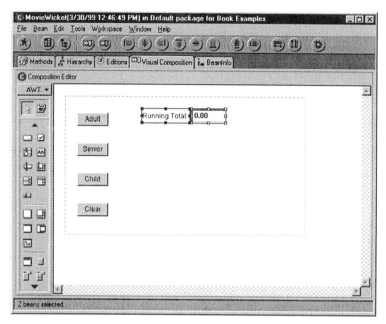

Figure 15.10 Vertically Centering *RunningTotalLabel* and *RunningTotal* Beans

Now add another *Button* bean below the labelled text field with *beanName* "PrintTicket" and the *label* "Print Ticket". Resize the button to fit the new label. Then add a *Label* bean with *beanName* "TotalLabel" and *text* "Total". Change its alignment to *CENTER* and font to "24 point bold". Figure 15.11 shows the *Properties* dialog box for the label with the *font* property selected. Resize the label to fit the text.

A **text area** is now created below the word "Total" for displaying the details of a customer's ticket. (*TextArea* is a GUI component that has not been used so far in this book. *TextArea* is a bean for displaying text in a **scrollable window**.) The *TextArea* bean is located on the third row in the second column. It looks like a window with scroll bars. Place the *TextArea* bean under "Total" and size it to fit in the Applet Viewer Window (the dashed rectangle). Because its default size is quite large, you may have to drag the text area into the center of the free-form drawing surface, resize it appropriately, and then drag it under the *TotalLabel* label. In Figure 15.12 the three beans: the *PrintTicket* button, the *TotalLabel* label, and the text area have been selected and the *Align-Centers* icon in the tool bar clicked.

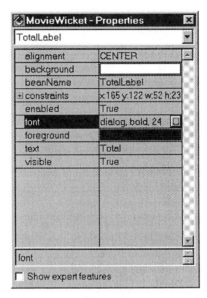

Figure 15.11 Changing Font Size of *TotalLabel* Label

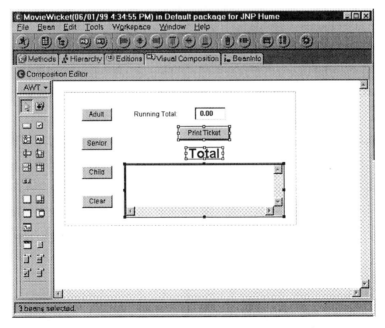

Figure 15.12 Horizontally-Center-Aligning Three Beans

15.5 Adding Methods to the Applet

So far the *Visual Composition Editor* alone has been used to create the applet. In most cases, however, it is necessary to write code as well. This code is in the form of methods that will be called by the *Visual Composition Editor* in response to button clicks.

To begin the process of creating your own methods, click the *Methods* tab (in the row below the tool bar) in the class window. The window changes and a different tool bar appears at the top. The rightmost icon in the tool bar has an F on it. This is the *Create Field* icon. Click it.

In the *Create Field* dialog box that appears, enter the Field Name *children* as a **protected int** with an Initial Value of 0. Then do the same for *seniors* and *adults*. Figure 15.13 shows the dialog box where the field *children* is created.

Figure 15.13 Adding the *children* field to MovieWicket

Repeat the process for a field *total* of data type **double**.

Now click on the *Hierarchy* tab (the one beside the *Methods* tab) and select *MovieWicket* in the upper pane. Add the line

> **import** *java.text.**;

after the other two **import** statements and save (*Control+S*). This **import** statement is necessary because we will be using the *NumberFormat* and *DataFormat* classes of the *java.text* package.

We have now created the fields of the *MovieWicket* class that represent the number of children, seniors, and adults. Next, we must create the five methods that will be called as each of the five buttons is clicked. The methods responding to the clicking of the *Adult*, *Senior*, and *Child* buttons add one to the corresponding field and increase the total ticket cost by the appropriate amount. Each returns a string representing the current total. Each method is entered by the *Create Method* icon. Figure 15.14 shows the *Create Method* dialog box for the *addAdult* method. To set the **protected** attribute for the method, the *Next>* button must be clicked to display the *Attributes* dialog box where the *protected* attribute can be selected.

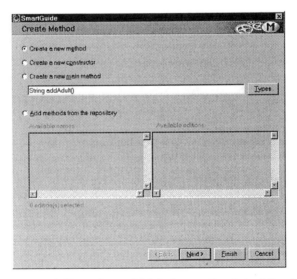

Figure 15.14 Adding the *addAdult* method to MovieWicket

Here are the five methods that must be entered.

```
protected String addAdult ()
{
    adults++;
    total += 8.00;
    NumberFormat form = new DecimalFormat ("0.00");
    return form.format (total);
}
```

```
protected String addSenior ()
{
    seniors++;
    total += 4.50;
    NumberFormat form = new DecimalFormat ("0.00");
    return form.format (total);
}

protected String addChild ()
{
    children++;
    total += 3.50;
    NumberFormat form = new DecimalFormat ("0.00");
    return form.format (total);
}

protected void clearAll ()
{
    adults = 0;
    seniors = 0;
    children = 0;
    total = 0;
}

protected String printTicket ()
{
    String result;
    NumberFormat form = new DecimalFormat ("0.00");
    result = "Adults: " + adults + " \nSeniors: " + seniors +
                "\nChildren: " + children + "\nTotal: " +
                form.format (total);
    clearAll ();
    return result;
}
```

In the first three methods, the value of *total* (which is real) is returned as a string with two decimal places by these statements:

```
NumberFormat form = new DecimalFormat ("0.00");
return (form.format (total));
```

In the *printTicket* method the \n used in the *result* is the end-of-line character.

After the methods are all created, return to the *Visual Composition Editor* by clicking the *Visual Composition* tab and select *Save Bean* from the *Edit* menu. This saves the beans and causes the *Visual Composition Editor* to generate the Java to run the applet.

At this stage, it is time to specify the size of the applet viewer window. Click the *Hierarchy* tab in the class window and select the *Properties* menu item from the *Classes* menu. This brings up the *Properties* dialog box for *MovieWicket* (See Figure 15.15). Set the width of the applet viewer to be 450.

It is now possible to test the buttons even though the applet is not complete. To do this, click the *Run* button (the first button in the tool bar) to try out the clicking of your button beans.

The *Applet Viewer* window appears with all the beans in position. Click any button and see that it is depressed. Nothing will happen in response to the button presses because the connections between the buttons, the methods, the text field, and text area have not yet been made.

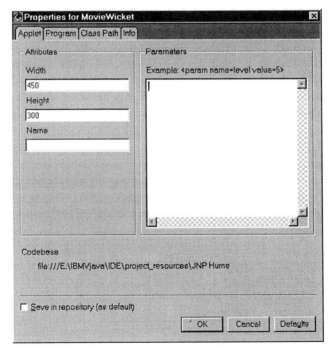

Figure 15.15 The Applet Settings Dialog Box for MovieWicket

15.6 Adding Connections Between Beans

We now need to add the connections between beans. The first connection will be between the *Adult* button and the text field labelled "Running Total".

To make this connection, click on the *Adult* button and then press the right button on the mouse (button 2) to bring up a menu. In this menu, select *Connect* and then select *actionPerformed* from the sub-menu. Figure 15.16 shows the menus for making the connection.

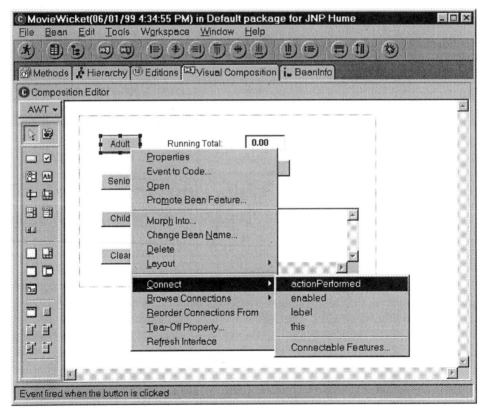

Figure 15.16 Selecting the Type of Connection from the *Adult* Button

When the *actionPerformed* has been selected, a dashed connection line is drawn from the *Adult* button to the current mouse location with a little "spider" on the end of it. Move the mouse to the text field, currently set at "0.00", and click the mouse button. Figure 15.17 shows the connecting line and the spider just before the mouse button is clicked.

A pop-up menu now appears as shown in Figure 15.18. Select *text* from the menu. The text is what is changed when the *Adult* button is clicked. The connection now becomes a dashed line with an arrow head pointing from the *Adult* button to the text field with "0.00" in it. Figure 15.19 shows the completed text field connection.

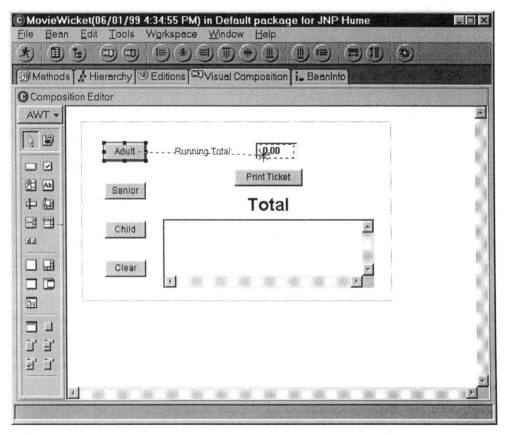

Figure 15.17 Attaching the Connection to the *RunningTotal* TextField

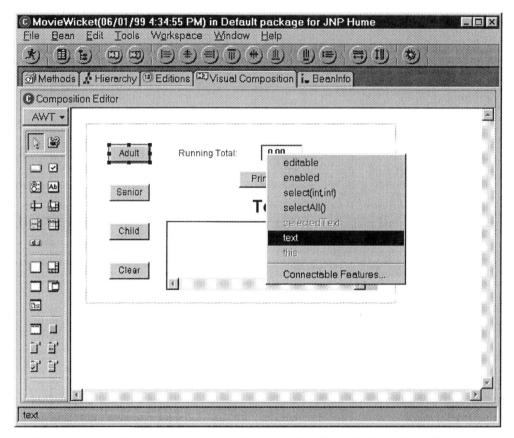

Figure 15.18 Selecting the Attribute of the TextField to be Changed

A connection is now established between the *Adult* button and the text of the *RunningTotal* text field. A second connection must be created between this connection and the method *addAdult* to specify what the text will be changed to when the button is pressed. The text will be set to the String returned by *addAdult*.

To make this second connection, click the existing connection itself and press the right button on the mouse to bring up a menu. Select *Connect* and then select *value* from the sub-menu. Selecting the *value* item indicates that this connection will be setting a value to the previous connection. Figure 15.20 shows the selected menu items for the new connection.

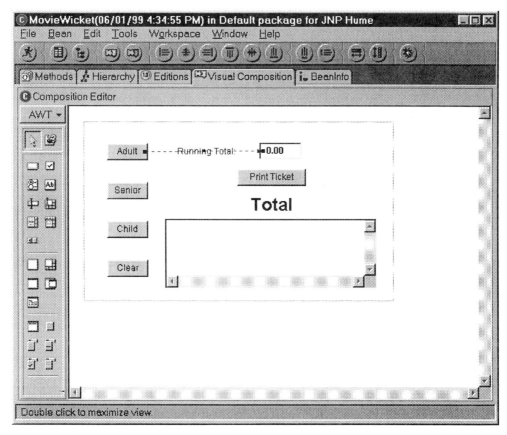

Figure 15.19 The Button to TextField Connection Completed

Another connection line appears starting at the first connection line and ending with a spider at the mouse's current location. Move the mouse off the drawing area which is outlined by a gray box. As you do this, a red dashed box appears surrounding the gray box. Setting the end of the connection outside the drawing surface specifies that the connection is to be external to the already-placed beans.

Now, click the mouse button in the area between the two boxes shown in Figure 15.21. When you release the mouse button a sub-menu appears. Select *Parameter from Code...* to specify that the value to be sent to the other connection is the result of a method. Figure 15.22 shows the menu with *Parameter from Code...*

A second dialog box (shown in Figure 15.23) comes up with the methods that can be used. These include the ones you have created. Select *addAdult* and press OK. The two connection lines now become solid (Figure 15.24). The connection line going outside the drawing area is drawn to a box containing the name of the method used by the connection. The solid connection indicates that all of the needed elements are in place. (The connection had been dashed before to indicate that you had not yet supplied a value for *RunningTotal*.)

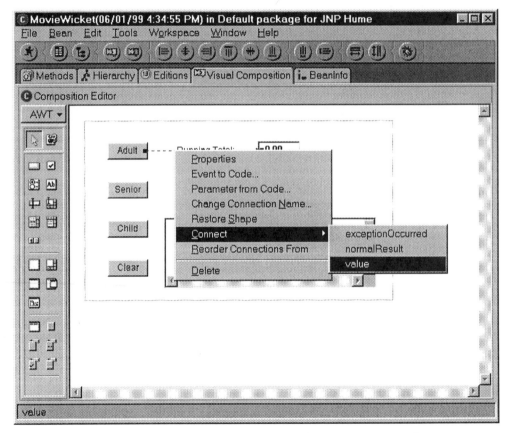

Figure 15.20 Setting the Value for *RunningTotal*

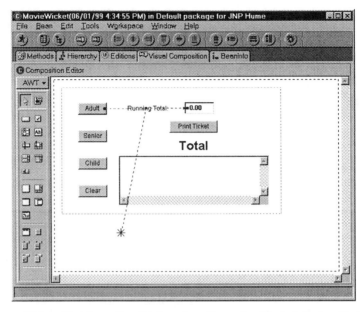

Figure 15.21 Setting the Value for *RunningTotal* to be External

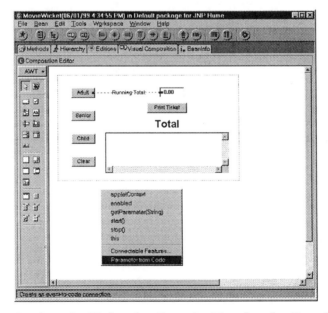

Figure 15.22 Setting the Value for *RunningTotal* to be Result of Method

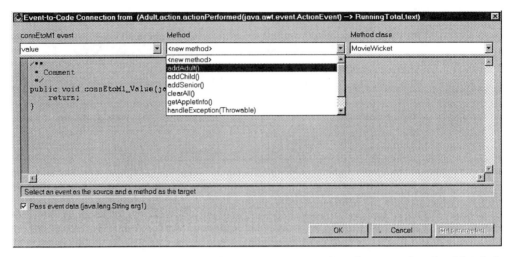

Figure 15.23 Setting the Value for *RunningTotal* to be Result of *addAdult*

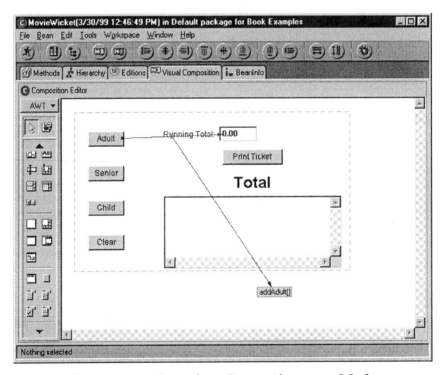

Figure 15.24 Complete Connection now Made

To test what you have done so far, select the *Run* icon button. Now that the adult button connection has been made, try clicking the *Adult* button and watch the running total go up by 8 dollars each time you click.

The same set of connections for the *Senior* and *Child* buttons must be made to the *addSenior* and *addChild* methods. See Figure 15.25.

Once again, save the beans and run the applet to see that the three buttons work correctly.

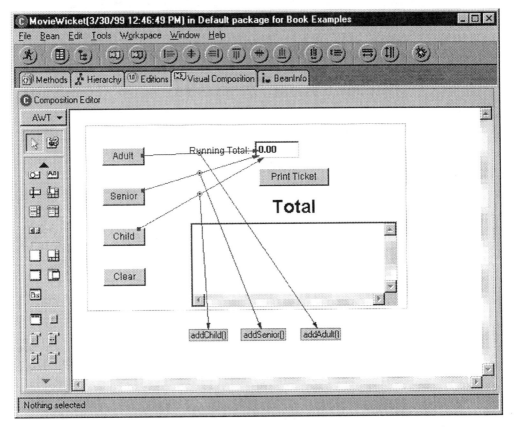

Figure 15.25 Connections from Other Buttons Now Made

A similar connection is made from the *PrintTicket* button to the text area (labelled "Total"). You connect the *actionPerformed* method, shown in Figure 15.16, to the *text* method of the text area and then connect that newly-made connection from the *value* to outside the drawing area as shown in Figure 15.20. Now, select the *Parameter from Code...* menu item (see Figure 15.22) and choose the *printTicket* method shown in Figure 15.23. It should now look like Figure 15.26.

Clicking the *PrintTicket* button sets a value for the *Total* text area. This value is specified as the string that is returned from the *printTicket* method (see *printTicket* method).

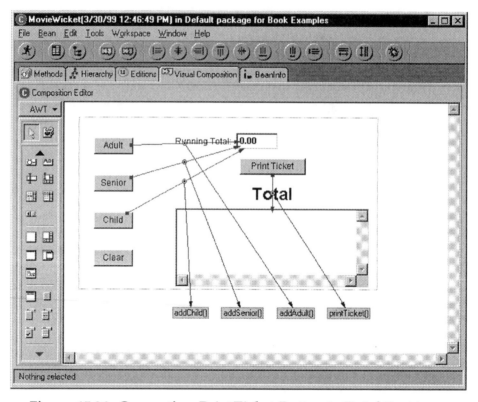

Figure 15.26 Connecting *PrintTicket* Button to *Total* TextArea

The *Clear* button performs three functions when pressed:

- sets the value of adults, children, seniors, and total to zero by calling the *clearAll* method,
- changes the *RunningTotal* text field to "0.00", and
- clears the contents of the *Total* text area.

To implement the *Clear* button, you need to connect it to the *clearAll* method. To do this, place the mouse over the *Clear* button and push the button on the mouse's right side. From the menus that now appear, select *Connect* and *actionPerformed*. Now click the other side of the connection to outside the drawing area as illustrated in Figure 15.27.

Clicking outside the drawing area brings up a new menu. Select *Event to Code...* This specifies that a method should be called when the button is pressed. Figure 15.28 shows the menu where *Event to Code...* can be selected.

Once you select *Event to Code...* a dialog box appears that lets you select the *clearAll* method. Figure 15.29 shows the dialog box and Figure 15.30 shows the results.

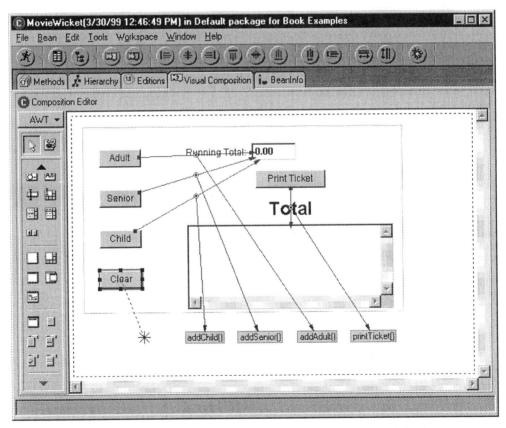

Figure 15.27 Connecting the *Clear* Button to Outside Area

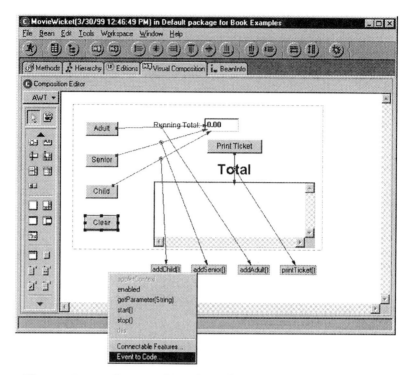

Figure 15.28 Connecting the *Clear* Button to a Method

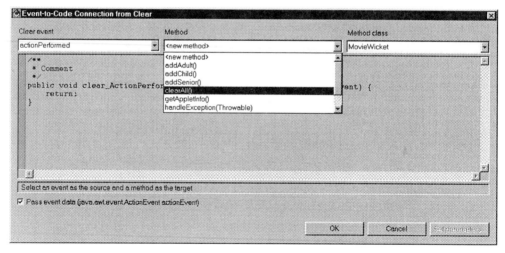

Figure 15.29 Connecting the *Clear* Button to a *clearAll* Method

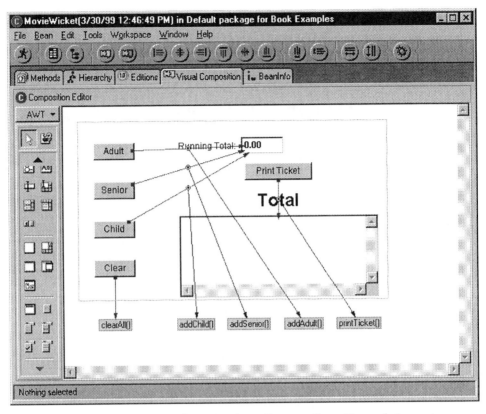

Figure 15.30 *Clear* **Button Connection Complete**

The *Clear* button must also set the running total to zero. Make a connection between these two as with the *Adult* button (A single button click can activate multiple connections).

You now click on the connection and select the *Properties* menu item. This brings up the *Event-to-method connection* dialog box with *actionPerformed* and *text* already selected (Figure 15.31). There is no need to use *Connect* because *RunningTotal* will always be set to the same value ("0.00"). Click the *setParameters* button at the bottom of the dialog box that appears. This brings up yet another dialog box in which you set the *value* for the running total to "0.00". Figure 15.32 shows the dialog box for the *Constant Parameter Value Settings*. Once this is done, click the *OK* buttons of the two dialog boxes to dismiss them.

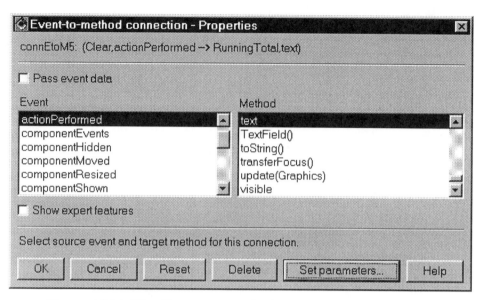

Figure 15.31 The *Event-to-method connection* Dialog Box

Figure 15.32 Setting *RunningTotal* to Constant Value of Zero

After the *PrintTicket* button has been pressed, when any of the four buttons (*Adult*, *Child*, *Senior*, and *Clear*) is clicked, the *Total* text area must first be set to a blank so that the previous ticket will be erased before the next ticket is entered.

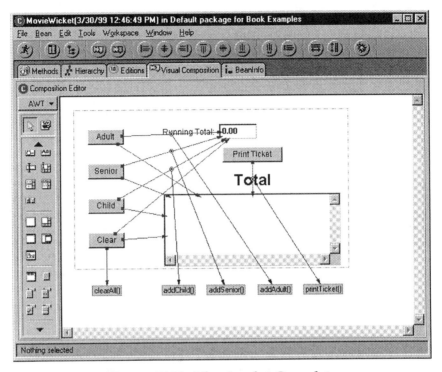

Figure 15.33 The Applet Complete

To set the *Total* text area to blank, make four connections, one from each of the four buttons on the left, to the text area and set the *value* for each to be a space (" "). This clears the total. Figure 15.33 shows the final result.

Save the beans again and you are ready to test the final applet. This process of making connections may seem complicated at first but will become routine with repeated use.

15.7 Using Other JavaBeans

When you use the *Visual Composition Editor*, a dashed rectangle appears on the free-form surface. This is the *Applet* bean. It can be adjusted in size, just as any other bean can, by selecting it and dragging on a selection handle. The size of the applet can also be changed by editing the *constraint* property of the Applet, which specifies the applet's height and width. If the applet's size is changed, then the width and height of the Applet Viewer should also be changed (as was done in Section 15.5).

When the mouse pointer is loaded with a bean it changes to a cross-hair. If you have selected the wrong bean you can **unload** it by selecting the correct bean or by clicking the **Selection** tool (the one with the diagonal arrow) at the top of the bean palette.

Not all beans are listed in the bean palette. To select a bean that is not in the palette (for example, the *Canvas* bean), click the **Choose Bean** tool beside the Selection tool. This brings up a dialog box where the full name of the bean can be entered (for example, java.awt.Canvas). Clicking *OK* loads the mouse cursor with the specified bean.

You can open a bean's *Properties* window by double clicking on the bean or right-clicking the bean and selecting *Properties* from the pop-up menu. You change the bean's font by selecting the *font* property, and then selecting the button that appears in the *value* column for *font*. This opens a *Fonts* window in which the font name, point size, and style can be entered. Figure 15.34 shows the *Fonts* window.

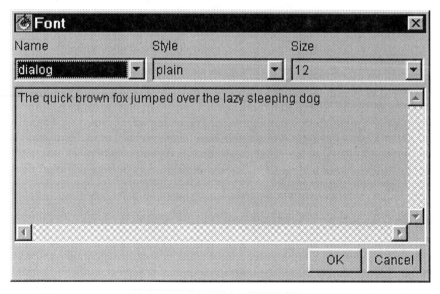

Figure 15.34 Font Window

Chapter 9 contained an example applet that drew an oval or a rectangle on a canvas depending on which of two buttons was pressed, filled or not depending upon whether a *filled* checkbox was checked or not, and in a color controlled by a group of three radio buttons labelled *red*, *blue*, and *green*. The components were in panels.

Icons for these four new beans: *Panel*, *Canvas*, *Checkbox*, and *CheckboxGroup* (used to create radio buttons) can be chosen from the bean palette.

- The *Panel* is the first icon in the second group of icons (it looks like an empty square).
- The *Canvas* must be selected using the *Select Bean* tool.
- The *Checkbox* is in the top group.
- The *CheckboxGroup* is also in top group.
- A radio button is a *Checkbox* that has been associated with a *CheckboxGroup*.

When you are creating applets without the Visual Builder (as in Chapter 9) *Panels* help you layout the applet more easily. When you use the Visual Builder, however, there is less need to use *Panels*. *Panels* are still useful for evenly placing beans. If you place several beans on a *Panel* bean, then the *Distribute-Vertically* and *Distribute-Horizontally* tools will distribute the beans evenly over the panel rather than the entire applet.

To assign text to a *Checkbox*, you enter the text in the *value* field of the *text* property in the *Checkbox* property sheet. To establish the initial state of a checkbox (checked or not), you then set the *state* property to *true* or *false*. The default state is *false*.

To associate a checkbox with a group, connect the *CheckboxGroup* **this** property to the *CheckboxGroup* property of the *Checkbox* for each *Checkbox* bean. This makes it a radio button. To define the default checkbox, connect the *Checkbox's* **this** property to the *selectedCheckbox* property of the *CheckboxGroup*.

There are many other beans available, including: Menu, Choice, Dialog, Frame, List, PopupMenu, Scrollbar, and Window.

15.8 Connections

In *VisualAge for Java* you draw connections between beans to define their interaction. As each connection is made, bean **features** from each end point are selected. The types of features – property, method, event, or code – at each end give the type of connection.

The first end point of the connection is called the **source**, the second end is called the **target**. A colored connection line appears when both ends of the connection have been made. The color depends on the features that have been selected.

The types of connections and colors are:

- **Property-to-property** connection; when the value of the source property changes, a value of the target property changes. (blue)

- **Event-to-method** connection; when the event takes place in the *source*, a method of the *target* bean is called. For example, when the *Adult* button is pressed, call the *TextField's setText* method. (green)

- **Event-to-code** connection; when an event takes place in the *source*, a user written method is called. For example, when the *Clear* button is pressed, call the *clearAll* method. (green)

- **Parameter-from-property** connection; uses a property as a parameter. Target is a connection. (purple)

- **Parameter-from-code** connection; uses the result of a call to a user-written method as a parameter. Target is a connection. For example, in the connection from the *Adult* button to the *RunningTotal TextField*, the parameter for *setText* is determined by the return value of the *addAdult* method. (purple)

- **Parameter-from-method** connection; uses the result of a method in a bean as a parameter to a connection. Target is a connection. (purple)

Try experimenting with connections. Can you categorize the connections in the example *MovieWicket*? Follow through the example a step at a time and watch the color of the connections.

15.9 Chapter Summary

Programmers have come to expect the user-friendliness of a good graphical user interface in a professional program. Building such interfaces in Java requires the use of the Java library **Abstract Windowing Toolkit** (awt). In Chapter 9 we showed how interfaces can be built directly by programming in Java using the methods of *java.awt*. *VisualAge for Java* provides the means for building a graphical user interface visually. This Visual Builder uses the *Visual Composition Editor*.

JavaBeans

A *JavaBean* (**bean**) is a standard component model for Java and is the basis of *VisualAge for Java*. The *Visual Composition Editor* allows you to assemble beans from a standard **palette** of beans.

You select beans by selecting the actual bean from the bean palette. You use the mouse to move the beans one-by-one into an applet window shown with a gray outline on a free-form surface beside the beans palette.

Before you begin, however, you must design an interface. Once the design is completed, the appropriate beans are moved, sized, and aligned to produce the desired interface. In the example shown in detail in this chapter, we used *Label*, *Button*, *TextField*, and *TextArea* beans.

Status Area

Along the bottom of the *Visual Composition Editor* window is an area where information is displayed to indicate what is currently selected.

Tool Bar

A row of icon buttons across the top of the *Visual Composition Editor* window provides a means of aligning and spacing beans that have been placed in the *Applet* window.

Connections

After the beans have been laid out in the window, the logical connections between the beans must be drawn using the mouse. These connections will not appear in the final interface, but allow the Visual Builder to create the required Java code. Connections go from one component – the **source** to another – the **target**. In some cases the connection itself is the source and the target is either a method or a component which is then connected to a method. The lines of the connections are in different colors depending on the type of connection being made.

Other Java Beans

Other beans referred to in this text but not in the example are given. These include: *Panel, Canvas, Checkbox,* and radio buttons which use *CheckboxGroup*.

15.10 Exercises

1. Build a class called *MovieWicket2* exactly as is done with *MovieWicket* in this chapter to see that you have followed the various steps. Note the colors of the connections to see what kind of connections they are.

2. Use the *VisualAge for Java* Visual Builder to program an applet equivalent to the *ControlDraw* class of Chapter 9.

3. Try printing the *MovieWicket* class to see if you can follow what is being produced automatically by the Visual Builder.

4. Use the *VisualAge for Java* Visual Builder to create an interface and an applet that has the user:

   • enter two real numbers in two text fields,
   • select a radio button to indicate the operation,
   • add, subtract, multiply, and divide as required,
   • press a button to cause the calculation to be done, and
   • display the result in a third text field.

Chapter 16

Advanced GUIs:
The Console Class

In previous chapters we discussed programming applets in Java. A window, called the *Applet Viewer*, is provided for displaying graphical user interfaces, receiving input, and showing output, as well as showing graphics. A Java application program, however, requires users to set up their own windows.

Throughout this book, we have been using the *Console* class developed by Holt Software Associates (*hsa*) to create a window, and to provide methods for input and output, and drawing graphics. In this chapter, we will examine the structure of a class that is similar to the *Console* class as an example of a large Java class.

16.1 The Console Class

When instantiated in an application program, the *Console* class provides a window for user interaction. There is a border around the window to frame it. At the top of the window is a panel that contains a single button labelled "Quit". Below is a pane that is used for both text input and output, and graphics. Figure 16.1 shows the window.

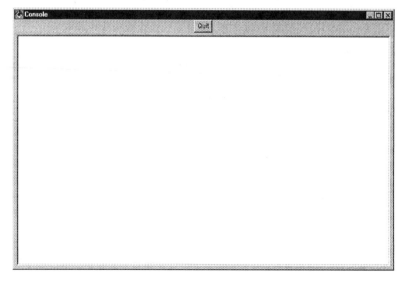

Figure 16.1 A *BaseConsole* Window

In Java all input is by characters or lines of characters. When necessary, these characters or lines of characters must be parsed and changed to integers, reals, booleans, and so on. Java standard output is also as strings of characters. All primitive classes must therefore be converted to strings for output.

The *Console* class has methods for reading all the primitive data types. To accomplish this task, the *Console* class must read characters and do the conversions. Where the required conversion is not possible, for example if a real number is input instead of an integer, the *Console* must give an error message and halt execution.

Graphics in Java are drawn on a canvas which also must be instantiated and sized. The *Console* class pane can be used as a window for text 25 rows by 80 columns, or a canvas for graphics that is *getWidth* pixels wide and *getHeight* pixels high. The size of the canvas is determined by the font size used for characters.

The complete *Console* class with the *ConsoleCanvas* class that it uses are highly complex and so we have distilled the essence of these classes into two simpler classes that we call the *BaseConsole* class and the *BaseConsoleCanvas* class. We will now examine these simpler classes and explain many of their features. The classes are shown in segments interspersed with explanations. Some of the Java library classes that these classes use (such as the *Frame* class) have not been covered in previous chapters of this book.

By looking more closely at these example classes, you should gain a better understanding of the nature of very large Java classes.

16.2 The BaseConsole Class

The *BaseConsole* class is a subclass of the Java *Frame* class. A *Frame* object is automatically instantiated when the *BaseConsole* class is instantiated in an application program (as happens with the full *hsa Console* class in all our application program examples).

The *BaseConsole* constructor instantiates a window (a Frame) that has a panel at the top with a button labelled "Quit". The panel is instantiated, has its color set to *lightGray*, and is laid out across the top of the window using a *FlowLayout* manager. The *Quit* button is added to it and the panel is centered. A canvas is instantiated from the *BaseConsoleCanvas* class big enough to hold

25 rows and 80 columns of text. The panel and canvas are then placed in the frame using the default *BorderLayout* manager of *Frame*, with the panel in the "North" position and the canvas in the "Center" position.

The *Frame* is then moved using its *setLocation* method so that its top-left corner is at the screen origin. Its background color is then set to *lightGray*. The Frame is declared as not resizable, and then displayed. In this part of the *BaseConsole* class various variables are declared for reading input from the keyboard. All input is buffered in two steps using: the **keyboard buffer** and the **line buffer**.

Here is the *BaseConsole* class so far.

```
// The "BaseConsole" class.
import java.awt.*;
import java.io.*;
import java.text.*;

public class BaseConsole extends Frame
{
    protected static final int CONSOLE_ROWS = 25;
    protected static final int CONSOLE_COLS = 80;

    // The "Quit" button at the top of the console.
    Button quitButton = new Button ("Quit");

    // The actual drawing pane on the console.
    BaseConsoleCanvas pane;

    // Initialize text variables.
    int gCurrentRow = 1, gCurrentCol = 1;
    int gActualRow = 1, gActualCol = 1;
    int gMaxRow = 0, gMaxCol = 0;
    int gStartCol = 0, gStartRow = 0;

    // Keyboard buffer variables. All input is buffered in two steps
    // the keyboard buffer and the line buffer.
    protected static final int kBufferSize = 2048;
    protected static final int kEmptyBuffer = -1;
    char [] gKbdBuffer = new char [kBufferSize];
    int gKbdBufferHead = 0, gKbdBufferTail = 0;
    char [] gLineBuffer = new char [kBufferSize];
    int gLineBufferHead = 0, gLineBufferTail = 0;
```

```
    int gUngetChar = kEmptyBuffer;

    // Initialize the default graphics color.
    Color gGraphicsColor = Color.black;

    // Constructor.
    public BaseConsole ()
    {
        super ("Base Console");     // Calls Frame class constructor.

        // Instantiate an object of the BaseConsoleCanvas class.
        pane = new BaseConsoleCanvas (CONSOLE_ROWS,
            CONSOLE_COLS);
        gMaxRow = CONSOLE_ROWS;
        gMaxCol = CONSOLE_COLS;

        // Add quitButton to lightGray panel using FlowLayout.
        Panel quitPanel = new Panel ();
        quitPanel.setBackground (Color.lightGray);
        quitPanel.setLayout (new FlowLayout (FlowLayout.CENTER, 0, 0));
        quitPanel.add (quitButton);

        // Add quitPanel and pane to Frame using BorderLayout.
        add ("North", quitPanel);
        add ("Center", pane);

        // Move the console window to the upper left corner of screen.
        setLocation (0, 0);

        // Do layout and display Frame using Frame methods.
        setBackground (Color.lightGray);
        setResizable (false);
        pack ();
        show ();
    } // BaseConsole constructor

    // Method to close the console window.
    public void close ()
    {
        dispose ();
    } // close method
} /* BaseConsole class */
```

16.3 Methods of BaseConsole for Graphics

The complete *Console* class contains more graphics methods than included here. In this example we will use only *drawLine, drawRect, fillRect, drawOval,* and *fillOval.*

Each one of these methods calls a similarly named method of the *BaseConsoleCanvas* class which has been instantiated as the *pane* object in the first part of the code for the *BaseConsole* class.

Here is the part of the *BaseConsole* class that has the graphics methods.

```
// Method to draw a line on the pane from (x1, y1) to (x2, y2).
public void drawLine (int x1, int y1, int x2, int y2)
{
    pane.drawLine (x1, y1, x2, y2, gGraphicsColor);
} // drawLine method

// Method to draw an oval on the pane in the rectangle from (x, y)
// to (x + width, y + height).
public void drawOval (int x, int y, int width, int height)
{
    pane.drawOval (x, y, width, height, gGraphicsColor);
} // drawOval method

// Method to draw a rectangle on the pane from (x, y) to
// (x + width, y + width).
public void drawRect (int x, int y, int width, int height)
{
    pane.drawRect (x, y, width, height, gGraphicsColor);
} // drawRect method

// Method to draw a filled oval on the pane in the rectangle
// from (x, y) to (x + width, y + height).
public void fillOval (int x, int y, int width, int height)
{
    pane.fillOval (x, y, width, height, gGraphicsColor);
} // fillOval method
```

```
// Draws a filled rectangle on the pane from (x, y) to
// (x + width, y + width).
public void fillRect (int x, int y, int width, int height)
{
    pane.fillRect (x, y, width, height, gGraphicsColor);
} // fillRect method

// Method for returning the width of the drawing area in pixels.
public int getWidth ()
{
    return pane.getWidth ();
} // getWidth method

// Method for returning the height of the window in pixels for graphics.
public int getHeight ()
{
    return pane.getHeight ();
} // getHeight method

// Method to set the foreground color for any graphics.
public void setColor (Color pmColor)
{
    gGraphicsColor = pmColor;
} // setColor method
```

16.4 Methods of BaseConsole for Basic Text Input

Here are the basic text methods of the *BaseConsole* class.

- The *clear* method uses the *BaseConsoleCanvas* method *clearScreen* to clear the canvas and set the cursor position to row 1, column 1.
- The *erasePreviousChar* method erases the previous character in a line of input when the user presses a backspace when typing.
- The *handleEvent* method handles both keystrokes and the "Quit" button being pressed. When "Quit" is the event, the application is stopped and all open windows closed.

- The *handleKeystroke* method places a keystroke in the keyboard buffer. The method is labelled **synchronized** so that values cannot be placed in and removed from the keyboard buffer at the same time. This method relies on the *notify* method of *Frame* class to wake up any processes that are **sleeping** while waiting for keyboard input.
- The *setCursor* method sets the cursor at a particular row and column.
- The *readChar* method reads a single character from one of the keystroke buffers.

```
// Method to clear the pane and move the cursor to the top–left corner.
public void clear ()
{
    pane.clearScreen ();
    gCurrentRow = 1;
    gCurrentCol = 1;
    gActualRow = 1;
    gActualCol = 1;
    pane.setCursorPos (gCurrentRow, gCurrentCol);
} // clear method

// Method to erase the previous character in a line of input.
// Called when the user presses backspace when typing.
private void erasePreviousChar ()
{
    if (gCurrentCol > 1)
    {
        gCurrentCol--;
    }
    else
    {
        if (gCurrentRow > 1)
        {
            gCurrentRow--;
            gCurrentCol = gMaxCol;
        }
    }
    gActualRow = gCurrentRow;
    gActualCol = gCurrentCol;
```

```
        pane.drawText (gCurrentRow, gCurrentCol, " ");
        pane.setCursorPos (gCurrentRow, gCurrentCol);

        if ((gCurrentCol == 1) && (gCurrentRow != gStartRow))
        {
            gCurrentCol = gMaxCol + 1;
            gCurrentRow--;
        }
    } // erasePreviousChar method

    // Overrides the handleEvent method of Frame. Method to handle both
    // keystrokes and the Quit button being pressed.
    // Overrides the handleEvent method of Frame.  Method to handle both
    // keystrokes and the Quit button being pressed.
    public boolean handleEvent (Event evt)
    {
        switch (evt.id)
        {
            case Event.KEY_PRESS:
                handleKeystroke ((char) evt.key);
                return (true);
            case Event.ACTION_EVENT:
                if (evt.target == quitButton)
                {
                    System.exit (0);
                }
                break;
            case Event.WINDOW_DESTROY:
                System.exit (0);
                break;
        }
        return super.handleEvent (evt);
    } // handleEvent method
```

```
// Method to place a keystroke in the keyboard buffer. It is
// synchronized so that there can't be a problem with input being
// taken off the keyboard buffer and placed on the keyboard buffer
// at the same time.
private synchronized void handleKeystroke (char ch)
{
    // Place the keystroke into the keyboard buffer.
    gKbdBuffer [gKbdBufferHead] = ch;
    gKbdBufferHead = (gKbdBufferHead + 1) % kBufferSize;

    // The following statements wakes up any processes that are
    // sleeping while waiting for keyboard input.
    notify ();
} // handleKeystroke method

// Method to reads a single character from the one of the keystroke
// buffers.
public synchronized char readChar ()
{
    char result, ch;

    // If a character in the "ungot" buffer, return that.
    if (gUngetChar != kEmptyBuffer)
    {
        result = (char) gUngetChar;
        gUngetChar = kEmptyBuffer;
        return (result);
    }

    // If there are characters in the line buffer, return the head of the
    // buffer.
    if (gLineBufferHead != gLineBufferTail)
    {
        result = gLineBuffer [gLineBufferTail];
        gLineBufferTail = (gLineBufferTail + 1) % kBufferSize;
        return (result);
    }

    gStartRow = gCurrentRow;
    gStartCol = gCurrentCol;
    if (gCurrentRow > gMaxRow)
    {
```

```
        gStartRow++;
        gCurrentCol = 1;
    }


    // Wait for a character to be entered.
    while (true)
    {
        while (gKbdBufferHead == gKbdBufferTail)
        {
            try
            {
                wait ();
            }
            catch (InterruptedException e) { }
        }

        // Once there's a character in the keyboard buffer, transfer it
        // to the line buffer until we reach a newline.
        ch = gKbdBuffer [gKbdBufferTail];
        gKbdBufferTail = (gKbdBufferTail + 1) % kBufferSize;

        if (ch == '\n')
        {
            print ("\n");
            gLineBuffer [gLineBufferHead] = '\n';
            gLineBufferHead = (gLineBufferHead + 1) % kBufferSize;
            break;
        }
        if (ch == '\b')
        {
            if (gLineBufferHead != gLineBufferTail)
            {
                gLineBufferHead =
                    (gLineBufferHead + kBufferSize - 1) % kBufferSize;
                erasePreviousChar ();
            }
        } // if backspace
        else
        {
            print (ch);
            gLineBuffer [gLineBufferHead] = ch;
            gLineBufferHead = (gLineBufferHead + 1) % kBufferSize;
```

```
        }
    } // while

    // The line buffer is now full.  Return the head of the buffer.
    result = gLineBuffer [gLineBufferTail];
    gLineBufferTail = (gLineBufferTail + 1) % kBufferSize;

    return result;
} // readChar method

// Method to move the cursor to a specified row and column.
public void setCursor (int pmRow, int pmCol)
{
    gCurrentRow = pmRow;
    gCurrentCol = pmCol;
    gActualRow = pmRow;
    gActualCol = pmCol;
    pane.setCursorPos (gCurrentRow, gCurrentCol);
} // setCursor method
```

The *readChar* method first attempts to read a character from the "ungot" character buffer (a one-character buffer where a character is placed when one more character than necessary has been read). If the "ungot" character buffer is empty, *readChar* attempts to read from the line buffer. If the line buffer is empty, *readChar* attempts to read a line of input from the keyboard buffer. If the keyboard buffer is empty, a line of input is then read. The *readChar* method calls the *wait* () method of the *Frame* class. The *wait* sits until the *notify* () method of *Frame* is called.

Whenever a key is pressed, Java calls the *handleEvent* method of the *Frame* class where the component that caused the event is tested. If the event is a keystroke, the *handleKeystroke* method is called. This method in turn puts the character into the keyboard buffer and calls *notify* (). If the *BaseConsole* has called the *wait* () method, *notify* () wakes the **thread** up. (A thread is a process waiting for execution.) If the keystroke does not finish the line of input, *readChar* adds the keystroke in the keyboard buffer to the line buffer and calls *wait* () again. Once there is a full line of input, the next set of calls to *readChar* will return immediately with a character from the line buffer until it is empty.

16.5 Methods of BaseConsole Class for Output

There are a number of output methods in the *BaseConsole* class named *print*. The *print* method is said to be overloaded. This means that the particular *print* used depends on the number and data types of its arguments. The *println* methods are similar to the *print* methods except that they put an end of line after the last character's output.

The methods are rather long because many of them include output format items such as field size and number of decimal places. All output in Java must be converted to strings so that the *print* method for printing a string is called by all the other print methods.

Here is the method for printing a string.

```
// Method to print a character (a "char") in the pane.
public void print (char theChar)
{
    print (String.valueOf (theChar));
} // print method

// Method to print a String in the pane.  All other print methods
// eventually call this routine to print the output to the pane.
// This routine handles setting the cursor properly, scrolling the
// pane if necessary and displaying the text.
public void print (String text)
{
    int index = 0;
    int len = text.length ();
    int start = 0;
    char ch;

    // Each time through the loop we try to print all the characters
    // in the string to be printed up to either the end of the line on
    // the pane or a newline in the string.
    while (true)
    {
        index = start;
```

```
if (index == len)
{
    pane.setCursorPos (gActualRow, gActualCol);
    return;
}
ch = text.charAt (index);
while ((index < len) && (text.charAt (index) != '\n') &&
    (index – start < gMaxCol – gCurrentCol))
{
    index++;
}

// We have reached the end of the string, the end of the line
// in the pane, or a newline.
if (start != index)
{
    // Draw what we have so far.
    pane.drawText (gCurrentRow, gCurrentCol,
        text.substring (start, index));
    gCurrentCol += index – start;
    gActualCol = gCurrentCol;
}

// If we've reached the end of the string, set the cursor and
// return.
if (index == len)
{
    pane.setCursorPos (gActualRow, gActualCol);
    return;
}

// We've either reached a newline or the end of the line
// on the pane.
if (text.charAt (index) == '\n')
{
    if (gCurrentRow < gMaxRow)
    {
        gCurrentCol = 1;
        gCurrentRow++;
        gActualCol = gCurrentCol;
        gActualRow = gCurrentRow;
    }
```

```
        else
        {
            pane.scrollUpALine ();
            gStartRow--;
            gCurrentCol = 1;
            gActualCol = gCurrentCol;
        }
    }
    else
    {
        if (gCurrentCol <= gMaxCol)
        {
            pane.drawText (gCurrentRow, gCurrentCol,
                text.substring (index, index + 1));
            if (gCurrentCol < gMaxCol)
            {
                gCurrentCol++;
                gActualCol = gCurrentCol;
            }
            else
            {
                if (gCurrentRow < gMaxRow)
                {
                    gCurrentCol++;
                    gActualCol = 1;
                    gActualRow++;
                }
                else
                {
                    gCurrentCol++;
                }
            }
        }
        else
        {
            if (gCurrentRow < gMaxRow)
            {
                gCurrentRow++;
            }
            else
            {
                pane.scrollUpALine ();
```

```
                gStartRow--;
            }
            pane.drawText (gCurrentRow, 1,
                    text.substring (index, index + 1));
            gCurrentCol = 2;
            gActualCol = gCurrentCol;
            gActualRow = gCurrentRow;
        }
    }
    start = index + 1;
    } // while
} // print method
```

Many of the statements of this *print* method have to do with starting a new line automatically when the last column is reached, or scrolling the output if necessary.

Here are the other *print* and *println* methods.

```
// Method to print a double precision floating point number (a "double")
// in the pane.
public void print (double theDouble)
{
    print (String.valueOf (theDouble));
} // print method

// Method to print a double precision floating point number (a "double")
// with a specified field size in the pane.
public void print (double theDouble, int fieldSize)
{
    double posValue = Math.abs (theDouble);
    int placesRemaining  = fieldSize;
    String format = null, numStr;
    StringBuffer padding = new StringBuffer ();

    if (theDouble < 0) placesRemaining--; // Space for the minus sign.
    if (posValue < 10.0) format = "0";
    else if (posValue < 100.0) format = "00";
    else if (posValue < 1000.0) format = "000";
    else if (posValue < 10000.0) format = "0000";
    else if (posValue < 100000.0) format = "00000";
```

```
        else if (posValue < 1000000.0) format = "000000";
        else if (posValue < 10000000.0) format = "0000000";
        else if (posValue < 100000000.0) format = "00000000";

        if (format == null)
        {
            // We're using scientific notation.
            numStr = String.valueOf (theDouble);
        }
        else
        {
            // Add a decimal point, if there's room.
            placesRemaining -= format.length ();
            if (placesRemaining > 0)
            {
                format = format + ".";
                placesRemaining--;
            }

            // For any additional room, add more decimal places.
            for (int cnt = 0 ; cnt < placesRemaining ; cnt++)
            {
                format = format + "#";
            }

            // Convert the number.
            NumberFormat form = new DecimalFormat (format);
            numStr = form.format (theDouble);
        }

        // If the number is not long enough, pad with spaces.
        for (int cnt = 0 ; cnt < fieldSize – numStr.length () ; cnt++)
        {
            padding.append (' ');
        }
        print (padding + numStr);
    } // print method
```

```java
// Method to print a double precision floating point number (a "double")
// with a specified field size and a specified number of decimal places
// in the pane.
public void print (double theDouble, int fieldSize, int decimalPlaces)
{
    double posValue = Math.abs (theDouble);
    int placesRemaining = fieldSize;
    String format = null, numStr;
    StringBuffer padding = new StringBuffer ();

    if (theDouble < 0) placesRemaining--;  // Space for the minus sign.
    if (posValue < 10.0) format = "0";
    else if (posValue < 100.0) format = "00";
    else if (posValue < 1000.0) format = "000";
    else if (posValue < 10000.0) format = "0000";
    else if (posValue < 100000.0) format = "00000";
    else if (posValue < 1000000.0) format = "000000";
    else if (posValue < 10000000.0) format = "0000000";
    else if (posValue < 100000000.0) format = "00000000";

    if (Math.abs (theDouble) >= 100000000.0)
    {
        // We're using scientific notation.
        numStr = String.valueOf (theDouble);
    }
    else
    {
        format = "0.";

        // For any additional room, add more decimal places.
        for (int cnt = 0 ; cnt < decimalPlaces ; cnt++)
        {
            format = format + "0";
        }

        // Convert the number.
        NumberFormat form = new DecimalFormat (format);
        numStr = form.format (theDouble);
    }

    // If the number is not long enough, pad with spaces.
    for (int cnt = 0 ; cnt < fieldSize - numStr.length () ; cnt++)
    {
```

```
            padding.append (' ');
        }
    print (padding + numStr);
} // print method

// Method to print an integer (an "int") in the pane.
public void print (int theInt)
{
    print (String.valueOf (theInt));
} // print method

// Method to print an integer (an "int") with a specified field size
// in the pane.
public void print (int theInt, int fieldSize)
{
    String numStr = String.valueOf (theInt);
    StringBuffer padding = new StringBuffer ();

    for (int cnt = 0 ; cnt < fieldSize – numStr.length () ; cnt++)
        {
            padding.append (' ');
        }
    print (padding + numStr);
} // print method

// Method to print a String with a specified field size in the pane.
public void print (String text, int fieldSize)
{
    StringBuffer padding = new StringBuffer ();

    for (int cnt = 0 ; cnt < fieldSize – text.length () ; cnt++)
        {
            padding.append (' ');
        }
    print (text + padding);
} // print method

// Method to print a boolean (a "boolean") in the pane.
public void print (boolean theBoolean)
{
    print (String.valueOf (theBoolean));
} // print method
```

```java
// Method to print an newline in the pane.
public void println ()
{
    print ("\n");
} // println method

// Method to print a character (a "char") followed by a newline
// in the pane.
public void println (char theChar)
{
    println (String.valueOf (theChar));
} // println method

// Method to print a double precision floating point number (a "double")
// followed by a newline in the pane.
public void println (double theDouble)
{
    println (String.valueOf (theDouble));
} // println method

// Method to print a double precision floating point number (a "double")
// with a specified field size followed by a newline in the pane.
public void println (double theDouble, int fieldSize)
{
    print (theDouble, fieldSize);
    print ("\n");
} // println method

// Method to print a double precision floating point number (a "double")
// with a specified field size and a specified number of decimal places
// followed by a newline in the pane.
public void println (double theDouble, int fieldSize, int decimalPlaces)
{
    print (theDouble, fieldSize, decimalPlaces);
    print ("\n");
} // println method

// Method to print an integer (an "int") followed by a newline
// in the pane.
public void println (int theInt)
{
    println (String.valueOf (theInt));
} // println method
```

```
// Method to print an integer (an "int") with a specified field size
// followed by a newline in the pane.
public void println (int theInt, int fieldSize)
{
    String numStr = String.valueOf (theInt);
    StringBuffer padding = new StringBuffer ();

    for (int cnt = 0 ; cnt < fieldSize – numStr.length () ; cnt++)
    {
        padding.append (' ');
    }
    println (padding + numStr);
} // println method

// Method to print a String followed by a newline in the pane.
public void println (String text)
{
    print (text);
    print ("\n");
} // println method

// Method to print a String with a specified field size followed
// by a newline in the pane.
public void println (String text, int fieldSize)
{
    StringBuffer padding = new StringBuffer ();

    for (int cnt = 0 ; cnt < fieldSize – text.length () ; cnt++)
    {
        padding.append (' ');
    }
    println (text + padding);
} // println method

// Method to print a boolean (a "boolean") followed by a newline
// in the pane.
public void println (boolean theBoolean)
{
    println (String.valueOf (theBoolean));
} // println method
```

When an integer is output with a field size specified, the integer is first converted to a string and then padded on the left with blanks to the specified size. Strings are padded on the right.

Output of **float** items is more complicated. By default Java's *toString* method for float numbers converts to about 16 decimal places. To make the format more manageable, a **decimal formatter** (already shown in the *MovieWicket* class in Chapter 15) is used with these statements

> *NumberFormat form* = **new** *DecimalFormat (formatString);*
> *String numberString = form.format (number);*

The *formatString* gives the format as a number of zeros in quotes with the position of the decimal point shown, for example, as "0000.00". If this formatting is used, the *java.text* package must be imported. Once the **float** number is converted to a string, padding by blanks adjusts it to the field size.

16.6 Methods of BaseConsole for Input

As mentioned, the *Console* class and its simplified relative the *BaseConsole* class have methods for reading all the primitive data types. These input methods in turn use the *BaseConsole* class method *readToken*. The method *readToken* skips over white space and reads characters until it hits whitespace again. This white space indicates the end of the token. White space is a space, tab, or end of line.

Here is the *readToken* method.

```
// Method to read a token from the keyboard. It skips over whitespace
// then reads characters until it hits whitespace again, which
// indicates the end of a token.
private String readToken ()
{
    char ch;
    String s = "";

    // Skip white space.
    do
```

```
    {
        ch = readChar ();
    }
    while ((ch == ' ') || (ch == '\n') || (ch == '\t'));

    // Read all the non–whitespace characters.
    do
    {
        s = s + ch;
        ch = readChar ();
    }
    while ((ch != ' ') && (ch != '\n') && (ch != '\t'));

    // Place the whitespace character that terminated the token in the
    // "ungot" buffer.
    gUngetChar = (int) ch;

    return (s);
} // readToken method
```

Here are the input methods for the various data types.

```
// Method to read a boolean from the keyboard (either "true" or "false").
public boolean readBoolean ()
{
    String s;

    s = readToken ().toLowerCase ();
    if (s.equals ("true"))
    {
        return (true);
    }
    else if (s.equals ("false"))
    {
        return (false);
    }
    else
    {
        System.out.println ("Unable to convert \"" + s + "\" to a boolean");
        System.exit (0); // Quit.
    }
```

```
        return (false);
} // readBoolean method

// Method to read a double precision floating point number (a "double")
// from the keyboard.
public double readDouble ()
{
    Double d;
    String s;

    s = readToken ();
    try
    {
        d = Double.valueOf (s);
        return (d.doubleValue ());
    }
    catch (NumberFormatException e)
    {
        System.out.println ("Unable to convert \"" + s + "\" to a double");
        System.exit (0); // Quit.
    }
    return (0.0);
} // readDouble method

// Method to read a 32-bit integer (a "int") from the keyboard.
public int readInt ()
{
    String s = readToken ();

    try
    {
        return (Integer.parseInt (s));
    }
    catch (NumberFormatException e)
    {
        System.out.println ("Unable to convert \"" + s + "\" to a int");
        System.exit (0); // Quit.
    }
    return (0);
} // readInt method

// Method to read a full line of text from the keyboard.
```

```
public String readLine ()
{
    char ch;    // The character being read in.
    String s = ""; // The string typed in.

    // Skip whitespace up to the first newline.
    do
    {
        ch = readChar ();
    }
    while (ch == ' ');

    if (ch == '\n')
    {
        ch = readChar ();
    }

    while (ch != '\n')
    {
        s = s + ch;
        ch = readChar ();
    }

    return (s);
} // readLine method

// Method to read a String from the keyboard.
public String readString ()
{
    return (readToken ());
} // readString method
```

16.7 The BaseConsoleCanvas Class

The *BaseConsoleCanvas* class is complicated to program because a complete copy of the canvas must be kept separately from what appears on the screen. This is done in case the console window is overwritten by another window.

When the obscuring window is removed, the *update* method of *BaseConsole* is automatically called to redraw the hidden parts. The border of the window, including the *Quit* button, is also redrawn. There is no need to keep a backup copy of this.

The backup copy of the canvas is in an **offscreen bitmap**. This offscreen image is copied into the onscreen window by the second last line of *doDraw*.

The size of the canvas depends on the particular computer platform being used and must be passed to *BaseConsoleCanvas* by *BaseConsole*.

Here is the *BaseConsoleCanvas* class.

```java
// The "BaseConsoleCanvas" class.
import java.awt.*;

class BaseConsoleCanvas extends Canvas
{
    protected static final int FONT_SIZE = 14;

    protected static final int MARGIN = 2;
    protected static final int DEPTH = 3;
    protected static final int GRAY_MARGIN  = 5;

    int originX, originY;
    int canvasMaxHeight, canvasMaxWidth; // Max size of canvas.
    Font font = null;
    Image offscreenImage;

    // Console variables
    int numRows, numCols;
    int numXPixels, numYPixels; // Size of drawing surface.
    int fontWidth = 0, fontHeight = 0, fontBase = 0;
    int gCursorRow = 1, gCursorCol = 1;
    // Constructor of BaseConsoleCanvas.
    public BaseConsoleCanvas (int rows, int columns)
    {
        numRows = rows;
        numCols = columns;
        font = new Font ("monospaced", Font.PLAIN, FONT_SIZE);
```

```
// Set the canvas size to the appropriate size based
// on the font size.
FontMetrics fm;
fm = Toolkit.getDefaultToolkit ().getFontMetrics (font);
fontHeight = fm.getHeight () + fm.getLeading ();
fontBase = fm.getDescent ();

// Determine maximum character width.
fontWidth = 0;
for (int ch = 0 ; ch < 256 ; ch++)
{
    fontWidth = Math.max (fontWidth, fm.charWidth (ch));
}

// Set the dimensions of the BaseConsoleCanvas.
numXPixels = numCols * fontWidth;
numYPixels = numRows * fontHeight;
canvasMaxWidth =
    numXPixels + 2 * (MARGIN + DEPTH + GRAY_MARGIN);
canvasMaxHeight =
    numYPixels + 2 * (MARGIN + DEPTH + GRAY_MARGIN);
setSize (canvasMaxWidth, canvasMaxHeight);

originX = MARGIN + DEPTH + GRAY_MARGIN;
originY = MARGIN + DEPTH + GRAY_MARGIN;
} // BaseConsoleCanvas constructor

// Overrides addNotify of Frame class in order to set up the platform
// dependent features (such as font size).
public void addNotify ()
{
    Graphics offscreenGraphics;

    super.addNotify ();

    // Create the offscreen bitmap.
    offscreenImage = createImage (numXPixels, numYPixels);
    offscreenGraphics = offscreenImage.getGraphics ();
    offscreenGraphics.setFont (font);

    // Clear the canvas to white.
    offscreenGraphics.setColor (Color.white);
```

```
        offscreenGraphics.fillRect (0, 0, numXPixels, numYPixels);
} // addNotify method

// Method to redraw the canvas (including the margins).
private void doDraw (Graphics onscreenGraphics)
{
    int cnt;
    int marginSize = MARGIN + DEPTH + GRAY_MARGIN;

    toggleCursor ();

    // Draw the grey area surrounding.
    int [] x = { − marginSize, getSize ().width,
        getSize ().width, − marginSize, − marginSize,
        − MARGIN − DEPTH, − MARGIN − DEPTH,
        numXPixels + MARGIN + DEPTH,
        numXPixels + MARGIN + DEPTH, − marginSize};
    int [] y = { − marginSize, − marginSize, getSize ().height,
        getSize ().height, − MARGIN − DEPTH, − MARGIN − DEPTH,
        numYPixels + MARGIN + DEPTH,
        numYPixels + MARGIN + DEPTH,
        − MARGIN − DEPTH, − MARGIN − DEPTH};
    onscreenGraphics.translate (originX, originY);
    onscreenGraphics.setColor (Color.lightGray);
    onscreenGraphics.fillPolygon (x, y, 10);

    // Draw the 3D Margin.
    for (cnt = MARGIN + 2 ; cnt <= MARGIN + DEPTH ; cnt++)
    {
        onscreenGraphics.draw3DRect (− cnt, − cnt,
            numXPixels + 2 * cnt − 1, numYPixels + 2 * cnt − 1, false);
    }
    onscreenGraphics.setColor (Color.black);
    onscreenGraphics.drawLine (− MARGIN − 1, − MARGIN − 1,
        numXPixels + MARGIN, − MARGIN − 1);
    onscreenGraphics.drawLine (− MARGIN − 1, − MARGIN − 1,
        − MARGIN − 1, numYPixels + MARGIN);
    onscreenGraphics.setColor (Color.lightGray);
    onscreenGraphics.drawLine (numXPixels + MARGIN,
        − MARGIN − 1, numXPixels + MARGIN,
        numYPixels + MARGIN);
    onscreenGraphics.drawLine (− MARGIN − 1,
```

```
        numYPixels + MARGIN, numXPixels + MARGIN,
        numYPixels + MARGIN);

    // Draw white margins.
    onscreenGraphics.setColor (Color.white);
    for (cnt = 1 ; cnt <= MARGIN ; cnt++)
    {
        onscreenGraphics.drawRect (– cnt, – cnt,
            numXPixels + 2 * cnt – 1, numYPixels + 2 * cnt – 1);
    }

    // Copy offscreen image.
    onscreenGraphics.drawImage (offscreenImage, 0, 0, this);

    toggleCursor ();
} // doDraw method

// Overrides the paint method to redraw the canvas using doDraw.
public void paint (Graphics g)
{
    doDraw (g);
} // paint method

// Overrides the update method to redraw the screen using doDraw.
public void update (Graphics g)
{
    doDraw (g);
} // update method
} /* BaseConsoleCanvas class */
```

Java provides some classes for creating offscreen bitmaps. First, in the declaration of instance variables, *offscreenImage* is declared as an object of the *Image* class and in the method *addNotify* is instantiated by the statement

offscreenImage = createImage (numXPixels, numYPixels);

Image itself is an abstract class and *createImage* must be used to instantiate an image. The values giving the size of the canvas, *numXPixels* and *numYPixels*, are calculated from the details of the font used. The canvas size is set to hold text of 25 rows and 80 columns and this is translated into the size in pixels.

Once the *offscreenImage* is created, the *Graphics* context *offscreenGraphics* is obtained using the *getGraphics* method of the *Canvas* class. The offscreen image does not include the console window's border (or margin).

Once the offscreen bit map is created in *addNotify*, it is used in all the drawing methods of *BaseConsoleCanvas*. Here is a note on the *addNotify* method:

> Java operates at one level removed from the computer's operating system, which is why it is so portable. When a canvas is instantiated initially, there is no canvas created by the actual operating system it is running. That takes place a short time later. Until the operating system equivalent (called a **peer** in Java) is created, some information about the system cannot be determined, for example, the font sizes. Since the canvas size depends on the font size, its creation must await the creation of the peer. Java calls *addNotify* when creation of the peer has been accomplished. In our *addNotify* (which overrides the *addNotify* of the *Frame* class) the first statement is to call the *addNotify* of *Frame* which will await the creation of the peer.

There are a number of methods in *BaseConsoleCanvas* for drawing graphics, each of which is called by the corresponding method of *BaseConsole*. For example, the *drawLine* of *BaseConsole* calls the *drawLine* of *BaseConsoleCanvas*.

Here are the graphics methods of the *BaseConsoleCanvas* class.

```
// Method to clear the pane to white.
public void clearScreen ()
{
    Graphics offscreenGraphics = offscreenImage.getGraphics ();
    Graphics onscreenGraphics = this.getGraphics ();

    // Erase the offscreen bitmap.
    offscreenGraphics.setColor (Color.white);
    offscreenGraphics.fillRect (0, 0, numXPixels, numYPixels);

    // Erase the onscreen window.
    toggleCursor ();
    onscreenGraphics.translate (originX, originY);
    onscreenGraphics.setColor (Color.white);
```

```
        onscreenGraphics.fillRect (0, 0, numXPixels, numYPixels);
        toggleCursor ();
} // clearScreen method

// Method to draw a line from (x1, y1) to (x2, y2) in specified color.
public void drawLine (int x1, int y1, int x2, int y2, Color color)
{
        Graphics offscreenGraphics = offscreenImage.getGraphics ();
        Graphics onscreenGraphics = this.getGraphics ();

        // First draw the line to the offscreen image.
        offscreenGraphics.setColor (color);
        offscreenGraphics.drawLine (x1, y1, x2, y2);

        // Then draw the line to the onscreen image.
        toggleCursor ();
        onscreenGraphics.translate (originX, originY);
        onscreenGraphics.setColor (color);
        onscreenGraphics.drawLine (x1, y1, x2, y2);
        toggleCursor ();
} // drawLine method

// Method to draw an oval on the screen in the rectangle from
// (x, y) to (x + width, y + height) in specified color.
public void drawOval (int x, int y, int width, int height, Color color)
{
        Graphics offscreenGraphics = offscreenImage.getGraphics ();
        Graphics onscreenGraphics = this.getGraphics ();

        // First draw the line to the offscreen image.
        offscreenGraphics.setColor (color);
        offscreenGraphics.drawOval (x, y, width, height);

        // Then draw the line to the onscreen image.
        toggleCursor ();
        onscreenGraphics.translate (originX, originY);
        onscreenGraphics.setColor (color);
        onscreenGraphics.drawOval (x, y, width, height);
        toggleCursor ();
} // drawOval method
```

```
// Method to draw a rectangle on the screen from (x, y) to
// (x + width, y + height) in specified color.
public void drawRect (int x, int y, int width, int height, Color color)
{
    Graphics offscreenGraphics = offscreenImage.getGraphics ();
    Graphics onscreenGraphics = this.getGraphics ();

    // First draw the line to the offscreen image.
    offscreenGraphics.setColor (color);
    offscreenGraphics.drawRect (x, y, width, height);

    // Then draw the line to the onscreen image.
    toggleCursor ();
    onscreenGraphics.translate (originX, originY);
    onscreenGraphics.setColor (color);
    onscreenGraphics.drawRect (x, y, width, height);
    toggleCursor ();
} // drawRect method

// Method to draw a filled oval on the screen in the rectangle
// from (x, y) to (x + width, y + height) in specified color.
public void fillOval (int x, int y, int width, int height, Color color)
{
    Graphics offscreenGraphics = offscreenImage.getGraphics ();
    Graphics onscreenGraphics = this.getGraphics ();

    // First draw the filled oval to the offscreen image.
    offscreenGraphics.setColor (color);
    offscreenGraphics.fillOval (x, y, width, height);

    // Then draw the filled oval to the onscreen image.
    toggleCursor ();
    onscreenGraphics.translate (originX, originY);
    onscreenGraphics.setColor (color);
    onscreenGraphics.fillOval (x, y, width, height);
    toggleCursor ();
} // fillOval method
```

```
// Method to draw a filled rectangle on the screen from (x, y) to
// (x + width, y + height) in specified color.
public void fillRect (int x, int y, int width, int height, Color color)
{
    Graphics offscreenGraphics = offscreenImage.getGraphics ();
    Graphics onscreenGraphics = this.getGraphics ();

    // First draw the line to the offscreen image.
    offscreenGraphics.setColor (color);
    offscreenGraphics.fillRect (x, y, width, height);

    // Then draw the line to the onscreen image.
    toggleCursor ();
    onscreenGraphics.translate (originX, originY);
    onscreenGraphics.setColor (color);
    onscreenGraphics.fillRect (x, y, width, height);
    toggleCursor ();
} // fillRect method

// Method for returning height of the drawing area in pixels.
public int getHeight ()
{
    return numYPixels;
} // getHeight method

// Method for returning width of the drawing area in pixels.
public int getWidth ()
{
    return numXPixels;
} // getWidth method
```

In the *drawLine* of *BaseConsoleCanvas* a graphics context for the *offscreenImage* is created in the first declaration. The line is first drawn to the offscreen image. The *setColor* and *drawLine* methods of the *Graphics* class are called to draw this line.

Creating the onscreen image is more complicated because you need to turn off the cursor (*toggleCursor*) so that the cursor and the picture do not interfere with each other. Then the coordinates must be translated to allow for the margins, the color set, and the line drawn before the cursor is turned back on by *toggleCursor*. The *clearScreen* method clears both the offscreen and onscreen images to white.

As well as the methods for drawing graphics, *BaseConsoleCanvas* contains methods for handling text. These methods include: *drawText, scrollUpLine, setCursorPos,* and *toggleCursor*. They are used in *BaseConsole*.

Here is the method to draw text to the pane.

```
// Method to draw the specified text to the pane at the specified
// row and column.
public void drawText (int pmRow, int pmCol, String pmText)
{
    int x = (pmCol – 1) * fontWidth;
    int y = (pmRow – 1) * fontHeight;
    Graphics offscreenGraphics = offscreenImage.getGraphics ();
    Graphics onscreenGraphics = this.getGraphics ();

    // First draw it to the offscreen image.

    // Erase the area on which the image will appear.
    offscreenGraphics.setColor (Color.white);
    offscreenGraphics.fillRect (x, y, fontWidth * pmText.length (), fontHeight);

    // Draw the text.
    offscreenGraphics.setColor (Color.black);
    offscreenGraphics.setFont (font);
    offscreenGraphics.drawString (pmText, x, y + fontHeight – fontBase);

    // Then draw the string to the onscreen image.

    // Erase the area on which the image will appear.
    toggleCursor ();
    onscreenGraphics.translate (originX, originY);
    onscreenGraphics.setColor (Color.white);
    onscreenGraphics.fillRect (x, y, fontWidth * pmText.length (), fontHeight);
```

```
        // Draw the text.
        onscreenGraphics.setColor (Color.black);
        onscreenGraphics.setFont (font);
        onscreenGraphics.drawString (pmText, x, y + fontHeight − fontBase);
        toggleCursor ();
    } // drawText method

    // Method to scroll the canvas up a line.  The blank space at
    // the bottom is filled is filled in white.
    public void scrollUpALine ()
    {
        Graphics offscreenGraphics = offscreenImage.getGraphics ();
        Graphics onscreenGraphics = this.getGraphics ();

        // First scroll the offscreen image.

        // Scroll the screen up.
        offscreenGraphics.copyArea (0, fontHeight, numXPixels,
            numYPixels − fontHeight, 0, − fontHeight);

        // Erase the last line.
        offscreenGraphics.setColor (Color.white);
        offscreenGraphics.fillRect (0, numYPixels − fontHeight, numXPixels,
            fontHeight);

        // Then scroll the onscreen image.

        // Update the onscreen image from the offscreen image.
        // We cannot use copyArea because there may be windows in front
        // of the console obscuring the screen.
        // Copy offscreen image.
        onscreenGraphics.translate (originX, originY);
        onscreenGraphics.drawImage (offscreenImage, 0, 0, this);

        toggleCursor ();
    } // scrollUpALine method
```

```
// Method to set the cursor to the specified row and column.
public void setCursorPos (int pmRow, int pmCol)
{
    toggleCursor ();
    gCursorRow = pmRow;
    gCursorCol = pmCol;
    toggleCursor ();
} // setCursorPos method

// Method to toggle the cursor on the canvas off or on.
private void toggleCursor ()
{
    int x = (gCursorCol − 1) * fontWidth;
    int y = (gCursorRow − 1) * fontHeight;
    Graphics onscreenGraphics = this.getGraphics ();

    onscreenGraphics.translate (originX, originY);
    onscreenGraphics.setColor (Color.white);
    onscreenGraphics.setXORMode (Color.black);
    onscreenGraphics.fillRect (x, y, fontWidth, fontHeight);
    onscreenGraphics.setPaintMode ();
} // toggleCursor method
```

16.8 Chapter Summary

This chapter explained the structure of the *hsa Console* class and the *ConsoleCanvas* class used in this text. It illustrated some of the more advanced features of the graphical user interface (GUI) components and provided an extended example of a Java class.

The BaseConsole Class

A somewhat simplified version of the *Console* class called the *BaseConsole* class, was examined. The *BaseConsoleCanvas* class, used by the *BaseConsole* class, was also discussed. Most of the features of the *Console* and *ConsoleCanvas* classes were included but limited to allow for clearer presentation. For example, the graphics methods included were limited to drawing lines, and filled and unfilled rectangles and ovals. The complete range available in the *Console* class can be found in the appendix. The Java *Graphics* class has nearly the same graphics methods.

Text Handling

The *BaseConsole* class was used to illustrate the details of text conversion and formatting. The standard Java input and output is by reading or writing characters or lines of characters. The *BaseConsole* and *BaseConsoleCanvas* classes contain methods for performing these operations so that all the primitive data types may be input and output without burdening the programmer with conversions. These classes have the added advantage of providing easy formatting of output.

Primitive data types must be input as strings and then converted by the process of **parsing** to their actual types. On output, they are converted back to strings.

Windows

The console window's size is fixed by the font size being used on the particular computer platform where the program is run. This must be computed and a canvas size established to hold 25 rows of 80 columns of characters. The corresponding size for the graphics screen is then fixed.

Because a window can be overwritten during the lifetime of a program, all details of what is recorded in the console window must be kept in a backup **offscreen image** as well as in the **onscreen image**.

Additional complications in these console classes involve the limitations of text spilling over the line length, requiring **wraparound**, and exceeding the line capacity of the screen, requiring **scrolling**.

16.9 Exercises

1. What methods must be added to the *BaseConsole* and *BaseConsoleCanvas* classes to permit the inclusion of the *drawArc* graphics method? The signature of *drawArc* is:

    drawArc (**int** *x,* **int** *y,* **int** *width,* **int** *height,* **int** *startAngle,* **int** *arcAngle*)

    where the meaning of *x, y, width,* and *height* are the same as for *drawOval.* The parameter *startAngle* is the angle in degrees measured from the horizontal, in the counterclockwise direction, where the *arc* is to start and *arcAngle* is the angle at the center made by the arc (positive if counterclockwise, negative if clockwise from the start).

2. Use inheritance to extend the *BaseConsole* and *BaseConsoleCanvas* classes to include the *drawArc* capability and test the result by instantiating this improved console in an application program.

3. Test the wrap-around feature of the simplified console classes by inputting a line that is longer than 80 columns and the scrolling feature by inputting more than 25 lines of text.

4. Modify the console classes to limit the canvas size to hold only 5 lines of 20 characters each.

5. Modify the console classes to have the margins of the window drawn in cyan.

Appendices

Appendix A : Reserved Words

This is the list of reserved words in Java. They cannot be used as identifiers.

abstract	boolean	break	byte
byvalue	case	cast	catch
char	class	const	continue
default	do	double	else
extends	final	finally	float
for	future	generic	goto
if	implements	import	inner
instanceof	int	interface	long
native	new	operator	outer
package	private	protected	public
rest	return	short	static
super	switch	synchronized	this
throw	throws	transient	try
var	void	volatile	while

This is the list of reserved identifiers in Java.

true	false	null

Appendix B : Java Class Library

This is the list of the classes found in the Java class libraries that are used in this book along with their associated methods.

Classes Sorted by Package

java.applet
    Applet

java.awt
    BorderLayout
    Button
    Canvas
    Checkbox
    CheckboxGroup
    CheckboxMenuItem
    Color
    Component
    Dialog
    Dimension
    Event
    FileDialog
    FlowLayout
    Font
    FontMetrics
    Frame
    Graphics
    GridLayout
    Image
    Label
    Menu

java.awt (continued...)
    MenuBar
    MenuItem
    Panel
    Point
    Scrollbar
    TextArea
    TextField
    Toolkit

java.io
    BufferedReader
    DataInputStream
    DataOutputStream
    FileInputStream
    FileOutputStream
    FileReader
    FileWriter
    IOException
    PrintWriter

java.lang
    Boolean
    Character
    Double

java.lang (continued...)
    Integer
    Math
    Object
    Runnable
    RuntimeException
    String
    StringBuffer
    System
    Thread

java.text
    DecimalFormat

java.util
    StringTokenizer
    Vector

Descriptions

This is the list of selected methods available for use in each class, along with a short description. In some of these cases, the methods listed will actually be methods defined in a parent class but commonly used in the listed class.

Applet   java.applet   Extend this class to create an applet.

void **init** ()
   Called by the system when the applet is loaded.

void **start** ()
   Called by the system when the applet is made active.

void **stop** ()
   Called by the system when the applet is made inactive.

void **destroy** ()
   Called by the system when the applet is discarded.

void **paint** (Graphics g)
   Called by the system when the applet drawing surface must be redrawn.

void **showStatus** (String message)
   Displays *message* in the status bar.

void **setLayout** (LayoutManager layout)
   Sets the Applet's layout manager to *layout*.

void **add** (Component comp)
   Adds Component *comp* to the Applet using the Applet's layout manager.

void **add** (String direction, Component comp)
   Used when the Applet's layout manager is BorderLayout. Add component *comp* to the frame in the area specified by *direction*. Possible values for *direction* are "North", "South", "East", "West", and "Center".

boolean **setVisible** (boolean visible)
   Used in the Applet's start and init methods to make the surface visible before drawing to it.

void **setBackground** (Color c)
   Sets the background color of the applet to the color *c*.

Graphics **getGraphics** ()
   Returns the graphics context of the applet. Used for drawing in the applet when not in the paint method.

Dimension **getSize** ()

> Returns the size of the applet's allocated drawing surface in pixels. The size is specified by the HTML's HEIGHT and WIDTH attribute in the APPLET tag. Dimension has two fields, *height* and *width*. The applet's height is returned by getSize ().height and the applet's width by getSize ().width.

Image **createImage** (int width, int height)

> Creates an offscreen bitmap of the specified width and height.

boolean **action** (Event evt, Object arg)

> Called by the system when a button is clicked or an ENTER in pressed in a text field in the Applet. The Button or TextField object that was clicked or had Return pressed is passed as the *target* field in *evt*. The method must return true if the event was handled and false if the event was not handled.

boolean **mouseDown** (Event evt, int x, int y)

> Called by the system when the mouse button is pressed. The location of the mouse click is passed as *x* and *y*.

boolean **keyDown** (Event evt, int key)

> Called by the system when a key is pressed. The keystroke pressed is passed as *key*.

boolean **handleEvent** (Event evt)

> Called by the system when an event occurs. Used for handling scrollbar events.

Boolean   java.lang   Wrapper class for **boolean** primitive data type.

Boolean (boolean b)

> Constructor.

boolean **booleanValue** ()

> Returns the boolean value contained by the object.

static Boolean **valueOf** (String s)

> Returns a Boolean object holding the value represented by *s*.

BorderLayout   java.awt   Places components along edges and in the center.

BorderLayout ()

> Constructor.

BorderLayout (int hgap, int vgap)
Constructor – Specifies the horizontal gap *hgap* and the vertical gap *vgap* between components.

BufferedReader   java.io   Reads ASCII data from file.

BufferedReader (FileReader reader)
Constructor – Opens *reader* for reading of ASCII text.

void **close** () throws IOException
Closes the file.

int **read** () throws IOException
Reads a character from the file. Returns –1 if the end-of-file was reached.

String **readLine** () throws IOException
Returns a line of input from the file (without the Return). Returns null if the end-of-file was reached before reading any characters.

Button   java.awt   A GUI button.

Button (String label)
Constructor – Creates a Button with label set to *label*.

String **getLabel** ()
Returns the Button's label.

void **setEnabled** (boolean enabled)
Sets whether the button is enabled or disabled. Disabled buttons cannot be pressed.

void **addActionListener** (ActionListener listener)
Attaches an ActionListener object to the Button. Causes the actionPerformed method of the listener to be called whenever the button is clicked.

Canvas   java.awt   Extend this class to create a surface on which to draw.

Canvas ()
Constructor.

void **addNotify** ()
Called by the system when the Canvas peer is created.

void **paint** ()
Called by the system when the Canvas must be redrawn.

void **setSize** (int width, int height)
> Changes the canvas to have width *width* and height *height*.

Dimension **getSize** ()
> Returns the size of the canvas in pixels. Dimension has two fields, *height* and *width*. The canvas' height is returned by getSize ().height and the canvas' width by getSize ().width.

Character   java.lang   Wrapper class for **char** primitive data type.

Character (char ch)
> Constructor.

char **charValue** ()
> Returns the boolean value contained by the object.

static char **toUpperCase** (char ch)
> Converts *ch* to uppercase.

static char **toLowerCase** (char ch)
> Converts *ch* to lowercase.

Checkbox   java.awt   A GUI check box.

Checkbox (String label)
> Constructor – Creates a checkbox with label set to *label*.

Checkbox (String label, CheckboxGroup group, boolean state)
> Constructor – Creates a radio button checkbox with label set to *label*. If *state* is true, the checkbox is checked, otherwise it is unchecked. This constructor is used for creating radio buttons.

String **getLabel** ()
> Returns the checkbox's label.

Boolean **getState** ()
> Returns true if the checkbox is checked.

void **setState** (Boolean state)
> Sets the checkbox to checked if *state* is true, unchecks the checkbox if *state* is false.

void **setEnabled** (boolean enabled)
> Sets whether the checkbox is enabled or disabled. Disabled checkboxes cannot have their state changed.

CheckboxGroup   java.awt   Makes check boxes into radio buttons.

CheckboxGroup ()
> Constructor.

CheckboxMenuItem java.awt   A checkable menu item.

CheckboxMenuItem (String itemName)
> Constructor – Creates a menu item called *itemName* that can be marked with a checkmark.

boolean **getState** ()
> Returns true if the menu item is marked with a checkmark.

void **setEnabled** (Boolean newEnabled)
> Enables (make the menu item selectable) if *newEnabled* is true. Disables (dims the menu item and makes it unselectable) if *newEnabled* is false.

void **setState** (boolean newState)
> Marks the menu item with a checkmark if *newState* is true. Eliminates the checkmark if *newState* is false.

Color   java.awt   A color.

Color (int red, int green, int blue)
> Constructor – Creates a Color with specified *red*, *green*, and *blue* components. Values must be in range 0 – 255.

final static Color **black, blue, cyan, darkGray, gray, green, lightGray, magenta, orange, pink, red, white, yellow**
> Predefined colors.

Component   java.awt   Base class for GUI components.

Toolkit **getToolkit** ()
> Returns the Toolkit used by the component.

Graphics **getGraphics** ()
> Returns the graphics context of the component.

Dimension **getSize** ()
> Returns a Dimension object specifying the width and height of the component.

Image **createImage** (int width, int height)
> Creates an offscreen bitmap of the specified width and height.

DataInputStream   java.io   Reads binary data from a file.

DataInputStream (FileInputStream stream)
>   Constructor – Opens *stream* for reading of binary data.

boolean **readBoolean** () throws IOException
>   Returns a boolean value read from the file. Throws an EOFException if end-of-file was reached when attempting to read from the file.

char **readChar** () throws IOException
>   Returns a char value read from the file. Throws an EOFException if end-of-file was reached when attempting to read from the file.

double **readDouble** () throws IOException
>   Returns an 8-byte double value read from the file. Throws an EOFException if end-of-file was reached when attempting to read from the file.

void **readFully** (byte[] buffer) throws IOException
>   Reads *buffer.length* bytes into *buffer*. Throws an EOFException if end-of-file was reached when attempting to read from the file.

int **readInt** () throws IOException
>   Returns a 32-bit int value read from the file. Throws an EOFException if end-of-file was reached when attempting to read from the file.

String **readLine** () throws IOException
>   Returns a line of input from the file (without the Return). Returns null if the end-of-file was reached before reading any characters.

DataOutputStream   java.io   Writes binary data to a file.

DataOutputStream (FileOutputStream stream)
>   Constructor – Opens *stream* for writing of binary data.

void **write** (byte[] buffer) throws IOException
>   Writes *buffer.length* bytes from *buffer* into the file.

void **writeBoolean** (boolean val) throws IOException
>   Writes the boolean value *val* into the file.

void **writeChar** (char val) throws IOException
>   Writes the character *val* into the file.

void **writeDouble** (double val) throws IOException
>   Writes the 8-byte double *val* into the file.

void **writeInt** (int val) throws IOException
>   Writes the 32-bit int *val* into the file.

DecimalFormat   java.text   Used to format floating point numbers.

DecimalFormat (String formatString)
> Constructor – Creates a formatter based on *formatString*.
>
> | | |
> |---|---|
> | # | Digit, zeros show as absent. |
> | 0 | Digit, zeros show as 0. |
> | . | Decimal place. |
> | – | Locale-specific negative sign. |

String **format** (double number)
> Returns the String of the number formatted in accordance with the *formatString* specified in the constructor.

Dialog   java.awt   Extend this class to create a dialog.

Dialog (Frame parent, String title, boolean modal)
> Constructor.

void **setVisible** (boolean visible)
> Makes the dialog appear or disappear.

void **dispose** ()
> Hides and destroys the dialog.

void **setLayout** (LayoutManager layout)
> Sets the Dialog's layout manager to *layout*.

void **add** (Component comp)
> Adds component *comp* to the Dialog using the Dialog's layout manager.

void **add** (String direction, Component comp)
> Used when the Dialog's layout manager is BorderLayout. Adds component *comp* to the Dialog in the area specified by *direction*. Possible values for *direction* are "North", "South", "East", "West", and "Center".

void **pack** ()
> Lays out all the component placed in the Dialog using their respective LayoutManagers and then shrinks the Dialog to the smallest size that fits all the components.

void **setSize** (int width, int height)
> Changes the Dialog to have width *width* and height *height*.

void **setLocation** (int x, int y)
> Moves the Dialog to have its upper-left corner at (x, y) with respect to the upper-left corner of the screen.

Dimension **getSize** ()
> Returns the size of the Dialog in pixels. Dimension has two fields, *height* and *width*. The Dialog's height is returned by getSize ().height and the Frame's width by getSize ().width.

boolean **action** (Event evt, Object arg)
> Called by the system when a button is clicked or ENTER is pressed in a text field in the Dialog. The Button or TextField object that was clicked or had ENTER pressed is passed as the *target* field in *evt*. The method must return true if the event was handled and false if the event was not handled.

boolean **handleEvent** (Event evt)
> Called by the system when any event occurs in the Dialog. The *id* field of Event *evt* is set to Event.WINDOW_DESTROY when the Close button (the X on the right hand side of the Dialog's title bar) has been pressed in the Dialog. The method must return true if the event was handled and false if the event was not handled.

boolean **mouseDown** (Event evt, int x, int y)
> Called by the system when the mouse button is pressed. The location of the mouse click is passed as *x* and *y*.

boolean **keyDown** (Event evt, int key)
> Called by the system when a key is pressed. The keystroke pressed is passed as *key*.

Dimension   java.awt   Specifies a size (height and width).

> A Dimension object is returned by methods that return an object's size.
> e.g. Toolkit.getDefaultToolkit ().getScreenSize ()

int **height, width**
> The height and width of the size.

Double   java.lang   Wrapper class for **double** primitive data type.

Double (double d)
> Constructor.

boolean **doubleValue** ()
> Returns the double value contained by the object.

static Double **valueOf** (String s) throws NumberFormatException
> Returns a Double object holding the value represented by *s*.

static String **toString** (double d)
> Returns a String containing the string representation of *d*.

Event   java.awt   Passed to action, handleEvent, mouseDown, and keyDown methods.

Object **target**
> The object that generated the event. The Button object if a button was pressed or the TextField object if Return was pressed in a text field.

int **id**
> The type of event. This is set to the constant Event.ACTION_EVENT for a button click or a Return pressed in a text field. id is set to Event.WINDOW_DESTROY if the Close button (the X on the right side of the Frame's title bar) is clicked.

final static int **ACTION_EVENT**
> The value of the id field of the Event object when a button is clicked or Return is pressed in a text field.

final static int **WINDOW_DESTROY**
> The value of the id field of the Event object when the Close button on a Frame is clicked.

final static int **SCROLL_LINE_DOWN, SCROLL_LINE_UP, SCROLL_PAGE_DOWN, SCROLL_PAGE_UP, SCROLL_ABSOLUTE**
> The value of the id field of the Event object when a scrollbar has been changed using the scroll arrows, clicking in the scrollbar or dragging the scrollbox.

FileDialog   java.awt   Creates a file dialog box to allow the user to specify a file to be loaded or saved.

FileDialog (Frame parent, String title, int mode)
> Constructor – Creates a file dialog. The *mode* parameter is one of FileDialog.LOAD or FileDialog.SAVE.

void **show** ()
> Makes the dialog appear and blocks until the dialog is dismissed. The system will hide the dialog when the dialog is dismissed.

String **getFile** ()
> Once the file dialog has been shown, getFile returns the filename selected or null if the Cancel button was pressed.

String **getDirectory** ()
> Once the file dialog has been shown, getDirectory returns the directory that the selected file is located in or null if the Cancel button was pressed.

FileInputStream   java.io   Opens a file to be used as a DataInputStream.

FileInputStream (String fileName) throws FileNotFoundException
> Constructor – Creates a FileInputStream object for the file of name *fileName*. The object can then be used as an argument to the DataInputStream constructor.

FileOutputStream   java.io   Opens a file to be used as a DataOutputStream.

FileOutputStream (String fileName) throws IOException
> Constructor – Creates a FileOutputStream object for the file of name *fileName*. The object can then be used as an argument to the DataOutputStream constructor.

FileReader   java.io   Opens a file to be used as a BufferedReader.

FileReader (String fileName) throws FileNotFoundException
> Constructor – Creates a FileReader object for the file of name *fileName*. The object can then be used as an argument to the BufferedReader constructor.

FileWriter   java.io   Opens a file to be used as a PrintWriter.

FileWriter (String fileName) throws IOException
> Constructor – Creates a FileWriter object for the file of name *fileName*. The object can then be used as an argument to the PrintWriter constructor.

FlowLayout   java.awt   Places components left-to-right, top-to-bottom.

FlowLayout ()
> Constructor.

FlowLayout (int alignment)
>   Constructor – Sets the alignment of the components to *alignment*.
>   *alignment* must be one of the constants defined in the FlowLayout class.

FlowLayout (int alignment, int hgap, int vgap)
>   Constructor – Sets the alignment of the components to *alignment* and the
>   horizontal and vertical gaps between the components to *hgap* and *vgap*.
>   *alignment* must be one of the constants defined in the FlowLayout class.

final static int **LEFT, CENTER, RIGHT**
>   Allowed values for *alignment* in the FlowLayout constructors.

Font   java.awt   A font for drawing text.

Font (String name, int style, int size)
>   Constructor – Creates a font with the font name of *name*, the font style set
>   to *style*, and point size set to *size*. *style* must be one or a combination of the
>   constants defined in the Font class.

final static int **BOLD, ITALIC, PLAIN**
>   Allowed values for *style* in the Font constructor. To get bold italic, use the
>   style Font.BOLD+Font.ITALIC.

FontMetrics   java.awt   The measurements of a font.

>   A FontMetrics object is returned by the getFontMetrics () method in the
>   Applet, Frame, Component or Toolkit class.
>   e.g. Toolkit.getDefaultToolkit ().getFontMetrics (font)

Figure B.1 The FontMetrics attributes

int **charWidth** (char ch)
>   Returns the width of the character *ch* in pixels.

int **getAscent** ()
>   Returns the font's ascent in pixels.

int **getDescent** ()
> Returns the font's descent in pixels.

int **getHeight** ()
> Returns the font's total height in pixels.

int **stringWidth** (String text)
> Returns the width of the String *text* in pixels.

Frame

java.awt   Extend this class to create a window.

Frame ()
> Constructor.

Frame (String title)
> Constructor – Creates a Frame with the window title set to *title*.

void **setVisible** (boolean visible)
> Makes the frame appear or disappear.

void **dispose** ()
> Hides and destroys the window.

void **setLayout** (LayoutManager layout)
> Sets the Frame's layout manager to *layout*.

void **add** (Component comp)
> Adds component *comp* to the Frame using the Frame's layout manager.

void **add** (String direction, Component comp)
> Used when the Frame's layout manager is BorderLayout. Adds component *comp* to the Frame in the area specified by *direction*. Possible values for *direction* are "North", "South", "East", "West", and "Center".

void **pack** ()
> Lays out all the component placed in the Frame using their respective LayoutManagers and then shrinks the Frame to the smallest size that fits all the components.

void **setSize** (int width, int height)
> Changes the Frame to have width *width* and height *height*.

void **setLocation** (int x, int y)
> Moves the Frame to have its upper-left corner at (x, y) with respect to the upper-left corner of the screen.

Dimension **getSize** ()
> Returns the size of the Frame in pixels. Dimension has two fields, *height* and *width*. The Frame's height is returned by getSize ().height and the Frame's width by getSize ().width.

Toolkit **getToolkit** ()
> Returns the Toolkit used by the component.

Image **createImage** (int width, int height)
> Creates an offscreen bitmap of the specified width and height.

boolean **action** (Event evt, Object arg)
> Called by the system when a button is clicked or a Return is pressed in a text field in the Frame. The Button or TextField object that was clicked or had Return pressed is passed as the *target* field in *evt*. The method must return true if the event was handled and false if the event was not handled.

boolean **handleEvent** (Event evt)
> Called by the system when any event occurs in the Frame. The *id* field of Event *evt* is set to Event.WINDOW_DESTROY when the Close button (the X on the right hand side of the Frame's title bar) has been pressed in the Frame. The method must return true if the event was handled and false if the event was not handled.

boolean **mouseDown** (Event evt, int x, int y)
> Called by the system when the mouse button is pressed. The location of the mouse click is passed as *x* and *y*.

boolean **keyDown** (Event evt, int key)
> Called by the system when a key is pressed. The keystroke pressed is passed as *key*.

Graphics   java.awt   A graphics context that can be drawn upon.

> A Graphics object is passed as a parameter to the paint method or is returned by the getGraphics methods of various Components.
> > e.g. canvas.getGraphics ()

void **clearRect** (int x, int y, int width, int height)
> Clears the rectangle to the background color.

void **draw3DRect** (int x, int y, int width, int height, boolean raised)
> Draws a 3-D rectangle. It appears raised if *raised* is true.

void **drawArc** (int x, int y, int width, int height, int startAngle, int arcAngle)
> Draws an arc. The arc is inscribed in the rectangle defined by the upper-left corner (x, y) with width of *width* and height of *height*. It starts at *startAngle* degrees and goes counterclockwise for *arcAngle* degrees.

void **drawImage** (Image img, int x, int y, ImageObserver observer)
> Draws an image onto the graphics context with the upper-left corner of the image located at (x, y). The *observer* parameter is usually set to **null**.

void **drawImage** (Image img, int x, int y, int width, int height,
     ImageObserver observer)
>   Draws an image onto the graphics context with the upper-left corner of
>   the image located at (x, y). The image is scaled so that it appears on the
>   graphics context with the specified width and height. The *observer*
>   parameter is usually set to **null**.

void **drawLine** (int x1, int y1, int x2, int y2)
>   Draws a line from $(x1, y1)$ to $(x2, y2)$.

void **drawOval** (int x, int y, int width, int height)
>   Draws an ellipse. The ellipse is inscribed in the rectangle defined by the
>   upper-left corner (x, y) with width of *width* and height of *height*.

void **drawPolygon** (int[] xPoints, int[] yPoints, int numPoints)
>   Draws a polygon. The *xPoints* and *yPoints* arrays define the coordinates of
>   the array of vertices. *numPoints* specifies the number of vertices in the
>   polygon.

void **drawRect** (int x, int y, int width, int height)
>   Draws a rectangle with upper-left corner at (x, y) with width of *width* and
>   height of *height*.

void **drawRoundRect** (int x, int y, int width, int height, int arcWidth, int
     arcHeight)
>   Draws a rectangle with rounded corners with upper-left corner at (x, y)
>   with width of *width* and height of *height*. The *arcWidth* and *arcHeight*
>   parameters are the width and height of the ellipse used to draw the
>   rounded corners.

void **drawString** (String str, int x, int y)
>   Draws the string *str* at the starting point (x, y). The *y* coordinate is the base
>   line of the text.

void **fill3DRect** (int x, int y, int width, int height, boolean raised)
>   Draws a filled 3-D rectangle. It appears raised if *raised* is true.

void **fillArc** (int x, int y, int width, int height, int startAngle, int arcAngle)
>   Draws a filled arc. The arc is inscribed in the rectangle defined by the
>   upper-left corner (x, y) with width of *width* and height of *height*. It starts at
>   *startAngle* degrees and goes counterclockwise for *arcAngle* degrees.

void **fillOval** (int x, int y, int width, int height)
>   Draws a filled ellipse. The ellipse is inscribed in the rectangle defined by
>   the upper-left corner (x, y) with width of *width* and height of *height*.

void **fillPolygon** (int[] xPoints, int[] yPoints, int numPoints)
>   Draws a filled polygon. The *xPoints* and *yPoints* arrays define the
>   coordinates of the array of vertices. The *numPoints* parameter specifies the
>   number of vertices in the polygon.

void **fillRect** (int x, int y, int width, int height)
> Draws a filled rectangle with upper-left corner at (x, y) with width of *width* and height of *height*.

void **fillRoundRect** (int x, int y, int width, int height, int arcWidth, int arcHeight)
> Draws a filled rectangle with rounded corners with upper-left corner at (x, y) with width of *width* and height of *height*. The *arcWidth* and *arcHeight* parameters are the width and height of the ellipse used to draw the rounded corners.

void **setColor** (Color c)
> Sets the color of the graphics context. The color is used for any draw methods.

void **setFont** (Font f)
> Sets the font of the graphics context. The font is used with the drawString method.

void **setPaintMode** ()
> Sets the graphics context into paint mode. All drawing in the graphics context draws over the background.

void **setXORMode** (Color c)
> Sets the graphics context into XOR mode. All drawing in the graphics context is XOR'd with the background. The color specified by *c* is a special color so that any drawing done on a background of color *c* will not be changed.

GridLayout

java.awt   Places components on a grid of identically-sized cells.

GridLayout (int rows, int columns)
> Constructor – Specifies the number of rows and columns when laying out the components.

GridLayout (int rows, int columns, int hgap, int vgap)
> Constructor – Specifies the number of rows and columns when laying out the components and sets the horizontal and vertical gaps between components to be *hgap* and *vgap*.

Image

java.awt   An offscreen bitmap.

> An Image object is created by the createImage method of the Applet or Component class.
>> e.g. this.createImage (200, 400);

Graphics **getGraphics** ()
  Returns the Images graphics context.
int **getWidth** (ImageObserver observer)
  Returns the image's width if it is known, otherwise it returns –1. It starts
  the image loading if the image is not already loaded. The *observer*
  parameter can be null.
int **getHeight** (ImageObserver observer)
  Returns the image's height if it is known, otherwise it returns –1. It starts
  the image loading if the image is not already loaded. The *observer*
  parameter can be null.

Integer   java.lang   Wrapper class for **int** primitive
                                                          data type.

Integer (int i)
  Constructor.
boolean **intValue** ()
  Returns the double value contained by the object.
static Integer **valueOf** (String s) throws NumberFormatException
  Returns an Integer object holding the value represented by *s*.
static int **parseInt** (String s) throws NumberFormatException
  Returns the int represented by *s*.
static String **toString** (int i)
  Returns a String containing the string representation of *i*.

IOException   java.io   An exception involving I/O

Ancestor class of **EOFException** and **FileNotFoundException**. Read and write
errors are of the class IOException.

Label   java.awt   A GUI label.

Label (String label)
  Constructor – Creates a Label with its text set to *label*.
Label (String label, int alignment)
  Constructor – Creates a Label with its text set to *label* and its alignment set
  to *alignment*. *alignment* must be one of the constants defined in the Label
  class.
final static int **LEFT, CENTER, RIGHT**
  Allowed values for *alignment* in the Label or constructor.

String **getText** ()
>   Returns the Label's text.

void **setFont** (Font font)
>   Sets the font of the Label to *font*.

Math   java.lang   Class for math methods. Note all methods are static.

static int **abs** (int a)
static double **abs** (double a)
>   Returns the absolute value of *a*.

static double **sin** (double a)
static double **cos** (double a)
static double **tan** (double a)
>   Returns the sine, cosine, or tangent of angle *a* in radians.

static double **sqrt** (double a)
>   Returns the square root of *a*.

static long **round** (double a)
>   Returns *a*, rounded to the nearest 64-bit integer (long).

static int **min** (int a, int b)
static double **min** (double a, double b)
>   Returns the minimum of *a* and *b*.

static int **max** (int a, int b)
static double **max** (double a, double b)
>   Returns the maximum of *a* and *b*.

static double **pow** (double x, double y)
>   Returns x^y.

static double **random** ()
>   Returns a random number from 0.0 (inclusive) to 1.0 (exclusive).

Menu   java.awt   A single menu in a menu bar.

Menu (String menuName)
>   Constructor – Creates a menu called *menuName*.

void **add** (MenuItem menuItem)
>   Adds *menuItem* to the end of the menu.

MenuBar

java.awt   The menu bar at the top of the window.

MenuBar ()

Constructor – Creates a menu bar. It must be placed in the Frame by calling the Frame method setMenuBar.

void **add** (Menu menuName)

Adds *menuName* to the end of the menus on the menu bar.

MenuItem

java.awt   A menu item in a menu.

MenuItem (String itemName)

Constructor – Creates a menu item called *itemName*.

void **setEnabled** (Boolean newEnabled)

Enables (make the menu item selectable) if *newEnabled* is true. Disables (dims the menu item and makes it unselectable) if *newEnabled* is false.

Object

java.lang   Base class for all Java classes.

Object **clone** ()

Creates a copy of the object. User-written classes must implement their own version of clone.

boolean **equals** (Object obj)

Returns true if *obj* is equivalent to the object. User-written classes must implement their own version of equals.

int **hashCode** ()

Computes a hashcode from the object's data. User-written classes must implement their own version of hashCode.

String **toString** ()

Returns a String representation of the object. User-written classes must implement their own version of toString.

Panel

java.awt   Allows nesting of a layout within another layout.

Panel ()

Constructor.

void **setLayout** (LayoutManager layout)

Sets the Panel's layout manager to *layout*.

void **add** (Component comp)

Adds component *comp* to the Panel using the Panel's layout manager.

void **add** (String direction, Component comp)
> Used when the Panel's layout manager is BorderLayout. Adds component *comp* to the Panel in the area specified by *direction*. Possible values for *direction* are "North", "South", "East", "West", and "Center".

Point
java.awt   Specifies a location (x and y).

> A Point object is returned by methods that return an object's location.
> e.g. frame.getLocation ()

int **x, y**
> The x and y coordinates of the location.

PrintWriter
java.io   Writes ASCII data to a file.

PrintWriter (FileWriter writer)
> Constructor – Opens *writer* for writing of ASCII text.

void **close** ()
> Closes the file.

void **print** (boolean b)
> Prints out boolean *b* as "true" or "false".

void **print** (char c)
> Prints out character *c*.

void **print** (double d)
> Prints out double *d*.

void **print** (int i)
> Prints out integer *i*.

void **print** (String str)
> Prints out string *str*.

void **println** (boolean b)
> Prints out boolean *b* as "true" or "false" followed by a Return.

void **println** (char c)
> Prints out character *c* followed by a Return.

void **println** (double d)
> Prints out double *d* followed by a Return.

void **println** (int i)
> Prints out integer *i* followed by a Return.

void **println** (String str)
> Prints out string *str* followed by a Return.

Runnable

java.lang   Java interface for making a class concurrent.

void **run** ()
> Called in a new thread of execution when the start method of the Thread instantiated from the object is called.

RuntimeException

java.lang   Exceptions caused by the JVM.

Ancestor class of **ArithmeticException, ClassCastException, NumberFormatException, ArrrayIndexOutOfBoundsException, EmptyStackException, StringIndexOutOfBoundsException, NegativeArraySizeException**, and **NullPointerException**. RuntimeExceptions need not be indicated in the throw clause of a method's signature.

Scrollbar

java.awt   Java GUI Scrollbar.

Scrollbar (int orientation, int value, int visible, int min, int max)
> Constructor – The *orientation* parameter is one of Scrollbar.HORIZONTAL or Scrollbar.VERTICAL. The *value* parameter is the initial value of the scrollbar. The *visible* parameter is the amount of the item being scrolled that is visible in the viewport. The *min* and *max* parameters are the minimum and maximum values between which the scrollbar can range.

int **getValue** ()
> Returns the current value of the scrollbar.

String

java.lang   Java Strings.

String (String str)
> Constructor – Creates a String object with value of *str*.

boolean **equals** (String str)
> Returns true if the String object is equal to *str*.

boolean **equalsIgnoreCase** (String str)
> Returns true if the String object is equal to *str* with case ignored.

int **compareTo** (String str)
> Returns the result of the String object compared to *str*. If the String object is less than *str*, it returns a negative value, if they are equal, it returns 0, if the String object is greater than *str*, it returns a positive value.

boolean **endsWith** (String str)
> Returns true if the String ends with *str*.

boolean **startsWith** (String str)
> Returns true if the String starts with *str*.

char **charAt** (int index)
> Returns the character at position *index* of the String object.

String **subString** (int startPosition)
> Returns the string starting from position *startPosition* of the String object.

String **subString** (int startPosition, int endPosition)
> Returns the string starting from position *startPosition* and ending at position *endPosition* − 1 of the String object.

String **concat** (String str)
> Returns the result of the String object concatenated with *str*.

int **indexOf** (int ch)
> Returns the index of the first occurrence of *ch* in the String object.

int **indexOf** (int ch, int position)
> Returns the first occurrence of *ch* in the String object starting from the position *position*.

int **indexOf** (String str, int position)
> Returns the first occurrence of *str* in the String object starting from the position *position*.

int **length** ()
> Returns the length of the String object.

String **toLowerCase** ()
> Returns a String object which is the original String object converted to lower case.

String **toUpperCase** ()
> Returns a String object which is the original String object converted to upper case.

static String **valueOf** (boolean b)
static String **valueOf** (int i)
static String **valueOf** (double d)
> Static method to convert a boolean, integer, or double to a String.

char **charAt** (int position)
> Returns the character at position *position* of the String object.

StringBuffer   java.lang   String buffer where the contents can be changed.

StringBuffer ()
> Constructor.

StringBuffer (String str)
>   Constructor – Initializes buffer to value *str*.

StringBuffer **append** (boolean b)
StringBuffer **append** (int i)
StringBuffer **append** (double d)
StringBuffer **append** (String str)
>   Appends the string representation of the argument to the StringBuffer and
>   then returns a reference to the StringBuffer.

StringBuffer **insert** (int offset, boolean b)
StringBuffer **insert** (int offset, int i)
StringBuffer **insert** (int offset, double d)
StringBuffer **insert** (int offset, String str)
>   Inserts the string representation of the argument at location *offset* of the
>   StringBuffer and then returns a reference to the StringBuffer.

void **setCharAt** (int position, char ch)
>   Sets the character at position *position* to character *ch* in the StringBuffer
>   object.

StringBuffer **reverse** ()
>   Reverses the characters in the StringBuffer and then returns a reference to
>   the StringBuffer.

int **length** ()
>   Returns the number of characters in the StringBuffer.

String **toString** ()
>   Returns a String representing the contents of the StringBuffer.

StringTokenizer   java.util   Breaks a String down into
                                            tokens separated by white
                                            space.

StringTokenizer (String str)
>   Constructor – Creates a StringTokenizer object to tokenize *str*.

int **countTokens** ()
>   Returns the number of tokens remaining in the StringTokenizer.

boolean **hasMoreTokens** ()
>   Returns true if there are more tokens to be read from the StringTokenizer.

String **nextToken** ()
>   Returns the next token from the StringTokenizer.

System

java.lang

Class for system functions.
Note all methods are static.

static void **exit** (int exitCode)
> Immediately terminates the Java program.

static final InputStream **in**
> Standard input. Open as a DataInputStream to read lines from the console.

static final PrintStream **out**
> Standard output. PrintStream supports most of the same methods as the PrintWriter class.

TextArea

java.awt

A GUI text area with scrollbars for displaying large quantities of text.

TextArea (int rows, int cols)
> Constructor – Creates a TextArea *rows* rows deep and *cols* columns wide.

TextArea (String str, int rows, int cols)
> Constructor – Creates a TextArea *rows* rows deep and *cols* columns wide with initial value set to *str*.

void **setText** (String str)
> Sets the text in the TextArea to *str*.

String **getText** ()
> Returns the String containing the text in the TextArea.

void **appendText** (String str)
> Appends *str* to the text in the TextArea.

void **insertText** (String str, int pos)
> Inserts the String *str* into the text in the TextArea before position *pos*.

void **replaceText** (String str, int startPosition, int endPosition)
> Replaces the text in the TextArea from position *startPosition* to *endPosition* – 1 with String *str*.

void **select** (int selectionStart, int selectionEnd)
> Selects the text in the TextArea between *selectionStart* and *selectionEnd* (inclusive). If *selectionStart* = *selectionEnd*, the selection is just a cursor position.

void **selectAll** ()
> Selects all the text in the TextArea.

TextField   java.awt   A GUI text area for displaying
                                               editabled text.

TextField (int cols)
> Constructor – Creates a TextField *cols* columns wide.

TextField (String str, int cols)
> Constructor – Creates a TextField *cols* columns wide with initial value set
> to *str*.

void **setText** (String str)
> Sets the text in the TextField to *str*.

String **getText** ()
> Returns the String containing the text in the TextField.

Thread   java.lang   Used to create multiple threads
                                               of execution.

Thread (Runnable obj)
> Constructor – Creates a Thread object based on the Runnable object.

void **start** ()
> Creates a new thread of execution running the Thread's run method.

void **stop** ()
> Stops the thread of execution associated with the Thread.

void **suspend** ()
> Suspends execution of a thread associated with the Thread.

void **resume** ()
> Allows the resumption of execution of a thread associated with the
> Thread.

void **run** ()
> The main body of the thread. The method executed in a new thread when
> the Thread's start method is called.

static void **sleep** (int millis) throws InterruptedException
> Causes the current thread to sleep for *millis* milliseconds.

Toolkit   java.awt   Implements platform specific
                                               functionality.

> A Toolkit object is returned by the getDefaultToolkit method of the
> Toolkit class or the getToolkit method of the Component class.
> e.g. Toolkit.getDefaultToolkit ()

static Toolkit **getDefaultToolkit** ()
>   Returns the Toolkit object used by this platform.

String [] **getFontList** ()
>   Returns an array of strings containing the names of all the fonts.

FontMetrics **getFontMetrics** (Font font)
>   Returns the font metrics for *font*.

Dimension **getScreenSize** ()
>   Returns the dimensions of the screen.

Vector   java.util   Java's implementation of a list.

Vector ()
>   Constructor.

int **size** ()
>   Returns the number of elements in the Vector.

void **addElement** (Object obj)
>   Adds *obj* to the end of the list of elements.

void **insertElementAt** (Object obj, int index)
>   Inserts *obj* before the index'th element. If index is 0, then obj is inserted at
>   the beginning of the lost of elements.

void **setElementAt** (Object obj, int index)
>   Changes the *index*'th element to *obj*.

Object **elementAt** (int index)
>   Returns the *index*'th element of the list.

int **indexOf** (Object obj)
>   Returns the index of the element containing *obj*. Returns –1 if *obj* is not
>   found.

boolean **isEmpty** ()
>   Returns true if the vector contains no elements.

void **removeElement** (Object obj)
>   Removes *obj* from the list of elements.

void **removeElementAt** (int index)
>   Removes the *index*'th element of the list.

Appendix C : HSA Class Library

The *hsa* package consists of three applications and nine classes. The applications make marking easier and provide some utilities for users moving between different Java environments.

The classes make it easier for users to begin writing programs that explore the basic concepts of computer science before coming to terms with the input and output methods of the Java class library.

To ensure the easiest possible transition from using the *hsa* package to using only the Java class library, wherever possible we have made the graphics methods in the *Console* class identical to those in the Java *Graphics* class. The *print* and *println* methods of the *Console*, *Stdout*, and *TextOutputFile* are also the same as those in the Java *PrintWriter* class. In a number of cases the classes in the *hsa* package contain extra methods.

See Appendix G for information on installing the *hsa* package.

To use the *hsa* classes in a Java class, the following line must appear in the class header:

> **import** *hsa.**;

Applications

Submit

A Java application program used to submit student's assignments for marking.

This brings up dialog boxes to allow the user to enter the name of the program to be submitted, the names of the Java text files that make up the program, and the namesof the test data files. It then prints the Java text files, the input files, and the output produced from running the program.

PrintFiles

A Java application program used to print Java files. It can paragraph (indent) the file, bold keywords, and italicize identifiers in the printout if requested.

PrettyPrint

A Java application program to indent (paragraph) Java programs.

PrettyPrint paragraphs (indents) Java files to make them suitable for printing or use in many environments.

Classes

Console
The Console window can hold 25 lines of 80 column text. The user can input data directly in the Console window. The output of the program appears there also. Formatted text output is provided. It supports all the basic Java Graphics class methods plus two more to draw stars and maple leaves (suitable for flags).

The Console class window has three buttons. The "Save" button saves the contents of the screen as a ".bmp" (Windows Bitmap) file. The "Print" button prints out the contents of the window. The "Quit" button quits the program immediately. It gives visual notification when the program is finished execution by changing the label in the "Quit" button to "Close".

TextConsole
The TextConsole window is a 25x80 window used for text output. As the output scrolls off the top of the window, a scroll bar is activated that allows users to view all output from the program. The TextConsole class differs from the Console class in that all text output is kept and can be saved and printed.

The user can input data directly in the TextConsole window. The output of the program appears there also. Formatted text output is provided.

The TextConsole class window has three buttons. The "Save" button saves all the output sent to the window to a text file. The "Print" button prints out the all the output. The "Quit" button quits the program immediately. It gives visual notification when the program is finished execution by changing the label in the "Quit" button to "Close".

Stdin
This is a non-instantiated class to allow users to read all the Java primitive data types from standard input before they have learned about exception handling and the intricacies of the Java primitive wrapper classes. It also makes it possible to read several primitives from one line of input without having to know the StringTokenizer class.

Stdout
This is a non-instantiated class to allow users to output formatted data to standard output without having to learn the java.text.NumberFormat class. Users can write data to fixed length fields and with a fixed number of decimal places.

TextInputFile
This class makes it easier to read from text files. It allows the user to read any Java primitive data type from a text file and does all the conversions, string tokenizing, and exception handling automatically.

TextOutputFile

This class makes it easier to write to text files. It's major convenience is that it handles formatted output. Users can specify field length when outputting primitive data type as well as the number of decimal places when outputting real numbers.

FatalError

This is a class to display fatal errors. When instantiated, it displays a window with a specified message and a button labelled "Quit". When the button is pressed, the program immediately exits.

Helpful for users who want to add error checking to their program but are not yet familiar with Frames and the rest of the Java class library.

Message

This is a class to display messages. When instantiated, it displays a window with a specified message and a button labelled "OK". When the button is pressed, the program continues execution.

Status

A quick way of displaying changing status messages without having to learn about Frames, and so on.

hsa Applications - Execution

To execute the *Submit*, *PrettyPrint* or *PrintFiles* programs, a Java Virtual Machine (JVM) must exist on your computer. As well, the *hsa* package must be made available to the JVM. For Sun's Java Development Kit (JDK), the *hsa* directory must be copied from the disk that accompanies this text into one of the directories listed in the CLASSPATH environment variable. See Appendix G for more information on installing the *hsa* package.

With the *Submit* program, the Java text files (".java" files) and class files (".class" files) of the program that you wish to Submit and any classes that the program uses must be available. For *PrintFiles* and *PrettyPrint*, the Java text file (".java" files) to be printed or paragraphed must be available.

To execute any of these program from Sun's JDK, you must enter DOS, move to the directory containing the files to be submitted, printed, or paragraphed, and type:

java hsa.*Application-Name*

where the *Application-Name* is *Submit*, *PrettyPrint*, or *PrintFiles*.

Failure of the JDK to find the program indicates that the *hsa* directory has not been correctly placed in one of the directories listed in the CLASSPATH. Check the documentation for Sun's JDK for more information on the CLASSPATH variable.

hsa Applications - Setting Options

You can also enter a number of options to modify the behavior of any of the *hsa* applications. These options are listed with the instructions for each of the programs. You can enter options in one of three ways.

The simplest way is to specify the options on the command line. This is done by entering the option after the name of the program, for example,

java hsa.Submit –nobold –noitalic

stops Submit from bolding keywords and italicizing identifiers when it prints out Java programs.

The second way is to change the options in the *Options* dialog box. Once you have started the program, each of the *hsa* application programs comes up with an *Options* dialog box which has checkboxes, radio buttons, and text fields for the basic options you can select. It also has a menu labelled "Options". The *Options* menu allows you to get information about the program, see only the basic options, see the advanced options, and save the options so the current set of options become the default values the next time the program is run.

The third way to enter options is to edit a file called "hsa.config" located in the your home directory. This file is read for options every time any of the *hsa* programs are executed and options are saved to this file when the user selects the *Save Options* menu item. There is a section in the file for each of the three applications. Each section is prefaced with either "[Submit]", "[PrettyPrint]" or "[PrintFiles]". An example "hsa.config" file might look like:

```
[Submit]
–nobold
–noitalic
[PrettyPrint]
–indent  2
```

Options selected in the *Options* dialog box override options specified on the command line which override options specified in the "hsa.config" file. To skip the *Options* dialog box, you can use the option **–nooptions** in the command line or in the "hsa.config" file.

You can determine the location that the *hsa* package will look for the *hsa.config* file by starting any of the applications and selecting the *About* menu item in the *Options* menu.

The *Console* and *TextConsole* class use the *PrettyPrint* options to determine the printer margins and default save directory.

Here is the list of all the available options. The default options are listed in bold face. Items in curly braces can be included zero or more times.

–program *classname*   Submit
> Sets the program to be submitted to *classname*. If this option and –*nooptions* is set the initial *Submit* dialog box does not appear.

–sourcedir *sourcedirectory*   All
> Sets the initial directory to *sourcedirectory* for the *Select Source Files* (Submit), *Select Files to Print* (PrintFiles), or *Select Files To Indent* (PrettyPrint) dialog box. If no option is specified, the initial directory is set to the current directory.

–source *sourcefile* {*sourcefile*}   All
> Sets the source files to be printed (Submit, PrintFiles) or paragraphed (PrettyPrint) to be the *sourcefiles* specified. If this option is used, the *Select Source Files* (Submit), *Select Files to Print* (PrintFiles), or *Select Files To Indent* (PrettyPrint) dialog box does not appear.

–inputdir *inputdirectory*   Submit
> Sets the initial directory to *inputdirectory* for the *Select Input Files* dialog box. If no option is specified, the initial directory is set to the last directory used in the *Select Source Files* dialog box.

–input {*inputfile*}   Submit
> Sets the input data files to be used to run the submitted program. If this option is used, the *Select Input Files* dialog box does not appear. You do not need to specify any *inputfile*, in which case the submitted program is run once with no input.

–echo   Submit
> Echoes input read from file into the program's output.

–noecho   Submit
> Does not echo input read from the file into the program's output.

–indent   Submit, PrintFiles
    Indents the programs using PrettyPrint before printing them.

–noindent   Submit, PrintFiles
    Does not indent the programs before printing them.

–print   Submit, PrintFiles
    Prints to the printer (see *–preview* for sending all output to a window instead).

–preview   Submit, PrintFiles
    Sends all output to a window rather than to the printer. This option is useful for reviewing the results of a Submit without wasting paper.

–bold   Submit, PrintFiles
    Prints Java keywords in bold face when printing programs.

–nobold   Submit, PrintFiles
    Does not print Java keywords in bold face when printing programs.

–italic   Submit, PrintFiles
    Prints identifiers in italics when printing programs.

–noitalic   Submit, PrintFiles
    Does not print identifiers in italics when printing programs.

–defaultmargin   Submit, PrintFiles
    Makes printing assume that Java has set the printer margins correctly. Due to some irregularities in the way Java (all environments) does printing, there is no way to know whether the upper-left corner of the printing area is the upper-left corner of the page, or the upper-left corner of the printable area.

    If your printouts are being cut off on the top and left sides, use the *–margin* option to set the margins.

–margin *{leftmargin topmargin}*   Submit, PrintFiles
    Causes Submit and PrintFiles to add their own margins when printing. *leftmargin* and *topmargin* are specified in inches. If they are not specified (*leftmargin* and *topmargin* are optional), the left and top margins are set to 0.35".

    If your printouts are being cut off on the top and left sides, use this option to set the margins. If necessary, specify *leftmargin* and *topmargin* to get printing to be placed correctly on the page.

–indentsize *indentSize*   All
    Sets the size of each indentation when paragraphing to *indentSize* spaces. This defaults to 4. This option is only relevant if the *–toother* option is selected (which it is by default).

–usetabs   PrettyPrint

Converts groups of 8 spaces into tabs when the paragraphed program is saved. This option is only relevant if the *–toother* option is selected (which it is by default).

–usespaces   *(use spaces)*   PrettyPrint

Does not converts spaces into tabs.

–fromva   *(from va)*   All

Makes *hsa* programs assume that source files have been exported from the *VisualAge for Java* environment and that tabs are set at 0.25″ apart.

–fromother   *(from other)*   All

Makes *hsa* programs assume that source files have come from other environments and that tabs are set 8 spaces apart.

–tova   *(to va)*   PrettyPrint

Saves PrettyPrinted (indented) file in format suitable for importation into *VisualAge for Java*. Each level of indentation is one tab, and tabs are assumed to be 0.25″ apart. Assume lines are 70 columns across.

–toother   *(to other)*   PrettyPrint

Saves PrettyPrinted (indented) file in a format suitable for printing or use in another environment. Indentation is specified by the *–indentsize* option and spaces are converted to tabs if the *–usetabs* option is specified. Tabs are assumed to be 8 spaces apart. Assume lines are 80 columns across.

–compact   All

Leaves the opening curly brace at the end of a line.

–expanded   All

Places an opening curly brace on a line of its own, indented at the same level as the previous line.

–nooptions   *(no options)*   All

Does not display any options at all.

–basic   All

Displays the basic options for the *hsa* program.

–advanced   All

Displays all the available options for the *hsa* program.

Submit

To execute Submit (which must be run from outside of *VisualAge for Java*) you must run the program **hsa.Submit**.

The *Submit* dialog box appears (see Figure C.1). You must enter the name of the Java program to be submitted. Enter only the class name without a ".class" or ".java" suffix. You can also select a number of options as described in the previous section. Pressing the *OK* button in this dialog box closes the *Submit* dialog box and makes the *Select Source Files* dialog box appear.

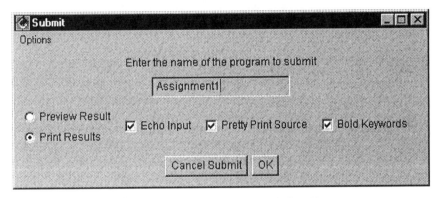

Figure C.1 The *Submit* Dialog Box

The *Select Source Files* dialog box (See Figure C.2) contains two lists of files, the files found on the disk and the list of Java text files to be printed. The dialog box only lists directories and those files that end in ".java" (which should be the case for all Java text files). To select files to be printed, you can either double click on the file name, or click once on the file name and then click the *Copy >* button. To move to a different directory, click on the directory name (all directory names are enclosed in square brackets). The name of the current directory is listed above the file name list on the left side. To switch to a different drive, select the drive from the pop-up menu beneath the list of files in the current directory.

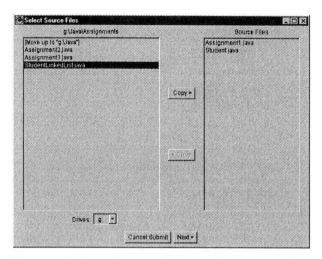

Figure C.2 **The** *Select Source Files* **Dialog Box**

If you accidently select a Java text file to be printed that should not be included, double clicking on the filename in the right hand list of files will remove it. Once all the Java text files that the program uses have been entered, click the *Next >* button. The list of Java text files to be printed appears in a window labelled "Source Files" in the upper-left corner of the screen. The *Select Input Files* dialog box appears in the center of the screen (Figure C.3).

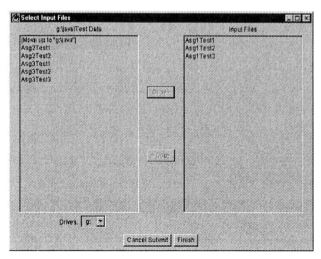

Figure C.3 **The** *Select Input Files* **Dialog Box**

This dialog box allows you to select files that will be used as input to the submitted program when it runs. The submitted program will be run once for each input file selected. For each run, instead of reading from standard input (or the *hsa* Console class), the submitted program will read from the input file. If no input files are selected, the submitted program will be run once using no input. Any text file can be used as an input file. Once all the files are selected, click the *Finish* button.

At this point, the *Submit* program will close the *Select Input Files* dialog box, display a small dialog box called *TestInputFiles* in the upper-right corner of the screen listing the selected input files and start printing. The printout contains a copy of all the Java text files selected, and then for each input file, the input file and the output from the submitted program using that input file. When it is finished printing, the *Submit* program quits. The printout can be submitted for marking by your instructor.

PrintFiles

To execute PrintFiles, you must run the program **hsa.PrintFiles**.

The *PrintFiles Options* dialog box appears (see Figure C.4). You can change any options at this point as described in the *Setting Options* section. Once the appropriate options are set (usually you will not need to change any of them from the default setting), click the *OK* button in the dialog box. The *PrintFiles Options* dialog box closes and the *Select Files To Print* dialog box appears.

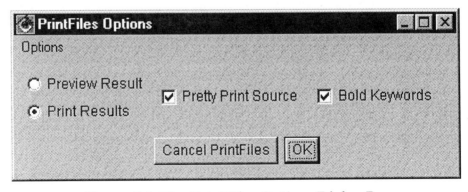

Figure C.4 The *PrintFiles Options* Dialog Box

The *Select Files To Print* dialog box (see Figure C.5) contains two lists of files, the files found on the disk and the list of Java text files to be printed. The dialog box only lists directories and those files that end in ".java" (which all Java text files should end in). To select files to be printed, you can either double click on the file name, or click once on the file name and then click the *Copy >* button. To move to a different directory, click on the directory name (all directory names are enclosed in square brackets). The name of the current directory is listed above the file name list on the left side. To switch to a different drive, select the drive from the pop-up menu beneath the list of files in the current directory.

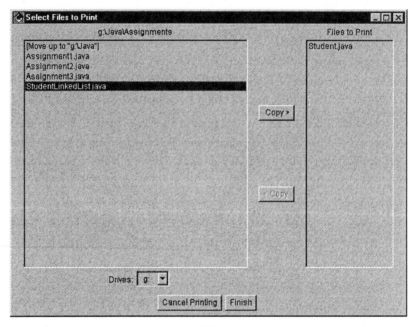

Figure C.5 The *Select Files to Print* Dialog Box

If you accidently select a Java text file to be printed that should not be included, double clicking on the filename in the right hand list of files will remove it. Once all the Java text files that the program uses have been entered, click the *Finish* button. The selected files are now printed.

PrettyPrint

To execute PrettyPrint you must either run the *PrettyPrint* program found in the *hsa* package in the *Holt Software* project from within *VisualAge for Java* or run the program **hsa.PrintFiles** using another environment such as Sun's JRE.

The *PrettyPrint Options* dialog box appears (see Figure C.6). You can change any options at this point as described in the *Setting Options* section. Once the appropriate options are set (usually you will not need to change any of them), click the *OK* button in the dialog box. The *PrettyPrint Options* dialog box closes and the *Select Files To Indent* dialog box appears.

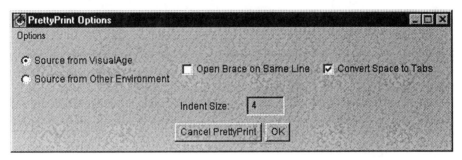

Figure C.6 The *PrettyPrint Options* Dialog Box

The *Select Files To Indent* dialog box (see Figure C.7) contains two lists of files, the files found on the disk and the list of Java text files to be printed. The dialog box only lists directories and those files that end in ".java" (which all Java text files should end in). To select files to be printed, you can either double click on the file name, or click once on the file name and then click the *Copy >* button. To move to a different directory, click on the directory name (all directory names are enclosed in square brackets). The name of the current directory is listed above the file name list on the left side. To switch to a different drive, select the drive from the pop-up menu beneath the list of files in the current directory.

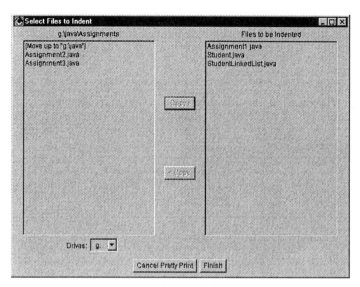

Figure C.7 The *Select Files to Indent* **Dialog Box**

If you accidently select a Java text file to be printed that should not be included, double clicking on the filename in the right hand list of files will remove it. Once all the Java text files that the program uses have been entered, click the *Finish* button. The selected files are then indented and saved with the same name as before. You can now copy the Java text files to a different environment.

Console

Console - General Methods and Constructors

Console ()
Constructor.

Console (int fontSize)
Constructor – Creates a Console window with the text size set to *fontSize*.

Console (int rows, int cols)
Constructor – Creates a Console window with width of *cols* columns and height of *rows* rows.

Console (int rows, int cols, int fontSize)
>   Constructor – Creates a Console window with width of *cols* columns, height of *rows* rows, and the text size set to *fontSize*.

Console (String title)
>   Constructor – Creates a Console window and sets the window title to *title*.

Console (int fontSize, String title)
>   Constructor – Creates a Console window with the text size set to *fontSize* and sets the window title to *title*.

Console (int rows, int cols, String title)
>   Constructor – Creates a Console window with width of *cols* columns, height of *rows* rows, and the window title set to *title*.

Console (int rows, int cols, int fontSize, String title)
>   Constructor – Creates a console window with width of *cols* columns, height of *rows* rows, the text size set to *fontSize*, and the window title set to *title*.

void **close** ()
>   Closes the Console window and disposes of its contents.

Console - Graphics Methods

void **clearRect** (int x, int y, int width, int height)
>   Clears the rectangle to the background color.

void **copyArea** (int x, int y, int width, int height, int deltaX, int deltaY)
>   Copies the rectangle defined by the upper-left corner (*x, y*) with width of *width* and height of *height* to a position moved by *deltaX* and *deltaY* pixels.

void **draw3DRect** (int x, int y, int width, int height, boolean raised)
>   Draws a 3-D rectangle. It appears raised if *raised* is true.

void **drawArc** (int x, int y, int width, int height, int startAngle, int arcAngle)
>   Draws an arc. The arc is inscribed in the rectangle defined by the upper-left corner (*x, y*) with width of *width* and height of *height*. It starts at *startAngle* degrees and goes counterclockwise for *arcAngle* degrees.

void **drawLine** (int x1, int y1, int x2, int y2)
>   Draws a line from (*x1, y1*) to (*x2, y2*).

void **drawMapleLeaf** (int x, int y, int width, int height)
>   Draws a maple leaf. The maple leaf is inscribed in the rectangle defined by the upper-left corner (*x, y*) with width of *width* and height of *height*.

void **drawOval** (int x, int y, int width, int height)
>   Draws an ellipse. The ellipse is inscribed in the rectangle defined by the upper-left corner (*x, y*) with width of *width* and height of *height*.

void **drawPolygon** (int[] xPoints, int[] yPoints, int numPoints)
Draws a polygon. The *xPoints* and *yPoints* arrays define the coordinates of the array of vertices. *numPoints* specifies the number of vertices in the polygon.

void **drawRect** (int x, int y, int width, int height)
Draws a rectangle with upper-left corner at (x, y) with width of *width* and height of *height*.

void **drawRoundRect** (int x, int y, int width, int height, int arcWidth, int arcHeight)
Draws a rectangle with rounded corners with upper-left corner at (x, y) with width of *width* and height of *height*. *arcWidth* and *arcHeight* are the width and height of the ellipse used to draw the rounded corners.

void **drawStar** (int x, int y, int width, int height)
Draws a star. The star is inscribed in the rectangle defined by the upper-left corner (x, y) with width of *width* and height of *height*.

void **drawString** (String str, int x, int y)
Draws the string *str* at the starting point (x, y). The *y* coordinate is the base line of the text.

void **fill3DRect** (int x, int y, int width, int height, boolean raised)
Draws a filled 3-D rectangle. It appears raised if *raised* is true.

void **fillArc** (int x, int y, int width, int height, int startAngle, int arcAngle)
Draws a filled arc. The arc is inscribed in the rectangle defined by the upper-left corner (x, y) with width of *width* and height of *height*. It starts at *startAngle* degrees and goes counterclockwise for *arcAngle* degrees.

void **fillMapleLeaf** (int x, int y, int width, int height)
Draws a filled maple leaf. The maple leaf is inscribed in the rectangle defined by the upper-left corner (x, y) with width of *width* and height of *height*.

void **fillOval** (int x, int y, int width, int height)
Draws a filled ellipse. The ellipse is inscribed in the rectangle defined by the upper-left corner (x, y) with width of *width* and height of *height*.

void **fillPolygon** (int[] xPoints, int[] yPoints, int numPoints)
Draws a filled polygon. The *xPoints* and *yPoints* arrays define the coordinates of the array of vertices. *numPoints* specifies the number of vertices in the polygon.

void **fillRect** (int x, int y, int width, int height)
Draws a filled rectangle with upper-left corner at (x, y) with width of *width* and height of *height*.

void **fillRoundRect** (int x, int y, int width, int height, int arcWidth, int arcHeight)

>Draws a filled rectangle with rounded corners with upper-left corner at (x, y) with width of *width* and height of *height*. *arcWidth* and *arcHeight* are the width and height of the ellipse used to draw the rounded corners.

void **fillStar** (int x, int y, int width, int height)

>Draws a filled star. The star is inscribed in the rectangle defined by the upper-left corner (x, y) with width of *width* and height of *height*.

int **getWidth** ()

>Returns the width of the drawing surface of the Console window in pixels.

int **getHeight** ()

>Returns the height of the drawing surface of the Console window in pixels.

void **setColor** (Color c)

>Sets the color of the graphics context. The color is used for any draw methods.

void **setFont** (Font f)

>Sets the font of the graphics context. The font is used with the drawString method.

void **setPaintMode** ()

>Sets the graphics context into paint mode. All drawing in the graphics context draws over the background.

void **setXORMode** (Color c)

>Sets the graphics context into XOR mode. All drawing in the graphics context is XOR'd with the background. The color specified by *c* is a special color so that any drawing done on a background of color *c* will not be changed.

Console - Text Input and Output Methods

void **clear** ()

>Clears the entire Console window and sets the cursor to the upper-left corner.

int **getMaxColumns** ()

>Returns the width of the Console window in columns.

int **getMaxRows** ()

>Returns the height of the Console window in rows.

int **getColumn** ()

>Returns the column number of the current cursor position.

int **getRow** ()
> Returns the row number of the current cursor position.

void **print** (byte b)
void **print** (short s)
void **print** (int i)
void **print** (long l)
void **print** (float f)
void **print** (double d)
void **print** (boolean b)
void **print** (char c)
void **print** (String s)
> Outputs the argument to the Console window beginning at the cursor position.

void **print** (byte number, int fieldSize)
void **print** (short number, int fieldSize)
void **print** (int number, int fieldSize)
void **print** (long number, int fieldSize)
> Outputs *number* to the Console window in a field of width *fieldSize* beginning at the cursor position. If the number (when converted to String) is larger than *fieldSize*, *fieldSize* is ignored. The output is right justified within the field.

void **print** (float number, int fieldSize)
void **print** (double number, int fieldSize)
> Outputs *number* to the Console window in a field of width *fieldSize* beginning at the cursor position. The method adjusts the number of decimal places displayed to fit in the field, if possible. If the argument (when converted to String) is larger than *fieldSize*, *fieldSize* is ignored. The output is right justified within the field.

void **print** (boolean b, int fieldSize)
void **print** (char c, int fieldSize)
void **print** (String s, int fieldSize)
> Outputs the argument to the Console window in a field of width *fieldSize* beginning at the cursor position. If the argument (when converted to String) is larger than *fieldSize*, *fieldSize* is ignored. The output is left justified.

void **print** (double number, int fieldSize, int decimalPlaces)
void **print** (float number, int fieldSize, int decimalPlaces)
> Outputs *number* to the Console window in a field of width *fieldSize* with *decimalPlaces* number of decimal places beginning at the cursor position. The field width is ignored if the number will not fit. The output is right justified.

void **println** ()
> Outputs a Return at the cursor position to the Console window.

void **println** (byte b)
void **println** (short s)
void **println** (int i)
void **println** (long l)
void **println** (float f)
void **println** (double d)
void **println** (boolean b)
void **println** (char c)
void **println** (String s)
void **println** (byte b, int fieldSize)
void **println** (short s, int fieldSize)
void **println** (int i, int fieldSize)
void **println** (long l, int fieldSize)
void **println** (float f, int fieldSize)
void **println** (double d, int fieldSize)
void **println** (boolean b, int fieldSize)
void **println** (char c, int fieldSize)
void **println** (String s, int fieldSize)
void **println** (float f, int fieldSize, int decimalPlaces)
void **println** (double d, int fieldSize, int decimalPlaces)

> Identical to **print** method with same arguments, except that a Return is output after the argument.

byte **readByte** ()

> Returns the byte value (–128 to 127) read from the keyboard.

short **readShort** ()

> Returns the 2-byte integer (–32,768 to 32,767) read from the keyboard.

int **readInt** ()

> Returns the 4-byte integer (–2,147,483,648 to 2,147,483,647) read from the keyboard.

long **readLong** ()

> Returns the 8-byte integer read from the keyboard.

float **readFloat** ()

> Returns the 4-byte float read from the keyboard.

double **readDouble** ()

> Returns the 8-byte double read from the keyboard.

boolean **readBoolean** ()

> Returns the boolean value (either "true" or "false", case insensitive) read from the keyboard.

char **readChar** ()

> Returns the character read from the keyboard.

String **readString** ()

> Returns the String read from the keyboard.

String **readLine** ()
> Returns the entire line of input read from the keyboard without the Return.

char **getChar** ()
> Returns the character read from the keyboard. Does not wait for **Enter** to be pressed.

void **setTextColor** (Color c)
> Sets the color for text output from print and println methods.

void **setTextBackgroundColor** (Color c)
> Sets the background color for text output from print and println methods.

void **setCursorVisible** (boolean visible)
> Shows or hides the text cursor according to the *visible* parameter.

void **setCursor** (int row, int col)
> Sets the cursor position to row *row* and column *col*.

Console - Example

```
import java.awt.*;
import hsa.Console;

public class TestConsole
{
    public static void main (String[] args)
    {
        Console c = new Console ();
        c.print ("Enter the radius of the circle: ");
        int radius = c.readInt ();
        c.setColor (Color.green);
        c.fillOval (c.getWidth () / 2 - radius,
            c.getHeight () / 2 - radius, radius * 2, radius * 2);
    } // main method
} /* TestConsole class */
```

TextConsole

TextConsole - General Methods and Constructors

TextConsole ()
> Constructor.

TextConsole (int fontSize)
> Constructor – Creates a TextConsole window with the text size set to *fontSize*.

TextConsole (int rows, int cols)
> Constructor – Creates a TextConsole window with width of *cols* columns and height of *rows* rows.

TextConsole (int rows, int cols, int fontSize)
> Constructor – Creates a TextConsole window with width of *cols* columns, height of *rows* rows, and the text size set to *fontSize*.

TextConsole (String title)
> Constructor – Creates a TextConsole window and sets the window title to *title*.

TextConsole (int fontSize, String title)
> Constructor – Creates a TextConsole window with the text size set to *fontSize* and sets the window title to *title*.

TextConsole (int rows, int cols, String title)
> Constructor – Creates a TextConsole window with width of *cols* columns, height of *rows* rows, and the window title set to *title*.

TextConsole (int rows, int cols, int fontSize, String title)
> Constructor – Creates a TextConsole window with width of *cols* columns, height of *rows* rows, the text size set to *fontSize*, and the window title set to *title*.

void **close** ()
> Closes the TextConsole window and disposes of its contents.

TextConsole - Text Input and Output Methods

void **print** (byte b)
void **print** (short s)
void **print** (int i)
void **print** (long l)
void **print** (float f)
void **print** (double d)
void **print** (boolean b)
void **print** (char c)
void **print** (String s)
> Outputs the argument to the TextConsole window beginning at the cursor position.

void **print** (byte number, int fieldSize)
void **print** (short number, int fieldSize)
void **print** (int number, int fieldSize)
void **print** (long number, int fieldSize)
> Outputs *number* to the TextConsole window in a field of width *fieldSize* beginning at the cursor position. If the number (when converted to String) is larger than *fieldSize*, *fieldSize* is ignored. The output is right justified within the field.

void **print** (float number, int fieldSize)
void **print** (double number, int fieldSize)
> Outputs *number* to the TextConsole window in a field of width *fieldSize* beginning at the cursor position. The method adjusts the number of decimal places displayed to fit in the field, if possible. If the argument (when converted to String) is larger than *fieldSize*, *fieldSize* is ignored. The output is right justified within the field.

void **print** (boolean b, int fieldSize)
void **print** (char c, int fieldSize)
void **print** (String s, int fieldSize)
> Outputs the argument to the TextConsole window in a field of width *fieldSize* beginning at the cursor position. If the argument (when converted to String) is larger than *fieldSize*, *fieldSize* is ignored. The output is left justified.

void **print** (double number, int fieldSize, int decimalPlaces)
void **print** (float number, int fieldSize, int decimalPlaces)
> Outputs *number* to the TextConsole window in a field of width *fieldSize* with *decimalPlaces* number of decimal places beginning at the cursor position. The field width is ignored if the number will not fit. The output is right justified.

void **println** ()
> Outputs a Return at the cursor position to the TextConsole window.

void **println** (byte b)
void **println** (short s)
void **println** (int i)
void **println** (long l)
void **println** (float f)
void **println** (double d)
void **println** (boolean b)
void **println** (char c)
void **println** (String s)
void **println** (byte b, int fieldSize)
void **println** (short s, int fieldSize)
void **println** (int i, int fieldSize)
void **println** (long l, int fieldSize)
void **println** (float f, int fieldSize)

void **println** (double d, int fieldSize)
void **println** (boolean b, int fieldSize)
void **println** (char c, int fieldSize)
void **println** (String s, int fieldSize)
void **println** (float f, int fieldSize, int decimalPlaces)
void **println** (double d, int fieldSize, int decimalPlaces)
> Identical to **print** method with same arguments, except that a Return is output after the argument.

byte **readByte** ()
> Returns the byte value (–128 to 127) read from the keyboard.

short **readShort** ()
> Returns the 2-byte integer (–32,768 to 32,767) read from the keyboard.

int **readInt** ()
> Returns the 4-byte integer (–2,147,483,648 to 2,147,483,647) read from the keyboard.

long **readLong** ()
> Returns the 8-byte integer read from the keyboard.

float **readFloat** ()
> Returns the 4-byte float read from the keyboard.

double **readDouble** ()
> Returns the 8-byte double read from the keyboard.

boolean **readBoolean** ()
> Returns the boolean value (either "true" or "false", case insensitive) read from the keyboard.

char **readChar** ()
> Returns the character read from the keyboard.

String **readString** ()
> Returns the String read from the keyboard.

String **readLine** ()
> Returns the entire line of input read from the keyboard without the Return.

TextConsole - Example

```
import java.awt.*;
import hsa.TextConsole;

public class TestTextConsole
{
    public static void main (String[] args)
    {
```

```
TextConsole c = new TextConsole ();
c.print ("Enter the times table: ");
int multiplier = c.readInt ();
for (int count = 1 ; count <= 10 ; count++)
{
    c.print (count, 3);
    c.println (count * multiplier, 4);
}
} // main method
} /* TestTextConsole class */
```

Stdin

static boolean **close** ()
Closes standard input to prevent further reading.

static boolean **eof** ()
Returns true if the next thing to be read from the keyboard is the end-of-file marker. (You can generate an end-of-file by pressing either Ctrl+Z or Ctrl+D.)

static byte **readByte** ()
Returns the byte value (–128 to 127) read from the keyboard.

static short **readShort** ()
Returns the 2-byte integer (–32,768 to 32,767) read from the keyboard.

static int **readInt** ()
Returns the 4-byte integer (–2,147,483,648 to 2,147,483,647) read from the keyboard.

static long **readLong** ()
Returns the 8-byte integer read from the keyboard.

static float **readFloat** ()
Returns the 4-byte float read from the keyboard.

static double **readDouble** ()
Returns the 8-byte double read from the keyboard.

static boolean **readBoolean** ()
Returns the boolean value (either "true" or "false", case insensitive) read from the keyboard.

static char **readChar** ()
Returns the character read from the keyboard.

static String **readString** ()
Returns the String read from the keyboard.

static String **readLine** ()
>   Returns the entire line of input read from the keyboard without the
>   Return.

Stdin - Example

>   See Stdout example.

Stdout

static void **print** (byte b)
static void **print** (short s)
static void **print** (int i)
static void **print** (long l)
static void **print** (float f)
static void **print** (double d)
static void **print** (boolean b)
static void **print** (char c)
static void **print** (String s)
>   Outputs the argument to standard output.

static void **print** (byte number, int fieldSize)
static void **print** (short number, int fieldSize)
static void **print** (int number, int fieldSize)
static void **print** (long number, int fieldSize)
>   Outputs *number* to standard output in a field of width *fieldSize*. If the
>   number (when converted to String) is larger than *fieldSize*, *fieldSize* is
>   ignored. The output is right justified within the field.

static void **print** (float number, int fieldSize)
static void **print** (double number, int fieldSize)
>   Outputs *number* to standard output in a field of width *fieldSize*. The
>   method adjusts the number of decimal places displayed to fit in the field, if
>   possible. If the argument (when converted to String) is larger than
>   *fieldSize*, *fieldSize* is ignored. The output is right justified within the field.

static void **print** (boolean b, int fieldSize)
static void **print** (char c, int fieldSize)
static void **print** (String s, int fieldSize)
>   Outputs the argument to standard output in a field of width *fieldSize*. If the
>   argument (when converted to String) is larger than *fieldSize*, *fieldSize* is
>   ignored. The output is left justified.

static void **print** (double number, int fieldSize, int decimalPlaces)
static void **print** (float number, int fieldSize, int decimalPlaces)
>   Outputs *number* to standard output in a field of width *fieldSize* with
>   *decimalPlaces* number of decimal places. The field width is ignored if the
>   number will not fit. The output is right justified.

static void **println** ()
>   Output a Return to standard output.

static void **println** (byte b)
static void **println** (short s)
static void **println** (int i)
static void **println** (long l)
static void **println** (float f)
static void **println** (double d)
static void **println** (boolean b)
static void **println** (char c)
static void **println** (String s)
static void **println** (byte b, int fieldSize)
static void **println** (short s, int fieldSize)
static void **println** (int i, int fieldSize)
static void **println** (long l, int fieldSize)
static void **println** (float f, int fieldSize)
static void **println** (double d, int fieldSize)
static void **println** (boolean b, int fieldSize)
static void **println** (char c, int fieldSize)
static void **println** (String s, int fieldSize)
static void **println** (float f, int fieldSize, int decimalPlaces)
static void **println** (double d, int fieldSize, int decimalPlaces)
>   Identical to **print** method with same arguments, except that a Return is
>   output after the argument.

Stdout - Example

```
import hsa.*;

// Reads and writes number to standard input and output.
public class TestStdinStdout
{
    public static void main (String[] args)
    {
        Stdout.println ("Calculate square roots");
        while (true)
        {
            Stdout.print ("Enter a number: ");
            if (Stdin.eof ()) break;
```

```
                        double number = Stdin.readDouble ();
                        if (number < 0)
                        {
                            // Instantiating a FatalError object displays an
                            // error window and then quits the program.
                            new FatalError ("Attempted to take the square " +
                                            "root of a negative number");
                            // Never reaches here.
                        }
                        Stdout.println ("The square root of ");
                        Stdout.print (number);
                        Stdout.print (" is ");
                        Stdout.println (Math.sqrt (number), 8, 5);
                    }
                } // main method
            } /* TestStdinStdout class */
```

TextInputFile

TextInputFile ()
> Constructor – Opens standard input as a TextInputFile.

TextInputFile (File file)
> Constructor – Opens *file* as a TextInputFile.

TextInputFile (String fileName)
> Constructor – Opens file with name *fileName* as a TextInputFile. If *fileName* is "Standard Input", "Keyboard" or "Stdin" (case irrelevant), standard input is opened as a TextInputFile.

void **close** ()
> Closes the TextInputFile to prevent further reading.

boolean **eof** ()
> Returns true if the next thing to be read from the file is the end-of-file marker. (When reading from standard input, you can generate an end-of-file by pressing either Ctrl+Z or Ctrl+D.)

byte **readByte** ()
> Returns the byte value (–128 to 127) read from the file.

short **readShort** ()
> Returns the 2-byte integer (–32,768 to 32,767) read from the file.

int **readInt** ()
> Returns the 4-byte integer (–2,147,483,648 to 2,147,483,647) read from the file.

long **readLong** ()
Returns the 8-byte integer read from the file.
float **readFloat** ()
Returns the 4-byte float read from the file.
double **readDouble** ()
Returns the 8-byte double read from the file.
boolean **readBoolean** ()
Returns the boolean value (either "true" or "false", case insensitive) read
from the file.
char **readChar** ()
Returns the character read from the file.
String **readString** ()
Returns the String read from the file.
String **readLine** ()
Returns the entire line of input read from the file without the Return.

TextInputFile - Example

```
import hsa.*;

// Reads a file of integers and calculates their square roots.
public class TestTextInputFile
{
    public static void main (String[] args)
    {
        String fileName;
        TextInputFile f;
        int lineNumber = 1;
        Stdout.print ("Enter the file to be read: ");
        fileName = Stdin.readLine ();
        f = new TextInputFile (fileName);
        while (!f.eof ())
        {
            double number = f.readDouble ();
            Stdout.print (number, 10, 4);
            Stdout.print (" ");
            Stdout.println (Math.sqrt (number), 10, 4);
        }
        f.close ();
    } // main method
} /* TestTextInputFile class */
```

TextOutputFile

TextOutputFile ()
> Constructor – Opens standard output as a TextOutputFile.

TextOutputFile (File file)
> Constructor – Opens *file* as a TextOutputFile.

TextOutputFile (String fileName)
> Constructor – Opens file with name *fileName* as a TextOutputFile. If *fileName* is "Standard Output", "Screen" or "Stdout" (case irrelevant), standard output is opened as a TextOutputFile.

TextOutputFile (File file, boolean append)
> Constructor – Opens *file* as a TextOutputFile. If *append* is true, any output will be appended to *file*.

TextOutputFile (String fileName, boolean append)
> Constructor – Opens file with name *fileName* as a TextOutputFile. If *append* is true, any output will be appended to the file. If *fileName* is "Standard Output", "Screen" or "Stdout" (case irrelevant), standard output is opened as a TextOutputFile.

void **close** ()
> Closes the TextOutputFile to prevent further writing.

void **print** (byte b)
void **print** (short s)
void **print** (int i)
void **print** (long l)
void **print** (float f)
void **print** (double d)
void **print** (boolean b)
void **print** (char c)
void **print** (String s)
> Outputs the argument to the file.

void **print** (byte number, int fieldSize)
void **print** (short number, int fieldSize)
void **print** (int number, int fieldSize)
void **print** (long number, int fieldSize)
> Outputs *number* to the file in a field of width *fieldSize*. If the number (when converted to String) is larger than *fieldSize*, *fieldSize* is ignored. The output is right justified within the field.

void **print** (float number, int fieldSize)
void **print** (double number, int fieldSize)
> Outputs *number* to the file in a field of width *fieldSize*. The method adjusts the number of decimal places displayed to fit in the field, if possible. If the

argument (when converted to String) is larger than *fieldSize, fieldSize* is ignored. The output is right justified within the field.

void **print** (boolean b, int fieldSize)
void **print** (char c, int fieldSize)
void **print** (String s, int fieldSize)

Outputs the argument to the file in a field of width *fieldSize*. If the argument (when converted to String) is larger than *fieldSize, fieldSize* is ignored. The output is left justified.

void **print** (double number, int fieldSize, int decimalPlaces)
void **print** (float number, int fieldSize, int decimalPlaces)

Outputs *number* to the file in a field of width *fieldSize* with *decimalPlaces* number of decimal places. The field width is ignored if the number will not fit. The output is right justified.

void **println** ()

Output a Return to the file.

void **println** (byte b)
void **println** (short s)
void **println** (int i)
void **println** (long l)
void **println** (float f)
void **println** (double d)
void **println** (boolean b)
void **println** (char c)
void **println** (String s)
void **println** (byte b, int fieldSize)
void **println** (short s, int fieldSize)
void **println** (int i, int fieldSize)
void **println** (long l, int fieldSize)
void **println** (float f, int fieldSize)
void **println** (double d, int fieldSize)
void **println** (boolean b, int fieldSize)
void **println** (char c, int fieldSize)
void **println** (String s, int fieldSize)
void **println** (float f, int fieldSize, int decimalPlaces)
void **println** (double d, int fieldSize, int decimalPlaces)

Identical to **print** method with same arguments, except that a Return is output after the argument.

TextOutputFile - Example

```
import hsa.*;

// Saves a Times table to a file.
public class TestTextOutputFile
```

```
{
    public static void main (String[] args)
    {
        String fileName;
        TextOutputFile f;
        int lineNumber = 1;
        Stdout.print ("Enter the file to be written: ");
        fileName = Stdin.readLine ();
        f = new TextOutputFile (fileName);
        f.print (" ", 6);                    // Print 6 spaces
        for (int i = 1 ; i <= 12 ; i++) // Print numbers across top
        {
            f.print (i, 4);
        }
        f.println ();
        for (int i = 1 ; i <= 12 ; i++)
        {
            f.print (i, 4);
            f.print (" ");
            for (int j = 1 ; j <= 12 ; j++)
            {
                f.print (i * j, 4);
            }
            f.println ();
        }
        f.close ();
    } // main method
} /* TestTextOutputFile class */
```

FatalError

FatalError (String message)
> Constructor – Displays *message* in a window titled "Fatal Error" centered on the screen. When the "Quit" button is pressed, the program exits immediately.

FatalError (String message, Frame frame)
> Constructor – Displays *message* in a window titled "Fatal Error" centered on the Frame *frame*. When the "Quit" button is pressed, the program exits immediately.

FatalError - Example

See Stdout example.

Message

Message (String message)
Constructor – Displays *message* in a untitled window centered on the screen. When the "OK" button is pressed, execution returns from the call to the constructor.

Message (String message, String title)
Constructor – Displays *message* in a window titled *title* centered on the screen. When the "OK" button is pressed, execution returns from the call to the constructor.

Message (String message, Frame frame)
Constructor – Displays *message* in a untitled window centered on Frame *frame*. When the "OK" button is pressed, execution returns from the call to the constructor.

Message (String message, String title, Frame frame)
Constructor – Displays *message* in a window titled *title* centered on Frame *frame*. When the "OK" button is pressed, execution returns from the call to the constructor.

static void **beep** ()
Causes the computer to beep. Useful for catching the user's attention.

Message - Example

```java
import hsa.*;

// Brings up four message windows, one after another.
public class TestMessage
{
    public static void main (String[] args)
    {
        new Message ("This is the first message", "First message");
        new Message ("This is the second message",
            "Second message");
        new Message ("This is the third message",
            "Third message");
        new Message ("This is the last message", "Last message");
    } // main method
} /* TestMessage class */
```

Status

Status (String message)
> Constructor – Displays *message* in a untitled window centered on the screen. The window only disappears when the hide () method is called or the user clicks the window's Close button (the X on the right hand side of the window's title bar). Execution returns from the call to the constructor immediately.

Status (String message, String title)
> Constructor – Displays *message* in a window titled *title* centered on the screen. The window only disappears when the hide () method is called or the user clicks the window's Close button (the X on the right hand side of the window's title bar). Execution returns from the call to the constructor immediately.

Status (String message, Frame frame)
> Constructor – Displays *message* in a untitled window centered on Frame *frame*. The window only disappears when the hide () method is called or the user clicks the window's Close button (the X on the right hand side of the window's title bar). Execution returns from the call to the constructor immediately.

Status (String message, String title, Frame frame)
> Constructor – Displays *message* in a window titled *title* centered on Frame *frame*. The window only disappears when the hide () method is called or the user clicks the window's Close button (the X on the right hand side of the window's title bar). Execution returns from the call to the constructor immediately.

void **setMessage** (String message)
> Changes the message in the window to *message*.

void **hide** ()
> Hides the window.

void **show** ()
> Shows the window.

void **dispose** ()
> Hides the window and disposes of its contents.

Status - Example

```
import hsa.*;

// Count number of lines in a file.
public class TestStatus
{
    public static void main (String[] args)
    {
        String fileName;
        TextInputFile f;
        Status status;
        int lineNumber = 1;
        Stdout.print ("Enter the file to have lines counted: ");
        fileName = Stdin.readLine ();
        f = new TextInputFile (fileName);
        status = new Status ("Reading " +
            fileName);              // Open status window.
        while (!f.eof ())
        {
            f.readLine ();
            status.setMessage ("Reading line number " +
                lineNumber);    // Change status message.
            lineNumber++;
        }
        status.dispose ();          // Close status window.
        f.close ();
        Stdout.println ("There were " + lineNumber + " lines in " +
            fileName);
    } // main method
} /* TestStatus class */
```

Appendix D : Operators

This is a list of the operators available in Java and their precedence.

Mathematical Operators

Operator	Operation	Result Type
Prefix +	Identity	Same as Operands
Prefix −	Negative	Same as Operands
+	Addition	Same as Operands
−	Subtraction	Same as Operands
*	Multiplication	Same as Operands
/	Division	Same as Operands
%	Remainder	**int**
<	Less Than	**boolean**
>	Greater Than	**boolean**
= =	Equals	**boolean**
< =	Less Than or Equal	**boolean**
> =	Greater Than or Equal	**boolean**
! =	Not Equal	**boolean**

Boolean Operators

Operator	Operation	Result Type
!	Negation	**boolean**
&&	And	**boolean**
| |	Or	**boolean**

Bit Manipulation Operators

Operator	Operation	Result Type
&	Bitwise and	Same as Operands
|	Bitwise or	Same as Operands
^	Bitwise XOR	Same as Operands
<<	Shift left	Same as Operands
>>	Shift right	Same as Operands
>>>	Shift right (fill with 0)	Same as Operands

Operator Precedence

Highest precedence operators first.

(1)   [ ], ., (*params*), *expr++*, *expr--*
(2)   + +*expr*, --*expr*, +*expr*, -*expr*
(3)   **new**, (*type*) *expr*
(4)   *, /, %
(5)   +, -
(6)   <<, >>, >>>
(7)   < =, <, >, > =, **instanceof**
(8)   = =, ! =
(9)   &
(10)   ^
(11) |
(12)   &&
(13) | |
(14)   ? :
(15)   =, + =, - =, * =, / =, % =, >> =, << =,
       >>> =, &=, ^ =, | =

Some of these operators were not introduced in this text.

Appendix E : Applet Syntax

An applet is a Java program capable of being loaded and executed over the internet using an Java-enabled web browser. To create an applet, the class must extend the Applet class found in the java.applet package. What follows is a template for a Java applet class.

```java
// The "AppletPlate" class.
import java.applet.Applet;
import java.awt.*;

public class AppletPlate extends Applet
{
    // Place instance variables here.

    public void init ()
    {
        // Any code placed here is executed when the page is loaded.
    } // init method

    public void start ()
    {
        // Any code placed here is executed when the applet is started.
    } // start method

    public void stop ()
    {
        // Any code placed here is executed when the applet is stopped.
    } // stop method

    public void destroy ()
    {
        // Any code placed here is executed when
        // the applet is removed from memory.
    } // destroy method

    public void paint (Graphics g)
    {
        // Any code placed here is executed whenever the applet
        // window is revealed or when the applet runs the first time.
    } // paint method
```

```
public boolean action (Event e, Object o)
{
    // Any code placed here is executed when a button is clicked
    // or a Return is typed in a TextField.
    return true;
} // action method
} /* AppletPlate class */
```

Any method in the template that is not modified can be omitted entirely.

The HTML file can have any number of other HTML elements. To load and execute the applet, it must have the following two lines:

```
<APPLET CODE = "class-name" WIDTH=width HEIGHT=height >
</APPLET>
```

The *class-name* must be in quotation marks and is the name of the Java class file, which ends in ".class", not the Java text file, which ends in ".java". The *width* and *height* fields are the size of the applet's display area on the web page. An applet cannot change the size of the drawing surface it will be using.

The user must then create the HTML file to run the applet. When the HTML file is loaded in an Internet browser, the file *class-name* will be loaded and executed. If no path name is specified in *class-name*, the Java class files must be in the same directory as the HTML file.

Here is a template for the HTML file.

```
<HTML>
<BODY>
<APPLET CODE = "class-name" WIDTH=width HEIGHT=height >
</APPLET>
</BODY>
</HTML>
```

Appendix F : Application Syntax

An application is a Java program capable of being run without the presence of an Internet browser. To create an application, the class must have a *main* method with the parameter of *String*[] *args*. When the application is executed, the system calls the *main* method with any command line arguments passed as a parameter to *main*.

A Java application does not have a built-in drawing surface. The application can either use standard input and output or create its own *Frame*.

What follows is a template for a Java application class.

```
// The "BoilerPlate" class.
import java.awt.*;

public class BoilerPlate
{
    static public void main (String [] args)
    {
        // Any code placed here is executed whenever
        // the application is run.
    } // main method
} /* BoilerPlate class */
```

Appendix G : Installing VisualAge for Java

Licensing Agreement

You **must** read and agree to the licensing agreement found in appendix H in order to use the CD provided with this book. If you do not agree to the licensing agreement, you are not entitled to use the software bundled with this book.

Note that you may use the software provided in this book only in connection with your use of this book and/or academic course work related to the book. You may not give or sell the software to anyone else.

Hardware Requirements

Minimum:
- Pentium 90 Processor
- 48MB RAM
- CD-ROM Drive
- 800x600 Resolution Display
- 100MB Disk Space (Large drives may require more space.)
- 30MB Swap/Paging Space

Recommended:
- Pentium 90 Processor
- 64MB RAM
- CD-ROM Drive
- 1024x768 Resolution Display
- 130MB Disk Space (Large drives may require more space.)
- 30MB Swap/Paging Space

If you are uncertain as to the amount of RAM on your system, select the *Settings* menu item from the *Start* menu. Select *Control Panel* from the sub-menu that appears. From the list of Control Panels, select *System*. The *System Properties* window appears. Select the *General* tab. Near the bottom of the window the total amount of RAM on your system will be listed.

Software Requirements

- Microsoft Windows 95, 98 or
- Microsoft Windows NT 4.0 with Service Pack 3
- TCP/IP must be up and running.

Installing *VisualAge for Java*

1. Quit all other Windows applications by closing all open windows. You can tell when you have done so by making certain that there are no other applications listed in the task bar.

2. Make certain that TCP/IP is up and running. If you are uncertain as to how to do this, read the README.TXT file found on the CD-ROM. To read the file, start the installer by placing the *VisualAge for Java* CD in the drive and clicking on *View Readme.txt*. This opens README.TXT in Notepad. The necessary information about configuring TCP/IP is found approximately two-thirds of the way through the file.

3. Place the *VisualAge for Java* CD in your CD-ROM drive. After a few seconds, the *VisualAge for Java* installation program automatically starts and the *Install Selection* window appears (see Figure G.1).

Figure G.1 The *Install Selection* Window

4. *VisualAge for Java* requires a browser capable of displaying frames to display the on-line help. If you do not have a frames-capable browser, click the *Install Netscape Navigator, Version 4.04* and follow the on-screen instructions. This installs Netscape Navigator 4.04.

5. Start the installation by clicking on *Install VisualAge for Java, Version 2.0*. A *Welcome* window with some introductory information appears. Click the *Next >* button in the *Welcome* window to continue.

6. The *Software Licencing* window appears. Note that you are bound by this agreement and the agreement in Appendix H if you wish to use the software. Click the *Yes* button and confirm when the *Licence Confirmation* window appears.

7. The *Choose Destination Location* window appears (see Figure G.2). If you want to change the location of where *VisualAge for Java* is to be installed, click the *Browse* buttonand select a new folder. When done, or if the default location is acceptable, click the *Next >* button.

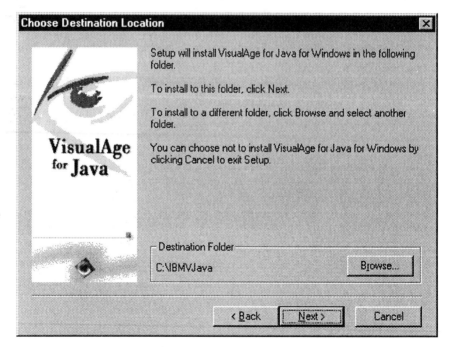

Figure G.2 The *Choose Destination Location* Window

8. The *Setup Type* dialog box appears (see Figure G.3). You can choose your form of setup, although we suggest choosing "Full". When you are satisfied with the type of installation and the location, click the *Next >* button.

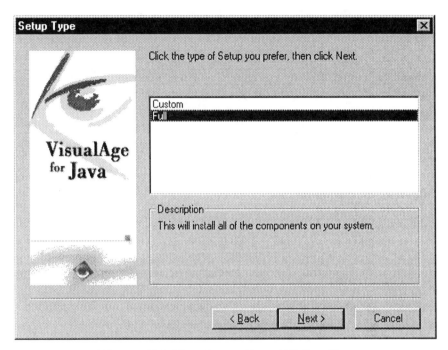

Figure G.3 The *Setup Type* Dialog Box

9. The *Select Program Folder* dialog box appears allowing you to specify where in the *Start* menu the program icons for *VisualAge for Java* should appear (see Figure G.4). In general, the default value supplied need not be changed. Once you have selected a folder (or more likely chosen the default folder name), click the *Next >* button.

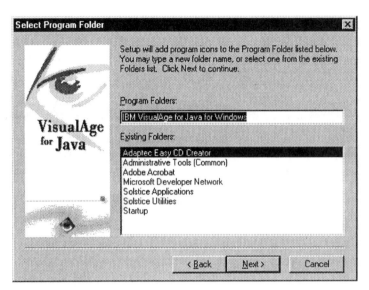

Figure G.4 The *Select Program Folder* Window

10. The *Start Copying Files* dialog box appears (see Figure G.5). This gives you one last chance to review the installation before proceeding. If you are ready to proceed, click the *Next >* button in the *Start Copying Files* dialog box.

Figure G.5 The *Start Copying Files* Dialog Box.

11. The installer starts copying the files to your hard drive (see Figure G.6). This can take several minutes.

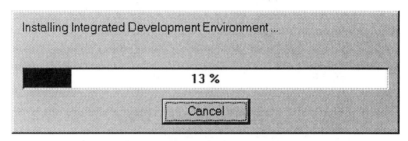

Figure G.6 Copying Files Progress Window

12. Once the files have been copied to your hard drive, the *Setup Complete* dialog box appears (see Figure G.7). You can now register your software and read the ReadMe file. Select the desired checkboxes and click the *Finish* button.

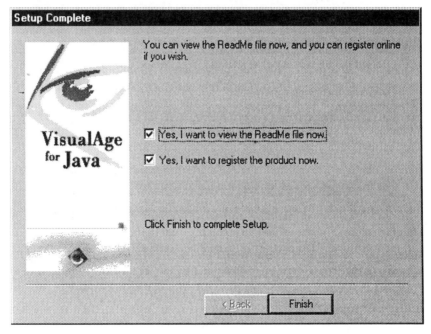

Figure G.7 The *Setup Complete* Dialog Box

13. After you register the software and read the ReadMe file, a last dialog box appears, also labelled "Setup Complete" (see Figure G.8). This dialog box reminds you that your computer must be restarted before using *VisualAge for Java*. It allows you to either restart your computer immediately or exit the installer and restart your computer later. We suggest restarting your computer immediately. Choose either option and click the *Finish* button.

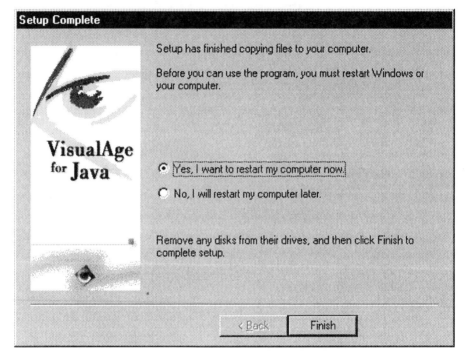

Figure G.8 The *Setup Complete* Window

14. Some editions of this book may contain a directory labelled "updates" on the CD. If present, the *updates* directory contains patches, fixes, and upgrades to the *VisualAge for Java, Professional Edition, Version 2.0* software. Check the contents of the *updates* directory for information on how to apply the fixes. For the most recent updates available, check the *VisualAge for Java* website at **www.software.ibm.com/ad/vajava**.

Installing the *Holt Software* and the *Book Examples* Projects

The CD accompanying this book contains not only *VisualAge for Java, Professional Edition, Version 2.0,* but also additional materials developed by Holt Software for use with this book. These are found on the CD in the root directory and consist of:

- The *book* directory, which contains all the ".java" and ".class" files for all examples classes in the book.
- The *hsa* directory, which contains all the ".java" and ".class" files for the *hsa* package used in this book (and documented in Appendix C).
- The *hsa examples* directory, which contains ".java" and ".class" files for example programs using the *hsa* package.
- The *hsa html* directory, which contains the HTML version of the documentation found in Appendix C. If the *hsa* package is updated, documentation of any changes will be found here.
- The *updates* directory, which may contain updates of *VisualAge for Java.*
- The *hsa.dat* file. This is a *VisualAge for Java* repository file containing the book examples and the *hsa* package.

The remainder of the section covers the details on importing the book examples and the *hsa* package into *VisualAge for Java.*

The classes in *hsa.dat* files are organized into two *VisualAge for Java* projects, The *Holt Software* project and the *Book Examples* project.

The *Holt Software* project contains two packages: the *hsa* package used by many of the programs in this book and the *Default Package for Holt Software* package, which contains example programs for each of the classes in the *hsa* package demonstrating the methods available in the class. The *hsa* package is fully described in Appendix C.

The *Book Examples* project contains one package, *Default Package for Book Examples.* This package contains all the classes that are used in this book.

VisualAge for Java must already be installed at this point. See the previous section for instruction on how to install *VisualAge for Java.*

1. If you have removed the VisualAge for Java CD from the machine, replace it in the CD-ROM drive. The VisualAge for Java installer will start again. Select *Exit* when the *Install Selection* window appears.

2. Open the *Windows Explorer* by opening the *Start* menu and selecting *Windows Explorer* from the *Programs* sub-menu.

3. Double click on the CD-ROM drive on the left side of the *Windows Explorer* window (see Figure G.9). The CD-ROM is labelled *Programming_conc*. The contents of the CD-ROM appear on the right side of the *Explorer* window. (The contents is a series of directories labelled *book, hsa, hsa examples, hsa html, ivj20, Netscape, updates* and the files *autoplay.ini, autorun.inf, hsa.dat, readme.txt, setup.bmp,* and *setup.exe*.)

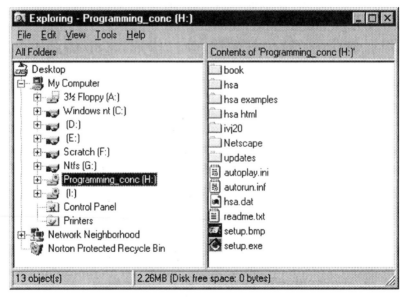

Figure G.9 The Explorer Window

4. Click the icon labelled *hsa.dat* (or *hsa*) that appears on the right side of the *Explorer* window and drag it your main hard drive (most probably C:) on the left side. When dragging the file to the left side, note that the name of the drive or directory in which the file will appear is highlighted. When the correct drive is highlighted, release the mouse button. The file is then copied (see Figure G.10).

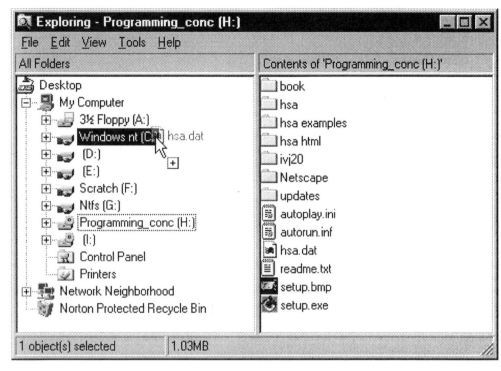

Figure G.10 Copying hsa.dat to Drive C

5. On the left side of the *Explorer* window, double click the icon of the hard drive to which you copied the file. The contents of the drive appears on the right side of the *Explorer* window. Scroll down until the *hsa.dat* (or *hsa*) file appears. Click the right mouse button on the *hsa.dat* (or *hsa*) file. A submenu appears. Select *Properties* from the submenu.

6. A dialog box labelled *hsa.dat* (or *hsa*) *Properties* appears (see Figure G.11). At the bottom of the dialog box is a series of checkboxes for the various file attributes. A checkbox labelled *Read-only* is checked. Click once in the checkbox to leave the checkbox blank. Click the *OK* button to close the dialog box.

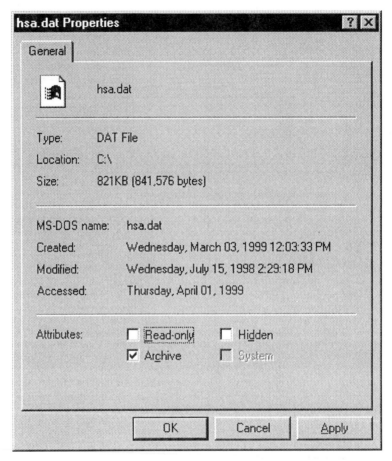

Figure G.11 The *hsa.dat Properties* Dialog Box

7. Start *VisualAge for Java*. (Found in the *Programs* submenu of the *Start* menu.) Close the *VisualAge Quickstart* dialog box by selecting the *Go to the Workbench* radio button and clicking the *OK* button.

8. Select *Import* from the *File* menu. The *Import* dialog box appears (see Figure G.12). Select the *Repository* radio button and click the *Next >* button.

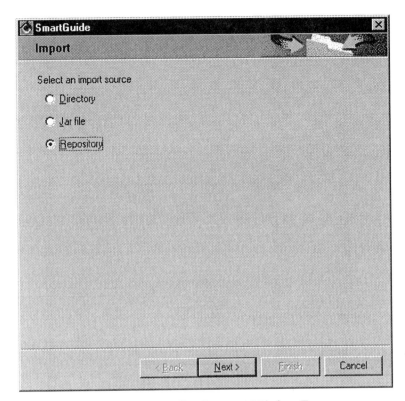

Figure G.12 The *Import* Dialog Box

9. The *Import from another repository* dialog box appears (see Figure G.13). In the file name field, enter "c:\hsa.dat" (unless you copied *hsa.dat* onto a different drive). Make certain the *Projects* radio button is selected. Once the file name is entered, click the *Details* button. The *Project import* dialog box appears with the *Book Examples* and *Holt Software* projects listed (see Figure G.14). Select both projects and press the *OK* button. The *Import from another repository* dialog box now lists "2 selected" beside the *Details* button. Click the *Finish* button to import the two projects.

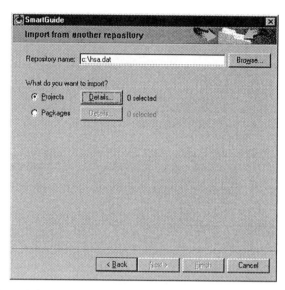

Figure G.13 The *Import from another repository* Dialog Box

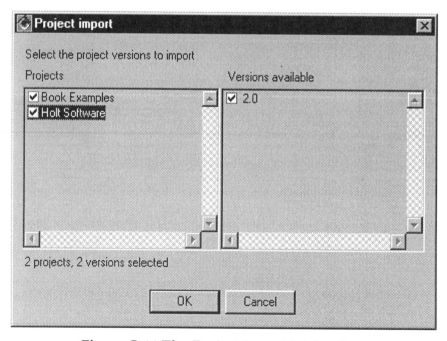

Figure G.14 The *Project import* Dialog Box

10. The project is imported into the repository. It still does not appear in the *Workbench* window. Now click the *Add Project* button in the tool bar (the fourth buton from the left that looks like a file folder). The *Add Project* dialog box appears (see Figure G.15). Click on *Add project(s) from the repository*. This displays a list of the projects available in the repository. Select the *book Examples* and *Holt Software* project and click the *Finish* button. The two projects are then placed in the workspace and can now be used.

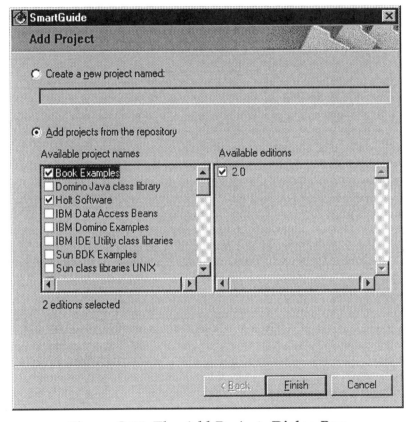

Figure G.15 The *Add Projects* Dialog Box

11. You must now add the *Holt Software* project to the list of projects *VisualAge for Java* checks for packages when compiling. In the *Workbench*, select the *Options* menu item from the *Window* menu. This brings up the *Options* dialog box (see Figure G.16). On the left is the list of options that can be changed. Select *Resources* from the list. The right side of the *Options* dialog box displays a text field labelled *Workspace class path:*. Enter *Holt Software* into the text field and click the *Apply* button. Then click the *OK* button. You can now import the *hsa* class into any of your classes in *VisualAge for Java*.

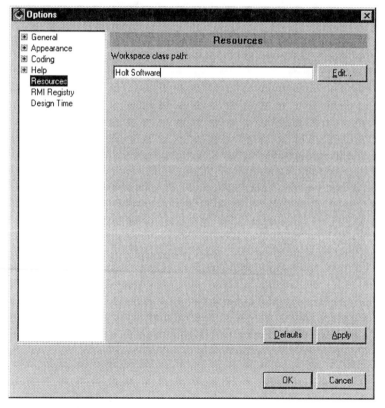

Figure G.16 The *Options* Dialog Box

12. Once the installation is completed, you can drag the *hsa.dat* file found on your main drive to the Recycler.

Using the *hsa* Package and the Book Examples in Other Environments

To use the *hsa* package in other environments, you must copy the Java text files and class files from the CD into appropriate directories on your hard disk. The actual location of the files on your hard disk is determined by the other Java environment that you will be using.

Most Java environments use a variable called CLASSPATH which is a list of directories that Java uses to look for classes to execute. The *hsa* directory must be copied into one of the directories in the CLASSPATH for Java to find the *hsa* package. Check the documentation of the Java environment that you are using to determine the CLASSPATH and the best location to install the *hsa* directory.

The exact location of the *book* directory is less important. In most environments, the CLASSPATH contains the current directory. As long as you are in the *book* directory when you run any of the book examples, Java will likely be able to find the program. The *hsa* and *book* directories can be found on the CD-ROM at the top level. Each contains all the Java text files and class files for all the files in the *hsa* and *Default Package for Book* packages.

To copy the directories to your hard drive, open up the CD-ROM in the *Windows Explorer*. Click once on the *hsa* directory (found at the top level) to select it (not open it). Click the right mouse button and select the *Copy* menu item from the pop-up menu that appears. Now select the directory where you want the *hsa* directory to be placed. Click the right mouse button and select the *Paste* menu item from the pop-up menu that appears. The *hsa* directory is now copied from the CD-ROM to the selected location on the hard drive. Now repeat this process for the *book* directory to move it to the desired location.

A third directory, *hsa examples*, contains all the example programs for the *hsa* package that are located in the *Default Package for Holt Software* package. Like the *book* directory, this can be copied where desired.

You have now copied the directories successfully. Remove the CD-ROM and store it in a safe place.

Appendix H : License Agreement for VisualAge for Java

International License Agreement for Evaluation of Programs

PLEASE READ THIS AGREEMENT CAREFULLY BEFORE USING THE PROGRAM. IBM WILL LICENSE THE PROGRAM TO YOU ONLY IF YOU FIRST ACCEPT THE TERMS OF THIS AGREEMENT. BY USING THE PROGRAM YOU AGREE TO THESE TERMS. IF YOU DO NOT AGREE TO THE TERMS OF THIS AGREEMENT, PROMPTLY RETURN THE UNUSED PROGRAM TO IBM.

The Program is owned by International Business Machines Corporation or one of its subsidiaries (IBM) or an IBM supplier, and is copyrighted and licensed, not sold.

The term "Program" means the original program and all whole or partial copies of it. A Program consists of machine-readable instructions, its components, data, audio-visual content (such as images, text, recordings, or pictures), and related licensed materials.

1. License

Use of the Program

IBM grants you a nonexclusive, nontransferable license to use the Program.

You may use the Program on only one machine at any one time, solely in connection with your use of the book entitled "Programming Concepts in Java" (copyright Holt Software Associates Inc. 1999) and/or academic course work related to the book. You agree to ensure that anyone who uses the program (accessed either locally or remotely) does so only for your authorized use and in compliance with the terms of this Agreement.

You may 1) copy the Program for backup and 2) merge the Program into another program. The terms of this license apply to each copy you make. You will reproduce the copyright notice and any other legends of ownership on each copy, or partial copy, of the Program.

You may not 1) use, copy, modify or distribute the Program except as provided in this Agreement; 2) reverse assemble, reverse compile, or otherwise translate the Program except as specifically permitted by law without the possibility of contractual waiver; or 3) sublicense, rent, or lease the Program.

This license begins with your first use of the Program and ends on the termination of this license in accordance with the terms of this Agreement. You will destroy the Program and all copies made of it within ten days of when this license ends.

2. No Warranty

SUBJECT TO ANY STATUTORY WARRANTIES WHICH CANNOT BE EXCLUDED, IBM MAKES NO WARRANTIES OR CONDITIONS EITHER EXPRESS OR IMPLIED, INCLUDING WITHOUT LIMITATION, THE WARRANTY OF NON-INFRINGEMENT AND THE IMPLIED WARRANTIES OF MERCHANTABILITY AND FITNESS FOR A PARTICULAR PURPOSE, REGARDING THE PROGRAM OR TECHNICAL SUPPORT, IF ANY. IBM MAKES NO WARRANTY REGARDING THE CAPABILITY OF THE PROGRAM TO CORRECTLY PROCESS, PROVIDE AND/OR RECEIVE DATE DATA WITHIN AND BETWEEN THE 20TH AND 21ST CENTURIES.

This exclusion also applies to any of IBM's subcontractors, suppliers or program developers (collectively called "Suppliers").

3. Limitation of Liability

NEITHER IBM NOR ITS SUPPLIERS ARE LIABLE FOR ANY DIRECT OR INDIRECT DAMAGES, INCLUDING WITHOUT LIMITATION, LOST PROFITS, LOST SAVINGS, OR ANY INCIDENTAL, SPECIAL, OR OTHER ECONOMIC CONSEQUENTIAL DAMAGES, EVEN IF IBM IS INFORMED OF

THEIR POSSIBILITY. SOME JURISDICTIONS DO NOT ALLOW THE EXCLUSION OR LIMITATION OF INCIDENTAL OR CONSEQUENTIAL DAMAGES, SO THE ABOVE EXCLUSION OR LIMITATION MAY NOT APPLY TO YOU.

4. General

Nothing in this Agreement affects any statutory rights of consumers that cannot be waived or limited by contract.

IBM may terminate your license if you fail to comply with the terms of this Agreement. If IBM does so, you must immediately destroy the Program and all copies you made of it.

You may not export the Program.

Neither you nor IBM will bring a legal action under this Agreement more than two years after the cause of action arose unless otherwise provided by local law without the possibility of contractual waiver or limitation.

Neither you nor IBM is responsible for failure to fulfill any obligations due to causes beyond its control.

There is no additional charge for use of the Program for the duration of this license.

IBM does not provide program services or technical support, unless IBM specifies otherwise.

The laws of the country in which you acquire the Program govern this Agreement. In Canada, the laws in the Province of Ontario govern this Agreement. In the United States and Puerto Rico, and People's Republic of China, the laws of the State of New York govern this Agreement.

Appendix I : Web Resources for Java

Holt Software

This is the website for the publisher of *Programming Concepts in Java*.

www.holtsoft.com

IBM VisualAge for Java

This is a website for IBM's VisualAge for Java development environment.

www.software.ibm.com/ad/vajava

IBM Academic Program for Java

This site contains a number of useful resources for educators teaching with Java (course notes, sample projects, and demos).

www.ibm.com/java/academic

Java Everything Site

This website contains an extremely large collection of Java resources (classes, example code, applets, and reference material).

www.gamelan.com

Java FAQ

These are files which contain the answers to frequently asked questions about Java. They can be very helpful if you are looking for answers to specific technical questions.

sunsite.unc.edu/javafaq/javafaq.html

www.best.com/~pvdl/javafaq.html

Java from Sun Microsystems

This is the website belonging to Sun Microsystems, the company that created and maintains the Java language. It provides the latest information about changes to the Java language.

java.sun.com

Java Development Kit

You can download the Java development Kit (JDK) from this website for free. JDK is a compiler and virtual machine.

java.sun.com/products/jdk

Java Newsgroups

These are Internet newsgroups for discussion of the Java language.

comp.lang.java.setup
comp.lang.java.programmer
comp.lang.java.api
comp.lang.java.tech

Index